John D. Voelker
June 29, 1903 - March 18, 1991

TROUT
MADNESS

John D. Voelker

TROUT
MADNESS

*Being a Dissertation on the Symptoms
and Pathology of This Incurable Disease
by One of Its Victims*

John D. Voelker

N

Northmont Publishing Company, Inc.
West Bloomfield, Michigan

ISBN 1-878005-47-2 Cl

CONTENTS

Preface

THERE is a lot of amiable fantasy written about trout fishing, but the truth is that few men know much if anything about the habits of trout and little more about the manner of taking them. And still fewer of these occasional wise men will spare any time from their fishing devotionals to write about it. Our knowledge of trout is like man's tenancy on this planet: precarious and tentative. In a world where men scarcely know each other, and are at pains to fight endless wars to confirm this somber fact, it is perhaps a gratuitous display of ignorance for any man to pretend extensive knowledge of the sly and secretive trout. They are dwellers on another planet. I have fished for trout since I was a boy and I admit I still know little or nothing about them. Indeed this is one of the special fascinations of pursuing them. Perhaps it is also the beginning of trout wisdom.

This book is the story of a lawyer gone wrong; of a man possessed of a fourteen-carat legal education who has gaily neglected it to follow the siren call of trout. It has been wisely observed that many lawyers are frustrated actors, but I know of one, at least, who is simply an unfrustrated fisherman. For lawyers, like all men, may be divided into two parts: those who fish and those who do not. All men who fish may in turn be divided into two parts: those who fish for trout and those who don't. Trout fishermen are a race apart; they are a dedicated crew—indolent, improvident, and quietly mad.

The true trout fisherman is like a drug addict; he dwells in a tight little dream world all his own, and the men about him, whom he observes obliviously spending their days pursuing money and power, genuinely puzzle him, as he doubtless does them. He prides himself on being an unbribed soul. So he is by way of being a philosopher, too, and sometimes he fishes not because he regards fishing as being so terribly important but because he suspects that so many of the other concerns of men are equally unimportant. Under his smiling coat of tan there often lurks a layer of melancholy and disillusion, a quiet awareness—and acceptance—of the fugitive quality of man and all his enterprises. If he must chase a will-o'-the-wisp he prefers that it be a trout. And so the fisherman fishes. It is at once an act of humility and small rebellion. And it is something more. To him his fishing is an island of reality in a world of dream and shadow. . . . Yet he is a species of unregenerate snob, too, and it pains him endlessly even to *hear* the name King Trout linked in the same breath with bass, pike, muskies, or similar representatives of what he is more likely to lump ungenerously as members of the lobster family.

All of these yarns are laid in the Upper Peninsula of Michigan, where I was born, a remote and sprawling region lying farther north than many points in Canada; a rugged land practically surrounded by the waters of two inland seas, Lake Superior and Lake Michigan. Many modest cities have larger populations than the whole U. P., a forgotten region which was virtually ignored in the westward surge of population. The canny lumber and steel barons, however, did not ignore the U. P., and they have doggedly hacked and clawed away at it for generations. Despite their best efforts, however, they still haven't quite been able to cut it down or blast it out. The brooding hills and gloomy swamps and endless waterways are still here. And the beaver. The people who inhabit the place are mostly from northern regions: Finns, Scandinavians, French-Canadians, with a generous sprinkling of the ubiquitous Irish, resourceful Cornish iron and copper miners, who were followed by the volatile Italians, and a mixed scattering of peoples from central Europe.

The simple truth is that the U. P. is one of the best hunting and fishing areas in the United States. It possesses three of nature's noblest creations: the ruffed grouse, the white-tailed deer, and the brook trout. Besides that there are sharp-tailed grouse, rabbits and black bears galore, some excellent rainbow and brown trout fishing, not to mention shoals of such tourist fish as bass, walleyes, muskies, crappies, bluegills and assorted stuff like that.

This fact, thank the Lord, is not yet widely known. It would be ironic—and a hideous thought to contemplate—if this little book should help bring about the discovery of the "forgotten" Upper Peninsula. Yet I take comfort when I reflect that the people who might find and deflower my native heath rarely hold still long enough to read books. And, I may ruefully add, they seem to have developed a special resistance to reading fishing books, like books of poetry, and somewhat like mosquitoes that finally learn to thrive on D.D.T. Apparently all that these people will willingly read are billboards, speedometers, funny books, road maps and signs proclaiming more Kozy Kabins five hundred yards ahead. They obediently race through here all summer long, sightlessly hissing along their labeled channels of concrete, bent only upon making five hundred miles a day, an achievement which somehow seems to ease the peculiar nature of their pain. They know not of the existence of the true U. P. They've never really been there.

In my view the best time to go trout fishing is when you can get away. That is virtually the only dogma you will be exposed to in this book. If you seek sage dilations on lunar tables, tidal impulses, wind phases, exotic fly patterns, tinted leaders, barometric pressures, and the like, then gently close this book and go fishing instead. Nor will you find herein any pictures of one big fish holding aloft another, the victor being identified largely by his triumphant grin. To this fisherman the fish in fishing happens to be what the onion is to onion soup: one of the main ingredients, yes, but far from everything. I fish mainly because I love the environs where trout are found: the woods; and further because I happen to dislike the environs where crowds of men are found: large cities; but if, heaven forbid, there were no trout and men were everywhere few, I would still doubtless prowl the woods and streams because it is there and only there that I really feel at home.

Successful fly fishing for trout is an act of high deceit; not only must the angler lure one of nature's subtlest and wariest creatures, he must do so with something that is false and no good—an artificial fly. Thus fake and sham lie at the heart of the enterprise. The amount of Machiavellian subtlety, guile, and sly deception that ultimately becomes wrapped up in the person of an experienced trout fisherman is faintly horrifying to contemplate. Thus fiendishly qualified for a brilliant diplomatic career he instead has time only to fish. So lesser diplomats continue to grope and bumble and their countries continue to fall into war. The only hope for it all, I am afraid, is for the Lord to drive the trout fishermen into diplomacy or else drive the diplomats to trout fishing. My guess is that either way we'd be more apt to have more peace: the fishermen-turned-diplomats would hurriedly resolve their differences on the trout stream so that they might return to their fishing, while the diplomats-turned-fishermen would shortly become so absorbed in their new passion they'd never again find time for war.

In this book I will lie a little, but not much, and I would prefer to hide my lapses under the euphemism "literary license," my excuse being that I find it difficult to inject drama into a series of fishing stories unless *somebody* occasionally gets on to a good fish. Quite frequently, you know, we fishermen don't.

ROBERT TRAVER

Trout Madness

1

The First Day

THE true fisherman approaches the first day of fishing with all the sense of wonder and awe of a child approaching Christmas. There is the same ecstatic counting of the days; the same eager and palpitant preparations; the same loving drafting of lists which are succeeded in turn by lists of lists! And then—when time seems frozen in its tracks and one is sure the magic hour will never arrive—lo, 'tis the night before fishing! Tomorrow is the big day! Perhaps it is also the time for a little poetry, however bad . . .

> 'Twas the night before fishing
> When all through the house
> Lay Dad's scattered fishing gear
> As though strewn by a souse . . .

Dad will of course have been up a dozen times during the night, prowling the midnight halls, peering out at glowering skies, creeping downstairs and pawing through mounds of duffel for the umpteenth last-minute checkup, crouching over the radio listening to the bright chatter of the all-night disk jockeys, ritualistically tapping the barometer—and perhaps even tapping his medicinal bottle of Kentucky chill-chaser. . . . It is this boyish quality of innocence, this irrepressible sense of anticipation, that makes all children and fishermen one. For after all, aren't fishermen merely permanently spellbound juveniles who have traded in Santa Claus for Izaak Walton?

Just as no Christmas can ever quite disappoint a youngster, however bleak and stormy the day, so no opening day of fishing can ever quite disappoint his grown-up brother. The day is invested with its own special magic, a magic that nothing can dispel. It is the signal for the end of the long winter hibernation, the widening of prison doors, the symbol of one of nature's greatest miracles, the annual unlocking of spring.

Since this fisherman dwells at Latitude 45 it should come as no great shock to learn that on most opening days I am obliged to draw rather heavily on this supply of magic to keep up my own drooping spirits. It is sometimes difficult to remain spellbound while mired to the hub caps in mud. *Our* big opening-day problem is twofold: to know where to find ice-free open water; and then be able to get there. During the ordeal we are sometimes driven to drink.

Our opening day is the last Saturday in April, ordinarily a disenchanting season of the year that finds most back roads badly clogged if not impassable, and a four-pound ice chisel a more promising weapon with which to probe our trout waters than a four-ounce fly rod. Our lakes and ponds are usually still ice-locked; our rivers and streams are usually in their fullest flood; and the most sensible solution is to try to remember a partially open spring-fed pond or beaver dam— and then spend a good part of the day trying to get there. Hence it is that my fishing pals and I usually take several pre-season reconnaissance trips on snowshoes. But regardless of the day, always we bravely go forth, come fire, flood, or famine—or the fulminations of relatives by marriage.

On many opening days I have had to trek into the chosen spot on snowshoes. I remember one recent spring when I stood on the foot-thick ice of a pond on my snowshoes— and took eight respectable trout on *dry* flies from a small open spring-hole less than thirty feet away, skidding them home to daddy over the ice! If you don't believe it, don't let it bother you; I'm not quite sure that I believe it myself.

Since 1936 I have kept a complete record of every fishing trip I have taken. It is amazing how I can torture myself during the winter reading over this stuff, recreating once again those magic scenes, seeing again the soft velvet glitter of trout waters, hearing once again the slow rhythmic whish of the fly lines. . . . From these records one thing emerges rather clearly: past opening days were more apt to lean to the mildly tragic than the magic. Here is the actual depressing account, omitting only the technical data on barometric pressures, water temperatures, wind direction, and the like.

1936: Snowshoed into Flopper's Pond with Clarence Lott. Pond partly open. No rises, no fish, no errors. Two flat tires on way out. "Oh, what fun it is to run . . ."

1937: Same way to same place with Mike DeFant. Reluctantly kept five wizened fryers out of low peasant pride.

1938: Slugged into Werner Creek beaver dam with mudhooks on Model A. Same fellows plus brother Leo. Caught 3 small trout and a touch of double pneumonia.

5

1939: Hiked into Wilson Creek beaver dams on snowshoes with Bill Gray. No rises, no takers. Bill took 6 fryers on bait. Spent balance of day coaxing the old fish car back across broken bridge. Finally did it with oats soaked generously in rum.

1940: Louie Bonetti, Nes Racine and Leo and I to O'Neil's Creek dam. A beautiful day succeeded by an even more beautiful hangover. No rises, no fish, several errors.

1941: Tom Cole and Vic Snyder and I drove out to the "Old Ruined Dams." Roads open, ponds free of ice. Fair rise. Beautiful day. Tom (6), Vic (7) and I (9), all honest fryers. All day long wedges of geese honking over like crazy, sounding remarkably like the weirdly demented yowlings of a distant pack of coyotes.

1942: Same gang plus Leo, to same place, same conditions. I kept 5 fryers. Vic filled out on bait. Had fish fry that night in camp. Lost $2.50 at rum. Tossed and turned all night.

1943: (No fish and no entry of just where I went. My, my. Must have gone straight up! Maybe no gas coupons.)

1944: South camp with usual opening gang. Bucked drifts last 2 miles. High water. Picked arbutus on south hillsides. No fish in crowd. Drowned our sorrows in mead and wore twisted garlands of arbutus in our hair.

1945: To Ted Fulsher's camp with Bill Gray and Carl Winkler. Raw, cold. Northeast wind. Didn't wet a line. Won $17.00 at poker. Slept like a log.

1946: To Frenchman's Pond with gang. Our fly lines froze in the guides. Thawed lines and drove to South Camp where Leo broke out a bottle of rare old brandy. Evidently it was *too* old; after the third round I suddenly rose and clapped my hand to my mouth—and ran outside. Guess I had better stick to the reliable brands of medium rare one-year-old cookin' whisky, the kind designed for peasants of distinction—bent on extinction.

1947: Snowshoed 5 miles with Dick Tisch in to Nurmi's Pond. Snow still 3 feet deep in woods. Got caught in bitter cold mixed rain and snow. Came down with chills and vapors and spent three days in bed with a nurse. Enervating but fun. Must try same next year. Her name was Lulu.

1948: Chopped way through the winter's bountiful supply of windfalls into O'Leary's Pond with Gipp Warner and Tom Bennett. Saw 2 wobbly young bear cubs and 17 deer. Caught 2 nice trout right off bat. Chuckled mirthlessly and twirled my waxed mustaches. Then caught in sudden hailstorm, which ended all fishing. On to Birchbark Lodge, one of those quaint Paul Bunyanish roadside tourist-traps cluttered to the eaves with stuffed owls and yawning dead bass impaled on varnished boards—and possessing the cutest iddy bitty bar, made, we were solemnly assured, out of *real logs*. Next morning, snug in my doghouse, I suspected the whisky was, too.

1949: Snowshoed into Scudder's Pond with Joe Parker. Pond partly open over bubbling springs. Fish dimpling. Stood on ice and took 8 on tiny dry flies! 'Twas a miracle. Skidded them over the ice. *Skidding at Scudder's!* by George Bellows. . . . Joe took only 1 on spinning gear, the wrong medicine.

1950: To Alger County with Marquette gang. Felt like a midget. Out of seven men I was the shortest, at six feet. A tall tale! Snow, ice and high water everywhere. Didn't wet a line. Wet whistle instead. Excursion degenerated into a pub crawl. Lost count after the 17th. Heard 8 million polkas and hillbilly laments—all miraculously sung through the left nostril. Love and despair, your spell is everywhere. . . . The inventor of the juke box is a cross between a banshee and a fiend. May he and his accomplices roast in the bottom-most pits of Hell.

1951: Slugged way through deep snow into Scudder's Pond led by proud Expedition Commander Frank Russell and his new jeep. The man *searched* for snowdrifts to charge! There is a new form of lunacy abroad in the land, the victims of which are called Jeepomaniacs. They're afraid of nothing. . . . Pond ice locked as tight as a bull's horns, as the saying doesn't go. Al Paul caught 2 in outlet—trout, not bull's horns. Surprise-attacked by party of friendly natives. Entire expedition got half shot and retired in vast disorder.

7

Trout Madness

1952: Mud-hooked way into Frenchman's Pond with Hank Scarffe and 2 boats. Nice intermittent "business" rise. Hank and I filled out, carefully selecting our trout. Fish fat and sassy. One of the most dramatic first-day rises I ever recall. Had but 2 bottles of beer all day. La, such a fine, contrite broth of a boy. Funny thing, I become a hell of a good fisherman when the trout decide to commit suicide. This is truly a fascinating pond.

And here is a later entry:

There have been 4 hauntingly lovely days in a row, the earth smoky and fragrant with the yeast of spring, the sky cut by the curling lash of endless flights of honking geese. Last night the wind swung abruptly to the east and the thermometer and barometer joined hands in a suicidal nose dive. Hank Scarffe, Al Paul, and I set out in 34° weather, the rainy sleet freezing to the windshield upon landing. All plans awry, we foolishly tried to reach the Moose Creek beaver dams, but got stuck up to the radiator in the first charge of a drift. We then retreated west and pushed and slugged our way through acres of rotten snow into Frenchman's Pond, where Hank and I huddled like wet robins and watched Al and his new telescope girder vainly test the pond with worms. Then came the snow, and there were *whitecaps* on the pond! Al folded his girder and we looked at each other and shrugged and slunk silently away. No one proposed even a drink. Once home I drained the fish car radiator, took a giant slug of whisky, and leapt morosely into bed, pulling the covers over my head. There I remained until nightfall, dreaming uneasily that I was a boy again and lo, it was Christmas—and I had just found my stocking filled with coal. I awoke to hear the blizzard screaming insanely outside. "Whee-e-e-e . . ." I crept downstairs in my bathrobe and drew every shade in the place, lit a roaring fire in the Franklin stove, built a foot-high highball, put on a mile-long piano concerto by Delius, and settled down with a book about hunting in Africa by a guy named, of all things, John A. Hunter. There were no pictures of fish! Was charmed to

8

learn that the pygmies of the Ituri forest cure eye infections by urinating in the bad eye. Found myself wishing that the red-eyed weather man would just sorta kinda drop in. Ho hum, only 8 more months 'til Christmas.

But enough of this dreary recital of frustration, hangover, and rue. As you may by now suspect, the first day of fishing in my bailiwick is something of a gamble. Usually it is considerably more devoted to drinking than fishing, a state of affairs against which I maintain a stern taboo when the fishing really gets under way. *Then* any drinking—usually a nightcap or two—comes only *after* the fishing is over and done. To me fly fishing is ordinarily quite difficult and stimulating enough without souping up the old motor. . . . But the first day is different; it is mostly a traditional spring get-together of congenial souls, an incidental opportunity to try out and find the bugs in one's equipment, and a chance to stretch one's legs and expand one's soul. I regret that it also frequently affords an excellent opportunity to entrench oneself early and firmly in the doghouse. Then comes the time for all middle-aged fishermen to sow their rolled oats. All of which brings on a final seizure of dubious poetry.

'Twas the morning after the first day
When all through the house
Echoed the moaning and groaning
Of poor daddy—the louse!

9

2

The Fish Car

SHE was born on an assembly line in Detroit in 1928. After a bitter childhood involving many harrowing misadventures, she was found and adopted by me on a rainy spring day in 1935. It was then that I discovered my beloved orphan, forlorn and neglected, weeping silently in an obscure corner of a used-car lot. I stared at her and she stared mournfully back at me, dripping tears. With us I guess it was a case of love at first sight. Appraisingly squinting an eye and stroking my chin, I kicked her once on a rear tire—lo! there was air in it—and then told the man I'd take her. (Why do all prospective purchasers of used cars invariably kick at one of the tires?) The adoption papers cost me one hundred dollars. The superintendent of the used-car orphanage signed and gave me her birth certificate. We formally shook hands, and I somehow drove her away under her own power. Pedestrians paused and stared at us. Once home

Trout Madness

I broke a bottle of beer across her radiator and christened her "Buckshot."

She was a little two-door sedan with wire wheels and twenty-one-inch tires. (For my money she is also a mobile testimonial and the most enduring monument I know to the mechanical genius of Henry Ford. How many cars of other make and like vintage does one still encounter regularly on the road?) When I got her she not only looked like a tramp, she was a tramp. Among many other things, her lights, brakes, horn, muffler, and charger didn't work; you could throw a creel through the leaky roof; a wildcat had evidently been let loose at her upholstery; the clanking engine sounded like the cardiac thumpings of an expiring thresher; a cardboard carton appropriately advertising a deodorant took the place of the glass missing from the driver's door; her windshield was cracked and completely fogged over, like a pair of dime-store sun glasses, giving the driver a wavering surrealist vision of the occasional larger objects he was able to behold.

But her heart and mind and spirit were essentially sound, and when I was done with her she was a glittering mechanical dream, a sight to behold. By that time, too, the original price I paid for her had faded into a Scotchman's tip compared to the national debt. As for her owner, he was poor but proud, and not unlike a widowed mother who takes in washing and sacrifices all to support a lazy daughter in indolence and sloth.

Since then my rejuvenated Buckshot and I have spent some of the best years of our lives together. We have hunted and fished together, explored and prospected for uranium, and gathered berries and pine knots together; there have been baseless dark rumors that we have even got drunk together. . . . But mostly we have fished; yes, year after year, season in and season out, come hell or high water, we have fished. Her radiator is adorned with two leaping tin fish I stole from my youngest daughter.

When Buckshot became old and discreet enough to vote, a few years back, I rewarded her coming of age by letting her rest after each bird season. All winter long I let her just sit in the garage, with southern exposure. There she basks like Man O' War let out to pasture. It is a kind of partial retirement, a sort of annual winter vacation with pay, in recognition of her long years of valor under fire. Now she is pure fish car and she loves it. When fishing season rolls around she snorts and trembles and backfires like an old fire horse at the sound of the bell.

She is loyal to me and in my way I am loyal to her. Last spring I had a chance to adopt a sturdy and handsome young jeep at a bargain price. I was jubilant; now I could ford rivers and scale mountains. But when it came right down to signing the adoption papers and getting rid of faithful old Buckshot on the trade-in, I fell to mentally reviewing our misspent youth together. Shortly I got all sentimental and choked up. We two had been through so *much* together. . . . "The d-deal's off," I finally told the astounded jeep man, sniffling and patting patient ol' Buckshot on the fanny. I felt so guilty for wavering that all summer long I fed Buckshot on nothing but the best ethyl gas. All was forgiven and I now suspect that our marriage shall last till old age—or jeeps—do us part. Not only is she cheap at half the price; she's a jeep at half the price.

I don't mean to imply that our romance hasn't had its darker moments. There were times when I could have reared back and given her a swift kick in the differential. No, Buckshot, I haven't forgotten the occasions when you sulked and pouted and even broke down and forced your poor old boss man to walk back to town from hell's half acre. 'Member the time you developed that—er—sudden female complaint way up north off the Yellow Dog plains? 'Member how I had to walk nearly twenty miles before I hitched a ride?—and then had to fetch a doctor from the garage, along with one of those expensive wrecker-ambulances to tote you in? And then paid nearly a hundred bucks for your operation?

Eh? How's that, Buckshot? What's that you just now said? Oh, that if I'd lay off swiggling beer when I was guiding you and watched closer where I was driving, you wouldn't develop nearly so many of those aches and pains and sudden fainting spells? Well I declare—now that's gratitude for you. My, my . . . I'm truly surprised at you, Buckshot. And in front of perfect strangers, too!

My fish car is probably one of the most complete fish cars in the world. Perhaps she is *the* completest, but then I don't like to brag. This I do know: All I have to do is to get into her and drive away—and we can stay out fishing for a week. There is no further preparation and nothing I can forget (unless I forget Buckshot herself) because I always leave all of my treasures in her custody. When she and I shove off we are a sort of Abercrombie & Fitch on the march. Here is only a partial list of the gear we *always* carry; it's standard equipment: Four fly rods and a spinning rod, all of which ride snugly on rubber slings suspended from the inside roof; binoculars, a camera, a magnifying glass (for studying the birds and the bees and the stomach content of trout), four sizes of flashlights (from pencil size to Lindbergh Beacon), and even one of those old Stonebridge candle lanterns for emergencies; waders and hip boots and low boat boots, and of course all the usual endless fishing gear (*that* would take a page itself), complete with patching cement, ferrule cement, and all the many odds and ends; eight miles of miscellaneous sizes and lengths of rope; a complete set of detailed county maps of Michigan based upon late air photos and showing all waters and side roads; a bedroll and spare blanket; rain clothes and a complete change of woods clothes; a tarpaulin and pup tent; a Primus stove and nesting cook kit with all the many trimmings; assorted water canteens; a small portable icebox; grub for a week, mostly bottled or canned; and, last but not least, always a supply of beer and a bottle or two of whisky—*always* when I leave, that is.

In addition I carry two spare tires and some extra tubes; enough small spare parts to start a neighborhood garage; a hand-cranked tugger that could yank a Patton tank out of a mudhole, complete with assorted logging chains and snatch blocks and "come-alongs" and U-bolts and towing cables, together with an old car axle to drive in the ground and use as a towing anchor in treeless terrain. I also carry enough tools and assorted junk to build and furnish a ranch house. On the roof I carry my rubber boat and inside the car the boat gear including anchors, jointed paddles, kapok cushions, air pump, etc. Then I carry two axes, one hatchet, one head-hunting brush knife, two sizes of pruning shears for cleaning out difficult "hot spots," an all-size leather punch, two handsaws, nails and hammers, and enough pry bars and wrecking tools to convict me of intended sabotage and burglary. To keep in character for my felonies I usually tote a .38 special revolver. Then, to top it off, there is a six-volt overhead light bulb in the car that is so bright I can read the fine print on a bill of lading without my glasses.

And where does the driver sit? one may sensibly ask. Incredibly enough, I somehow manage to keep *both* front seats free for driver and passenger. Of course with this mound of

15

equipment piled behind us we are usually obliged to converse in guarded whispers, lest our voices jar loose the poised glacier and bury us in the avalanche. Indeed, sometimes I have even managed to squeeze an adventurous small fisherman in the *back* seat, stashing the stuff around him, though I always thoughtfully furnish him a breathing pipe so that he does not perish on the way. "Fisherman drowned in tidal wave of fishing equipment!" is one headline we seek to avoid.

As I read over this modest inventory I am struck by the number of items I have left out. I haven't even hinted about the assorted barometers, thermometers, and depthometers, the toilet, gaming and first-aid kits, the fishtail propellers, transistor radios, and folding camp stools; nor yet about the red flares and collapsible canvas pails, the crow calls, Audubon birdcalls and Indian love calls—not to mention the aluminum waterscope I use leeringly to watch mermaids. And when my pals and I really go on a prolonged expedition and take along the trailer and all *three* of my boats, that is something to behold. Then I pile most of the gear in the flat-bottomed trailer boat, and lash the third boat on top. *Ship ahoy!* Admiral Dewey is about to steam into Manila harbor.

Last summer as I was about to shove off on big safari, Grace came out on the back porch to see me off. She studied the caravan rather thoughtfully for quite a while. She spoke slowly.

"You look," she said quietly, "you look like the addled commander of a one-man army about to launch a rocket invasion of Mars."

"Nope," I corrected her. "I'm the Ringling Brothers on my way to merge with Barnum & Bailey. Good day, Madam. Giddap, Buckshot!"

16

3

✦✦✦

Big Secret Trout

No MISANTHROPIST, I must nevertheless confess that I like and frequently prefer to fish alone. Of course in a sense all dedicated fishermen must fish alone; the pursuit is essentially a solitary one; but sometimes I not only like to fish out of actual sight and sound of my fellow addicts, but alone too in the relaxing sense that I need not consider the convenience or foibles or state of hangover of my companions, nor subconsciously compete with them (smarting just a little over their success or gloating just a little over mine), nor, more selfishly, feel any guilty compulsion to smile falsely and yield them a favorite piece of water.

There is a certain remote stretch of river on the Middle Escanaba that I love to fish by myself; the place seems made for wonder and solitude. This enchanted stretch lies near an old deer-hunting camp of my father's. A cold feeder stream—"The Spawnshop," my father called it—runs through

17

the ancient beaver meadows below the camp. After much gravelly winding and circling and gurgling over tiny beaver dams the creek gaily joins the big river a mile or so east of the camp. Not unnaturally, in warm weather this junction is a favorite convention spot for brook trout.

One may drive to the camp in an old car or a jeep but, after that, elementary democracy sets in; all fishermen alike must walk down to the big river—*even* the arrogant new jeepocracy. Since my father died the old ridge trail has become overgrown and faint and wonderfully clogged with windfalls. I leave it that way. Between us the deer and I manage to keep it from disappearing altogether. Since this trail is by far the easiest and closest approach to my secret spot, needless to say few, secretive, and great of heart are the fishermen I ever take over it.

I like to park my old fish car by the camp perhaps an hour or so before sundown. Generally I enter the neglected old camp to look around and, over a devotional beer, sit and brood a little over the dear dead days of yesteryear, or perhaps morosely review the progressive decay of calendar art collected there during forty-odd years. And always I am amazed that the scampering field mice haven't carried the musty old place away, calendars and all. . . . Traveling light, I pack my waders and fishing gear—with perhaps a can or two of beer to stave off pellagra—and set off. I craftily avoid using the old trail at first (thus leaving no clue), charging instead into the thickest woods, using my rod case as a wand to part the nodding ferns for hidden windfalls. Then veering right and picking up the trail, I am at last on the way to the fabulous spot where my father and I used to derrick out so many trout when I was a boy.

Padding swiftly along the old trail—over windfalls, under others—I sometimes recapture the fantasies of my boyhood:

once again, perhaps, I am a lithe young Indian brave—the seventh son of Chief Booze-in-the-Face, a modest lad who can wheel and shoot the eye out of a woodchuck at seventy paces—now bound riverward to capture a great copper-hued trout for a demure copper-hued maiden; or again, and more sensibly, I am returning from the river simply to capture the copper-hued maiden herself. But copper fish or Indian maid, there is fantasy in the air; the earth is young again; all remains unchanged: there is still the occasional porcupine waddling away, bristling and ridiculous; still the startling whir of a partridge; still the sudden blowing and thumping retreat of a surprised deer. I pause and listen stealthily. The distant blowing grows fainter and fainter, *"whew"* and again *"whew,"* like wind grieving in the pines.

By and by the middle-aged fisherman, still gripped by his fantasies, reaches the outlet of the creek into the main river. Hm . . . no fish are rising. He stoops to stash a spare can of beer in the icy gravel, scattering the little troutlings. Then, red-faced and panting, he lurches up river through the brambles to the old deer crossing at the gravel ford. Another unseen deer blows and stamps—this time across the river. *"Whew,"* the fisherman answers, mopping his forehead on his sleeve, easing off the packsack, squatting there batting mosquitoes and sipping his beer and watching the endless marvel of the unwinding river. The sun is low, most of the water is wrapped in shadow, a pregnant stillness prevails. Lo, the smaller fish are beginning to rise. Ah, there's a good one working! Still watching, he gropes in the bunch grass for his rod case. All fantasies are now forgotten.

Just above this shallow gravel ford there is a wide, slick, still-running and hopelessly unwadable expanse of deep water—a small lake within the river. I have never seen a spot quite like it. On my side of this pool there is a steep-sloping

19

sandy bank surmounted by a jungle of tag alders. On the far opposite bank there is an abrupt, rocky, root-lined ledge lined with clumps of out-curving birches, rising so tall, their quivering small leaves glittering in the dying sun like a million tinkling tambourines. But another good fish rises, so to hell with the tambourines. . . . For in this mysterious pool dwell some of the biggest brown trout I know. This is my secret spot. Fiendishly evasive, these trout are not only hard to catch but, because of their habitat, equally hard to fish. The fisherman's trouble is double.

A boat or canoe invariably invokes mutiny and puts them down—at least any vessel captained by me. My most extravagant power casts from the ford below usually do the same or else fall short, though not always. The tall fly-catching tag alders on my side discourage any normal bank approach consistent with retaining one's sanity. (Hacking down the tag alders would not only be a chore, but would at once spoil the natural beauty of the place and erect a billboard proclaiming: BIG TROUT RESIDE HERE!) Across the way the steep rocky bank and the clusters of birches and tangled small stuff make it impossible properly to present a fly or to handle a decent trout if one could. The place is a fisherman's challenge and a fisherman's dream: lovely, enchanted, and endlessly tantalizing. I love it.

Across from me, closer to the other side and nicely out of range, there is a slow whirl-around of silky black water, endlessly revolving. Nearly everything floating into the pool —including most natural flies—takes at least one free ride around this lazy merry-go-round. For many insects it is frequently the last ride, for it is here that the fat tribal chieftains among the brown trout foregather at dusk to roll and cavort. Many a happy hour have I spent fruitlessly stalking these wise old trout. The elements willing, occasionally I even outwit one. Once last summer I outwitted two—all in the same ecstatic evening. Only now can I venture coherently to speak of it.

I had stashed my beer in the creek mouth as usual and had puffed my way through the tangle up to the deep pool. There they were feeding in the merry-go-round, *both* of them, working as only big trout can work—swiftly, silently, accurately—making genteel little pneumatic sounds, like a pair of rival dowagers sipping their cups of tea. I commanded myself to sit down and open my shaking can of beer. Above and below the pool as far as I could see the smaller brook trout were flashily feeding, but tonight the entire pool belonged to these two quietly ravenous pirates. "Slp, slp" continued the pair as I sat there ruefully wondering what a Hewitt or LaBranche or Bergman would do.

"They'd probably rig up and go fishin'," at length I sensibly told myself in an awed stage whisper. So I arose and with furious nonchalance rigged up, slowly, carefully, ignoring the trout as though time were a dime and there were no fish rising in the whole river, dressing the line just so, scrubbing out the fine twelve-foot leader with my bar of mechanic's soap. I even managed to whistle a tuneless obbligato to the steady "Slp, slp, slp. . . ."

And now the fly. I hadn't the faintest idea what fly to use as it was too shadowy and far away to even guess what they were taking. Suddenly I had *the* idea: I had just visited the parlor of Peterson, one of my favorite fly tiers, and had persuaded him to tie up a dozen exquisitely small palmer-tied creations on stiff gray hackle. I had got them for buoyancy to roll-cast on a certain difficult wooded pond. Why not try one here? Yet how on earth would I present it?

Most fishermen, including this one, cling to their pet stu-

21

pidities as they would to a battered briar or an old jacket; and their dogged persistence in wrong methods and general wrongheadedness finally wins them a sort of grudging admiration, if not many trout. Ordinarily I would have put these fish down, using my usual approach, in about two casts of a squirrel's tail. Perhaps the sheer hopelessness of the situation gave me the wit to solve it. Next time I'll doubtless try to cast an anvil out to stun them. "The *only* controlled cast I can possibly make here," I muttered, hoarse with inspiration, "is a *roll* cast . . . yes—it's that or nothing, Johnny me bye." If it is in such hours that greatness is born, then this was my finest hour.

Anyone who has ever tried successfully to roll-cast a dry fly under any circumstances, let alone cross-stream in a wide river with conflicting currents and before two big dining trout, knows that baby sitting for colicky triplets is much easier. For those who know not the roll cast, I shall simply say that it is a heaven-born cast made as though throwing an overhand half-hitch with a rope tied to a stick, no backcast being involved. But a roll cast would pull my fly under; a decent back cast was impossible; yet I had to present a floating fly. *That* was my little problem.

"Slp, slp, slp," went the trout, oblivious to the turmoil within me.

Standing on the dry bank in my moccasins I calmly stripped out line and kept rolling it upstream and inshore— so as not to disturb my quarry—until I figured my fly was out perhaps ten feet more than the distance between me and the steadily feeding trout. And that was plenty far. On each test cast the noble little gray hackle quickly appeared and rode beautifully. "God bless Peterson," I murmured. Then I began boldly to arc the cast out into the main river, gauging for distance, and then—suddenly—I drew in my breath and drew up my slack and rolled out the fatal business cast. *This was it*. The fly lit not fifteen feet upstream from the top fish—right in the down whirl of the merry-go-round. The little gray hackle bobbed up, circled a trifle uncertainly and then began slowly to float downstream like a little major. The fish gods had smiled. Exultant, I mentally reordered three dozen precious little gray hackles. Twelve feet, ten feet, eight . . . holding my breath, I also offered up a tiny prayer to the roll cast. "Slp, slp . . ." The count-down continued—five feet, two feet, one foot, "slp"—and he was on.

Like many big browns, this one made one gorgeous dripping leap and bore down in a power dive, way deep, dogging this way and that like a bulldog shaking a terrier. Keeping light pressure, I coaxed rather than forced him out of the merry-go-round. Once out I let him conduct the little gray hackle on a subterranean tour and then—and then—I saw and heard his companion resume his greedy rise, "Slp, slp." *That* nearly unstrung me; as though one's fishing companion had yawned and casually opened and drunk a bottle of beer while one was sinking for the third time.

Like a harried dime-store manager with the place full of reaching juvenile delinquents, I kept trying to tend to business and avoid trouble and watch the sawing leader and the other feeding trout all at the same time. Then my trout began to sulk and bore, way deep, and the taut leader began to vibrate and whine like the plucked string of a harp. What if he snags a deadhead? I fretted. Just then a whirring half-dozen local ducks rushed upstream in oiled flight, banking away when they saw this strange tableau, a queer man standing there holding a straining hoop. Finally worried, I tried a little more pressure, gently pumping, and he came up in a sudden rush and rolled on his side at my feet like a length of cordwood. Then he saw his tormentor and was down and away again.

The nighthawks had descended to join the bats before I had him folded and dripping in the net, stone dead. "Holy old Mackinaw!" I said, numb-wristed and weak with conquest. A noisy whippoorwill announced dusk. I blew on my matted gray hackle and, without changing flies, on the next business cast I was on to his partner—the senior partner, it developed—which I played far into the night, the nighthawks and bats wheeling all about me. Two days later all three of us appeared in the local paper; on the front page, mind you. I was the one in the middle, the short one with the fatuous grin.

Next season I rather think I'll visit my secret place once or twice.

4

Green Pastures

FISHERMEN are a perverse and restless lot, constantly poised to migrate to greener pastures, ever helpless recruits for the wild-goose chase. They're apt to be up and away at the drop of an idle rumor. Indeed this willingness to pursue the will-o'-the-wisp of the true trout fairyland, this curious readiness to chase bubbles, mirages, and rainbows up and down the land, seems to make up half the lure of fishing. Some wild-eyed mosquito-crazed character sidles up to another fisherman and furtively mumbles, "I just heard of a place where they splash waves in your face"—and off they zoom to the moon, gaily negotiating seven cedar swamps on the way.

Any fisherman with red fish blood in his veins has himself made these wild excursions, only to return, flushed and fishless, "when the day is far spent, smelling of strong drink, and the truth is not in him." All of us are guilty. Fishermen who

25

no longer heed these siren calls have either become ex-fishermen or old fishermen. . . . On the other hand some of the best trout spots I have ever known were divulged to me quite by accident, and frequently were disclosed when my mind was miles—well, anyway six inches—away from thoughts of trout.

There was the historic occasion when I drove to the remote logging village of McFarland to settle a workmen's compensation accident case with a game-legged tobacco-chewing fellow who'd injured his knee. Inasmuch as I was a fishing stranger in those distant parts, it looked as if any serious fishing was shot for the day. And on the way there I hadn't even crossed a decent creek. Certainly all this was a dubious prelude to the discovery of some of the most fabulous brook trout fishing I have ever encountered. My man signed the release papers, I gave him his check, and he spat. Thus unpouted, he managed to thank me and then tried to pay me some money for my trouble. Pushing Satan behind me, I thanked him and virtuously explained that my fee was being paid by the other side, by whom I was retained. My grateful chum still insisted.

"Here, take ten bucks, anyway." He squinted discerningly. "Go buy yourself a coupla drinks—you kinda look like you could stand a few snorts."

"Look, friend," I said, mostly to avoid offending the gracious little man, and so that I might get going, "if you still insist on doing something nice for me, suppose some day when your leg gets better you take me out and show me a good trout spot in your bailiwick." It was one of those defensive and purposely vague fishing dates fishermen are always making and rarely keeping.

But my man was a pragmatist; efficient, purposeful, and a bear for action. "Hell, Mister," he said in an Is-that-all-you-

26

want tone of voice, "I'll take you *now!* Got your fishin' tackle along?"

"I always carry it—even to weddings," I announced truthfully. (My wife still bitterly suspects that I smuggled my fishing gear along on our honeymoon. Otherwise, where had I disappeared to, hours on end? The truth is that it was just some darned old fishing equipment I had meant to give away to some junior anglers and had instead forgotten and left in the back of the car. . . .)

"Come with me," he said, and I, putty in his hands, followed directions obediently. "An' don't you worry none about my leg," he added, winking. "I got my money, ain't I?"

After not more than thirty minutes of driving over a serpentine maze of dirt side roads my new chum stopped me at a dubious-looking foot-wide rivulet running through a galvanized-iron culvert, and then—his extravagant compensation limp now miraculously cured—plunged me upstream through a tangle of assorted brambles into a little jewel of a beaver dam—high and narrow, deep and black as India ink, crisscrossed with fallen cedars, and backed up as far as the eye could see.

"This is it," he said, wrenching apart the joints of a steel girder he was carrying—known in some quarters as a telescope pole—and threading a half-dozen of what he engagingly called "pork chops" (night crawlers to me) on to a bait hook the size and hue of half of a rusty ice tongs. This done he stomped up to the dam and, whirling the loose coils of line 'round and 'round him as though he were about to rope a bronco, finally lofted this fantastic blob of writhing bait out across the dam. It landed with the genteel plop of an anvil dropped from an airplane. "He must be aiming to *stun* them," I thought, shutting my eyes in quiet horror—

27

and opening them only to find him disengaging a plump twelve-inch brook trout from his harpoon.

"N-nice one," I ventured.

He spat an amber stream of Peerless juice that must have raised the dam six inches, looked up at the sky, shook his head, and spoke. "Nope, guess the big ones ain't hittin' yet. Too bright'n early."

He and his portable crane had miraculously horsed out five more nice trout before I was fairly rigged up, and then he stomped away and disappeared around a bend upstream. I teetered out onto the middle of the beaver dam, my hands shaking a little as I selected and tied on a small red and white candy-striped hair fly tied by Paul Young. If my chum could do *that* with worms and that steel beam he'd stolen from the Brooklyn Bridge . . .

"Here goes," I murmured, flipping her out on a preliminary non-business cast, not more than fifteen feet.

An ascending *cone* of trout rushed up and literally fought for the fly. It was by all odds the damndest thing of its kind I ever saw. In my delirium I nearly keeled back off the dam. The problem was not to get on to a trout; the *big* trick would have been to successfully snatch the fly away before one of them grabbed it. I stood there in the middle of the dam in a blazing sun and calmly—perhaps not so calmly—filled out, keeping nothing under ten inches and returning but two. And they were all plump, dark-backed native beauties with flaming flanks. All told it couldn't have taken a half-hour. They ran up to thirteen inches; not fabulous, I agree, but nice brook trout in any fisherman's league. I hadn't had fishing quite like it since I was a kid.

My chum and his girder finally clanked around the bend. His limp had totally disappeared and I reflected on the re-markable therapeutic properties of that faithful old miracle

28

drug: *money*. He found me sitting on a cedar log, smoking and watching the first trout beginning to roll, my own trout cleaned and neatly laid away in my creel, my rod taken down. He spat—"Plink!"—and spoke.

"What luck?" he chirped.

"Good," I chirped back, grinning smugly.

"How many?"

"Fifteen," I answered proudly.

"Hm. . . . Aintcha gonna ketch your limit?" he said, frowning.

"Whatcha mean, *limit*?" I said.

"Why, thirty," he said, "I only got twenty-seven. They ain't hittin' jest right today."

I sagged on the log but remained conscious. "Look, chum," I said, rallying a little. "Look, the present limit for one day is *fifteen*. Didn't you know? The legislature changed it recently—just about twenty-five years ago."

My new friend stood looking at me in amazement, chewing ruminantly and wagging his head incredulously. Then he spat a new stream that I feared would surely wash out the dam. "Well, whadya know, now whadya know," he murmured, completely baffled by all the newfangled legislative innovations seeping north out of Lansing. (The limit *now* is ten.)

For several years this beaver dam presented such wonderful but essentially rather boring fishing (it was so easy), that I christened the place "The Icebox." Never once did it fail, a rare phenomenon in the present crowded world of trout fishing. Then one spring I went there to find the main dam freshly blasted out, quite evidently the work of an illegal beaver trapper. All I could catch in the trickling ruined waters was an endless parade of wriggling chubs. I nearly wept with sorrow and rage that such a natural trout habitat should have been ruined to provide a fur coat for some silky blonde on Fifth Avenue. I've never been back, though I know I should return on the long chance that a new generation of beaver may also have returned—and in the further hope that the villainous trapper either tripped and snapped his whizzle string or else died or got religion.

Ah, yes, green pastures! One Saturday afternoon in a smoky bar, where I had gone to have a quick beer while my fish car was being gassed up, an amiable Finnish pulp cutter weaved uncertainly up to me and plucked at my sleeve and said, "Yonny, you the lawyer bucko who so crazy for fish, yes? You da fella what like for fish trouts, yes? You like me show you fine place for ketch big trouts, yes?"

"Yes," I confessed to the entire indictment as I tried to quell the familiar surge of juvenile excitement over the visions of a new fishing spot. "Here we go again," I thought, recognizing all the fatal symptoms. "W-when do we leave, Toivo?" I said, surrendering unconditionally.

Two hours and some thirty miles later Toivo and I jolted to a stop on a little sand hill overlooking a vast cranberry bog in the center of which a large crescent-shaped lake lay glittering in the late afternoon sun.

"Dis here is Loon Lake," Toivo said, yawning and curling up in the car to nurse the remnants of his pint bottle while I leapt out to conduct the assault. The next four hours I spent in leaping and bouncing around on the bedspring cranberry bog, like a trapeze performer on his safety net. I flung flies, spinning lures, flatfish and spoons—I would doubtless have hurled out knives and forks had I had them—until my arm ached. Not only were there no takers, but I saw nary a sign of a fish during the entire siege. A snoring Toivo roused himself when I dragged myself back to the car.

"How many?" he grunted, blinking.

"No luck," I grunted back.

"No *luck*?" he said, astounded.

"No luck, Toivo," I repeated patiently, putting the place down as just another of those wild-goose chases. I felt one small comfort; at least there would be one less goose to chase that season. Inevitably each year there seems to be a certain number.

"What kind vorms you using?" he inquired.

"I never use worms," I replied, drawing myself up haughtily. I charitably concluded that Toivo was unaware that fishermen have become involved in duels for insinuating less.

"Oh, but you gotta use vorms," Toivo said, shaking his head over such perverse stupidity. "Dose big yuicy night crawlers—he vork da best."

I was glum and preoccupied as I unrigged. It was nearly dark as I nosed the throbbing Model-A around to take off. I silently wished for a plague to visit this malarial spot.

"*Look!*" Toivo said, pointing back at the lake.

I looked and in the gathering gloom I saw that the whole vast lake had suddenly come to a boil; it was alive with leaping and mighty rises. The fish were huge and there must have been scores and hundreds of them. It was fierce, spectacular, unbelievable. *Never* have I seen a trout rise to equal it, anywhere, and I have fished for years in Canada as well as here. . . .

"Toivo," I said, my voice grown beseeching. "C-can you wait till I rig up and t-try her again?"

Toivo shook his head. "No siree, Yonny, I can't vait no any longer. I'm late now, already. I got date my missus over vun hour ago. My missus she's big fat crabby an' if I vait nudder minoot I guess I better build camp an' stay."

31

Trout Madness

If Toivo had been just a trifle less potted I would have cheerfully given him the fish car and walked back. Anything to stay. But he was too far gone for me to entrust my beloved old Buckshot to his uncertain care.

"I see, Toivo," I said, for I dolefully saw. So I cast one last wistful farewell look at the miracle rise and drove sadly away. I've never been quite the same man since. I am charmed to report that Toivo's "big fat crabby" wife wasn't even ready when I finally delivered him and the remains of his bottle up to her tender mercies.

"Wat da hell you come home so soon for?" was the shrill opening shell she fired in her bombardment.

After that I virtually moved my law office out to Loon Lake. I haunted it by day and by night. I ranged the bouncy shore like a crazed water buffalo, flinging flies and guttural oaths, but nary a pass or a strike—*and never did I see another solitary rise!* Then one evening I fetched my old bait-fishing friend, Louie Bonetti, elaborately swore him to secrecy, and sat him down on an old beer case and took off on my usual lunges. When I had made the course and returned he was in the act of derricking out a beauty with his pork chops. He had several more like it folded away in his big creel, the tails protruding. Toivo was right; worms were the medicine.

"Gooda place, Yon," beaming Louie said, grinning his million-dollar grin. "You lak borrow some pork chop?" he teased.

I then switched despondently to deep-running spinning lures and finally managed to dredge up several trout up to fourteen inches—juveniles compared with the whoppers I had seen that first enchanted evening. And anyway I wanted perversely to take them on flies. The thing had become an obsession. The truth was that Loon Lake was fast driving me loony.

Some anglers I know can't quite decide just what kind of green pastures are the most wearing on fishermen: those in the great majority that turn into wild-goose chases; those rarer ones that sometimes actually deliver; or those rarest ones of all, like Loon Lake, that are simply crawling with magazine-cover trout, and steadily defy one's best efforts to take them on flies.

As one angler this I do know. It was bad enough to find and lose that heavenly little "icebox" beaver dam, the one that became ruined, but offhand I am aware of no fishing torture quite like a fisherman *knowing* of a lake full of gorgeous trout, and not being able to so much as *lose* a fly to a single one of them! Sometimes in the middle of those warm summer nights, when the subdued crickets are quietly ticking and humming and a brooding sense of mystery pervades the air, I wake up with sudden cold sweats and lie there and think: Now, here, tonight—at this very moment— that lovely baffling lake is probably boiling with giant trout rises—and here I am, writhing in my moist bed of frustration. About then I shuffle down the hall and tilt the aspirin bottle.

I finally had to quit going to Loon Lake. I had to quit it in order to maintain three things: my wavering sanity, the remnants of my law practice, and that state of uneasy truce known as marriage. I'll venture there again only under one circumstance: Merely to guide some courageous fisherman who'll first promise under oath to use nothing but flies—and who honestly thinks he knows of a way to raise them on flies. The line of applicants will please form on the left.

As for me, when that happens I think I'll just curl up in

33

the fish car with my bottle, and when the first crazed volunteer bounces back to the firm ground of reality I'll hand out the bottle and leer red-eyed at him and say: "See! Didn't I tell you? It's just like Toivo said: Dose big yuicy night crawlers—he vork da best!"

5

Sinning Against Spinning

"THIS is the place, Frank," I said, ducking through the last wedge of intervening cedars.

It was a still summer evening and the sun was slowly curving down to bed. Frank Russell and I stood at last on the soggy, bedspring bank of a remote little jewel of a trout pond. A ragged unbroken wall of tall cedars literally pressed at our backs.

"See that nice trout feeding out there, Frank?" I said, pointing pondward some hundred feet.

"Barely," Frank answered cynically, shielding his eyes Indian fashion and peering through a dancing fog of delighted mosquitoes.

"Want to see me ketch 'im?" I bragged softly, ignoring both Frank's sarcasm and the feasting mosquitoes.

"I *dare* you to," Frank answered, glancing dubiously over his shoulder at the looming cedars. "But just how do you propose to drop a lure out there—by slingshot, balloon, or helicopter?"

"Watch!" I said with insufferable superiority, and I quickly assembled my magic new glass spinning rod, threaded on the hair-like monofilament nylon line, tied on a plastic casting bubble and a bare fly hook, impaled a live grasshopper on the hook, and triumphantly croaked, "Here goes!"

With one casual flip I cast the lure; it arched out truly over the rise—"plop"—; and I barely straightened out the spider-web line when the fish whammed it—and we were on to our first trout, and a nice one, too.

"Well, I'm a bowlegged tadpole!" Frank said, awestruck. "So *that's* what you call spinning?"

"Yup," I said, proudly reeling in and grinning fanatically. "Yup, this is the new love of my life."

This deathless drama unfolded some eight or ten years ago. As I recollect Frank and I each took several fair trout that evening, mostly on live grasshoppers and one or two on artificial flies. We missed at least twice as many strikes because of the inevitable slack and stretch in the spinning line—one of the smaller headaches in spinning—but despite all this Frank became an immediate and burning convert to spinning.

"Order me one of those outfits, Johnny!" he said as we ducked and threaded our way back to the fish car. "Do it *tomorrow!*"

"Your most idle whim is a command, sir," I said. "But how about our having a soothing beer to celebrate your initiation into the dark mysteries of spinning?"

As we rattled back to town, flushing the crouching night-hawks off the dirt road like mad, Frank sat in silence. Finally he spoke.

"You know, Johnny," he said. "These casting bubbles are

all right—novel as hell—but this spinning business would *really* be something if they could find a way to cast a lure— say a number eighteen dry fly—and have the casting weight fall off once the fly was floating 'way out there. That way there'd be no clumsy and distracting plastic float either to scare the fish upon landing or on the retrieve or to slow the strike when the fish hits."

Frank was catching on fast. "Smart boy," I said. "You've divined one of the main headaches of this form of spinning in one easy lesson. There's only one small hitch—how're you going to do it?"

"Yes," Frank continued thoughtfully, as though talking to himself. "Yes," he repeated, "the problem is to find some sort of expendable casting weight. Hm . . . now let's see. . . ."

Two days after he got his new spinning outfit, Frank Russell solved the problem of spin-casting even the tiniest dry flies fabulous distances and then, equally important, floating them. He's that kind of a guy. He solved it by use of an ingenious expendable lead casting weight that falls off immediately upon contact with the water, leaving the fly floating high and dry. He calls his simple contraption the Russell Castaway, but I shall not explain it in more detail here because his application for a patent has not yet been granted. Instead I shall pause and dilate a little on conventional spinning itself.

As everyone who has ever held a fish pole now knows, spinning (known as "threadlining" in England) is a fairly new method of sport fishing imported from Europe, the chief feature of which revolves about a free-stripping, fixed-spool, anti-backlash reel. A fine line, of leader thickness, is usually employed along with some sort of weight—whether in the lure or otherwise—to strip the line off the reel when the cast is made. For in spinning, unlike in fly-fishing, it is not the *line* that is cast but the *lure*. To this extent it is more nearly like bait-casting.

The practical advantages of spinning are manifold: even a child can cast a lure incredible distances; cautious big fish are thus more easily approached and more frequently caught off guard; little or no casting room is necessary for the out pitch; clumsy Mortimer Snerd himself couldn't foul the line; and normally unreachable water can thus be covered with deception and ease.

Back in the dear dead days of B. S. (before spinning), the line drums on all bait-casting reels revolved as the line was unwound with the cast, as though one were stripping off thread from a revolving spool held on a nail, much like the old Halloween rat-a-tats kids once used on the neighbors' windows. Frequently, however, the unwinding reel ran faster than the outgoing line, particularly near the end of the cast, creating that fisherman's horror known as the backlash. Every season I still run across an occasional fisherman sitting quietly on some remote bank, mumbling in his beard, still trying to unsnarl his casting line. "How's it coming, pal?" I usually whisper and quietly pass on. They never even look up. . . .

Then along came the revolutionary spinning reel with its stationary line-storage drum—and gone was that particular form of fishing madness. For in spinning, the line-storage drum (or spool) remains stationary as the line (or thread) is drawn off over the stationary *end,* not the revolving *side,* of the spool. There can be no backlash because the line merely dribbles off the end of the spool and, whether cast fast or slow, there is no possible way it can get snarled in the reel. Take an ordinary spool of thread and try it yourself.

38

The consequent decrease in casting resistance and lowered friction coupled with the general ease in casting thereby permits a child—and even ladies in slacks—to cast fabulous distances. Many of my old fly-fishing friends took up this comparatively new sport and some have become wedded to it to the virtual exclusion of their fly fishing. I became wedded, too, but I have since gotten a divorce and I'll tell you why.

With my customary childish curiosity and helpless compulsion to possess every new fishing gadget that comes along, I too fell for spinning—hook, line, and sinker. Some two-hundred-dollars-worth-of-equipment later I woke up, rubbed my eyes, and decided that I did not give a tinker's damn for this new method of taking trout. In fact I gave up spinning before many fishermen in these parts had even heard of it, and instead returned to my fly fishing with, if possible, an even greater sense of joy and dedication.

I admit everything that the increasingly numerous slaves to spinning claim for their new sport; and I recognize much of its charm and fascination. It is not so much that I hate spinning, but rather that I love fly fishing so much better. For one thing I happen to prefer to strike and play my fish on or near the surface, and typical spinning is generally done with deep-running lures for the reason that the conventional spinning lure *also* is the casting weight that is necessary to strip out the line. I have also long been familiar with and have used the various hookups of the floating plastic bubble (and similar devices) with a wet or dry fly, but I somehow do not like either casting or fishing with them. This Rube Goldberg business of using tiny swivels and bubbles and all leaves me cold.

Perhaps it is largely an hitherto unsuspected sense of neatness and fitness on my part, coupled with my delight in the

39

beauty and subtlety inherent in being part of a good cast with a fly rod, for one thing is certain: there is no doubt that these spinning get-ups can and do take fish that often cannot even be *reached* in any other way. Perhaps the dismaying sense of fishing with "hardware" offends me. Certainly I have had advantages few "spinners" possess, what with the free use of and part ownership in the fabulous but undeveloped Russell Castaway. I dunno, maybe I'm just a cream puff.

At any rate, another serious drawback to all methods of spinning, in my book, is the comparative length of time involved in making the retrieve. Perhaps a spinning reel with an automatic retrieve might partially answer this objection, but as things stand it gets my cork to paste out a beautiful hundred-foot spinning cast and then, while reeling in, stand there and helplessly watch a nice trout rising a mere fifty feet out there or over here or over there, and not be able to immediately paste one over him. Then, more often than not, by the time I have reeled in to cast at this last rise, the fish has either moved on or else when I cast at the spot he or another fish rises a few feet to one side or the other and fingers his nose at me—while there I am 'way out there again, grating my bridgework and reeling in like mad.

The point is that any competent fly fisherman can retrieve his fly and cast it out over a rising fish—assuming it is in casting range—much quicker than can his spinning brothers. Perhaps my basic lack of interest in spinning springs from the fact that I am a slave to attempting dainty casts over rising trout; and that those stout fellows who can stand and cast out and reel in, then cast out and reel in, stolidly raking non-rising water for hour after hour, arouse my respect for their dogged patience but not any desire to copy them. I will patiently stalk rising trout by the hour, but once they sulk and go down I am inclined to join them and go pout in the car and sob over my beer until they decide to come back up to the skylight of their homes.

But none of these objections goes to the heart of the matter and I suspect that I would still prefer to fly fish for trout with the conventional split bamboo fly rod and regular tapered silk or nylon line even if all the technical objections to spinning were solved. I rather think that the simplest statement is that I find the art and ritual of fly casting a joyous and poetic experience in itself, fish or no fish. Perhaps it is sheer sentimentality or conservatism on my part; perhaps it is a stubborn desire to do things the hard way; but somehow or other I like and prefer the sense of *personal involvement* and *immediacy* and *control* that I, at least, feel only when I am delicately casting my fly over likely trout waters. By comparison I find that this thing called spinning is strictly for the birds.

There—I've finally said it! The line of dedicated and appalled spin-fishermen who wish to stone me for my heresy will please form on the left.

6

Lost Atlantis

IT WAS a hot lazy afternoon in mid-August. The small fry had the radio turned on full blast, blaring out the first game of a doubleheader between the New York Yankees and, I guess, the Green Bay Packers. The game had reached a pretty pass: there were two down and the bases were loaded; some character or other from Gap Tooth, Kentucky, was coming to bat; the din was terrific. I was enchanted to learn that this man of destiny weighed 193 pounds, stood 5 feet 11, had been rejected by the draft for night sweats, and boasted a batting average of .315. But horror of horrors, he had popped out in the last two times at bat. . . .

I retreated to the side porch, dark with hatred of all organized sports in general and Sunday afternoon baseball in particular. "Try that favorite brew of millions!" the announcer bawled after me. "Try a cool bottle of Pssst's mel-

43

low, golden, *homogenized* beer!" Ah, science had invaded even the beer vats . . . I made a mental note forever to avoid the stuff and sat staring morosely at the unkempt lawn, hot, bored, and fidgety. It was too torrid to go fishing, and anyway, I generously concluded, a responsible husband and parent owes a certain moral duty to share some of his leisure hours with his wife and children. Especially the poor kids. . . . Yes, during their formative and impressionable years a man's children need dear old dad around to—well—to sort of quietly set them an example. After all, *fishing* wasn't everything in life . . . I gave a virtuous little sniff.

Just then Grace came to the screen door and suggested that the lawn needed currying. "The place," she added acidly, "is beginning to look like an abandoned graveyard." Poor girl, she still cherishes the dream that I can ever be housebroken—at least during fishing season.

"Let's tether a goat instead and be the show place of the neighborhood," I said, ducking a withering look.

"Muskrat swings and pops up to center field!" the radio tragically proclaimed, as though announcing the fall of Rome. I squeezed my eyes shut.

Grace weighed the troubled situation. "Will you promise to mow the lawn tomorrow after work if I let you go fishing now?" she countered, trading slyly on a certain weakness she had observed in her husband.

"Madam, it's a deal," I answered brightly, already halfway out to the old fish car. With a flourish I swung open the garage doors, nearly tripped over a lurking lawn mower, and leapt into the fish car. "Giddap, Buckshot," I chortled, free as the wind, and in nothing flat I was rattling out toward Moose Creek, one of my favorite trout streams. Growing children, I mused between bounces, needed to balance their character development with the rare vitamins found only in freshly caught trout. Yes, I reflected, young ideals can best be nurtured in sturdy young bodies. Far from walking out on the kids, then, this fishing expedition, like so many others, was essentially a sacrificial labor of love.

Moose Creek is no great shakes to look at, being for the most part narrow and brushy, but the stretch where I usually hit it is a wide, shallow stream formed by an ancient inactive beaver dam which backs up the water for nearly a mile. I had been fishing there off and on for over fifteen years. The place harbors some nice brook trout but they are a temperamental lot, scary and hard to catch.

For years I had been hitting Moose Creek at this very same place—at old Camp Alice—about a half-mile upstream from the old beaver dam. I had almost always confined my fishing between the camp and the dam. While a good deal of the stretch was wadable, the margins of it were inclined to be swampy and difficult and there were also some interesting crannies and hideouts that could only be reached from a boat because of the varying depth of the water or accumulation of silt. Consequently I usually threw my rubber boat on the roof of the car whenever I planned to fish there. I had it along today.

Once or twice in recent years I had ventured upstream a little way from the usual point of embarkation, but this upper stretch was so choked and clogged with lily pads and some sort of matted and clutching water grass that I soon gave up and deeded it back to the Indians. Yup, there was no doubt about it: downstream toward the dam was by far the better place to fish. It was true that old-time fishermen used to tell me about a wonderful spring-fed beaver dam near the headwaters—"way up there in the foothills," they'd wave vaguely—but years ago, it seemed, some low

45

genius in the conservation department had had a vision and
blasted the dam out as part of some newfangled stream-
improvement program. Here the old-timers would invariably
choke up and dolefully wag their heads as though to say:
"Mysterious are the devices of all game wardens . . ." So
the word was out that the fishing upstream was all shot; and
the fact was that the old fishing trails along the near bank
had long since grown in and become choked with tangles of
windfalls.

"Yep, yep," one old-time fisherman told me. "We'd only
taken barrels of beautiful trout out of that there upper
dam for nigh on to half a century—so those smart hammer-
heads in the State Capitol proved the fishing was bad—so
they up an' blasts her out!"

Thus it was that on a hot Sunday afternoon I reluctantly
decided to go upstream and survey the historic ruins for
myself. Boredom, not vision, was all that drove me to it.
I leisurely wrestled the rubber boat off the fish car, gave the
bladders an extra shot of air for my trip, loaded and strapped
my .38 around my waist, threw my fishing gear and an old
rod and a few cans of beer in my packsack, and shoved off.
I paddled upstream slowly in the blazing sun, craning and
listening, deliberately killing time. The voyage was on.

My first mild shock was to observe that the lily pads and
thick water grass petered out before I had gotten around
the second bend, the stream opening up into beautiful gravel-
bottomed water in which I could see numerous small trout
darting about. I had no doubt that their elders were lurking
not far away. Naturally in the hot sun and the calm no fish
were rising, but the spot was as trouty-looking as any stretch
I had seen on the creek. "My, my," I murmured, "where
has *this* place been all my life?" Of course my excuse was
that I'd only been fishing the same creek for fifteen years.

I slowly pushed on and gradually the prevailing swampy shore gave way to higher land flanked in turn by low ridges, the creek narrowing and deepening, the banks now being lined with as lovely a stand of mature white pine as I had seen in many a year. Calm as it was, the soft whish and whine of the wind sifting through the tall wavy tops sounded like the muted strains of faraway violins. After another half-mile or so of this haunting vagrant music the creek narrowed down sharply.

Then I came to my first beaver dam. It wasn't much of a dam, as dams go, but the thing that quickened my pulse was the fact that it was a live dam, with fresh beaver cuttings very much in evidence. Could it possibly be? I mused, pondering what might lie above. Hm . . . let's go see.

I tossed the old rubber boat up over the dam, which didn't hold back much water, and sat perspiring in the bright sunlight sipping a can of warm beer. The big pines had now given way to a lush jungle of tag alders, the low ridges some distance away being adorned by spruces and balsams and a sprinkling of mixed second growth. I shrugged and pushed onward and upward.

In the next hour I negotiated three more fresh beaver dams, all about as modest as the first, the creek all the while getting so narrow that several times I was tempted to call it quits and head back downstream for the evening rise. But there is no lunatic quite like a trout lunatic, so each time I resisted temptation and doggedly pushed on.

Then I began to hit a series of big old white-pine windfalls lying plump across the creek. Most annoying they were, being too low to pass under and being sufficiently high, with their scorched and jagged old branches, to give me a bad time with my boat and gear. After scaling a round dozen of these fire-scarred old giants I finally scuffed a

47

seat for myself among the layers of bird and animal guano on the last log and sat there sweltering and had another beer and wondered what in hell I was doing way up there on a narrow miserable creek in which any decent trout would have a hard time turning around. I mopped my brow and looked at my watch and figured I could still fish the evening rise below if I abandoned this foolish enterprise and made tracks. Yes, I'd turn around and flee this malarial bog.

Just then a slight breeze came up—I swear it was a miracle—and I heard the faint but unmistakable sound of distant running water, not a trickle, not the gentle splash of a little dam, but the dull steady moan of a considerable volume of falling water. Again I squatted in the rubber boat and paddled away and in a half-hour came to a beautiful live beaver dam, at least eight feet high, from where I sat crouched in the boat below and, it seemed, at least a hundred feet long. It was a gorgeous thing.

When I had excitedly clambered up the crisscrossed beaver cuttings and finally stood on the mud-packed crest of the vast dam, trembling like a girl, I felt like Magellan or somebody beholding a new continent. The dam was loaded to the scuppers, leaking over the top in some places, and backing up a beautiful expanse of mysterious deep water as far as the eye could see. Low ridges of jack pine fringed either side. The whole thing appeared to lie in a broad ancient beaver meadow, the dry margins still being lined with old water-killed trees reaching their rigid empty branches beseechingly into the air. It was plain that untold generations of beaver had dwelt and built their dams at this spot.

From this, and the occasional weathered old workings that I saw mixed with the fresh cuttings, I was pretty sure I was standing on the same old upper beaver dam blasted out years before by "those damned game wardens." The only trouble was that the oblivious beaver had ignored the fact that a dam in that place was officially *verboten*. Alas, they'd surely be arrested for violating . . . As I stood gaping, an exploring grasshopper foolishly lit on a sun-dried cutting near me. I caught and tossed him out in the dam. There was a quick swirl and a chunky trout whammed Mr. Grasshopper and flashed down and away. Hm. . . . Peering, I could see the wavering outline of a broad network of crisscrossed logs lying deep under water. The plot thickened.

Purely in the interest of science I rigged up my rod, tied on a number 12 Slim Jim—a quick-sinking wet fly—and pasted her out. *Clap!*—and I was onto a twelve-inch brook trout. Standing there in one spot on the dam in the blazing sun I took ten plucky brook trout running from ten to thirteen inches—missing twice that number—before my conscience smote me and I took down my rod. I sat and cleaned my fish, whistling while I worked, and then had my last can of beer to celebrate my new discovery. I then tossed my rubber boat over the dam, gave my bulging woven nylon creel a final loving pat, and pushed on. By then I couldn't stop and by that time, too, the sun was slacking off, and as I paddled upstream the trout were beginning to rise as far as I could see, some of them appearing larger than any I had taken or pricked. A pair of herons rose in noisy haste and flapped away in undulant flight. Ah, what a beautiful, isolated spot, I mused, delighted as a kid who had wandered into a fairy toyland.

I had not got two hundred feet above the splashing waters of my wondrous new dam before I heard something that made me nearly fall out of the boat—*the roaring rush of high-speed auto traffic!* Had mighty Magellan gone in circles and merely rediscovered Spain? I held my paddles to

49

listen. There m-must be some mistake, I told myself, sick with dismay.

There wasn't. Another car rushed by, stridently sounding its horn. Frantic now with mingled curiosity and concern for my new dream spot, I paddled upstream in the lengthening shadows through one of the most dramatic rises of brook trout I had seen in years, the primeval calm of the spot being broken only by the ever-nearing roar and clash of car traffic and wailing horns. The combination of pristine peace and screeching mechanical din was positively weird. And in Heaven's name how, in this day and age, could there be such fabulous fishing within a stone's throw of a public speedway?

Up, up I went, like a man possessed, through perhaps a half-mile of sporty but narrowing water with lovely trout dimpling all around me. The invisible rushing cars now seemed to be practically alongside me. Pretty soon the dwarfed creek narrowed and shallowed to a rivulet so that I could no longer row. Shrugging like one of Roger's resourceful Rangers I got out and splashed upstream, dragging the boat by the anchor rope. Shortly the ridges narrowed, grown tight with jack pines, and I got into a series of shallow and intensely cold gravelly feeder springs. I then knew that I was at the headwaters of Moose Creek. But precisely where in hell was *that*?

By now it was getting dusk and I was running out of towing water, so I philosophically took my paddles apart and stashed them in my packsack, shouldered my boat, and sloshed up the dwindling main channel. All the time I could still hear the Sunday traffic rushing mildly by. A quarter of a mile of this and my creek became a mere trickle, so I veered left toward the car sounds and, with all the airy grace of a man carrying a folded double mattress, fought my pregnant rubber boat up through the thick spruce and tamarack to the jack pine on top of the ridge. There I rested and heaved and blew and mopped the sweat away and sneaked a reassuring look at my glistening trout—and longed for a beer. Then I heard the mutter of voices close by. Leaving my boat and pistol and packsack hidden in the jack pine I walked toward the voices and in no time came out into an opening—and upon a whole family of Sunday blueberry pickers, complete with picnic hampers, parked Chevrolet, and Grandma.

"Hello," I said, peering engagingly through my damp and sweat-matted locks.

The nearest picker, a kneeling, butt-sprung lady clad in revealing if scarcely becoming tight slacks, wheeled and squealed and nearly dumped her pail of berries. She stood regarding me in moist horror, as though she had seen a ghost emerge from the woods. I didn't much blame her. Another unseen car rushed by.

"Hello," I repeated. "I've been out looking for berries and I guess I got a little mixed up," I partially lied. "What road is that?" I said, motioning toward the sounds of traffic.

By this time a red-faced, perspiring man, presumably the lady's husband, quickly moved up to defend her be-slacked virtue from the hot maniac emerged from the swamp. I repeated my suave falsehood as he squinted an appraising eye at me. "The traffic you hear is on the main road between Ishpeming and Gwinn, on Highway 35," he answered warily. "You're right at the Moose Creek turn off." I blinked and shook my head at that, for I had just come over the same road on the way out fishing, and was therefore less than three miles from my car. And after all those years I was charmed to learn, for the first time, that since the dawn of man—or at least since the last glacier—my creek had always

51

described a gigantic U. My chum kept staring skeptically at me. "What kind of berries you lookin' for in hip boots, fella?—cranberries? And what's in the bulging creel?"

Touché! I had forgotten to cache the telltale creel. I blushed prettily and piled on another whopper. "Oh, that . . . wa-water lilies! Yep, been out gathering water lilies, too . . . wife's crazy about 'em . . . got all tangled up in that awful swamp." I tittered a trifle hysterically and waved vaguely at my New Spain. "Don't ever go near it," I warned darkly. "Full of snakes and things." The lady of the slacks sidled away from me as from a crazed leper. "Look," I rattled on, swerving abruptly from water lilies and reptilian swamps, "how would you like to make yourself a fast two bucks—and have a coupla cold beers to boot?"

"Hm . . . *cold* beer? How do you mean?" he parried, devoutly rolling his eyes and moistening his lips and stroking his chin. Plainly I was now talking his language.

"For driving me over to my car on Moose Creek—at Camp Alice. What do you say?"

I think the visions of the cold beer rather than mere money turned the trick; in a half-hour I was back at the fish car and had loaded down my pal with cool foaming goodies and his cab fare and sent him on his way. As he started to drive away he leered out the window of his car, winked, and fired this parting shot: "Those are certainly the gamiest-smellin' water lilies I ever smelt, fella. If I was you I'd go clean 'em off down in the creek!"

I grinned and waved as he gunned the Chev away, and then sat down on the running board of the fish car and opened a heavenly cold beer. "A-a-ah . . ." I looked up and saw a thin slice of yellow moon. I held up the beer. "You've had a busy day, little man," I whispered. "Fish, drink, and be merry—for tomorrow we must cut the grass. *Skoal!*"

7

Back-Yard Trout Fishing

I T W A S one of those warm, soft, luminous summer evenings; the kind that commands fishermen to go forth and then makes them yearn for time to stop in its tracks. The sky was big and high and gloriously aflame, and the fanning shafts of sunlight sifting through the far-off piles of clouds looked like the very organ pipes of Heaven. I had stolen away after supper to get an hour or two of the evening rise on one of the nearby trout ponds. The old Model-A Ford and I were bumping along nicely down through the aquarium-green tunnel of an unkempt grove of second-growth maples, about three miles from my chosen pond, when—*pow!*—I had a flat, so I drew over bumpety-bump to the side of the dirt road, cursing softly as a steve-dore.

Here was a nice kettle of no fish. If I stopped to change the tire I'd have little time left over for fishing, and if I

53

hiked it, even less. What to do? I stood looking around. Hm . . . that bald "selectively" logged hill to the left looked vaguely familiar. . . . Then I realized that I was only about a quarter of a mile from Klipple Pond, a shallow and dying old mud puddle left from the ruins of an ancient beaver dam. I hadn't fished there since I was a kid. Should I give it a visit for old time's sake? The trout fishing in it used to be very good, yes, but that was true nearly everywhere in those distant days. Then there were dark rumors, too, that the pond had been dynamited and netted in recent years; and, anyway, none of the really *good* fishermen ever fished there any more or even mentioned the place. After all, how could a fisherman in his right mind expect to catch a decent trout these days less than nine miles from town, and only *six* miles by crow flight? Perish the thought.

Thus did I consider and mentally damn old Klipple Pond. I sighed and reached for the tire irons and then paused. *Must* I spend this enchanted evening wrestling with a flat? Here I had a night out and was dying to fish (I hadn't for a whole twenty-four hours!), so I shrugged and instead dug out the necessary tackle and gear and locked the car. At least I might as well go *look* at the place. . . . In less than ten minutes I had slipped and skidded down the old needle-covered deer trail on the steep root-lined hill and was standing on the soggy and twilit-margin of the old pond. Time had not stopped in its tracks; the organ pipes had disappeared.

The old pond lay in a deep glacial bowl scooped from between abrupt wooded hills. In the closing dusk its shallow waters looked as delicately thin and blue and uninviting as dairy milk in the bottom of a porridge bowl. It was the same old pond, all right: still no bigger than a small skating rink; still dotted with myriad islands of lily pads; still with the

same old grass-grown water-logged raft that had once nearly
drowned me still anchored to the near shore with the same
weathered upright pole. Yes, and there was still the same
dying sun shaded by the mixed spruce and maple hill across
from me; still the same rhythmically persistent jungle drum-
ming of the bullfrogs—*kwonky-kunk, kwonky-kunk!*—; and
still the plaintive evening calls and ghostly dartings of the
same mysterious birds whose names I had never sought nor
ever cared to know. . . .

I sat there reflecting that under the surface of those placid
waters endless battles raged, as fierce as any wars of men.
Insects fought insects; bloodsuckers fought bloodsuckers,
crayfish crayfish; salamanders salamanders; and all of them
warred on each other; and the trout (if still there were any)
fought all of them, all the while trying to avoid the fish ducks
and gulls and kingfishers, the cranes and ospreys, and all the
other swift dive bombers from out of the sky. And there was
always the fear of the wily and undulant otter. And then,
lo, a stray man now came along and sought to ensnare the
trout with cunning little deceits contrived of feathers and
fur. Yes, and he too was of the same species of lordly men
who still stupidly fought each other days without end. . . .

I sat there reflecting that there was something ageless and
timeless about a place like this; that it couldn't have changed
much since the dawn of the world; that it would probably
remain much the same after restless man, whose wisdom appeared unable to keep up with his brains, finally joined hands
with his fellows and soared heavenward, propelled thence
by the marvels of nuclear fission. Here, at this place, was
primeval solitude: the patient unfolding pattern of a sub-
limely indifferent nature which doubtless regarded man as
no more and no less important than a gnat.

As I sat there gripped by such lofty and poetic thoughts

Trout Madness

I heard the first splash. I crouched low and shaded my eyes against the waning sun and discerned an ever-widening wake not more than fifty feet out from me. Hm . . . Must have been a cavorting muskrat, I concluded, ready to flip my cigar pondward and flee the hungry mosquitoes. *"Plunk,"* it went again and this time—you've guessed it—I *saw* that it wasn't any mere muskrat at all, but the rise of a fine, careless, savage man-sized trout which was out after his supper and didn't give a tinker's damn who knew it.

With trembling hands I groped for my rod and clapped it together and threaded my line and tied on a leader and a pert little dry fly and teetered out a few feet in the muddy and treacherous ooze waiting for my ravenous friend to renew his challenge. All poetry and mosquitoes were forgotten.

"Plash!" he went again, and by this time I became blissfully aware of trout rises dimpling all over the pond. Rollcasting because of the halo of tag alders behind me, I began feeding out line to my near fish like a rodeo cowboy trying to lasso an escaping steer. Finally my stuff was out there, placed deliberately about ten feet to the right of him, so as not to put him down, and so that I might give it to him right on the nose the next time he rose—

"P-lunk!" he obediently rose, accepting the challenge, and I swiftly drew up the slack and rolled her like a hoop, the line rippling out like a fleeing serpent, the leader finally folding over, and the fly itself lighting upon the center of the feeding circle as gently as the wafted down of a thistle. There was a surge as my trout took it—*wham*—and I was on to him, fighting him, while all about me the frogs croaked—*kwonky-kunk*—, the birds darted and flashed and called, a ghostly owl hooted far up the valley, and the sun winked down out of sight. Then a fine rain started to fall. I stood there enthralled in the gathering gloom, my rod hooped and

straining, the fisherman sunk in the ancient muck and ooze, ever so slowly fighting him up to the net. Give him line, take in line, come, darling, please come to daddy. . . . In ten ecstatic minutes—or was it years?—he lay gleaming in the net, as mistily colorful as a slice of rainbow robbed from the sky. Nearly a foot and a half in length he was, the loveliest native brook trout I had seen in many a year. And all this, believe it or not, within six miles of my own back yard!

It is seldom that rational men whistle when they must change a tire, especially in the rainy dark, but I know of one lunatic who did that night as he kept glancing up at the dripping creel of trout that sagged from the door of his car. . . . Since then my pal Henry and I have fished the old pond many times, but I must confess that never since have we found the trout as much on the prod as they were on that first magic night of rediscovery.

The unlikely old pond is truly enchanted; nowhere is it deeper than five feet, though the mud must go clean to Singapore. It crawls with bloodsuckers and the only fish in it are adult native brook trout. Even stranger, from opening day until about mid-season the place is teeming with trout; but along about the Fourth of July, as soon as the real summer heat comes along, they disappear as though someone had rung down a curtain or—worse yet—poisoned the pond overnight. The Lord only knows where or precisely why they go—but each spring at opening day they are back bigger and better than ever. There is a respectable inlet and a good outlet, and I keep promising myself that one day I must explore these unknown stretches, but my reason (sometimes the poorest of fishing guides) plus my aerial maps tell me there shouldn't be any decent open water anywhere near there. (But aerial maps can't show cool, deep, trouty beaver dams hidden away in the shade of enfolding trees.) At any rate, each year since then I give up the old puddle about mid-season and rattle off to other and greener pastures.

Perhaps next fall during bird or duck season I'll take my shotgun and my hip boots and explore the front and back doors of this queer old pond and try to discover where those smart trout go on their annual summer vacation. But perhaps that would spoil all the mystery of the pond; perhaps it is better to accept its favors humbly and without question; perhaps it is well to rest a lovely enchanted old pond that permits one to try for gallant and fighting native brook trout practically in one's own back yard.

Moral: Flat tire or no flat tire, pause once in a while in the summer madness of fishing; pause and take inventory and simply *make* yourself revisit some of those long-neglected and "fishless" old trout waters. There may be some big surprises in store. With me, at least, it has just about gotten so that my best and most exciting fishing is had at these forgotten old places that are totally ignored by those "smart" fishermen who day after day roar by them at top speed and, then, standing shoulder to shoulder like herd bulls, lash the more popular distant waters to a froth as foamy as an ad of their favorite beer.

8

Little Panama

MY FATHER, Nicholas Traver, was a tall man with big hands and the disposition of a bilious gnu. He was also the world's most successful saloonkeeper: that is, he hunted and fished all the time and only visited his saloon to raid the iron safe and cuss out the bartenders and lay in more hooch. He spent the rest of his time roaming the woods with his pal, old Dan McGinnis. Mostly he and Dan went to the favorite of his three camps, the South Camp.

Old Dan was a quick, wiry, mustached Scotch-Irish iron miner, turned trapper, who had violated the game laws so long and so well that they had finally given him a job and a star and called him a state trapper.

It was Dan's boast that he had never owned a game or fish license from the time, years before, when he had inadvertently stumbled into the county clerk's office and, not knowing just what else to do, had applied for a license. When the young man at the desk asked him the color of his eyes, he promptly replied, "Bloodshot," whereupon, Dan avowed, "the young whippersnapper commenced laffin' so hard he couldn't stop, so out I walks from the damn place, an' I ain't never been back. Of all the insultin' young bastards!"

Anyway, when Dan got to be a state trapper he was supposed to roam around the woods and trap wolves and coyotes and other predatory beasts; but when he got the star and the salary he quit trapping, and instead he and my father would go out to camp and fish and get a little drunk and play cards and argue.

My father and Dan would drive out of our back yard in the old buckboard with a barrel-bellied bay mare called Molly, the oats and a bale of hay in the back, a lantern clamped on the dashboard, and a battered water pail dangling from the rear axle. When they got to the gate my father, suddenly remembering, would call back to my mother. She would come hurrying out from the kitchen, wiping her hands on her apron, and quietly stand there on the back porch shading her eyes.

"We'll just be gone for the weekend, Bess," my father would say.

My mother would nod her head quickly and smile and wave her hand gladly, but sometimes when she turned away I noticed tears in her gray eyes. I guess it was because she knew that the weekend meant that she wouldn't see my father until the following Wednesday or Thursday, when they would return home for more food and whisky and beer, and then shortly depart once again "for the weekend."

But we boys said very little about my father being in the woods so much, because when he wasn't in the woods he was so crabby and bad-tempered that we wished he were. And he had two good bartenders, a Frenchman and a Cornishman, to run the saloon for him when he was gone. I have never in my life seen a man so crazy about the woods, about hunting and fishing, as my father. Unless it was old Dan McGinnis, the state trapper who wouldn't trap.

On my father's land there was a lake in which there were no fish. On the county map it was called Lake Traver, and I think my father was very proud of this—though he never spoke of it—because when they first came out with the big maps with Lake Traver on them, he stuck one on the wall of the saloon, above the music box, near a gaslight, and made a big circle around his lake with a red crayon.

Lake Traver was the only body of water on his land. It was a deep glacial jewel, with its steep rocky banks on one side, above which towered straight Norway pine trees, their fallen needles lying thick on the moss-covered old rocks and in the crevices. The rest of the shore line was mostly wild cranberry marsh, with young cherry trees and poplars and maples reaching back to the pines. The lake was spring-fed, gravel-bottomed, without an inlet, and the water was very clear. It was always cool, even in the middle of the summer. But there were no fish.

From season to season my father and old Dan had planted barrels of brook trout in the lake—trout fry, fingerlings, even mature trout—but they were never seen again. Old Dan once suggested, during a feverish argument over this phenomenon, that the real reason the trout didn't survive was because they couldn't live in a lake owned by such a cantankerous, poisonous old buzzard as my father. But my father pounded the table and shook his head and shouted, "I'll make the bastards live in there yet." So the next spring would see him and old Dan lurching and tugging and cursing more cans of doomed trout into Lake Traver.

The funny part of it was that all they had to do was to hike over on almost any of the next forties, owned by the lumber company, and there the streams and ponds and beaver dams abounded with trout.

Just over the line, on the lumber company's land, in sight of my father's lake, was a big ancient beaver dam teeming with brook trout. My father tried to buy the land with the big beaver dam on it, but the lumber company wouldn't sell because there was a nice stand of young white pine coming along on it. They told him he could fish the dam all he liked, and treat it as his own, but they would not sell. So my father, overcome with humility and profound gratitude, roared at them to go plumb to hell. "You graspin' capitalist bastards!" The gnawing horrors of Wall Street were always a favorite theme of my father's.

My father was an independent man. He was in fact one of the most independent men I ever knew. And stubborn, too. He got so mad because he couldn't buy the beaver dam that he ceased to fish on any of the lumber company's land. Since they owned all the land for miles around his camp, this left him only his fishless lake to fish in. And he dearly loved to fish.

He couldn't somehow bring himself to believe there were no trout in his lake, despite the fact that old Dan, who could catch fish in a desert, had tried all kinds of bait, had flung flies all over the lake, and had even netted and dynamited to test the place, but nary a fish.

It really got pretty bad. He and Dan would hitch up old Molly and plod morosely out to camp for the weekend, and by and by, after a few preliminary drinks, old Dan would sneak over to the beaver dam with his fishing tackle, and then in a little while my father, cursing quietly to himself, would slip through the woods to his lake. There they'd be, in plain sight of each other, old Dan landing one beautiful trout after the other out of the beaver pond, and my father, no longer cursing quietly to himself, circling and circling his lake like a crazed water buffalo, his long legs buried in the cranberry marshes, wallowing and threshing, fishing like mad, with never a solitary rise.

Later, when they met back at camp, old Dan would cock his head sideways, comb his mustache with his fingers, and say, all pert and bright, "Have any luck today, Nick?"

"Hell, no. No bloody luck. They ain't risin' today. The wind ain't right—but I guess it'll change by night, Danny."

Then old Dan would dig in the damp grass of his creel and lay out the trout he had caught, smiling and allowing that the wind wasn't so bad over his way. "Let's build us a damn good drink, Nick," Dan might add, licking his mustache.

"Yes, Dan, we had a pretty hard day." My father would be staring at Dan's trout.

"You better come fishing with me tonight over on the beaver dam, Nick."

"You go high-dive to hell, you trespassin' ol' rum-pot," my father would say, stomping into the camp.

I knew that all this was going on because occasionally my father and old Dan would take me along, "for a fishing trip," they called it. My fishing consisted mainly of taking care of the old mare, Molly, front and rear, weeding the stunted vegetable garden—which my father evidently maintained to vary the diet of rabbit and porcupine—and of paring potatoes, filling lamps, hauling water and firewood, and making up the bunks.

And then there was the business of mixing those whisky

sours for my father and Dan, which they never seemed to tire of. I learned to mix them before I learned to drink them. Whisky sours were one thing that my father and old Dan fully agreed upon. Never in my whole life have I seen two men who drank more whisky sours than my father and old Dan McGinnis.

It was on such a trip that the vision, the big solution, came to my father. It was a beautiful evening in the early spring, the trees were not yet in leaf, dusk was closing in, the whip-poorwills had started, the mists were rolling up from the marshes. I had finished doing the supper dishes and had put fresh salt on the deer licks. Dan and my father were out fishing, old Dan as usual over at his beaver dam, my father gloomily stalking his lake. I was just getting out the fixings for the whisky sours.

Suddenly I could hear them shouting out there in the twilight, and then their stomping, and they burst into the camp.

"By the roarin' Jesus, Nick, I think you got it—*a canal's the thing!* We'll run the bloody beaver dam over into your lake—an' that'll freshen and change the water, jus' like you say—hell, an'—why then there'll be oodles of trout livin' at last in Lake Traver. Well, I'll be cow-kicked!"

My father seldom got excited unless he was drunk or mad. This night he was neither, but he was very excited. His eyes were shining and I saw how he must have looked when he was a boy.

"It come to me sudden-like, Dan," he kept saying in an awed voice.

He kept illustrating and waving with sweeps of his big hands how they would scoop out the canal and join the beaver pond to the lake; how they would build stop dams at either end to keep out the water while they were digging.

"Why, Dan—listen, Dan—we'll tell that bloody lumber company crowd to go run up a hemp rope." Then turning to me: "Son, mix up a mess of whisky sours—take one for yourself." And then I got excited, too, because it was the first whisky sour I ever had. It was not the last—not even the last that night.

Although it was only Monday and the weekend was barely half over, early the next morning we hitched up protesting old Molly and hustled her back to town. My father and old Dan could talk of and plan nothing but the new canal.

After that we didn't see my father around the house for days—not for a good part of the summer, in fact. The very day we got home, he and Dan visited all the saloons in town, rounding up out-of-work lumberjacks and thirsty bar flies to help dig the canal.

They bought boxes and boxes of dynamite, got second-hand scrapers and picks and shovels, and third-hand horses, and paraphernalia galore. With their motley crew they threw up a cook-shack and bunk-house tent—and then rooted and gouged and slashed away at their canal all the summer through. The leaves were tinted and falling, the fishing season was nearly over, when they had finally dug their ditch from the beaver dam over to Lake Traver.

All summer long fishermen came from miles around to view the proceedings; to watch my father, stripped to the waist, a fanatic with a shovel, throwing up vast clouds of dirt, shouting, sweating, straining at rocks—and at the same time carefully, tenderly feeding his sad-eyed bar-fly crew just enough whisky to keep them from deserting and yet not enough so that they would tumble into the ditch. He was foreman, engineer, laborer, wet nurse and all the rest, rolled into one.

And old Dan—here, there, and everywhere, like a hornet

—cursing the teamsters, bullying the blasters, dispensing the drinks—occasionally falling into the ditch. But finally the great canal was dug and done and thirsting for water.

Labor Day was the big day, the grand opening. It seemed that half the town was lined up and down the big canal. My father had a bar set up along about the middle of the ditch. His two bartenders were there, aproned and sweating, working like mad serving free drinks. At noon my father got ready to fire his rifle, the signal for the blasters at each end of the canal to blow out the stop dams so that the prolific waters of the beaver pond would pour through the canal into the new trout paradise, Lake Traver.

As the noon hour drew near, everyone began to gravitate toward the middle of the canal. My father and old Dan stood out sort of in front of the rest, nearest the canal. Everybody was laughing and singing and talking.

Old Dan had a haircut and a red necktie for the occasion. He kept peering at a big silver watch and a soiled piece of paper which he held in his hand, clearing his throat. My father stood very tall and straight, his rifle ready in his hands. Then Dan raised his hand and glared at the crowd for silence. Squinting at the piece of paper which he held, he began to read, slowly and with dignity:

"This here is the dedication of Nick Traver's canal. We worked goddam hard on this here canal of Nick Traver's. You folks who is crazy about fishin' owe lots to the visions and leadership of my friend Nick Traver."

Dan turned to my father. "Let her go, Nick," he said, very quietly, and my father let her go, stepping back and handing the smoking rifle to me. Old Dan still stood peering at his watch. It took about half a minute for the short fuses to burn —the scampering blasters . . . and then two dull booms, practically together, and the stop dams were out. The hushed crowd pressed forward to the canal to watch.

For a moment nothing happened. Then we could hear a low rumbling roar, like distant thunder, growling and gathering; then we could see the water surging in from both directions in mighty waves, from the dam and from the lake, thundering, pounding, roaring and then—crash!—the two streams met in the middle of the canal, the ground trembled, and a great muddy wave burst high into the air, blotting out the sun like a typhoon, raining down all over—over Dan and my father, over me, the crowd, the bartenders, the whisky sours, over everything. And still the water roared in, hissing and boiling, while the dripping crowd stood there hunched and silent, like men at a lynching.

Then it happened. You could sense it before you could see it. There was an enormous flood of water coming from the lake, more and more and more, and then suddenly we saw —*we saw that the water was flowing in the wrong direction!* There was no mistake; it was roaring wildly past us from the lake into the beaver dam. We could see the dam rising and the lake lowering before our very eyes.

I looked at my father. He stood there dripping and mud-covered, shrunken-looking, his hair in his eyes, his mouth hanging open, watching the torrent pound into the beaver pond. Then we could see it before we could hear it, a cloud of earth and sticks and stones—it was war, a bombardment— then nothing but the pulsing surge of the water racing past us. And all the while my father and old Dan and the rest of us stood there, silently watching the fishless waters of Lake Traver emptying into the lumber company's ruined beaver dam. *The beaver dam had washed out.*

My father turned to me. He had closed his mouth. Looking like a little boy, he slowly wiped his muddy face with the back of his hand.

"Pa," I said very quietly, hoping the others would not hear. "Listen, Pa."

"What's that, son?"

"Pa, it looks like the whole trouble is your lake was higher than the beaver dam."

My father seemed to consider this. He pursed his lips and shook his head with little nods, thinking hard.

"Yes, son," he said finally, "it sure kind of looks that way."

Then someone tittered in the crowd. I heard it plainly. My father heard it too, for the look left his face in a flash, and he almost knocked me over as he leaped toward the crowd.

"*Who done that?*" he roared. "What dirty bastard done that?" He howled and danced before them, clutching out with his big hands, the veins standing out on his neck—a very bad sign. "I'll lick the hull mother-beating bunch of you!" he bellowed. The crowd gave ground as he advanced. "I don't give a rattlin' goddam for the hull snivelin' pack of you! I'll—"

Just then old Dan let out a whoop, and my father and everyone turned around just in time to see him sailing his big silver watch into the canal. He was acting like a drunken man in a beehive, leaping, laughing, cursing, shouting. He ran up to the boiling ditch, tore off his jacket, flung it in, turned and hollered, "Nick! Nick! It's a goddam swell idea—*a perfect swimmin' hole!*"

With that he took a mighty running dive, his thin legs crooked frog-fashion in the air, disappearing into the muddy water of the canal. My father and the rest frantically rushed up to save him. "Thar she blows!" someone hollered, just as old Dan came up spitting, snorting, splashing, looking like an aged walrus, threshing and trumpeting.

"Yoo hoo, boys!" he shouted, waving his hand. "Come on in—the water's fine!"

And, like the possessed swine of Gadara, every man jack of us, led by my father, went leaping pell-mell into what has been known, even to this day, as Nick Traver's Folly.

9

Paulson, Paulson, Everywhere

F o r many years I was district attorney of this bailiwick, and during that time I naturally had much to do with game wardens and, of course, with overzealous citizens who collided with the hunting and fishing laws. Indeed, I discovered some of my best fishing spots through these uneasy encounters; and while the following yarn is scarcely a fishing story, in any sporting sense, it *is* about trout and about some of the trout waters I found while plying my D. A. trade.

Up my way old township politicians never die; they merely look that way. Instead they become justices of the peace. It is a special Valhalla that townships reserve for their political cripples and has the following invariable rules of admission: The justice of the peace must be over seventy; he must be deaf; he must be entirely ignorant of any law but never admit it; and, during the course of each trial, he must chew—and violently expel the juice of—at least one (1) full package of Peerless tobacco. It is preferable that he speak practically no English, and that with an accent, but in emergencies an occasional exception is permitted to slip by. Sometimes I preferred the former.

I could write a lament as thick as this book about the grotesque experiences I have had trying justice court cases out before some of these rural legal giants. It is a depressing thought. Instead I shall tell you about the trial of Ole Paulson before Justice of the Peace Ole Paulson.

Ole Paulson of Nestoria township was charged with catching forty-seven brook trout out of season with a net. Ole Paulson was in rather a bad way because it is never legal to take or possess forty-seven brook trout in one day; to fish for them in any manner out of season; or ever to take brook trout with a net, in or out of season. Ole Paulson promptly pleaded not guilty and the case was set for trial before His Honor, Justice of the Peace Ole Paulson, also of Nestoria. I drove up there to try the case rather than send one of my assistants, not because I panted to sit at the feet of Justice Paulson, Heaven knows, but largely because I was dying to find out precisely where a man could ever *find* forty-seven brook trout in one place, regardless of how he took them. It was also a riotously beautiful September day, and afforded the D. A. a chance to escape from that personal prison he inhabits called his office.

"Vell, hayloo, Yonny!" His Honor greeted me as I entered his crowded courtroom, a high-ceilinged, plaster-falling, permanently gloomy establishment from which he ordinarily dispensed insurance of all kinds, assorted tourist supplies, game and fish licenses, live bait, not to mention various and sundry bottled goods and rubber accessories. "Ve vas yoost satting here vaiting for yew!"

"Was you, Your Honor?" I cackled gleefully, warming up disgracefully to this local political sachem, pumping his limp hand, inquiring about his rheumatism—or was it his flaring ulcers?—respectfully solicitous over his interminable replies, making all the fuss and bother over him that both he and the villagers demanded whenever the District Attorney came to town to attend court. It was understood that we two initiates into the subtle mysteries of the law had to put on a show for the groundlings. . . . The courtroom was crowded, every adult male in the community having somehow gathered enough energy to forsake the village tavern for a few hours and move across the street for the trial.

I turned to the People's star witness, the eager young game warden who had arrested the defendant. "Is the jury chosen yet?" I asked him in a stage whisper that must have been audible to a farmer doing his fall plowing in the next township. There could be no sneaky professional secrets in Judge Paulson's court—the penalty was swift and sure defeat.

"Yes," the game warden answered, "I struck the jury this morning. The list of jurors was prepared by Deputy Sheriff Paulson here. The six jurors are all here now."

It had not escaped my notice that I seemed to be getting fairly well hemmed in by Paulsons, but it was a trifle late to get into that now. I'd have to trust to the Lord and a fast outfield. I turned to Justice Paulson and said: "Very well, Your Honor, the People are ready to proceed with the trial."

"Okay den," His Honor said, rapping his desk with a gavel ingeniously contrived from a hammer wrapped in an old sock. He pointed to six empty chairs against a far wall. "Yantlemen of da yury," he announced, "yew vill now go sat

73

over dare." Six assorted local characters scrambled for their seats, relaxed with a sigh, and were duly sworn by Justice Paulson. Allowing the jurors to sit for the oath was only one of his minor judicial innovations.

Justice Paulson, exhausted by administering the oath, opened a fresh package of Peerless and stowed away an enormous chew in his cheek. There was a prolonged judicial pause while he slowly worked up this charge. He spat a preliminary stream against a tall brass cuspidor. "*Spa-n-n-n-g!*" rang this beacon, clanging and quivering like an oriental summons to evening prayer. "Okay," His Honor said in a Peerless-muffled voice.

"The People will call Conservation Officer Clark," I announced, and the eager young game warden arose, was sworn, took the stand—and told how he had come upon the defendent, Ole Paulson, lifting the net from Nestoria creek just below the second beaver dam in Section 9. "I caught him red-handed," he added.

"Do you have the trout and the net?" I asked the young warden, slyly noting the latitude and longitude of this fabulous spot.

"Oh, yes," he answered. "The net is in my car outside— and the trout are temporarily in the icebox in the tavern across the street. Is it okay if I go over and get them now?"

I turned to His Honor, "Your Honor, the People request a five-minute recess," I said.

Judge Paulson, moon-faced and entirely mute now from his expanding chew of Peerless, whanged another ringer, banged his homemade gavel on his desk and, thus unpouched, managed to make his ruling. "Yentlemen, Ay declare fi'-minoot intermissin so dat dis hare young conversation feller kin go gat his fish." He turned to a purple and

74

bladdery bystander. "Sharley," he said, "go along vit him over an' unlock da tavern."

I gnawed restlessly on an Italian cigar while Charlie, the tavern owner and my sole witness, went across the street to fetch the evidence. The jury sat and stared at me in stolid silence. His Honor replenished his chew, like a starved Italian hand-stoking spaghetti. "*Whing!*" went the judge, every minute on the minute. A passing dog barked. The bark possessed a curious Swedish accent, not "woof" but "*weuf*"! I wondered idly whether "Sharley" and my man had got locked in a pinochle match when lo! they were back, the flushed tavern keeper appreciatively licking his moist chops over the unexpected alcoholic dividend he had been able to spear. The jury watched him closely, to a man corroded with envy. The young officer placed the confiscated net and a dishpan full of beautiful frozen brook trout on the judge's desk and resumed the witness chair.

"Officer, you may state whether or not this is the net you found the defendant lifting from Nestoria creek on the day in question?" I asked, pointing.

"It is," the officer testified.

Pointing at the fish: "And were all these fish the brook trout you removed from the net?"

"They were."

"Were the fish then living?"

"About half. But they were nearly done in. None would have survived."

"How many are there in the pan?"

"Forty-seven."

I introduced the exhibits into evidence and turned to Judge Paulson. "The People rest," I said.

"*Plink!*" acknowledged Judge Paulson, turning to the defendant. "Da defandant vill now race his right han' an' tell da yury *hiss* side of da story." It was not a request.

Ole Paulson was sworn and testified that it was indeed he who had been caught lifting the writhing net; that he had merely been patrolling the creek looking for beaver signs for the next trapping season when he had come across the illegal net; that the net was not his and was not set by him; and that he was just lifting the net to free the unfortunate trout and destroy the net when, small world, the conservation officer had come along and arrested him for his humanitarian pains. "Dat's all dare vere to it!" he concluded.

I badgered and toyed with the witness for several minutes, but it was an unseasonably hot September day and I could see that the fans were anxious to get back across the street to their hot pinochle games and cool beer, so I cut my cross-examination short. In my brief jury argument I pointed out the absurdity of the defendant's story that he was out prowling a trout stream in mid-September looking for beaver signs for a trapping season that opened the following March. I also briefly gave my standard argument that every time a game violator did things like this he was really no different from a thief stealing the people's tax money—that the fish and game belonged to *all* the people. . . . The members of the jury blinked impassively over such strange political heresy.

"*S-splank!*" went Judge Paulson, scoring another bull's-eye. Had any man moved carelessly into the crossfire he would have risked inundation and possible drowning.

The defendant's argument was even briefer than mine. "Yantleman of da yury," he said, rising and pointing scornfully at the fish net. "Who da hecks ever caught a gude Svede using vun of dem gol-dang homemade Finlander nets? *Ay tank you!*" He sat down.

"B-blink!" went the Judge, banishing the jury to the back room to consider their verdict.

The jury was thirstier than I thought. "Ve find da defandant *note gueelty!*" the foreman gleefully announced, two minutes later.

"Whang!" rang the cuspidor, accepting and celebrating the verdict.

After the crowd had surged tavernward, remarkably without casualty, I glanced over the six-man jury list, moved by sheer morbid curiosity. This was the list:

> Ragnar Paulson
> Swan Paulson
> Luther Paulson
> Eskil Paulson
> Incher Paulson
> Magnus Carl Magnuson

I turned to Deputy Sheriff Paulson. "How," I asked sternly, "how did this ringer Magnuson ever get on this jury list?"

Deputy Paulson shrugged. "Ve yust samply ran out of Paulsons," he apologized. "Anyvay, Magnuson dare vere my son's brudder-in-law. My son vere da defandant, yew know!"

"Spang!" gonged His Honor, like a benediction. "Dat vere true, Yonny," he said. "My nephew dare—da deputy sheriff— he nefer tell a lie!"

I lurched foggily across the street and banged on the bar. "Drinks fer da house!" I ordered, suddenly going native. "Giff all da Paulsons in da place vatever dey vant!"

10

The Haunted Pond

WHEN I was a kid there were no bass or German browns in our lakes and streams and, as nearly as I can recall, few if any rainbows. When a man said he was going fishing he meant he was going fishing for brook trout. Our waters were loaded with them. Then along came the bass. The advent of these sea monsters was greeted with shouts of wild delight by the bored native fishermen; here at last was *really* a big fighting fish; and soon throngs of sleepy fishermen were up all hours of the night greeting overdue trains, gaily acquiring assorted calluses and hernias as they unloaded can after can of wriggling government bass fry and fingerlings into waiting buckboards and Model-T Fords and rushed them out and dumped them into our lovely trout waters. It still makes me shudder to contemplate the fumbling midnight horror of this picture.

Needless to say, most of these fishermen lived to regret

their hot haste; and again needless to say, much of our good trout water was permanently usurped by the bass and eventually ruined for *all* fishing. It is only in comparatively recent years that state-directed poisoning programs have removed the bass from some of our natural trout ponds and lakes and retrieved these waters for the fish that really belong there. The bass-infested trout rivers and streams present another and more difficult problem, but in general it is perhaps fair to say that nature saw to it that the bass soon died out or became a negligible factor in the true trout streams, while those streams and rivers in which the bass have thrived were probably doomed as trout waters anyway.

I personally don't happen to care a whoop for bass fishing or bass; in fact I loathe it and them; but I have no quarrel with the queer people who do, only a sort of bewildered pity. My big gripe is that I believe bass should be confined to bass waters, and I weep and grit my teeth and see red when I find the ugly brutes fouling up and crowding out our vanishing trout waters.

The point is that for their own scaly sakes bass should not be planted in trout waters; they not only ruin the water for trout, but they themselves are ultimately doomed. It is now known that bass will thrive in these trout waters for the first few years, growing to huge and awesome dimensions, but by and by, after all of the rough natural food is consumed, they will inevitably languish and grow stunted so that nobody is happy, not even the dwarfed bass.

Alas, my own father was guilty of more than his share of planting bass in our trout waters. He lived to regret it and I have forgiven him much in this respect, but I have never rightly forgiven him for planting bass in the lovely natural trout waters we used to fish.

THE HAUNTED POND

One spring my father got authentic reports that the Winthrop boys had been winter-fishing the brook trout out at old Blair pond. "Aha, I'll fix 'em," my father said, so he and my older brother Leo quick got a load of bass and dumped them into the pond. (Bass mud down in the winter in a kind of quasi-dormant stupor and cannot readily be caught, at least up in this part of the state where winter doesn't fool.) At the time I did not know anything about this terrible deed, but it would not have done any good if I had because my father was not the kind of man who discussed his decisions with any man; he simply announced them.

My father indeed thwarted the Winthrop boys, all right, but it was a clear case of cutting off his nose to spite his face, because in two years not a single trout could be taken from the pond and after that it began to yield up the biggest and ugliest bass it has ever been my displeasure to look in the eye. For several years I used to lure bass fishermen out there with their chests of hardware in a vain hope that they might somehow fish the devilish monsters out. Many huge bass were winched in, and by and by they did disappear, only to be replaced by a race of midgets; and it shortly got so that one could take a mature undersized bass on nearly every cast, so stunted and hungry had they grown. At last I realized that the old place had been permanently ruined for all fishing. I nearly wept.

I should like to digress here and comment briefly on the various theories that account for what it is that makes trout disappear when bass take over their waters. For disappear they certainly do. One simple theory is that the bass eat all the trout (except for the very largest trout, who ultimately roll their eyes and die of loneliness); another that the trout perish of internal flat tires from eating the tiny spike-backed bass fry; another that the bass starve out the trout by their

81

swinish consumption of all available food. And there are doubtless other theories. I rather lean to the first theory, but I am willing to concede that the other things are probably contributing factors.

The only places I have ever seen bass and trout persist together are in those waters where the trout have an opportunity to get away from the bass to spawn and get their growth before they come back down to vie with the bass. Lorraine Lake in this county (with its various springs and deeps and shallows—and many inlets) is such a spot; all of which rather lends force to the theory that it is the bass eating the smaller trout that causes the latter's ultimate extinction and not the trout fatally eating the smaller bass. But to get back to my haunted and ruined pond.

Along about the summer of 1940, perhaps fifteen years after the bass were planted, I first met Dr. Albert Hazzard. He was and is director of the institute for fisheries research, a branch of the division of fisheries of the Michigan conservation department working in co-operation with the state university at Ann Arbor. Doc Hazzard is not only a scientifically trained fish man and a good one but, I soon discovered, a swell modest guy to boot. I cornered him and chokingly told him the sad and harrowing tale of Blair Pond. He said he'd like to look at the place as the state was keenly interested in reclaiming all and any good trout waters for public trout fishing. I quick glanced at my watch and said when.

One way and another it was the summer of 1941 before Doc and his boys got out to Blair Pond. They did their stuff —caught bass, tested for plankton and other food content, took temperatures, etc.—and the upshot was that Doc wrote me that while the bass were both stunted and diseased, the pond was "highly suitable for trout," a conclusion which did not astound me since I had caught scores of speckled beauties out of it when I was a kid. Doc went on to say that they would not be able to make their poison survey until the following August, following which they could then poison out the bass and restock with trout within a month or so. He wound up his letter with these magic words: ". . . and there should be some trout fishing as early as 1943." I let out a whoop and turned three handsprings and went fishing.

Then along came Pearl Harbor, which unsettled more than fishermen, and I was not surprised when Doc wrote me the following June that the government had frozen all stocks of fish poison (rotenone) for the duration. However, there was one note of hope: Doc promised to complete the survey that summer so that the pond would at least be up near the top of the list when and if the stuff again became available. Thus were the villainous bass reprieved until the war ended.

In the autumn of 1946 Doc's boys (now mostly ex-G. I.'s) marched back and poisoned out the pond, but it developed that the first post-war poison released to the state was far too weak, and everything but a few minnows managed to weather the Borgia blitz. The thing was necessarily put off until the following year. In 1947 the question of poisoning out the pond struck a new snag over the further question of public access to the pond, once it was poisoned out and re-stocked. The objection was most reasonable so I swallowed my disappointment and cheerfully helped Doc and the conservation department to clear up this snag. Then in 1948, lo and behold, Doc's boys came and re-poisoned the pond and restocked it with nice clean little trout. At long last the thing was done.

I deliberately avoided the place until the 1950 season and I can best summarize the situation I then found by quoting from a letter I wrote Doc:

Trout Madness

You will be interested to receive a progress report on Blair Pond. I fished it this year for the first time since the planting. The first time I fished it I found both dams in good shape and the water well up. There were no rises and a short interval of worm fishing produced nothing. Last Saturday I tried it again with flies, spinning lures and finally, in desperation, with worms. Sitting on the rock part of the dam on the lower pond my partner finally got a good bite but missed the strike. Hearing his shout I joined him from the upper pond and threw in my porkchop and got a good bite and hooked the fish. It was an 11-inch brook trout full of fight and unusually heavy for its length. I would say it went three-quarters of a pound and was very "deep-chested" and literally hump-backed with flesh. There was no evidence of lice in the gills. A few minutes later my partner hooked and landed a slightly larger brook trout, and a few minutes later while retrieving my hook a heavy trout nailed the almost bare hook and after a splendid fight (I was using a bare fly hook, fine leader and fly rod) I landed a beautiful brook trout that went exactly 13 inches and was as plump as a partridge and must have weighed a pound and a half, most unusual for a trout that length.

Yesterday I returned with 2 friends. There was a high wind which made fishing difficult and we finally settled down to worms. Right off the bat we caught 2 trout, both about 11 inches and both unusually plump and full of fight. The flesh was salmon pink on all the trout. We saw no rises although both days should have produced rises towards evening. Yesterday we caught 3 shiners, and I can only conclude that they worked up over the bottom dam or else came out of some slough above. The beaver had dammed one of the two small inlets, one of the dams being practically at the edge of the lake and I am wondering if this will interfere with spawning.

We saw literally hundreds of minnows from an inch and a half to two inches but were unable to catch any although we chose to think they looked and behaved like trout fry. I am simply delighted with the way the trout appear to have taken hold although I am a little puzzled by the lack of rises. If you or your boys are up this way this summer I think it would be interesting to do a little seining to see how many survived the original planting. Certainly those that did are in excellent shape and there is every evidence that they will be propagating.

Little did I realize that I was whistling my way past the cemetery.

Doc replied, thanking me for my report and stating that he was "disturbed" by my report of the small minnows, as he suspected that they were young chubs or shiners and not trout fry. Following the 1950 trout season I wrote Doc partly as follows:

The place now has me baffled. In May, as I wrote you, we took five beautiful fat brooks, 11 to 13 inches, but all on bait. During the summer I haunted the place and never took or saw another trout—on bait or otherwise. There are hundreds of what we call shiners. The place is loaded with them. I did not see a single authentic trout rise. I fished late and early, on the surface and on the bottom and in between. In July we hauled a boat in there and scoured the place. Surface temperatures averaged 70 degrees. This occurred after a comparatively warm spell. We could not locate, from surface temperatures, the springs you once found during your surveys.

I am afraid the place may be one of those early and late season places, but the thing that dismays me most is my inability to see or attract a trout at or near the surface. Bait fishing leaves me cold. . . . If you get up here next summer I hope you and I can go and take a look. The boat is still there —and few fishermen appear to have been near the place. If we hadn't caught those five beauties I'd swear there were no trout in there.

Doc wrote back that he would personally make a check in the summer of 1951. This we did—and our nets showed that the ponds were infested with hundreds of chubs, shiners and suckers—but nary a trout. Doc concluded that the rough fish had survived and come in from tiny spring feeders above. That fall Doc's boys again poisoned out the ponds—and all feeders—and not a single trout showed up. *We had caught the only 5 trout that survived the 1948 planting of several thousand fish!* By then I was about ready for the gas pipe—but I reckoned without Doc Hazzard.

The pond was again poisoned out and replanted in the spring—a monument to the persistence and vision of Doc Hazzard. I have resolved not to fish there for several years —and then—so help me, following the first trout I take on a fly I swear I'll swallow a fifth of Old Cordwood and jump in with my clothes on. For that will be a day. And I wish my old bass-loving father could be there to see it.

11

Crystal-Ball Fishing

IN THE watery and spectral half-world in-habited by trout fishermen there dwell many fanatic sects, each with its own stout band of followers, and each claim-ing exclusive possession of the one true ladder to trout heaven. At one time or another I have tarried with most of these sects and dallied with their doctrine: the disciples of lunar tables, the pilgrims who yield only to barometric pressures, the worshipers at the shrines of tidal impulses, wind directions, thermal dynamics, water strata, sun spots, spots before the eyes—and all the others. Then one day there came the light, and I became a lamb strayed from the fold, a renegade and a blasphemer. For I now embrace the heresy that the "best" time to go fishing is when you can get away. I have also concluded that Dr. Bile's Almanac (for 1911) is about as good a fishing guide as all the involved scientific claptrap with which so many present-day fishermen clutter their comings and goings.

87

Trout Madness

There is not the slightest doubt, of course, that the fishing is better on some days than it is on others, and that frequently certain parts of the day are better than others. All fishermen know that. My thesis is that I do not believe anyone can predict those times—at least for any appreciable period in advance—, and it both amuses and irks me to watch certain self-appointed native witch doctors blandly arrogate this authority to themselves. Any dolt with a head full of Crisco may suspect that the fishing *might* be lousy when he sets forth in the teeth of a belting northeast gale, with the barometers crashing all about him, but I am talking about those smug gentry who sit in skyscrapers in January and undertake to tell me what the fishing will be on Herkimer's Pond at 4:42 P.M. the following July 17. I just can't buy it and I'll try to tell you why.

The big trouble with all these trout swamis, in my book, is that they try to select and blow up one of the many admittedly important fishing *factors* into an exclusive revealed religion; that as a class they incline to ignore the fact that there are many variable factors that combine endlessly to influence trout fishing; and, perhaps most serious, that they tend to forget that even when all known factors are isolated and weighed and calibrated, that the unknown factors ever lurking in the weeds are likely as not to pop up and throw all their fine calculations into a tailspin.

If one must get into the act and couch this ill-natured swipe at the high priests of fishing in the argot of science, I'll venture to put it this way: mathematicians have not yet found a way to solve a problem when the necessary factors X and Y are unknown. That, I believe, is unassailably sound scientific doctrine. And it is my further belief that this maxim applies equally to fishing, and that it is a rare time when we go fishing that, at the very least, fish factors X and Y are not

88

only unknown but often totally unsuspected. I realize I'm drifting boldly into the realm of fish mysticism, but I further suspect that usually these unknown factors embrace a good part of the entire fishing alphabet. There is so incredibly much that all men, let alone we little fishermen, don't know and perhaps can't ever know.

I'll attempt to give just one example. Over a long period of years I have observed a certain strange fishing phenomenon—and one that I have yet to see mentioned or even hinted at in all the scores of fishing treatises and assorted revelations I have read. It is this: On some days the surface of the water possesses a peculiar gun-metal sheen, a kind of bland, polished, and impersonal glitter, a most curious sort of bulging look, coupled with the aloof, metallic quality and cold, glassy expression of a dowager staring down a peasant through her lorgnette. At the same time there is a deceitful appearance of warmth, an opaque expression of bland geniality, and the light reflects off the water in a curiously false-friendly way. It is all very subtle and confusing and hard to describe, yet when I see it I never for an instant mistake it. On such days, fortunately rare, I have learned that I might just as well leave my rod in the case and instead go chase butterflies or lurking girl-scout leaders.

Please don't ask me what all this means or why it is so or what causes it. I have seen it on the high barometer and the low; at the time of the full moon, the half moon and no moon at all; and at times when the swamis had predicted good fishing, medium fishing—or had even flatly recommended staying home and mowing the front lawn. In fact this strange phenomenon seems to have no discernible connection with any of the current theories of the Learned Society of Elder Swamis. I have come to sense dimly that it is simply one of the unknown factors of which I speak—or perhaps, more accurately, an end result or observable symptom of one or more of these unknown factors.

But there it is and when "it" is there the fishing is invariably lousy. If you want me to speculate about this and play a little at being a crystal-ball gazer myself, I'd *guess* that it may be simply that the unusual lighting somehow makes the fish wary and more easily seen by their natural foes, so that they sulk in their cyclone cellars. Or perhaps the peculiar lighting affects their eyes. Or perhaps their appetites. Or perhaps—but you see where we land when we thus try to penetrate the great fishing unknown? And the only way I can tell when "it" is there is to go look at the water. When it is present it seems to visit its blight indifferently upon all waters in the vicinity.

I suppose I could parley all this into quite an impressive fish religion, and perhaps even start a new sect. I do not intend to. For my part I'd rather spend my time in fishing than in missionary wooing of superstitious and gullible fishermen. It is bad enough for me to have to see it and sigh and shrug and open a can of beer and hope, usually vainly, that it will go away. Yet none of the official fish guessers seem ever to have seen or heard of it, let alone to have weighed or accounted for it when issuing their edicts. Nevertheless it is my opinion that this occurrence is simply a reflection of one of the many and infinitely varied unknown factors that constantly influence fishing (and doubtless many other things); factors that also just as constantly damn and ruin the "scientific" validity of all the incantations I have mentioned.

The more one fishes for trout, then, the more he is forced to the conclusion that no man knows even faintly when or why the fishing will be good or bad. Too often have all of us marched forth hopefully on those rare "perfect" days—

when all the licensed fish prophets were for once smiling and nodding in sweet accord—only to return wondering whether all the trout hadn't migrated to Mars. Or again, too often have we braved their collective frowns—and gone out and hit the jackpot. *Why?* I don't know why, otherwise I would set up shop as a swami myself—and henceforth tramp the trout circuits of the world, fishing away like mad on the proceeds of my sage revelations.

While we indeed live in an advanced age of science, and an alarming one at that, many men are too apt to think that therefore *all* the problems of living—and fishing—can be solved by applying the pragmatic methods of science to problems that are perhaps essentially insoluble. The same men laugh at the superstitions of our quaint ancestors and at the leaping witch doctors of present-day primitive tribes, yet themselves gladly swallow enough phony science every day to make even the dizziest witch doctor look like Dr. Einstein.

I hasten to add that most trout swamis are a serious, well-intentioned, and dedicated crew who genuinely love to fish; they are often highly intelligent men, perhaps lacking only in the saving perspective offered by a sense of humility and humor, whose pretensions after all cause little harm and possibly save quite a few trout. In a sense they are victims of their own hobbies. And sometimes their predictions are dead right, as they are occasionally bound to be, like a man who always plays the same number in roulette. They can't possibly always be wrong. Their occasional home runs are in fact the thing that keeps them in business.

There's one other thing that helps weld their flocks together. If, rightly or wrongly, a disciple of one of these fanatic fishing faiths *believes* that the fishing is going to be good, in that frame of mind he is naturally going to fish better—and that, too, is still a pretty important factor in all fishing. And should his favorite prophet say nay, the more devoted disciple generally doesn't even dare go fishing, so he is scarcely in a position to convict let alone accuse his holy man of treasonable error. Or if he goes fishing anyway, possibly because he has already planned the trip, his heart isn't in it, he is oppressed by a sense of sin for slumming among the heathen, his decalogue is shattered. One way or another he is less likely to be on the ball. Consequently he is apt to ascribe his subsequent fishing pratfall as still another triumph for his particular fishing saint. Thus, you see, his favorite prophet simply can't lose.

It's the same sort of thing as the fisherman and his "favorite" fly. The fly became a favorite, of course, because he or a pal once caught or raised a lot of trout with it; therefore he has faith in it, it is a "good" fly; therefore he fishes it more often and with greater care; therefore he is more likely to continue to take most of his fish on it; and therefore, to complete the vicious circle, he becomes more and more caught in the spell of his favorite fly. Or even take a strange deluded fellow who becomes depresssed when he thinks he sees a certain mysterious gun-metal sheen on the water. . . .

For my part it will be a sorry day when any character can ever tell me ahead of time what my fishing is going to be. To me the indescribable sense of anticipation and mystery in simply *going* fishing is almost half the fun. It is the beckoning lure of the unknown, the very unpredictability of the enterprise, that draws me on and on. Always I keep telling myself: This may be the big day when I'll get on—and stay on—to Grampaw. . . . And if ever some sly superswami comes along who can *really* tell me what I'm apt to do on Frenchman's Pond tomorrow night, he'd better quick gather up his crystal ball and start running. And he'd better not trip on his robes. Because I'm going to crack him and his crystal ball with my stoutest trout priest. I've now given him fair warning.

Have I told you my own new pet theory, the one about the influence of *bald spots* on trout fishing? Boy oh boy, it never fails! It's terrific! Oh, so you don't want to hear about it? So you prefer to worship at that eccentric rival angling church across the street—the one with bats in its belfry? Very well and *pardon* me. If you still want to blindly embrace such a weird collection of medieval fishing dogma and superstition, hop to it. See if I care. It's a free country. But as for me, *I'll* still cling to my precious bald spots. Because, you see, bald spots are milder. And, lordy, how they do satisfy!

12

Trout Heaven

THERE is a certain bass lake in these parts the water height of which is regulated by the whims of nature coupled with the variable needs of a certain incorporated benevolence known as an hydroelectric company. Since both parties are strangely uncommunicative and their moods are equally unpredictable, it is difficult for me to tell ahead of time just when the damn place will be ripe for fishing. I'm just not consulted. . . . But why, you may ask, why does this prideful fellow who dilates so interminably on being a trout-fishing purist—why should this untouchable take the slightest interest in waters inhabited by the miserable and lowly *bass*?

The reason, my friends, is that I am a member of a small secretive band of fishermen that knows that this so-called "bass" lake is also inhabited by trout—what is more, by big, savage, lantern-jawed, square-tailed, native brook trout! The gimmick—and the cross we must bear—is that one has a fighting chance to take these trout on flies *only* during those rare periods when the lake level is way down low. When that happens the usually flooded and submerged channel of a certain inlet becomes exposed; the banks become dried out; the mechanical aspects of fly-casting are then ideal; and for some mysterious reason that still baffles me—doubtless connected with food, temperatures, and protection—the big trout then come crowding pell-mell into this enchanted half-mile-long exposed channel in incredible numbers. Verily, it is so.

My theory is that as the lake waters continue to recede and the competition for food daily grows more keen, the trout perforce leave the cool deeps (where I suspect they normally dwell) and range out not only in search of food but also to avoid the ever-narrowing proximity with the bass. (You see, even the trout hate 'em!) I also suspect that as the waters dwindle the lake temperatures doubtless rise, and the sensitive trout, with their low toleration for rising temperatures, come crowding into the old river outlet to enjoy the concentrated coolness of fresh aerated waters pouring out of the deep woods. At any rate one thing is certain: given these conditions, the trout are *there;* and while the anguished and threadbare utility people prostrate themselves and beat their breasts and burn incense daily for rain, our little knot of initiated trout fishermen smile evilly and quietly foregather from miles around. For then it is we know that we are about to enter the very front door of trout heaven.

According to my fish records the last time Lake Enchantment (don't ever go *looking* for a lake of that name!) was "right" was back in mid-July, 1946. My entries for that period are faintly incredible. Here is an early and typical one:

TROUT HEAVEN

Tommy Cole, Pinky Strand, Raymond Friend and I outboarded up to the main inlet early this morning. What a wildly beautiful Canadian-type lake to be wasted on bass—with the tall balsams and spruces pressing right down to the normal shore line and with the brooding dark hills sweeping beyond. A magnificent buck in velvet stood on a wind-swept open point and disdainfully watched us out of sight, as motionless as an iron deer on a lawn. Four men in a stuttering and smelly boat weren't going to budge *him* from his mosquito-free haven. . . .

Weather cloudy and rather coolish. Barometer off but holding steady. Rather brisk northwesterly winds. Approaching the channel had to lift motor and paddle rest of way. Tommy sculls a paddle beautifully—even in this old scow. Deadheads everywhere, some big enough to stove the *Queen Mary*. Around noon made tea and lunched. Mysterious inky water now down a foot below top of banks of the winding old channel. Banks getting fairly dry except for few side pools and puddles. No rises. Saw two bald eagles sweeping and tacking far overhead, an incredibly graceful and lovely sight. Sometimes wish I were a little bald eagle instead of merely a little bald. . . . This desolate place, with the rigid crazily twisted limbs of the long-engulfed dead trees reaching witch-fingered in the air, looks like a deserted street in Hell.

Still no rises, Raymond busily gathering clam shells. Must be planning on renewing barter with the Indians. I housecleaned through my disordered fly boxes. Lordy, I carry enough flies to start a store. . . . It was around 5:00 when Tommy, doggedly casting blind with his own favorite Cole Special, a wet hair fly, pricked and rolled a tremendous trout. I swear I heard it growl. . . . First action of the day! *On the very next cast* the same fish hit again, in a maddened lunge, and this time Tommy was on to him, obliviously dancing his big-fish adagio, like he does, and chanting "Where oh where can my little dog be?" In less than ten minutes of superb handling he had nearly four pounds of copped dynamite folded and sagging in his net. He gave us a little sidelong glance. "The name is Cole, men," he said.

All of us then leapt to work except Raymond—who doesn't

97

fish, strange man—and then the real rise suddenly started! I had on a 14 Adams dry, but I believe they would have taken a red wig. The thing was incredible. Big mantelpiece trout obliviously flopping and rolling all around us, like suckers on a spawning run. They battled each other for our flies. There were few intervals when at least one of us wasn't on to a trout, and at one time I know all three of us—foolishly less than 100 feet apart—were on to tackle-busters at the same time. I lost mine, a real sleigh-dog of a trout, on a submerged deadhead trying craftily to move him down away from the others. Innocence is the best policy . . . Raymond let out an anguished Tarzan whoop in my ear. "You *lost* him," he said in an awed voice. I nodded grimly and wrapped on the first fly I could grab. It happened to be a Grizzly King the size of a pregnant mouse. I then proceeded to lose three different flies in a row to three other soakers on the strike—always and forever my biggest and most persistent fishing headache, especially under pressure. That, plus my insistence on using fine leaders.

In thirty minutes the rise ended as abruptly as it began. I was so weak I had to sit down, like the time when I chased and caught that fat boy who broke our window on Halloween. Box score: Tommy, 5 brook trout from 2 to 4 pounds; Pinky, 4 from 1 to 3 pounds; clumsy me, 2 measly fingerlings of about 1½ pounds each. . . . It was one of the fiercest, most thrilling and memorable jags of trout fishing I have ever been on anywhere. What a mad half-hour! That night in the gathering dusk as we nosed the boat quietly down through the maze of whale-sized deadheads, Tommy burst into song: "With his tail cut short and his hair cut long, where oh where can he be!" All joined in. The startled eagles drifted out from their pine-clad hills, the better to observe our dementia.

That magic year this sort of fabled fishing lasted nearly a month—until finally the prayers of the utility folks were answered, and a three-day young cloudburst hit us in early August. We were almost relieved that the fantasy was over; the fishing—and domestic—strain was beginning to tell. The

place gave us nearly every fishing experience in the book—
and a few I'd never heard of. Some days there was no rise
and no fishing; some days there was no rise and good fishing; some days a good rise and good fishing; and some days
a good rise and no fishing. Other days there was a little of
everything. And on a few days the fishing was simply fantastic. Most of these just bore down and headed out into the
lake till something gave way. I firmly believe that Doc
Thomas' old record could be smashed in this place—that is,
if a man could ever hold a record trout in all those deadheads.

While I'm in the grip of confession (I'll probably be
drummed out of the lodge for this) I'll tell you another secret.
Here it's only mid-March and there's practically no snow
left in the woods. The spring runoff is nearly over. Extremely
low water is plainly indicated. The graybeards predict a
long drought this summer. As for this fisherman, I'm busily
laying in some heavier leaders. (When the pinch comes I
probably won't use 'em.) And in the meantime I intend re-
ligiously to practice the difficult art of the sure but gentle
strike. For it looks as if the tattered utility people are about
to go into another long pout as we patient fisherfolk once
again stand expectantly on the threshold of trout heaven.
And this time I'm locking up my office and pitching a tent.
Watch out, Doc Thomas, here we come!

13

The Intruder

IT WAS about noon when I put down my fly rod and sculled the little cedar boat with one hand and ate a sandwich and drank a can of beer with the other, just floating and enjoying the ride down the beautiful broad main Escanaba River. Between times I watched the merest speck of an eagle tacking and endlessly wheeling far up in the cloudless sky. Perhaps he was stalking my sandwich or even, dark thought, stalking me. . . . The fishing so far had been poor; the good trout simply weren't rising. I rounded a slow double bend, with high gravel banks on either side, and there stood a lone fisherman—the first person I had seen in hours. He was standing astride a little feeder creek on a gravel point on the left downstream side, fast to a good fish, his glistening rod hooped and straining, the line taut, the leader vibrating and sawing the water, the fish itself boring far down out of sight.

Trout Madness

Since I was curious to watch a good battle and anxious not to interfere, I eased the claw anchor over the stern—*plop*—and the little boat hung there, gurgling and swaying from side to side in the slow deep current. The young fisherman either did not hear me or, hearing, and being a good one, kept his mind on his work. As I sat watching he shifted the rod to his left hand, shaking out his right wrist as though it were asleep, so I knew then that the fight had been a long one and that this fish was no midget. The young fisherman fumbled in his shirt and produced a cigarette and lighter and lit up, a real cool character. The fish made a sudden long downstream run and the fisherman raced after him, prancing through the water like a yearling buck, gradually coaxing and working him back up to the deeper slow water across from the gravel bar. It was a nice job of handling and I wanted to cheer. Instead I coughed discreetly and he glanced quickly upstream and saw me.

"Hi," he said pleasantly, turning his attention back to his fish.

"Hi," I answered.

"How's luck?" he said, still concentrating.

"Fairish," I said. "But I haven't raised anything quite like you seem to be on to. How you been doin'—otherwise, I mean?"

"Fairish," he said. "This is the third good trout in this same stretch—all about the same size."

"My, my," I murmured, thinking ruefully of the half-dozen-odd barely legal brook trout frying away in my sun-baked creel. "Guess I've just been out floating over the good spots."

"Pleasant day for a ride, though," he said, frowning intently at his fish.

"Delightful," I said wryly, taking a slow swallow of beer.

"Yep," the assured young fisherman went on, expertly feeding out line as his fish made another downstream sashay. "Yep," he repeated, nicely taking up slack on the retrieve, "that's why I gave up floating this lovely river. Nearly ten years ago, just a kid. Decided then 'twas a hell of a lot more fun fishing a hundred yards of her carefully than taking off on these all-day floating picnics."

I was silent for a while. Then: "I think you've got something there," I said, and I meant it. Of course he was right, and I was simply out joy-riding past the good fishing. I should have brought along a girl or a camera. On this beautiful river if there was no rise a float was simply an enforced if lovely scenic tour. If there was a rise, no decent fisherman ever needed to float. Presto, I now had it all figured out. . . .

"Wanna get by?" the poised young fisherman said, flipping his cigarette into the water.

"I'll wait," I said. "I got all day. My pal isn't meeting me till dark—'way down at the old burned logging bridge."

"Hm . . . trust you brought your passport—you really are out on a voyage," he said. "Perhaps you'd better slip by, fella—by the feel of this customer it'll be at least ten-twenty minutes more. Like a smart woman in the mood for play, these big trout don't like to be rushed. C'mon, just bear in sort of close to me, over here, right under London Bridge. It won't bother us at all."

My easy young philosopher evidently didn't want me to see how really big his fish was. But being a fisherman myself I knew, I knew. "All right," I said, lifting the anchor and sculling down over his way and under his throbbing line. "Thanks and good luck."

"Thanks, chum," he said, grinning at me. "Have a nice ride and good luck to you."

"Looks like I'll need it," I said, looking enviously back

over my shoulder at his trembling rod tip. "Hey," I said, belatedly remembering my company manners, "want a nice warm can of beer?"

Smiling: "Despite your glowing testimonial, no thanks."

"You're welcome," I said, realizing we were carrying on like a pair of strange diplomats.

"And one more thing, please," he said, raising his voice a little to be heard over the burbling water, still smiling intently at his straining fish. "If you don't mind, please keep this little stretch under your hat—it's been all mine for nearly ten years. It's really something special. No use kidding you —I see you've spotted my bulging creel and I guess by now you've got a fair idea of what I'm on to. And anyway I've got to take a little trip. But I'll be back—soon I hope. In the meantime try to be good to the place. I know it will be good to you."

"Right!" I shouted, for by then I had floated nearly around the downstream bend. "Mum's the word." He waved his free hand and then was blotted from view by a tall doomed spruce leaning far down out across the river from a crumbling water-blasted bank. The last thing I saw was the gleaming flash of his rod, the long taut line, the strumming leader. It made a picture I've never forgotten.

That was the last time ever that I floated the Big Escanaba River. I had learned my lesson well. Always after that when I visited this fabled new spot I hiked in, packing my gear, threading my way down river through a pungent needled maze of ancient deer trails, like a fleeing felon keeping always slyly away from the broad winding river itself. My strategy was twofold: to prevent other sly fishermen from finding and deflowering the place, and to save myself an extra mile of walking.

Despite the grand fishing I discovered there, I did not go back too often. It was a place to hoard and save, being indeed most good to me, as advertised. And always I fished it alone, for a fisherman's pact had been made, a pact that became increasingly hard to keep as the weeks rolled into months, the seasons into years, during which I never again encountered my poised young fisherman. In the morbid pathology of trout fishermen such a phenomenon is mightily disturbing. What had become of my fisherman? Hadn't he ever got back from his trip? Was he sick or had he moved away? Worse yet, had he died? How could such a consummate young artist have possibly given up fishing such an enchanted spot? Was he one of that entirely mad race of eccentric fishermen who cannot abide the thought of sharing a place, however fabulous, with even *one* other fisherman?

By and by, with the innocent selfishness possessed by all fishermen, I dwelt less and less upon the probable fate of my young fisherman and instead came smugly to think it was I who had craftily discovered the place. Nearly twenty fishing seasons slipped by on golden wings, as fishing seasons do, during which time I, fast getting no sprightlier, at last found it expedient to locate and hack out a series of abandoned old logging roads to let me drive within easier walking distance of my secret spot. The low cunning of middle age was replacing the hot stamina of youth. . . . As a road my new trail was strictly a spring-breaking bronco-buster, but at least I was able to sit and ride, after a fashion, thus saving my aging legs for the real labor of love to follow.

Another fishing season was nearly done when, one afternoon, brooding over that gloomy fact, I suddenly tore off my lawyer-mask and fled my office, heading for the Big Escanaba, bouncing and bucking my way in, finally hitting the

Trout Madness

Glide—as I had come to call the place—about sundown. For a long time I just stood there on the high bank, drinking in the sights and pungent river smells. No fish were rising, and slowly, lovingly, I went through the familiar ritual of rigging up: scrubbing out a fine new leader, dressing the tapered line, jointing the rod and threading the line, pulling on the tall patched waders, anointing myself with fly dope. No woman dressing for a ball was more fussy. . . . Then I composed myself on my favorite fallen log and waited. I smoked a slow pipe and sipped a can of beer, cold this time, thanks to the marvels of dry ice and my new road. My watching spot overlooked a wide bend and commanded a grand double view: above, the deep slow velvet glide with its little feeder stream where I first met my young fisherman; below a sporty and productive broken run of white water stretching nearly a half-mile. The old leaning spruce that used to be there below me had long since bowed in surrender and been swept away by some forgotten spring torrent. As I sat waiting the wind had died, the shadowing waters had taken on the brooding blue hush of evening, the dying embers of sundown suddenly lit a great blazing forest fire in the tops of the tall spruces across river from me, and an unknown bird that I have always called simply the "lonely" bird sang timidly its ancient haunting plaintive song. I arose and took a deep breath like a soldier advancing upon the enemy.

The fisherman's mystic hour was at hand.

First I heard and then saw a young buck in late velvet slowly, tentatively splashing his way across to my side, above me and beyond the feeder creek, ears twitching and tall tail nervously wigwagging. Then he winded me, freezing in midstream, giving me a still and liquid stare for a poised instant; then came charging on across in great pawing incredibly graceful leaps, lacquered flanks quivering, white flag up and waving, bounding up the bank and into the anonymous woods, the sounds of his excited blowing fading and growing fainter and then dying away.

In the meantime four fair trout had begun rising in the smooth tail of the glide just below me. I selected and tied on a favorite small dry fly and got down below the lowest riser and managed to take him on the first cast, a short dainty float. Without moving I stood and lengthened line and took all four risers, all nice firm brook trout upwards of a foot, all the time purring and smirking with increasing complacency. The omens were good. As I relit my pipe and waited for new worlds to conquer I heard a mighty splash above me and wheeled gaping at the spreading magic ring of a really good trout, carefully marking the spot. Oddly enough he had risen just above where the young buck had just crossed, a little above the feeder creek. Perhaps, I thought extravagantly, perhaps he was after the deer. . . . I waited, tense and watchful, but he did not rise again.

I left the river and scrambled up the steep gravelly bank and made my way through the tall dense spruces up to the little feeder creek. I slipped down the bank like a footpad, stealthily inching my way out to the river in the silted creek itself, so as not to scare the big one, *my* big one. I could feel the familiar shock of icy cold water suddenly clutching at my ankles as I stood waiting at the spot where I had first run across my lost fisherman. I quickly changed to a fresh fly in the same pattern, carefully snubbing the knot. Then the fish obediently rose again, a savage easy engulfing roll, again the undulant outgoing ring, just where I had marked him, not more than thirty feet from me and a little beyond the middle and obliquely upstream. Here was, I saw, a cagey selective riser, lord of his pool, and one who would not suffer fools gladly. So I commanded myself to rest him before casting. "Twenty-one, twenty-two, twenty-three . . ." I counted.

The cast itself was indecently easy and, finally releasing it, the little Adams sped out on its quest, hung poised in mid-air for an instant, and then settled sleepily upon the water like a thistle, uncurling before the leader like the languid outward folding of a ballerina's arm. The fly circled a moment, uncertainly, then was caught by the current. Down, down it rode, closer, closer, then—*clap!*—the fish rose and kissed it, I flicked my wrist and he was on, and then away he went roaring off downstream, past feeder creek and happy fisherman, the latter hot after him.

During the next mad half-hour I fought this explosive creature up and down the broad stream, up and down, ranging at least a hundred feet each way, or so it seemed, without ever once seeing him. This meant, I figured, that he was either a big brown or a brook. A rainbow would surely have leapt a dozen times by now. Finally I worked him into the deep safe water off the feeder creek where he sulked nicely while I panted and rested my benumbed rod arm. As twilight receded into dusk with no sign of his tiring I began vaguely to wonder just who had latched on to whom. For the fifth or sixth time I rested my aching arm by transferring the rod to my left hand, professionally shaking out my tired wrist just as I had once seen a young fisherman do.

Nonchalantly I reached in my jacket and got out and tried to light one of my rigidly abominable Italian cigars. My fish, unimpressed by my show of aplomb, shot suddenly away on a powerful zigzag exploratory tour upstream, the fisherman nearly swallowing his unlit cigar as he scrambled up after him. It was then that I saw a lone man sitting quietly in a canoe, anchored in midstream above me. The tip of his fly rod showed over the stern. My heart sank:

after all these years my hallowed spot was at last discovered.

"Hi," I said, trying to convert a grimace of pain into an amiable grin, all the while keeping my eye on my sulking fish. The show must go on.

"Hi," he said.

"How you doin'?" I said, trying to make a brave show of casual fish talk.

"Fairish," he said, "but nothing like you seem to be on to."

"Oh, he isn't so much," I said, lying automatically if not too well. "I'm working a fine leader and don't dare to bull him." At least that was the truth.

The stranger laughed briefly and glanced at his wrist watch. "You've been on to him that I know of for over forty minutes—and I didn't see you make the strike. Let's not try to kid the Marines. I just moved down a bit closer to be in on the finish. I'll shove away if you think I'm too close."

"Nope," I answered generously, delicately snubbing my fish away from a partly submerged windfall. "But about floating this lovely river," I pontificated, "there's nothing in it, my friend. Absolutely nothing. Gave it up myself eighteen-twenty years ago. Figured out it was better working one stretch carefully than shoving off on these floating picnics. Recommend it to you, comrade."

The man in the canoe was silent. I could see the little red moon of his cigarette glowing and fading in the gathering gloom. Perhaps my gratuitous pedagogical ruminations had offended him; after all, trout fishermen are a queer proud race. Perhaps I should try diversionary tactics. "Wanna get by?" I inquired silkily. Maybe I could get him to go away before I tried landing this unwilling porpoise. He still remained silent. "Wanna get by?" I repeated. "It's perfectly O.K. by me. As you see—it's a big roomy river."

"No," he said dryly. "No thanks." There was another long

109

pause. Then: "If you wouldn't mind too much I think I'll put in here for the night. It's getting pretty late—and somehow I've come to like the looks of this spot."

"Oh," I said in a small voice—just "Oh"—as I disconsolately watched him lift his anchor and expertly push his canoe in to the near gravelly shore, above me, where it grated halfway in and scraped to rest. He sat there quietly, his little neon cigarette moon glowing, and I felt I just had to say something more. After all I didn't *own* the river. "Why sure, of course, it's a beautiful place to camp, plenty of pine knots for fuel, a spring-fed creek for drinking water and cooling your beer," I ran on gaily, rattling away like an hysterical realtor trying to sell the place. Then I began wondering how I would ever spirit my noisy fish car out of the woods without the whole greedy world of fishermen learning about my new secret road to this old secret spot. Maybe I'd even have to abandon it for the night and hike out. . . . Then I remembered there was an unco-operative fish to be landed, so I turned my full attention to the unfinished and uncertain business at hand. "Make yourself at home," I lied softly.

"Thanks," the voice again answered dryly, and again I heard the soft chuckle in the semidarkness.

My fish had stopped his mad rushes now and was busily boring the bottom, the long leader vibrating like the plucked string of a harp. For the first time I found I was able gently to pump him up for a cautious look. And again I almost swallowed my still unlit stump of cigar as I beheld his dorsal fin cleaving the water nearly a foot back from the fly. He wallowed and shook like a dog and then rolled on his side, then recovered and fought his way back down and away on another run, but shorter this time. With a little pang I knew then that my fish was a done, but the pang quickly passed—it always did—and again I gently, relentlessly pumped him up, shortening line, drawing him in to the familiar daisy hoop of landing range, kneeling and stretching and straining out my opposing aching arms like those of an extravagant archer. The net slipped fairly under him on the first try and, clenching my cigar, I made my pass and lo! lifted him free and dripping from the water. "Ah-h-h . . ." He was a glowing superb spaniel-sized brown. I staggered drunkenly away from the water and sank anywhere to the ground, panting like a winded miler.

"Beautiful, *beautiful*," I heard my forgotten and unwelcome visitor saying like a prayer. "I've dreamed all this— over a thousand times I've dreamed it."

I tore my feasting eyes away from my fish and glowered up at the intruder. He was half standing in the beached canoe now, one hand on the side, trying vainly to wrest the cap from a bottle, of all things, seeming in the dusk to smile uncertainly. I felt a sudden chill sense of concern, of vague nameless alarm.

"Look, chum," I said, speaking lightly, very casually, "is everything all O.K.?"

"Yes, yes, of course," he said shortly, still plucking away at his bottle. "There . . . I—I'm coming now."

Bottle in hand he stood up and took a resolute broad step out of the canoe, then suddenly, clumsily he lurched and pitched forward, falling heavily, cruelly, half in the beached canoe and half out upon the rocky wet shore. For a moment I sat staring ruefully, then I scrambled up and started running toward him, still holding my rod and the netted fish, thinking this fisherman was indubitably potted. "No, no, no!" he shouted at me, struggling and scrambling to his feet in a kind of wild urgent frenzy. I halted, frozen, holding my sagging dead fish as the intruder limped toward me, in a curious sort of creaking stiffly mechanical limp, the uncorked

111

but still intact bottle held triumphantly aloft in one muddy wet hand, the other hand reaching gladly toward me.

"Guess I'll never get properly used to this particular battle stripe," he said, slapping his thudding and unyielding right leg. "But how are you, stranger?" he went on, his wet eyes glistening, his bruised face smiling. "How about our having a drink to your glorious trout—and still another to reunion at our old secret fishing spot?"

14

These Tired Old Eyes ...

THESE tired old eyes have beheld some fairly strange sights during the years they have guided this fisherman on his trout devotionals. Sometimes I suspect that fishermen while practicing their favorite vice are peculiarly well situated to observe nature with her hair down. Perhaps it is the very intentness and detachment of fishermen during their seizures. Perhaps their obliviousness to all but the business at hand somehow communicates itself to the rest of the forest and water dwellers so that they in turn are lulled into going about their normal pursuits with a calm they would rarely possess under the conscious search and scrutiny of the hunters or professional bird and animal watchers. At any rate fishermen are at least suffered if not accepted by the wild things of nature; and if they, the fishermen, would but look away more often from their fishing they would doubtless observe even stranger sights than they do. Here are some droll sights and experiences, just a few, that I have run across in my addled wanderings after trout.

On several occasions I have come upon a mother porcupine prone on her back nursing her young, a unique position which I have heard that the females of these prickly animals likewise maintain while begetting them—though my quill is somewhat uncertain on this latter point.

While on a fishing trip that I have mentioned elsewhere I have seen a skunk swim leisurely across a broad river, its tail arched proudly so as to keep its powder dry. I have also come upon rabbits and groundhogs nestling up in trees, an arboreal environment not normally associated with these creatures.

I have watched a pair of otter slip up over a beaver dam and assault and boldly gut the place of its trout while I stood there unarmed and helpless, trying vainly to drive them away with the few rocks I could find. It was a blitzkrieg and a harrowing spectacle to watch. One undulant otter patrolled the upstream escape outlet, flashing back and forth at incredible speed, while the other robber did the real dirty work, both chomping their jaws horribly each time they came up for air. Creation of panic and their lightning speed seemed to be their chief weapons. It was then that I learned thoroughly to loathe otter; so much so that I refuse to succumb to the obvious pun that there otter be a law against otter. If they would *only* confine their depredations to bass I'd start breeding them . . .

This was the same strange season that I swear I caught more birds and insects and assorted reptiles and flying things than trout. A typical entry follows:

"Caught a dragonfly on a 16 Trude on my back cast out at Frenchman's Pond. Kept pumping away at the forward cast and nothing happened, a creepy feeling. Looked back and

114

there was the dragonfly, himself pumping away like mad, trying vainly to drag my fly and flyline in the opposite direction. Put down rod, donned my rubber gloves, and performed minor surgery before order was restored. Dr. T. Wellington Cole scrubbed with me. Suspect this may be as much evidence of the nearsightedness of dragonflies as a tribute to the expertness of my fly-tier."

This same thing happened *three* times that same season; though it never happened before and hasn't since. That enchanted summer I also caught two bats and two unknown birds on my back casts, a swooping swallow-like bird on my forward cast, and three frogs, a fish duck, a snapping turtle and two garter snakes in the water. Toward the end of that season I find this wistful entry: "Must remember to start a zoo. It'll have everything but fish!"

On another expedition Gunnar Anderson, Tom Bennett, and Gipp Warner and I boated up the Big Dead basin. All of us were hilarious and feeling no pain. We put in at the eerily squawking heron rookery near the mouth of Wahlman's Creek to try for the big brook trout that sometimes lurk there. Long time nothing. Then I finally snubbed on to a fair trout on a sunken hair fly. Gunnar netted him and dressed him out and cast the entrails overboard, chortling, "This will bring the big ones around." Then he reached over to rinse off the trout. The trout slipped out of his hand—*pop* —and *swam* gracefully and deliberately down out of sight! We looked at each other wide-eyed and soberly weighed anchor and got the hell out of there. I know a little something about the possibility of muscular spasms, instinctive reactions, and habit responses and all that, but don't *ever* let it happen to you!

Here is another odd one for the book:

"At 5:30 this morning took a nice 13-inch brook at the

115

high sand-bank-bend on the East Branch. Number 12 Mc-Ginty, dry. Had court that day so reluctantly quit at seven. Cleaned out my trout at gravel ford by washed-out bridge. Found partly digested bait hook in gut of largest trout. Met Gipp in town that morning and, since he and I fish that stretch a lot, started to tell him about finding hook. He stopped me and said: 'You caught the fish at the high sand bank, didn't you? He was over twelve inches. The hook was an eagle claw, about number 8, snelled, with red wrappings, with about two inches of leader left above the shank?' He paused. 'My wife lost that fish at 9:30 last night.' "

It was the same fish, of course, but the point is that a trout started feeding again within such a few hours after such a harrowing experience (contrary to many fish dopesters) and further, that during that short time he had nearly digested a hook that would loom relatively the size of a whale harpoon in our own bellies. Small wonder that the more one fishes for trout the less he pretends to know about them.

Here is an entry from my fish notes:

"My old fishing pal, Louie Bonetti, took me on another of his celebrated goose chases, this time down the Fifteen Hill Creek. 'Are you *sure* I can fly fish down there, Louie?' I cross-examined him carefully before we started, still smarting over past wild-goose expeditions led by the dauntless and irrepressible Louie. 'Sure, sure t'ing, Yon,' Louie grinned, 'you can fly lak ever't'ing!' He was right. We hadn't proceeded a hundred yards through this jungle before I realized wryly that the only way to properly present a fly in that creek was to fly over and drop it from a balloon. I could hear Louie ahead of me, threshing along like a bull elephant in must, pausing here and there to drop his bait into the murky waters. It was like trying to fish in a green barrel. After ruining one leader and losing three flies I shrugged philosophically and folded my rod and creeled my net and bowed my head in defeat. I longed only to get out of there. I had been taken again. . . .

"'Yon!' Louie shouted. 'Luke at dis! Come queeck, luke at dis!' I finally crashed into a clearing big enough to accommodate a telephone booth, and there was Louie proudly holding a ten-inch brook trout he had just taken on a big nightcrawler. From the mouth of the still-wriggling trout protruded four inches of another trout's tail! As I watched, Louie pulled on the tail and extracted what was left of a seven-inch trout! A cannibalistic ten-inch trout had eaten— or was eating—a seven-inch trout, and still had found the greedy appetite and room to cram Louie's porkchop bait on top of that! 'W'at you tink?' Louie asked me. 'Me, I think it's time for a drink,' I said, reaching in Louie's knapsack for his trusty pint bottle."

Another day Louie Bonetti and I were boating up a remote stretch of the Middle Escanaba, when hawk-eyed Louie spotted a little spotted fawn lying amongst the water-worn rocks that lined the exposed shore line below a high tangled bank. We assumed that it and its mother had come down for a drink or for respite from flies, so we went merrily on our way, the discovered fawn watching us out of sight with its soft liquid eyes. Many hours later, floating back down in the dusk, we saw that the fawn was still there. I was about to shrug and float on but Louie insisted that we put in. "*Non, non*, we stop. Somet'ing goddam a wrong a dis place, Yon," he said.

There was. As we approached the shore the fawn stood up on its spindly, wavering legs and bleated in terror, at the same time pulling out to the end of a chain which anchored a large double-spring trap, the rusty jaws of which we discovered were clamped tightly across the right foreleg just above the exquisite tiny hoof. I held the trembling creature from plunging while Louie tenderly released the jaws of the trap. We then carried the bleating fawn up the high bank and set it upon level ground. It continued to bleat and cry piteously. "Ma-a-ma!" it called. "Whew," answered the unseen mother from deep in the woods. "*Whew, whew!*" we could hear her thudding back and forth in the thick cover, running in quick thumping nervous trots.

The fawn took a few tentative limping steps in the direction of the woods and then *ran* on all *four* legs to join its mother, bleating gaily. Louie and I grinned and nodded and resumed our twilit float down the misty Escanaba, both of us swollen with virtue over the good turn we had done an otherwise doomed fawn.

"Damma dose coyote trappers," Louie swore darkly. "Why dey leave a dose set trap lay 'round for poor little fella catcha his foot in?" *This* burst of sentiment was from a man who had shot more deer than most men have ever seen. . . .

On still another day Louie and I were fishing a rather tangled but productive brook up near Silver Lake. When we met back at the car at dusk, a puffing and breathless Louie announced he had just met a "beeg" black bear on the trail. Louie, who always acted out everything that ever happened to him, crouched down on all fours.

"I coma down trail an' ducka my head under t'ick bush lak a dis—an' w'en I stan' up dere's dis beeg blacka bear stan' right dere on front of me—so close I can see even his little red eyes lak peeg, an' smell his bad breat'."

"What'd you do, Louie?" I said, wondering how the lucky bear ever got away from Louie.

"Hm . . . Wan time I hear some place, I dunno, some people he say if man say somet'ing to wile animal he liable get scare an' run lak a hell."

118

"Yes?" I prompted.

"Well, dis a here beeg black bear he stan' dere an' luke at me an' I stan' dere luke at him—so den I queeck remember w'at I hear. '*Say* somet'ing, Louie!' I t'ink. So I tip my hat lak dis, real polite, an' smile real nice an' I say reala loud, 'Gooda mornin', Mister Bear!'"

"What'd the bear do?"

"Hm . . . he get scare lak da people say an' run lak a hell nudder way."

"What'd you do, Louie?"

"Hm . . . Louie he *stay* awful scare an' run lak a hell dis a way. . . . Boy oh boy, le's have da beeg drink!"

To attempt to do justice to this rare man Louie would require a five-foot shelf of books. *Everything* happened to Louie—including the final awful day two autumns ago when the bullet from an old friend's deer rifle unerringly found its way into Louie's belly. Louie had been mistaken for a deer. He died the next morning and the whole county went into mourning. But the saga of Louie Bonetti will cling to his name for many years. I can only faintly suggest the pungent flavor of the man here.

Perhaps the most moving woods spectacle I have ever seen while fishing happened several years ago and the record of which I quote from my fishing notes:

"Yesterday on Loon Lake I saw the unfolding of a thrilling and saddening forest tragedy. I was prowling the north side of the lake when suddenly I heard a great commotion and squawking from the southwest corner, nearly a half-mile away. Looking I saw a wild duck and a great loon engaged in battle. It was a case of David versus Goliath, the little duck seeming to be the aggressor. I quickly put my binoculars on them. I cannot describe the fierceness of the combat;

the incredible darting swiftness of it. At length the duck retreated, the loon following, the duck skeetering just over the top of the water as though wounded, always *just* out of reach of the pursuing loon. Then the truth dawned on me: this was a mother duck doubtless protecting her young and putting on the ancient lame-duck act. At any rate, the loon suddenly submarined and the duck, at the real risk of her life, still kept skeetering, flapping the very surface of the water, luring the loon on and away from her young, whose terrified cheeping now came thinly across the water. I never did see the young ducks. At length the mother duck rose in flight, and almost immediately the great loon popped out of the water where the duck had just been. The duck circled in low flight back to her young. She banked and skidded into a little bay and the terrified cheeping ceased.

"In the meantime I had ignored my fly and it had sunk to the bottom. I flipped the line to raise it—and was on to a good trout. While I was preoccupiedly landing this fish the loon returned to the ducks, and the very same battle ensued, except that this time the loon showed signs of giving up the pursuit and returning to the young. At this the lion-hearted mother duck again made a fierce frontal attack on the loon and again enraged it into following her virtually across the lake. And once again the loon rose from the water just as the duck lifted into flight and circled back to her young. Then I felt my rod bending and remembered I was on to a fish, my first trout on flies in tantalizing Loon Lake. I landed it. It was a plump fighting thirteen-inch brook. But I had lost all zest for fishing. I just sat and helplessly watched the distant drama, longing for a rifle to plug the bullying loon. Although the loon stalked the ducks all afternoon, schnorkeling in close, it evidently lacked the heart to again mix with the brave mother duck. At sundown I quietly folded my tent and stole away. There was no rise."

A few days later I returned, this time with a high-powered rifle with a scope sight. This is my entry for that day:

"Saturday back at Loon Lake I saw and heard a *pair* of loons giggling and cackling and diving, but no sign of the ducks. I fear the worst, namely, that the loons either ganged up and killed the gallant mother duck or else chased her away (though I think not) and ate her young. Certainly the young could not very well have flown or walked away. [NOTE: Since writing this I have indeed met a mother duck and her young walking along on land.] I was tempted to shoot the loons, but I was not sure there had been a murder or that they were the murderers. Anyway I was apparently too late. And, moreover, who was I to judge their guilt or appoint myself their executioner? I did not know that loons ate flesh, besides, possibly, fish, but now I am afraid they do. . . ."

Here I lapsed into a little gratuitous philosophizing which I shall throw in for good measure.

"The constant obscure savagery of nature seems always to lurk below the apparently placid surface of things. Probably even the lice on the loon's wings battle each other, while I know that the fish swimming below dwell in a subterranean welter of cannibalism. How can men hope for peace when combat and strife, not peace and calm, seem to be the basic norms of nature? In a real sense, then, peace is an unnatural state and all the elaborate plans of men to achieve it are, in this sense, in plain perversion of nature. Alas, peaceful men may be *unnatural* men, a fairly bleak prospect in the Atomic Age."

15

Grampaw Returners

"AT LAST the great-hearted trout lay dripping and sagging in my net, both of us gasping from the
scorching battle. I looked down at him and he rolled his
glistening wet eyes up at me. Then, carefully holding him
so [here follows a description in vast detail of the certified
way to lovingly hold trout] I tenderly removed the fly, which
miraculously hung by a bare sliver of bony cartilage, and
gently held the great fish upright in the water. There he lay,
fanning his great fins and desperately working his gills. After
a bit I gently touched his dorsal fin, just a little pat, and he
moved slowly down and away and became one with the
shadowy depths. 'Farewell, great fighting old fellow—farewell and good luck. . . .'"

For years I have been hearing and reading poetic dilations
like this from the great-hearted giants among fishermen, and
each time I get a powerful big lump in my throat. In fact

123

these men of heroic stature fill me with awe and I am inclined to break out all over with little goose pimples of inferiority in their presence. For I envy these gallant fishermen who are forever releasing their "big ones," and who then stand around all kind of misty-eyed and choked up while Grampaw (for whom they had been campaigning relentlessly for at least three seasons) regains his composure and swims majestically away. Indeed, some of these big fish seem to have been caught and released so often they have lost their amateur standing.

Yes, I envy these fishermen their greatness of heart and nobility of spirit but I cannot copy them. I regret that on these occasions I seem possessed of the heart of a woodtick and the spirit of a gnat. My craven character fails always to respond to the lofty challenge of the situation. I guess I simply lack the magnanimity of spirit and extravagance of soul. My really big fish are few and far between and I keep them. Furthermore, I wail like a banshee whenever I lose one.

I try to comfort myself for my deficiencies by reflecting that all trout are cannibals and that the big ones are almost exclusively so; and that by removing them from our trout waters I am really doing both the fish and my fellow fishermen a good turn. But try as I might to rationalize myself into gladness, in my secret heart I *know* that I can never really *belong;* that I am still an unregenerate and greedy peasant among true trout fishermen. Alas, *I don't return my big fish!*

But there is one thing that I do do that I don't hear quite so much about. I return a whale of a lot of small *legal* trout; and, when the prospects are good that I could have filled out, I frequently leave the stream or pond with less than my legal limit. I know that this dreary ruse will never qualify me for membership in the exclusive fishing fraternity of *Grampaw*

Returners, but I try to console myself with the notion that, as undramatic and unsung a thing as it is, and one not nearly so inflating to the fisherman's ego, it is perhaps a more sensible working fishing philosophy and one that really helps the fish and my fellow peasants.

16

Spots Before the Eyes

FISHERMEN are a cultured and worldly lot; their broad and diversified interests make them delightful and even absorbing companions; they'll talk about anything under the sun so long as it concerns fishing—preferably with themselves in a stellar role. They take a trout's-eye view of the world and see everything darkly through their own wavering, distorted, astigmatic lens of broken beer bottles. Spots and speckles dance constantly before their eyes. When they aren't fishing they gabble and prattle about fishing much as clusters of idle women run on about babies and clothes—and the witch-like tendencies of *other* women. So it is that the following grab bag of trout prejudice and gossip concerns itself not so much with actual fishing as with the trivia of fishing, like the chatter of earnest boy scouts who temporarily forsake the solemn business of tying bowlines and rubbing dry sticks together, to sit around the campfire

127

and compare the various wrenches and reamers and other burglar tools that adorn their respective scout knives. On with the small talk.

Outdoor Fish Fries: The flesh of the trout is a rare delicacy that comes from one of nature's most tender and perishable creatures. Trout were never designed to be embalmed along with the steaks and ox joints of the aristocracy of the new Ice Age in their well-larded deep freezers. Trout should be eaten not later than twenty-four hours after they are caught, else one might better eat damp swamp hay crowned with chain-store mayonnaise. But by far the best time to enjoy your trout is beside the waters where they are caught. Take a fry pan along and some bacon or shortening, and a little cornmeal and salt, and have yourself a feast fit for a deposed king—or an ulcerated millionaire. But first take a trout. . . .

Competition in Fishing: A trout stream is a poor place for gambling and much of the reflective charm of fishing is lost by making a surly competition out of the undertaking. I will have no part of a fishing party made up of those fishing prima donnas whose very manhood seems to depend on being top rod. Yet my regular trout pals and I have worked out a standing wager on our fishing, and far from making us surly it is surprising how much added zest and friendly fun this adds to our sport. Anyone that does get surly about it is fired out of the lodge. This is our bet: we each pay the winner a dollar for the longest trout over twelve inches. The loser's ante jumps to two bucks a head if the longest fish goes fifteen inches or over.

The net result of this is good; we find ourselves more and more frequently returning a lot of legal-sized trout we might otherwise have kept; and when we meet and decide to quit

"in just five minutes more" there is always the delicious uncertainty and the long chance that the Mister Tanglefoot of
the day will make one last desperate cast and—*whambo!*—
walk away with the honors. It has happened. Frequently,
of course, no fish qualify, but there have been times when
three or more of us have had to get out our calipers and
crouch to see just who had won the two-dollar bet. These
occasions have usually involved lunking browns or rainbows,
but it has also happened with brooks.

Trout Sense: There is no substitute for fishing sense, and if
a man doesn't have it, verily, he may cast like an angel and
still use his creel largely to transport sandwiches and beer.
I have friends whom I can mechanically outfish in practically every department of the sport yet who in their comparatively crude way still manage to tie into any big trout
that happen to be lying about. They also continue regularly
to relieve me of my wrinkled dollar bills. Then again I have
fishing friends—several of them holders of enviable casting
records—who can in turn outfish me in nearly every department but who sometimes even more sadly than I seem to
lack that indescribable sixth sense that guides the flies of
some fishermen into the very jaws of lurking "soakers."

Without growing mystic over this, some men seem to
"think like a fish" more than others. They are the smart ones
who can take one look at a pool or a riffle and sense immediately where to pause and plop their sloppy, ill-delivered
casts, when all the while we Fancy Dans are posturing
grandly over here or over there, unerringly sending out long
whistling dramatic casts over the favorite lies of old tomato
cans.

Once in a blue moon a fisherman comes along who combines this mysterious fish sense with superb casting ability

129

and all the rest. I have known one or two of these diabolical fellows. He is the magician we other fishermen should take up collections for in order to persuade *him* to take up golf. There is no other way to keep the trout away from him. He can catch fish in a rain barrel. My current fishing pal, Henry Scarffe, is fast moving into this class. Some men are said to have sex appeal; *these* characters possess trout appeal, and I swear that many a happily married lady trout will forsake even her snug spawning bed to succumb to his lure. He is also the suave one who makes all the rest of us pedestrian fishermen look like slipping and fumbling political hacks out taking creel census in borrowed waders.

Glass Rods: I am now reluctantly satisfied that glass fly rods are mechanically the equal of and perhaps often perform better than the best bamboo rods. Not only that, they are more reasonable in price; require little or no care; and apparently last forever. I'll concede all that, but never will I let another glass fly rod darken my door. Put it down, if you will, to a burst of girlish sentiment of the heart or middle-aged sediment on the kidneys—I'll take split bamboo. To my mind there is no fairy wand in creation more graceful and beautiful than a good bamboo fly rod. They *look* so good; they *feel* so good. Like fingerprints, no two bamboo rods are alike; each is an individual possessed of its own unique character and one that a fisherman can really get to know.

But these gleaming impersonal glass rods that some chemist has conceived in a laboratory out of skimmed milk and old box tops, these synthetic concoctions that are turned out on an assembly line as much alike as two peas in a pod, simply aren't for me. I'd sooner cast over glass *fish* than use one. I love my bamboo fly rods and I choose to think they have a sneaking yen for me. But I'm afraid I can never quite fall in love with a chemist's incestuous brain child. In short 'tis a pox I wish on all glass rods. (Adv.: I'll sell you a dandy for five bucks.)

Creels: Conventional bulging wicker creels are handy to carry beer in, and they also look nice and woodsy when freshly varnished and hanging from the wall of a den. Aside from that they are clumsy, brush-snagging, foul-smelling nuisances. Get yourself a *flat,* loose-meshed matting creel, one that will nicely accommodate your landing net for travel or brushy going. If you *must* remain a slave to synthetics, then get a flat plastic one, damn it. Either variety is easily washable and thus does not attract the sea gulls and blow-flies for miles around.

Simple Refrigeration: One of those tightly covered round popcorn tins the kids keep trundling home together with some of those little cans of solution you pre-freeze solid in your icebox (and use over and over) make a non-messy and fine combination for cooling beer and keeping perishables. They are also nice to preserve that big trout you bought from Julius the guide to prove to your wife you were not out wading with squaws or dallying with blondes.

Guides on Fly Rods: They're way too small and they should be made of chromium or some other bland non-abrasive metal. I believe as many fly lines are ruined by the constant sawing and rasping through these niggardly conventional fine-wire snake guides as are ruined by the twin plagues of mildew and improper storage. Since there are from nine to thirteen of these wizened hacksaw guides on the average fly rod, I sometimes suspect that the line and rod people must have conspired to continue using them. I have a seven-foot glass combination spinning and fly rod, and when fly fishing with it—I rarely do—I use a lovely torpedoed-in-series Marvin Hedge silk fly line. In places where I can get a decent backcast verily I believe I can paste out nearly as much line in a controlled cast as I can with my best bamboo fly rod. Part of this is due to the rippled torpedo feature, no doubt, but a good part I believe is due to the larger, smoother, free-running spinning guides. At any rate I can really shoot the cast. Next winter I'm going to try an experiment and have a set of spinning guides put on one of my bamboo fly rods. Perhaps I'll still shame these unimaginative and smug medieval fly-rod makers into following suit.

On Getting Lost: If you are really lost and it is dusk, build a rough camp and compose yourself until the thundering horde comes to find you. Most people seem to display a morbid sort of missionary zeal in finding lost brethren. Conserve your matches for smoke signals. If it is still daylight follow a trout stream, if you are on or near one, and you should soon come to a broad trail beaten by the army of faithful fishermen. More lost men come to grief from panic and exhaustion than anything else. Remember, when you are lost you are only temporarily in a state that was permanent to your hardy ancestors. Keep your chin up and your temperature down, and above all use your head before your legs.

An obvious clue overlooked by many confused fishermen is secondary roads and trails. If a road or trail you are following forks off into two or more roads or trails, you may safely conclude that you are going the wrong way and that "civilization" lies the other way. All roads and trails fork off *away* from home plate. Simply follow the point of the V. Think it over. . . . Again, if you see car tracks on a road with water puddles you can easily tell the direction the car has gone by the tire marks. The tracks are visible entering the puddle but become obliterated by the splashing cargo of water as they leave. Follow the car. If it has gone to camp it shouldn't be far; if it has gone to town, that's for you, too. And if, while following the tracks, you come to a fork, you can also thus confirm which way the car was heading, town or woodsward.

Leaders: Leaders are the problem child of fishing; they are far and away the weakest weapon in the fisherman's arsenal. All leaders are necessarily an uneasy compromise between the fisherman's normal desire to hold a decent fish if he gets on to one and his awareness that it is neither sporting nor productive of rises to employ a logging chain. Theoretically a leader should be invisible, and the only way to approach this diabolic goal is to keep using finer leaders. The main drawback with this strategy, however, is that the finer the leader the less liable it is to survive the initial shock of the strike; yet, *once a fish is on,* it is surprising how much strain even the finest leader can stand.

I have found a simple way to lessen this frequently fatal initial impact on fine leaders and, good fellow that I am, I pass it on to you. It is especially good on still clear waters where one must employ hair-thin leaders. It is this: Simply affix a common rubber elastic band between the end of your fly line and the butt end of your leader. It's the neatest little shock-absorber on the market. Think it over—and then go forth and try it.

Not only does this stratagem help with the initial shock but it also helps greatly to reduce the danger of loss in play during those thrilling moments when you discover that your

133

fish is heavier than you bargained for and it is touch and go whether you can hold on to him at all.

Slow Intermittent Rises: For good fishing give me these any time over the boiling and dramatic general rise. The latter is apt to be highly selective, and especially so on still waters. When trout are choosy every fly in the kit is apt to be the wrong one or else the right one is spurned if it is not presented and handled in precisely the right way. On the other hand a fairly steady but intermittent riser usually represents a fish gnawed by hunger and one more likely to snaffle any interesting morsel that drifts within its ken. Another thing, an occasional riser seems to range farther from his lie for food than does a rapid feeder on a particular fly hatch; hence the fisherman's cast need not be so delicately exact.

I remember a pair of such slow risers one evening at dusk on a deep, narrow run on the East Branch of the Escanaba. They were rising so seldom I almost passed them by. At first I tried approaching them from below but could not get within decent casting range because of brush and deep water. The approach from upstream was better but since they lay at the loop of a sharp double curve, the difficult slack-line downstream dry-fly float was not feasible. It looked as if I would practically have to go pat them on the nose to decently present a fly.

I did just that. I appproached them warily from above, the only way I could, inching along with infinite caution. When one would rise I'd move another foot closer. Finally they stayed down so long I thought I had put them down for good. Then both rose simultaneously. So, with scarcely more line out than twice the length of my rod, I dapped, not floated, a dry fly above the top riser. He immediately rose and nailed it. I powered him away from his cousin and fought him to net with only the leader showing. Without moving I tried the same strategy with the second riser—and also tied into him on the first try. They were a nice pair of fighting brook trout, but I perhaps wouldn't have had a Chinaman's chance to take either of them if they hadn't been hungry, less careful, and quite nonselective in their diet.

Another time I maneuvered for hours, it seemed, to get in casting position below a big intermittent riser on the Middle Branch. His lie was one of the many fisherman's headaches —inshore and directly under some low-lying tag alder branches—but I still saw a faint chance to float in a morsel over him. It was a delicate situation; one sloppy cast or false move would surely drive him down. In my mind's eye I could see him lying there just above me, fanning away and avidly watching everything, owly with hunger.

I concluded I had to do it on the first try or fail; it was all or nothing. So I made my false casts, back and forth, back and forth, measuring and calculating like a perspiring diamond cutter about to split a fabulous gem. Then, just as I released the business cast, the fly ticked a protruding tag alder twig and dropped like a sash weight, striking the water —*spat*—about four feet *below* my fish. Before I could let out an anguished yelp—or do anything else—that fish literally turned a somersault around and lunged downstream, nailing the fly. All hell couldn't have gotten it away from him! After a thrilling tussle amidst the awful tangle of half-submerged tag alder boughs I finally brought him to net. He was a monster brown with a yawning cannibalistic head like a tarpon. Part of his tail still stuck up out of the net, he was that big. And I *didn't* put him back. But the point is that I no more deserved to catch that fish than, I feel, I deserved to fail to catch so many others I have stalked and presented

135

the fly to perfectly—only to have them spurn my most adroit and gorgeous offerings.

One-Man Boats: Most so-called one-man boats designed for trout fishing on inland waters could be better employed in harpooning whales off the storm-lashed coast of Newfoundland. These craft are usually far too big and heavy. Indeed, the average man would be hard put to trundle their *oars* any distance. And their designers evidently think that fly-fishermen mount and employ a windlass to crank in their trout; at least they build their monstrosities accordingly. In fact these builders possess a positive low genius for not knowing what in hell they're doing. The requirements for a one-man trout boat are few and simple: it should be small, light, safe, silent, and easily portable. But try and find one.

There are some new light metal one- and two-man boats seeping into the market that are in all respects the candy rig except for two bad features—they cost nearly their weight in gold and, worse yet, they make too damn much noise. Either the fisherman is forever accidentally banging the thing with his paddle or the varying water pressures are bulging and buckling the metal hide. *"Clank, clunk!"* I have a spendthrift friend, proud fellow, who possesses a new one, and a gleaming thing it is. The only trouble is that his clanging progress along a trout stream or pond sounds not unlike that rural legal giant, Justice of the Peace Paulson, whanging away at his tall brass cuspidor. Remember? All the terrified trout for miles around promptly go down and stay down. Now when we two go a-boating for trout I usually spend half my time getting to hell away from him.

I have three fishing boats: a light canvas-covered duck boat that I occasionally use on placid trout ponds; then a sturdy nine-foot cedar boat that I use on rougher ponds and lakes and rocky rivers and also when I use my fishtail propeller; and then an eight-foot rubber boat with twin inflatable bladders, sort of like pregnant hot dogs laid end to end. This last is my pet and is the best all-around one-man trout boat I have ever seen. (Isn't it nice that I like my equipment?) It is light, safe and silent; I can easily carry it and my fishing gear a quarter or half mile, inflated, if the going isn't too thick; and if it is I can deflate and pack it in and then inflate it with a hand pump or air cartridge. It is tough (I bought it way before the War) and has never once snagged or punctured.

I always prefer to wade when wading is feasible but so much of our glaciated country possesses such suicidally unwadable waters that I think my best fishing waters would be reduced by at least half if it weren't for my faithful old rubber boat. I have waded certain stretches of our rivers right up the middle and been only ankle deep, while only a few yards away yawned deep watery craters large enough to engulf a cathedral, pigeon guano and all, and leave not a trace. In fact I suspect some of them do harbor sunken cathedrals because on quiet evenings I sometimes seem to hear the stifled pealing of far-off watery bells. . . . At any rate, these hidden river caverns may be nice hiding places for big fish but they're rather wearing on the nerve ends of big wading fishermen.

The only trouble with my rubber boat is that it is getting pretty battered and old and leaky—like its skipper—and the first money I get ahead I'm going to send and get me an exact duplicate. It's strictly a honey and when this book is hatched and flutters soundlessly upon a heedless world I at least expect to be invited by the maker to pose for a sleek portrait in *Field and Fen* endorsing his brand of rubber sausage. "Folks," I'll say, "I've rid and spun around in and

cursed this here now tough old sausage for nigh on to—"
It'll be a labor of love.

The Strangest Trout Spot in My World: Of all the many
weird places I know that harbor trout the Old Springhole
on the Whitefish River in Alger County is the strangest of
all. It is a veritable lake, a quarter-mile long and deep, set
down in the middle of a shallow river and fed winter and
summer from both sides by gushing ice-cold springs that
tumble down out of steep crumbly limestone ledges. Both
banks are crowded to the edges by a jungle of tangled cedars.
It is a devil of a place to get a boat into and nine devils of
a place to fly fish without a boat. There is one little fifty-foot
catwalk of limestone on one side that a good roll-caster might
cast from, provided he were only as tall as a midget. I once
tried it on my knees and, in that prayerful attitude and
doubtless due to divine intervention, was rewarded by taking
a lovely trout.

Bait-fishermen naturally haunt the place, and on a good
day the woods along both banks bristle with their protruding
steel girders, much like the peering artillery of rival troops
lined up for point-blank fire. I once came upon an old peg-
legged local character who had hacked a hole in the jungle
through which he was thrusting his girder, lowering a seven-
inch fish into the inky water.

"Just ketch one?" I said, making low fish talk.

"Naw," he replied. "That's my bait. Can't ya see it's a
chub?"

Lo, it *was* a chub. "Y-you mean you use *that* for bait?" I
gasped incredulously.

"Damn right I do!" he snapped. "Caught a twenty-two-
inch brook yesterday with a helluva bigger chub." He
squinted up at me in my diving suit and endless parapher-

nalia. "And how many like *that* do *you* ketch with them there goddam little house moths?"

I gulped and fought my way on downstream.

In the July or August dog days when the temperatures rise and the water levels go down, all the big trout for miles around seem to congregate in this fabulous trout haven. Some of the most dramatic big-fish rises I have ever seen occur there. (I have never caught an undersized trout there nor seen one come from the place.) Yet the few times I have found the hardihood to tote my rubber boat in there one wouldn't think a trout ever had dwelt there. That's fisherman's luck, of course, but someday I'll hit. . . .

Bears I've Never Met: I've seen dozens of them from cars but I'm delighted to report that never yet have I met one face to face while on foot. Yet I've heard them and smelled them—they smell like an unmanicured pig—and one time I even contrived to get myself caught between a feeding bear and a muddy, unwadable beaver dam. Here's how it happened: Tommy Cole and I had gone up to the Salmon Trout Creek to fish a certain productive beaver dam. Tommy and I rigged up while we watched a sprightly rise. I then left Tommy and crossed on the dam and worked my way upstream through a tangle of brambles and raspberry bushes, intently fishing all the while. I had creeled two trout when at length I heard Tommy crashing through the thick brambles right behind me.

"Come on out here, Tommy," I said. "The going's much better out here." The crashing continued. "Tommy," I called more urgently.

"Woof," Tommy grunted in my ear, and then I heard the greedy slurping of the unseen bear feeding on the rasp-

139

berries not more than two rod lengths behind me. He had been there all the while. . . .

"Taw-o-me!" I wailed like a banshee. The bear fell ominously silent.

"Halloo-oo!" Tommy answered, his voice floating thinly from far downstream, where I later found he'd gone to find a rumored new beaver dam.

"I—I'm a-coming!" I answered, and since I had successfully fished my way into this mess (the bear was doubtless just plain awed by my casting ability), I decided to fish my way out of it, though I'll admit I was glad no one was around making movies of my feverish casts.

This neck of the woods is crammed with black bears and yet I've heard of but two cases of a bear attacking a human —once from hunger (the bear stole a baby out of a forester's crib) and once because a man was molesting the bear's cubs. But I was plenty scared that day. The reason I had the hay up my neck with *this* bear was because I feared that he might think that I was challenging his possession of the raspberry patch. And raspberries were scarce that year. I wasn't, of course, and in fact I haven't ever been able to enjoy this wild fruit since—'though Tommy Cole still gives me the raspberry over the way I came charging pell-mell down creek to join him. He claims that on that day I joined the immortals: that I'm one of the few fishermen in captivity who ever made the 100-yard dash in ten seconds using hip boots for track shoes.

Getting Close to Trout: Wary as trout are, this can be done. It can be done because trout fishermen, including this one, constantly do it. Some fishermen, like Hewitt, get real chummy and even manage to touch them with their hands —"tickling" it's called—but I've never got quite that far, or rather, come that close. All river and stream trout normally lie facing upstream. It is surprising how close one can come to them by approaching from below. But Indian stealth and infinite patience are two absolute requirements.

I have approached solitary feeding trout so close that I could have reached out and touched their feeding circles with my rod tip, and in fact had finally to *retreat* in order to make a presentable cast. The noise of the current, the fact that the fish is facing away, and his concentration on feeding are doubtless all factors making this possible. And if a relatively clumsy fisherman can get this close it is small wonder, then, that the lightning otter can sneak up and grab a trout.

Again, believe it or not, I have on a number of occasions suddenly found myself in the midst of a wild general rise of big feeding trout—maddening rises in which I could not possibly match the hatch—where I was morally certain I would have had a much better chance if I merely reached out and tried to take them with my landing net, I was that close.

The moral of all this, if there is any, is that a man needn't be a whing-ding tournament distance caster to present a decent dry fly. All he needs to do is learn to stalk up close and make an *accurate* short cast before his fish. In the meantime he isn't scaring the bejabbers out of the *other* trout and keeping down *all* the dormant but potential risers that might lie between him and his distant riser. Most rookie fly casters (and too many experienced ones) try to handle way too much line. I raise twice as many fish within thirty feet or less, in my dry-fly work, than I ever do beyond that distance. Forget the histrionics and dramatics and the business of trying to impress your fellows with what a hell of a power-caster you are. It's worth repeating: work up close and make a short accurate cast. If you must show off take up amateur dra-

141

matics next winter. That slinky Naomi Goldfinch is simply dying to have you hold her in your big strong arms.

Tying Your Own: Alas, I've tried and I've sighed and all but cried, but I simply can't seem to tie a decent fly. Apparently I fell on my head when I was a baby or something. All my flies come out like old feather dusters. And I really envy those fishermen who can tie a good fly because it seems to me there is a special satisfaction, not to mention a delicate massage to the ego, in luring a trout with one's own creation; something akin to playing a solo part in one's own symphonic composition and watching the glittering ladies out front heaving and sighing and swooning with emotion.

Aside from these intangible values, however, there is a definite practical value in being able to tie up precisely the fly you want. After all, *you* are the only person that really knows what you want—you were there and saw the wondrous sights. There are flies I still dream about that are apparently so filmy and fugitive—or simple—that I cannot seem to impart my dream to any tier I know. Perhaps I merely confess the limitations and poverty of my prose.

There is one big compensation I have observed in *not* being able to tie flies: the few good fishermen-tiers I know seem to spend most of the season manacled to their vises; they consume more time in tying flies than in fishing. And I doubt that many fishermen save any money tying their own; many of them seem promptly to develop an occupational malady that results in a sort of evangelistic fervor, a missionary zeal, to promulgate some particular pattern. Most of the fishermen-tiers I know *give* away most of their flies.

Despite these minor vices of the fly vise, however, I'll take the chance on being manacled and evangelistic and all the rest; I still long to tie a fly that doesn't always contrive to look like a motheaten Fuller brush. Then what a whiz-kid I'd really be on a trout stream!

Leader Sinks: Try lava soap. However dark remains your soul and buoyant your leaders you'll at least keep your hands clean.

Fly Dope: If you are hardy enough, smoke Italian cigars. They smell like a burning peat bog mixed with smoldering Bermuda onions but they're the best damned unlabeled DDT on the market; all mosquitoes in the same township immediately shrivel and zoom to earth. (Fellow fishermen occasionally follow suit.) However, if you are soft and effete, use formula 448. On the other hand one of the most popular fly dopes on the market is the best little varnish remover I've ever seen.

Domestic Relations: Invite your wife to go fishing during the height of fly time. Press her to join you. Tell her the *only* real canker in your fishing is missing her bright presence by your side. Put a quaver in your voice. "It's nice to go fishing with the fellows and all, Honey, but . . ." is a good opening gambit. If successful in luring her give her sweetened water for fly dope. This harrowing experience will hold her nicely for a year. If she recoils in horror and refuses to go, still remembering the last time, she can nevertheless cherish the memory of that sweet generous gesture by her man. Either way you lay up red points and emerge as a real good guy. A sly fisherman can get a lot of domestic mileage from an occasional well-placed invitation of this kind.

Preservation of Fly Lines: Drunk or sober, always dry your fly line as soon as possible after leaving the water. In a pinch wind it around your whisky bottle, or else lay it out in loose coils in a shoe box. Even wrap it around yourself if necessary —or else mail it to me. More fishing equipment is ruined through thoughtless neglect than ever it is by use on laughing trout waters.

"You Shoulda Been Here Last Week!": Drill these whimsical characters between the eyes at forty paces.

Out-of-Town Guests Who Invite Themselves: Tell them you've given your fly rods to charity and taken up plug-casting for wormy bass—or else that, hurray, the doctor thinks those ugly spots on Junior may not be smallpox after all.

Out-of-Town Guests You Want to Come: Wire them that an eccentric old Finn west of here just showed you a secret pond where the trout measure three feet between the eyes —but that none of the bumpkins around here can ketch 'em, not even *you.* This challenge will fetch your man running every time.

Women Fishermen: Avoid them. One kind will quietly out-fish you and generally get in your hair while another variety will come down with the vapors and want to go home just when the rise gets under way. Avoid all of them like woodticks.

Trout Fishermen: Most people avoid *them* like woodticks. They're regarded in many quarters as tricky and deceitful, subtle and full of guile, and as men who lie just to keep their hands in. But don't blame fishermen: after all they devote their lives to practicing these black arts on the stream, a topsy-turvy world where these vices are hailed as virtues.

144

Be reasonable and reflect that fishermen just can't help acting the same way on the few occasions they mingle in the society of ordinary men. That is why so many normal people regard fishermen as being no damned good. Drat it, men, we're simply misunderstood.

17

The Old and the Proud

I HEARD the rhythmic whine and whish of his fly line before I saw him.

It was late afternoon and I was sitting on the edge of a flood-blasted high gravel bank overlooking a wide bend in the Big Escanaba River, leaning against one of a whispering stand of white pines, sipping a tepid can of beer and waiting for the evening rise. The sun was curving down and half of the river was already in shadow. *"Whish,"* sang the music of the unseen fly line, and I leaned forward craning to glimpse the sturdy fisherman who had penetrated to such a remote stretch on one of my favorite trout streams.

Then he rounded the bend below me, wading up over his waist, breasting the deep powerful current, inching along, a tottering old fisherman supporting and pushing himself along with a long-handled landing net which also served as a wading staff. As I sat watching, a good trout rose between

147

us. The old man saw it, too, and paused and braced himself against the current. He then paid out his line—false-casting to dry the fly and at the same time extend his line—and then, when I had about concluded he would never release the thing, whished out and delivered a beautiful curling upstream dry-fly cast. The fish rose and took the fly almost as it landed and I leaned forward watching the old fisherman as he expertly gathered in his slack, like a man harvesting grapes. He then suddenly whipped out his long-handled net and scooped in the fish as it passed him on its downstream run. It was a spanking beauty and I sat chewing my lip with envy.

The old fisherman held up his glistening fish and admired it and then creeled it. He then seemed to spend an interminable time selecting and tying on a new fly. He carried a little magnifying glass through which he peered at his fly boxes like a scientist bending over his retorts. In the meantime two more nice fish had risen between us, a circumstance which would have normally spurred me into action—not there, indeed, for this was now the old man's stretch—but I was held riveted to the spot by the sheer artistry and pluck of the old man's performance. The ritual of choosing and tying on the fly completed, it must have taken him another five or ten minutes to push and maneuver himself against the urgent river to assume his chosen casting position for the lower rising trout. Again there was the expert, careful, painstaking cast; again the obedient take on the first float; and again the sudden deft netting of the fish on its first downstream run. I thought the tottering old gentleman would surely founder and drown as he fought up through even deeper water to try for the third trout. He seemed to teeter in the current, like a wavering tightrope walker, and I restrained an impulse to shout a warning. Even *I*, a relative adolescent, had never dared wade up through this particular deep bend. . . . But the old man didn't drown and he calmly took the trout —again in as impressive a display of quiet fishing artistry as I had ever seen.

Here, I told myself, was a *real* fly fisherman, cool, deliberate, cagey, who for all the disabilities of his years could plainly fish rings around me and all the rest of my eager fishing pals. His performance was an illustrated lecture on one of the hardest of fundamentals for fishermen to learn: *easy does it*. But my heart went out to him as he continued to struggle manfully against the insistent current to reach still a new rise opposite and a little above me. On he came, like a man shackled by nightmare, still using his landing net as a staff. When he had fought his way opposite me I couldn't resist offering my nickel's worth of comment.

"Nice job of fishin'," I said, with all the foolhardy aplomb of the winner of a local dance marathon undertaking to compliment Nijinsky.

He glanced quickly up at me—one keen, appraising, wrinkled glance—and then away, as though I were a squirrel scolding and chattering on a bough. "Hm," he sniffed, that was all; just "Hm."

"Wouldn't it be a lot easier," I said, still filled with concern and still determined to take the fatal plunge, "wouldn't it be a lot easier if you fished downstream?"

The effect of this remark was as though I had deliberately impaled the old man with my fly or thrown a rock at his rising trout. His whole body seemed to shudder and recoil; then he stood stock-still and sighted me through his glasses, adjusting them, as though at last discovering that I was not a foolish squirrel but rather some new species of buzzing and pestiferous insect. "Harrumph," he snorted. "Listen, young fella," he said, "I'd sooner sit on my prat on the public dock at Lake Michigamme and plunk night crawlers for bass than *ever* fish a wet fly!"

Thus shriveled, I sat there red-faced and watched him teeter and struggle out of sight around the bend above. On the way he paused and took two more lovely trout.

This exchange of pleasantries between trout fishermen took place some fifteen years ago. Since then my anonymous old dry-fly purist has doubtless been gathered into the place where the meadows are always green and the trout always rising; but the lesson of our brief meeting was well learned. Ever since then my fellow fishermen may have at their trout from balloons or diving bells, for my part, without dredging up a single comment from me. And while I still fish the ignominious wet fly just as avidly as the lowly plunkers plunk for bass at Lake Michigamme, I have since learned that when dry-fly fishing is in season (alas, it frequently isn't in our chilly and temperamental northern waters) it is the most thrilling and rewarding—and exacting—of all methods of taking the fighting trout.

Whenever the day is dying and I find myself sitting on that particular high water-gouged bank on the Big Escanaba waiting for the evening rise, the brave words of that gallant old fisherman keep echoing and ringing in my ears—and lending them color, too. "Listen, young fella, I'd sooner sit on my prat on the public dock at Lake Michigamme and plunk night crawlers for bass than *ever* fish a wet fly!"

I have never forgotten this testy proud old man. In my mind's eye I can see him now. It is a still evening and he is breasting the deep celestial waters that run through green pastures. He is inching along with his glistening rod and his staff. A heavenly trout rises. He pauses and prepares to make one of his cool deliberate casts. His magic wand flashes and bends. "Whish," sings the line—"Whish," it goes, ever *"Whish."* . . .

18

Straight Up at Dinty's

A GOOD many people seem constitutionally unable to give proper directions. All want to; many yearn to; but, alas, few can correctly tell the way. The matter seems to have little or no connection with their intelligence or virtue; they simply can't coherently describe where they've been or how they got there.

Take the time last fall Jim Clancey and I were proceeding to Covington in the old fish car to hunt partridge. Trying to find a short cut we instead found ourselves snarled in a maze of windfallen and partridgy old logging roads. Away the birds flew, "Bang, *bang!*" our cannons blew. . . . We finally hewed and bombarded our way to the grand intersection of a dozen-odd roads flying off in all directions, all of them bad. At the very hub of this maze stood an old Finn sharpening an ax.

Jim leered out the car window. "My good man," he be-

153

gan suavely, and for a moment I thought he was going to recite "Woodman-spare-that-tree." "My good man," he repeated, "which of these roads can we take to Covington?"

The old Finn leered back, reflected and shrugged, then spat and spoke. "Any of dem, dat's all right, I doan care," he said, turning sadly away. Like ourselves, magnanimity could go no further. . . .

Yes, I have ruefully learned that many if not most people cannot properly direct their needy fellows, say, to an illuminated outhouse forty paces away. Especially is this true of woods directions. They might possibly remember that you should turn right at Macy's corner but not at that storm-blasted pine. They have simply never observed the storm-blasted pine. But they themselves can invariably find the place you seek, depending upon a vague and woolly sort of mental Braille, much as many people manage to remember phone numbers by a convoluted process of association that would shame Rube Goldberg.

Often have I been "directed" to secret trout streams in deep valleys and instead wound up on bald granite bluffs. At least in that way I saved lots of my favorite flies—and there was always the view. . . . Beware, too, of home-grown hand-loomed maps; they serve only to engrave the error and compound the confusion. Some hapless hunters and fishermen who have followed such maps have sprouted beards as long as those of gay Chamber of Commerce centennial celebrants before they were rescued and led away to the barber. Perhaps the biggest weakness in giving woods directions is the careful failure of the average director or cartographer to indicate (a) important turn-offs and (b) the roads or trails one *shouldn't* take. There was the day last spring that an amiable bartender undertook to direct me to Blair Pond in adjoining Baraga County. His fuzzy counsel was so typical it should have been preserved on tape.

"Blair Pond, hey? That's easy. Hm. . . . First you drive to the town of L'Anse," my guide began boldly.

"We now find ourselves in the sleepy logging village of L'Anse," I intoned in the soothing voice of the travelogue movies.

"Then you take and drive out just past that gas station and sorta turn off . . ." He paused and blinked. Ah, we were in trouble already.

Surprised: "Oh, so L'Anse has a *gas* station now? My, my . . . time marches on. . . . When in the world did they ever get *that?*"

Pouting: "You turn off at the Standard Oil station, dammit!"

Reflecting: "Hm. . . . Offhand I recall at least *three* Standard stations in the sleepy logging village of L'Anse."

Doggedly: "It's the one across from the Shell station."

"And pray tell where in hell is the Shell station?"

Triumphant: "Just across from the Standard station."

The man had me there. Indubitably. There was a long pause. Perhaps, I thought, it would be better if we started from scratch. Brightly, offhandedly: "Say, chum, could you tell me the way to Blair Pond?"

Rapidly: "You go to L'Anse and turn off at the Standard station."

"Hm. We two seem to have been there before. Did you ever, perchance, pump gas before you were promoted to pumping beer? No? Well anyway, do you sorta turn off to the left or to the right?"

"Neither. Sorta slantwise like . . ." He waved his hands vaguely, like an ultra-modern sculptor fashioning a buttock.

155

"Kind of a slow curve, see? Then you go two-three miles and you come to a farm with a white horse grazing in the pasture—"

Interrupting: "But suppose the white horse isn't hungry? Suppose he's out working? Or off running in the Derby? Or hanging around a New York advertising agency waiting to pose for a whisky ad? Or has dyed himself? Or has himself died? Or—?"

Grimly: "Look, fella, you want to know where this here place is at or don't you? I'm tryin' to do you a favor."

Softly: "I'm dying to."

Leaving the white horse at the turn: "You don't turn off where the white horse is grazing but keep going straight. A mile or two past there—or is it three?—you'll come to a place where a nice-looking Finnish girl is selling blueberries under a tree." He waved his hands some more and continued wistfully. "Yep, a fine-looking Finnish girl. . . . Then you sorta turn off just past her on a two-rut road and drive straight in to the pond. You can't miss it!"

"This Finnish girl—does she always sell her blueberries in May? Oh, I get it—they're preserved in Mason fruit jars. Tell me, must one leave a deposit on the jar? Does she do her stuff right under the tree? And what kind of a tree—?"

But my cowardly bartender was retreating to the back room, running, hurling his last words over his shoulder. "Gotta tap a new keg— Don't ketch 'em all. . . . Good luck. . . . So long, pal."

Naturally I never did find the fabled white horse or the Blueberry Girl, let alone Blair Pond. But I did miraculously avoid any bald granite bluffs. Instead I stumbled into a virgin beaver dam loaded with brook trout. Wanna find the

156

place? It's dead easy, friend. Just take and go to L'Anse and sorta turn off like when you see that big dumpling cumulus cloud. Park the car kinda off to the side of the cloud to avoid rain. The damn dam lies straight ahead. You can't possibly miss it!

19

The Old Fox

I T W A S about noon when I pulled out of the stream at the ruins of the old logging dam and fought my way to the top of the shattered old dam through the inevitable tangle of alders. There I sat and drank in the view, looking far up and down the sparkling and dancing Yellow Dog River, enjoying the comparatively cool breeze, and waiting for Carroll to join me for our noonday sandwich. I could still see evidences of the old dam lying jumbled all about me: great square rusty hand-forged spikes still protruding from the rotting timbers. I reflected that the nearly forgotten white pine lumberjacks were giants in their day, while today's so-called "lumberjacks" are merely unhappy mosquito-bitten mechanics caught far away from home. . . .

The remote Yellow Dog River is a fabulous little rocking-chair stream; as willful and turbulent and wenchy as a handsome native dancer; the kind of seductive trout stream that

159

keeps fishermen misty-eyed and mumbling to themselves trying to fathom its tempestuous moods and to realize its promise. But few are the fishermen that ever solve or subdue it. Its virtually unending series of shallow pockets and pools, gravelly riffles and rapids, wild chutes and quiet glides offer a bewildering variety of fishing and harbor some of the loveliest trout in Michigan. The *only* problem is to get on to them.

This particular day Carroll and I had been slugging away at the problem since shortly after sunup. I still didn't know how he was doing, but I ruefully knew that I, at least, was still several thousand light years away from the solution. Fishing mostly downstream I had caught or pricked scores of dancy, spittin' little trout. Out of desperation and low pride I had finally kept several seven- and eight-inchers for the fry pan (we had planned our usual stream-side trout fry to augment our sandwiches). But I hadn't so much as seen a decent rising trout much less raised one to the fly. Mostly I had fished downstream wet or occasionally slack-line dry because of the difficulty of making a decently controlled upstream cast in the brushy, unkempt little stream. I was getting a trifle despondent and anxious for Carroll to join me so that I could lay the sly preliminary groundwork for a move on to other more fishable if less fabulous trout waters. And I needed his vote.

But where was Carroll? I looked at my big silver watch, the kind that strikes the hour and the quarter hours, and saw that it was past twelve-thirty. A couple of partridge in the woods back of me suddenly decided to get into the time act, so they began beating their tom-toms, beginning in their slow deliberate rhythmic locomotive fashion, like a college cheer, and concluding in a rapid ecstatic ascending crescendo of fluttering wings. Out of boredom more than hunger

I fished out my sandwich and ate it; then I filled and tamped and lit my pipe and just sat there looking down the glittering serpentine course of the river waiting for tardy Carroll to join me. When Old Big Ben struck one I knocked out my pipe and ground out the embers and moved slowly down river along the heavily wooded bank in quest of the missing fisherman.

One-fifteen chimed; then one-thirty; then I began to get a little worried. Where was my man? Carroll was usually prompt in meeting at the agreed time and place. And this was pretty wild and woolly country. I got back away from the insistent noise of the stream on a little rise of ground so that I might better both see or hear him if he was in trouble. Still no Carroll. Big Ben tinkled one-forty-five and I was just about to vent one of my bloodcurdling shouts when through a thin grove of dappled poplars I saw a man plodding slowly up the river. I craned to look. Yes, it was Carroll all right; the Old Fox himself. But what was he doing? I peered more closely. Of all things, he was fighting a fish, and a good one, too, judging from the bow in his rod. Feeling like a wallflower at a prom I shook my head in envy and admiration as I watched him creel this handsome specimen. He always carries an old-fashioned rigid wicker creel about the size of a pack basket so there was no way to judge whether this was his sole catch of the day.

I was just about to shout a greeting and try to lure him elsewhere when I saw him tie on another fly and continue fishing. Hm . . . fishing must be fairly good. But where were the long whistling dry-fly casts for which he was locally famous? I quietly moved closer to the river. The old fox was intent as a real fox, stalking, squinting, inching—and delicately casting out *not more than fifteen feet of line!* As I watched him he rose and got on to a respectable trout—a

161

ten-eleven incher, at least—and released it before my in-
credulous eyes. Then I saw him change flies again and
stealthily inch a few more feet upstream. He paused below
a modest riffle and, still working the short line, rose and was
fast to a lovely trout on his first cast. He postured and turned
like a marionette during the whirling fight. His net sagged
under this specimen, and I stood there entranced while he
fumbled in his creel, as though counting, and then unhooked
and *released* this spanking fish! He then lit a cigarette and
suddenly quit the stream—almost walking into me stealthily
spying on him.

"Ah, good morning, Mister Bear," he said drily.

"You old fox," I said accusingly. "You sly, deceitful, rum-
soaked, double-dealing—er—foxy old fox—what have you been
up to now? I *saw* you release those fish. Have you finally
completely blown your top?"

"Spying on me, were you?" Carroll grew mock-indignant.
"Creeping up on me unbeknownst and ferreting out my
trade secrets, were you? Well, if you *must* know I threw
the first one back because he was too small—I've already put
back many bigger ones—and the last one because I discovered I already had my limit. I had merely lost count. But
how'd you do, Izaak Walton, Junior?"

I swallowed hard and ignored this barb. "Lemme see
'em," I demanded.

"Sure, sure," Carroll answered loftily. "The proof of the
pudding gathers no moss." He hefted his heavy pack basket
off his shoulder and *poured* out a torrent of big trout upon
the ferns—perhaps the loveliest catch I have ever seen, at
least outside of Canada.

I sank to my knees in an unfamiliar attitude of prayer and
stared at them in awe. Fifteen glistening trout they were—
mixed browns, rainbows, and brooks—and all of them two-

dollar fish, that is, fifteen inches or over. I shook my head. "My heavenly days," I murmured, a defeated and broken man, corroded with envy.

"How'd you do?" Carroll repeated sweetly, plunging the needle farther.

Reaching in my sweat-dampened pocket I fished out my answer—two wrinkled dollar bills—and bleakly handed them to him. "Kept four dwarfed grandchildren of your smallest fish," I said. "But how did you *do* it?" I went on, incredulously. "What'd you *use*, man—Parisian postcards?"

"Oh, I used only one fly," Carroll answered, stifling a yawn, as offensively modest as a man who'd just swum the Channel with one arm tied behind his back—and then refused to be photographed.

"You lying fox—I just *saw* you change flies twice."

"Don't be hasty, chum—I only used one fly pattern—but I put on a fresh fly after every fish. Today they were temperance trout—they wanted them strictly dry. I kept nothing under fifteen inches. Boy oh boy, what a day, what a stream."

"But what fly was it?" I demanded. "*Confess*, damn it!"

Carroll shrugged and widened his hands and bowed his head in mock surrender. "You've caught me, pal—it was the little Betty McNault—number 16."

Between them those two old foxes Tommy Cole and Carroll Rushton have perhaps taught me most of what I was ever able to absorb about the mysteries of fly fishing for trout. Carroll it was that initiated me into the roll cast, perhaps the only department of the sport in which I might excel him. Both he and Tommy are slow, deliberate, undramatic fishermen, almost sleepily casual performers, true disciples of the all-important *easy does it*. More than being excellent fishermen they are philosophers who fish. Both have fly-fished for many years and both are battle-scarred old foxes of the stream who possess to an astonishing degree that diabolical "fish sense" coupled with fishing dexterity that I have mentioned earlier. (Young Henry Scarffe, with whom I am currently "going steady"—as my wife calls my fishing romances—is another such comer.) And so it was that on that enchanted day on the Yellow Dog I learned once and for all the invaluable lesson of the short accurate dry-fly upstream cast. I've never forgotten it.

"Nobody but a magician can manage an accurate long cast in these brambles," Carroll finally relented and explained between mouthfuls of sandwich. "All you can accomplish is to put the fish down in those very intervening places where you might otherwise have a Chinaman's chance to take them—the ones lying there right before your patrician and alcoholic nose. So what do you do? You get disgusted and stubborn and careless and try to fish downstream and, in these clear waters, only manage to scare the pants off of every decent trout within fifty feet. You've thoughtfully been herding the big ones down to me all morning. And all you get are the Junior Leaguers. But don't you see— in these noisy tumbling waters from *below* you can almost walk up and pet these fish. Do you follow me, my disconsolate friend?"

"Yes, sir," I answered meekly.

"Therefore," he went on, "if you would only muster the wit and the patience to try, you will find that you can float a dainty cast directly over their suspected lies. And you don't miss nearly so many fish as on the imperceptibly delayed strike involved in long upstream casts on these fast shallow waters." Carroll paused. "But enough of this pompous lecturing. Class is dismissed. . . . Get going, now, while I clean out these fish. Here, take a half-dozen of these virgin Betties."

I took the flies humbly and followed instructions—and in little over a half-hour had taken six trout between ten and fifteen inches. I had also raised several more, one a spaniel. They were really on the prod that day, though needless to say the Yellow Dog doesn't always deliver that way. But it is a rare day when Carroll Rushton doesn't dredge up a companion old fox to enable him to relieve me of one or two of those officially engraved likenesses of George Washington so thoughtfully provided by the U. S. Mint.

As for the Betty McNault (I have seen it also variously spelled McNall and McNoll), it is a dainty little hackled hair fly, tied and appearing much like a minor variant of that old reliable, the Royal Coachman. It is a tremendously versatile fly; one that can be fished either wet or dry. Oddly enough, like so many effective flies it looks like no natural fly I've ever seen floating on a stream. Carroll always carries oodles of them, in all smaller sizes, but the number 16 is far and away his favorite—especially, as I wryly discovered, for stalking big trout upstream in the tumbling and fumbling Yellow Dog.

The only thing Carroll hasn't been able to impart to me, unfortunately, is perhaps the most important thing. It is this: how in the bloomin' blazes does he *know* where the favorite lies of the big trout are? Ah, there's the rub! That, alas, is one of the fascinating mysteries of fishing; here is an instinct, a secret sense, that no fisherman can ever divulge to another—even if he would. And so, to this day, I continue to pay him tribute regularly in damp one- and two-dollar installments. (I hope my wife never reads this.) But I have grown philosophical about it all—I now regard it as money well spent, a payment more in the nature of a deserved tuition, so to speak, to be able to study at the casting elbow of the Old Fox himself.

20

The Voyage

LOUIE BONETTI sidled up to my law office one beautiful August morning, bowing and scraping and grinning, hat in hand—"Gooda mornin', Mister Yon"—and slipped into the chair opposite me. For some obscure reason the dusty shelves of systematically unread law books and the various diplomas and certificates and somber pictures of notaries, dead fish, and politicians that adorned my walls seemed always unduly to impress Louie, because these were the only occasions I ever saw him remove his hat for anyone or anything—although you will remember, he did *tip* his hat when he said, "Gooda mornin', Mister Bear!"

"Luke, Yon," he said, grinning and puffing away at his gnarled Italian cigar. "Luke, I jes' talka some people over my a place, an' dey tella me confidench where dey catcha one hell of a beeg mess a brooka trout las' night."

"You *mean* it, Louie?" I said, suddenly sitting up all alert.

Trout Madness

Louie's "place" was his tavern, of course, run by his two strapping sons, Geno and Guido. I had learned that Louie heard many strange and wonderful tales from his arid customers—and also delivered himself of quite a few. "Do you mean it, Louie?" I repeated.

"Sure, sure t'ing—dese people gooda people, dey sometime tella da trut'." Louie shrugged and threw up both hands, palms up. "An' he's a nice a day an' you my gooda fran an' I t'ink maybe I take a you dere dis aft. W'at you t'ink?"

Louie had chosen and cast his lure well. "Do we need a boat, Louie?" I said, already mentally canceling appointments and rearranging my modest affairs.

"Ya, ya," Louie answered. "We gotta have da boat. He's a kinda bad a place. Dis here a spot he's a west of here on swampy stretch of Meedle Escanaba. Leedle feeder crick he come right in where da beeg a trout he hang aroun'. Dat's da dope."

"Can we make it in one afternoon, Louie?"

"Sure, sure," Louie reassured me. "Easy. . . . Udder people—gooda people—tella me confidench a shorta cut dat even dese people who tella me da place doan know."

It was all a little complicated, but by then my nostrils were flaring and my eyes were wide and awash with stardust. "When and where do we meet?" I said, as Louie moved to the door, hat still in hand.

"Hm. . . . Picka me up behind da place at twelva-t'irt— an' be sure you bring a da leedle boat."

"O.K., Louie," I said, and thus the great voyage was planned.

At 1:30 Louie and I rattled over the loose planking of the logging bridge of the Middle Escanaba in search of Louie's short cut. I stopped the fish car on the other side and grew

168

thoughtful. "Look, Louie," I said, "why don't we just put the boat in here and paddle up to the new hot spot?"

"*Non, non*," Louie answered, "Too far. An' maybe udder people dey see us on way an den dey fine our new a spot. Anyway, lak I tella you, I know da swella shorta cut. *Drive on!*"

Commander Bonetti had taken over, and few were the men who could resist his peculiar brand of hypnosis. He should have been a conjurer or a trial lawyer; he was a natural specialist in persuading the complete abdication of reason.

"Stoppa da car!" Louie ordered, after we had proceeded north on the dusty road nearly five miles. "Dis here da shorta cut." I slammed on the brakes and we were overtaken by our own dust storm.

We had stopped at a little tag-alder creek about four feet wide that girdled and squeezed itself to run under the dirt road through an iron pipe. Louie had already leapt out and was untying the cedar boat from the trailer.

I shook my head. "Looks pretty small to me for boating," I said, dubiously stroking my chin.

"*Non, non*, Yon." He widened his arms. "He gets a beeg beeg down jes' a leedle way. Anyway, he's a gooda shorta cut."

"Just how far down is it to this hot spot on the main river, Louie?" I asked.

"Hm . . . maybe two-t'ree 'ondred yard, maybe less," Louie answered airily. "Anyway, he's swella shorta cut."

I scratched the top of my head and squinted one eye. "Look, Louie," I said, "how in hell can the big river be only a few hundred yards away when we crossed the damned thing five miles *south* of here?"

Louie sighed over my obtuseness and crouched in the

169

middle of the sandy road and drew a map with his finger. He had now adopted the title of master cartographer of the expedition. "Luke, Yon," he lectured patiently, wagging his dusty map finger at me. "Da beeg riv' he runna easta-west across da breedge, yes, jes' lak a dis, see?"

"I see," I answered meekly, appropriately chastened.

"Den da riv' maka beeg a loop nort' up a dis a way, lak a dis, see?"—Louie the mapmaker described a big loop north —"an' almos' hita da road right here, see?"

"Yes."

"Den dis here a crick he runna two-t'ree 'ondred yard down dis a way, see?"

"Yes."

"Den we hita da hotta spot an feesh—an' den we feesh an' float an' float an' feesh all da way down da riv' to da breedge, see?"

"Yes," I answered. "But after we get down to the wooden bridge how'n hell do we get way back up *here* to get the car and trailer?" I thought I really had him there.

But Louie was equal to anything. "Hm . . . da lucky a man what get da beegest feesh—he sit on breedge an' watcha da feesh an' drinka da whisk'. *He doan walk.*"

"O.K., Louie," I said, accepting his challenge. We tossed off the boat and threw in our gear and prepared to shove off. Just as an afterthought I threw in an ax.

Commander Bonetti sat straight as an arrow in the bow of the nine-foot cedar boat, like his "Christa Columb." "Alla set, Yon?" he said, impatient to get at his big secret trout lying there in wait such a few feet away.

"All set, Louie," I said, shoving on the culvert with my paddle. The historic voyage was away. I glanced at my watch. It was 1:55.

THE VOYAGE

I cannot truthfully say that I have ever seen a river that ran uphill but I can say that I saw one creek that got smaller and smaller the farther down it one got. We were on it that day. By the time we had pushed and shoved and hacked our way downstream a hundred yards it was hideously plain that there was no turning back; even *Louie* couldn't have managed that.

"Kinda brushy, Louie," I said softly, avoiding his eyes and tossing a bushel or so of tag-alder branches out of the boat.

"On'y leedle farder," Louie grunted, leaping out of the boat in his hip boots and *pulling* the boat and me down through the next jungle of tag alders that loomed ahead. I leaned back like Cleopatra floating on the Nile.

I could go on and on, tracing each tortuous *mile* of that fantastic voyage; telling about the scores of times we had to stop and chop a path to get the boat through the horrible tangle, lift it over logs and endless tiny beaver dams, and of the scores of times we had to empty the boat of heaps of twigs and rotten branches. We were doubtless the only men in history, white or red, drunk or sober, who had ever been foolish enough to pull a boat down that particular creek. Rogers' Rangers had had a basket picnic.

"On'y leedle farder," Louie chanted each time we ran into a particularly discouraging new wall of obstruction. It was no longer a question of fishing; all that was long since sweated out of us. It had become a grim question of getting ourselves out of there and saving the boat.

At 9:58 that night—eight hours later—we gained the river, and while we couldn't even see each other any longer we could hear the big feeding trout flopping all around us.

By 10:17 we had negotiated the short easy float down to the wooden bridge! On the way wily Louie had surreptitiously run out his girder and caught himself an eight-inch trout. By midnight I had walked up to and returned with the fish car and trailer; and by 1:58 Louie and I were arm and arm in the back booth of his "place," sweat-stained and grimy, alder twigs coming out of our ears, and both drunker than skunks on but two rounds of bar whisky. The fishermen were home from the bog. . . .

The next morning grinning Louie sidled up to the office, hat in hand. "Yon," he announced, "da people my place jes' tella me 'bout gooda trout a place."

I groaned and recoiled arthritically in my chair. "Any short cuts, Louie?" I demanded.

"No shorta cuts," Louie answered, the grin spreading

"You swear?" I pressed him.

"Hones' crossa my heart, Yon," Louie answered, doing it.

I leaned back with a sigh. "Tell me about it, Louie—and can I *fly* fish there?"

"You can fly lak ever't'ing," Louie answered, still grinning and crossing his heart once more.

During my addled career as a trout fisherman I have gone on a lot of wild-goose chases, and I ruefully expect to go on a lot more before I hang up my waders. Only a fraction of these mad expeditions are confessed in this book, but you have now heard about the wild-goose chase that, in my considerable wry experience in chasing geese, I consider the goose chase to end all goose chases. I do not expect or want ever to equal or surpass it unless, perchance, one day I take off in search of the restless spirit of Louie or the moon.

Finally, I do not wish disloyally to leave the impression that A. Louis Bonetti was not a good woodsman. He was, in fact, one of the best I've ever known; one of those rare individuals who disdain compasses and such truck, who never forget a road or a trail or a marker, who always *know* where they are. He was a natural primitive. The main thing wrong with Louie was that he was gullible; he *listened* to other people; and the main thing wrong with me was that I am gullible; and I listened to Louie when he had been listening to other people. If Louie had once *been* to a place himself, he could remember every physical detail twenty years later, and no mistake; but when he listened to other people and I listened to Louie—together we made a soaring championship team of wild-goose chasers that could have taken on the world.

And you, Louie, wherever you are and whatever you may be doing—all is forgiven. I wouldn't have missed a single moment of our great voyage together. And may you have an unobstructed downstream float to paradise by the shortest cut of all.

21

The Last Day

EACH year it is the same: this time, we tell ourselves, the doze and stitch and murmur of summer can never end; this season time will surely stand still in its tracks. Yet the hazy and glorious days glide by on golden wings, and presently here and there the leaves grow tinted by subtle fairy paintbrushes and flash their red warnings of impending fall. Even the trout become more brilliant in hue and grow heavy and loaded with spawn. And then, lo, one day we tired fishermen drag ourselves abroad only to discover that the stricken summer has waned into colorful northern autumn, like a beautiful woman flushed with the fevers of approaching death. It is the last day of fishing; the annual hibernation is once again at hand.

To this fisherman, at least, with all of its sadness and nostalgia the end of fishing is not unmixed with a sense of relief and release. No more is one oppressed by the curious compulsion of the chase; no more the driving sense of urgency that fills the eyes of fishermen with flecks of stardust shot through with mad gleams of lunacy. Reason is temporarily restored. The precious rods can now be leisurely gone over and stashed; the lines cleaned and stored; the boots hung up by their feet, and all the rest of the sad ritual. Yes, and with a little luck perhaps diplomatic relations can even be restored with those strange but vaguely familiar ladies with whom we have been oh so absently sharing our bedrooms all summer long.

For many years I have speculated on the precise nature of the drives that possess a presumably reasonable man and turn him into that quietly mad creature we call a fisherman. I am satisfied that it is not merely the urge to kill and possess. In fact I now think—like Messrs. Gilbert and Sullivan—that this has nothing to do with the thing, tra la, has nothing to do with the thing. Most fishermen I know are poor or indifferent hunters; as a class they are apt to be a gentle, tweedy, and chicken-hearted lot; and, let us admit it, they are frequently reflective and poky to the point of coma. But allowing for all this I sometimes wonder whether they are not a more atavistic and elemental crew than most of their fellow men—even more so than their bombarding second cousins, the hunters.

All hunters, unless they have got themselves too loaded with cookin' whisky, invariably first *see* their quarry and know precisely what it is, and then deliberately sight and hurl a projectile at it—bullet, arrow, rock or what you will—while the fisherman rarely "sees" his fish in this sense, but rather must expend endless ingenuity and patience in approaching and luring his game to its fate. And perhaps most important, when he is successful he is in actual, pulsing, manual contact with his quarry through the extension of his hand that he calls his line. The real combat only *begins* when he "shoots" his game, that is, sinks the barb. This, to me, marks fishing as at once a more subtle and yet basically more primitive pursuit than hunting, or selling cars or TV sets on time—or even excelling in the absorbing mysteries of corporate financing.

At this late hour I don't want to go in over my waders and poach on the preserves of the psychiatrists. Thank heaven I have never been encouched and so am not qualified to. But sometimes I wonder whether the wild urge to pursue and lure a fighting fish isn't connected somehow with the— er—sexual urges of the fisherman himself. My, my, I've up and said it! Many frustrated and neglected wives of fishermen will doubtless rise up at this point and shout hoarsely, "*What* sexual urges?" Hm, let us see, let us see. . . .

Under the beneficent glow of our present pale tribal customs courtship and marriage can get to be, so my runners inform me, a pretty drab and routine affair; and I divine as though in a dream that some men there are among us who doubtless rebel at constantly laying siege to an already conquered citadel; and unless they are going in for collecting blondes of assorted shades and varying degrees of moral rectitude, fishing and all that goes with it may be the one pursuit that permits them to vent their atavistic impulses and still preserve the tatters of their self-respect. I do not labor the point, but smile evilly and cast my lure lightly upon the troubled waters—and quietly rejoin the drabber subject of the Last Day, the sad refrain upon which I seem to have opened this swan song.

On the last day all fishermen are akin to pallbearers; worse yet, they are pallbearers at their own funerals. Going out on the last day is a job that has to be done, like burying the dead; but their hearts aren't in the enterprise and the day is apt to be ruined by a future that looms ahead as bleak and hopeless as the grave. They may comfort themselves for the ordeal and brace themselves for the purgatory of waiting by telling themselves that it is all for the best. The fisherman's last-day funeral litany is a foggily beautiful and self-deceiving thing and runs something like this: the fishing is no longer sporting; the fisherman himself is dog-tired; the rise can no longer be depended on; the spawn-laden trout are far too easy to catch; and to take them now is to bite off one's nose. Amen.

Yes, on the last day we fishermen can try as we may to incant ourselves into hilarity and acceptance, but our hearts are chilled and our minds are numb. For what we fishermen really want is to go on fishing, fishing, fishing—yes, fishing forever into the great far blue beyond. . . . All that sustains us in our annual autumnal sorrow is the wry knowledge that spring is but two seasons removed. After all, we can sadly croak, it's *only* eight more months till the magic *First Day*!

THE

GOOD

CARBOHYDRATE

REVOLUTION

Also by Dr. Terry Shintani

The HawaiiDiet™

Available from POCKET BOOKS

THE

GOOD

CARBOHYDRATE

REVOLUTION

TERRY SHINTANI

M.D., J.D., M.P.H.

POCKET BOOKS
New York   London   Toronto   Sydney   Singapore

READ THIS FIRST

Before You Change Your Diet and Exercise Habits: Do not change your diet or exercise habits without guidance from your medical doctor, especially if you have health problems or are on medication. Do not change your medications without the guidance of your medical doctor. The information in this book is general information about your health and is not to be taken as professional advice, nor is it intended to serve as a substitute for medical attention. The advice in this book is directed toward reasonably healthy adults. Individual needs do vary. For those with special conditions or needs, or for children and pregnant women, modifications may be necessary and should be made under the guidance of your medical doctor or registered dietitian.

 POCKET BOOKS, a division of Simon & Schuster, Inc.
1230 Avenue of the Americas, New York, NY 10020

Library of Congress Cataloging-in-Publication Data

Shintani, Terry T., 1951–
    The good carbohydrate revolution / Terry Shintani.
        p. cm.
Includes bibliographical references and index.
ISBN: 0-7434-0598-6
    1. High-carbohydrate diet. 2. Reducing diets. I. Title.

RM237.59 .S554 2002
613.2'83—dc21

2001055416

First Pocket Books hardcover printing January 2002

10 9 8 7 6 5 4 3 2 1

POCKET and colophon are registered trademarks of
Simon & Schuster, Inc.

For information regarding special discounts for bulk purchases,
please contact Simon & Schuster Special Sales at 1-800-456-6798
or business@simonandschuster.com

Designed by Nancy Singer Olaguera

Printed in the U.S.A.

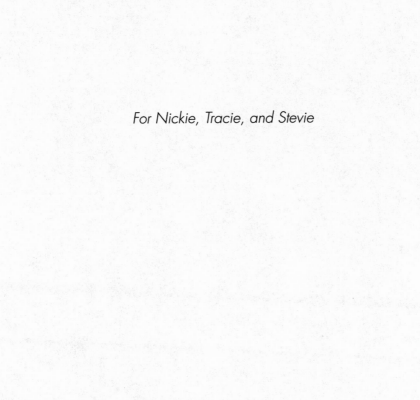
For Nickie, Tracie, and Stevie

IN MEMORY OF

Aveline and Maybelle

ACKNOWLEDGMENTS

Producing a book always takes more time than you might imagine. It also takes the effort, assistance, and the good will of many. While it is impossible to thank everyone who has had some influence on the creation of this book, I would like to acknowledge at least some of the efforts of those who have made this book and all the work that I do possible.

- Dr. Diane Nomura, administrator of the Hawaii Health Foundation, who keeps the wheels turning on our work to promote health.

- My managing editor, Jan Foster, who is also a first-class desktop publisher, took charge of the recipe chapter and put the final touches on the "how to" chapter of the book.

- My writer, Rebecca Saltzburg, who humanized my writing that at times was very scientific and complex.

- My researchers Angela Kusatsu, Jon Tang, Annette Sacksteder, Gloria Renda, M.P.H., R.D., and Quinn Ni, all of whom provided excellent in-depth research.

- Family and consumer science teachers Carol Devenot, Lynne Lee, and Jenny Choy, who have worked with me on recipes for this book.

- Barbara Gray, food designer and specialist who helped create, test, and edit many of my recipes.

- Claudia Neely, "The Vegan Gourmet," who makes excellent meals on contract for individuals; Ed and Wendy Esko, premier macrobiotic cooking teachers; and Ann Tang, who contributed recipes.

- Fran Moody of Austin, Texas, writer and cooking teacher, who helped me to write the "how to" section of this book.

- S. Y. Tan, M.D., J.D., Endocrinologist; John Westerdahl, Ph.D., R.D.; Ruth Heidrich, Ph.D.; Mae Isonaga, M.P.H., R.D.; and Ben Stackler; all of whom kindly shared their expertise on technical points.

- Dr. Diane Nomura, Bianca Kusatsu, and David McDonald, who reviewed the book.

- Ande Kawaiaea, who helped to transcribe early versions of the book.

- Tracy Sherrod, Editor at Pocket Books, whose excellent editing kept this book high in quality and easy to read and accessible to the readers.

- Ho'oipo DeCambra, Kenneth Brown, Kamaki Kanahele, Ronald Sakamoto, Esq. current board members of the Hawaii Health Foundation, and officers, Rodney Sato, Esq. and Marianne Glushenko, with whom I share the dream of Hawaii as a world center for health.

- The Waianae Coast Comprehensive Health Center, their owners, the Waianae Coast community, the Integrative Medicine Center there of which I am currently director, and their staff, especially Helen Kanawaliwali O'Connor and Sheila Beckham, M.P.H., R.D., who have worked with me for so many years in my research on traditional diets.

- All the contributors* to the Hawaii Health Foundation, who by their generosity help us promote health and peace in Hawaii and eventually around the world.

- Special thanks to Maybelle Roth and George Bonn.

- Zippy's Inc., and Cesari Response T.V., whose royalty contributions have helped the Hawaii Health Foundation and the Waianae Coast Comprehensive Health Center.

- All the organizations and individuals* that supported us or our programs "in kind" such as: Waianae Coast Comprehensive

---

*Names not listed because permission not obtained from all individuals.

Health Center; Ke Ola Mamo; Diagnostic Laboratory Services; Mokichi Okada Association; Hawaii State Department of Business; and Economic Development and Tourism.

- All the volunteers* of the Hawaii Health Foundation, who by their personal commitment and work have made many of the accomplishments of the Foundation possible.

- Michio and Aveline Kushi; and Herman and Cornelia Aihara, pioneers of low-fat, whole-food, vegan diets and the natural food movement in the United States. Their selfless lives have been an inspiration to me and millions of others.

- Kekuni Blaisdell, M.D., one of my professors and mentors, and one of the co-founders of the University of Hawaii John A. Burns School of Medicine. Frank Tabrah, M.D., one of my first mentors in the field of medicine, who is always there with his wise counsel.

- T. Colin Campbell, Ph.D., of Cornell University; Walter Willett, M.D., Dr.P.H., of Harvard University; Antonia Trichopolou, M.D., of the University of Athens; Lawrence Kushi, Dr.P.H., of University of Minnesota, and Claire Hughes, Dr.P.H., R.D., of the Hawaii State Department of Health, all of whom freely gave their consultation on some of my research on traditional diets.

- Kenneth Brown; Robert Oshiro, Esq.; and the Queen Emma Foundation, who have supported my efforts to promote health in Hawaii and around the world.

- The Honorable Benjamin J. Cayetano, Governor of the State of Hawaii; Lt. Governor Mazie Hirono; members of the Governor's cabinet, including Charles Toguchi, Susan Chandler, Herman Aizawa and Joseph Blanco; and State Senator Calvin Kawamoto, and members of the Papakolea community, who helped to make some of our community health programs successful.

I would also like to thank the following individuals and organizations who are at the top of their fields and were kind enough to take notice of our work; Robert Arnot, M.D., and *Dateline NBC;* Carolyn O'Neil and CNN; Mike Silverstein and ABC National Radio; Laura Shapiro and *Newsweek;* Ben DiPietro, Meki Cox, and Associated Press; Dick Allgire, Paula Akana, Pamela Young, and KITV;

Leslie Wilcox, Ron Mizutani, Manolo Morales, Bernadette Baraquio, Mary Zanakis, John Yoshimura, and KHON; Jade Moon and KGMB; Emme Tomimbang; Brickwood Galuteria, Laura Lott and "Hawaii's Kitchen"; Michael W. Perry, Larry Price, the Hawaiian Moving Company, the Perry and Price Show, and KSSK; Sam, Lina, and Ikaika and Local Kine Grindz; Ed Glassel and *Ohohia* magazine; the TV show *Lifestyle Magazine*; Linda Tomchuck and *Encyclopedia Brittanica*; Barbara Ann Curcio and *Eating Well* magazine; *Vegetarian Times* magazine; Steven Pratt and the *Chicago Tribune*; *Tufts Newsletter*; Diana Sugg and the *Sacramento Bee*; Barbara Burke, Dave Donnelly, Catherine Enomoto, Linda Hosek, Becky Ashizawa and the *Honolulu Star Bulletin*; Joan Nam Koong, Beverly Creamer, Chris Oliver and the *Honolulu Advertiser*; Debbie Ward and *Ka Wai Ola O OHA*; Janice Otaguro and *Honolulu* magazine; Ciel Sinnex and *MidWeek* magazine; Sally-Jo Bowman and *Aloha* magazine; Gwen Bataad and the *Hawaii Herald*; Betty Fullard-Leo and *Hawaii* magazine; Stu Dawrs and the *Honolulu Weekly*; Tracy Orillo-Donovan and the University of Hawaii, and many others whom I have forgotten to thank.

I would like to thank my brother, Arthur Shintani; and my *hanai* (adoptive) family, especially Mom, Agnes Cope, and brother, Kamaki Kanahele, who have always given me wise counsel.

Thanks to my wife, Stephanie; daughters, Tracie and Nickie; and their grandparents, Henry and Peggy Hong, for their support and patience while I was writing this book.

Thanks to my grandparents, Gunichi and Yukie Otoide, Kansuke and Miyo Shintani, and to my parents, Emi and Robert Shintani, who are always with me in spirit.

Last but most important, I thank our Almighty Father, who ultimately does all the healing, and who has provided us with good carbohydrates to help us along.

Contents

THE

GOOD
CARBOHYDRATE
REVOLUTION

CHAPTER 1

You Can Benefit from the Good Carbohydrate Plan

You can benefit from the Good Carbohydrate Plan because every-one—including those on high protein diets—eats carbohydrates. If you answer yes to any of the following questions, the Good Carbohydrate Plan will be of enormous benefit to you.

- Are you confused about carbohydrate, protein, and fat?
- Have you tried dieting and gained and lost weight over and over again?
- Do you have a lot of weight to lose, perhaps 20 to 50 pounds or more, and you are concerned that these pounds may contribute to health problems?
- Are you trying to lose those last, stubborn 5 to 20 pounds and can't seem to get them off?
- Have you been told that you have or are at risk for high blood sugar and you want to get it under control before it gets out of hand?
- Have you discovered that you have high cholesterol and you are concerned about heart disease risk, but you don't want to take

medication to control it? Or, are you already on medication for cholesterol and want to get rid of the need for medication?

- Do you feel tired and just not up to par all the time and you want to get your energy back?

My patients have followed the principles of the Good Carbohydrate Plan and have successfully met these health challenges—some of them in as little as three weeks. What's more, when they continue to follow the principles, they experience the results for a lifetime.

WHAT IS THE GOOD CARBOHYDRATE PLAN?

The Good Carbohydrate Plan is a high carbohydrate eating plan that helps you control your weight, your blood sugar, and your cholesterol permanently by changing the sources of carbohydrates in your diet. I have used this plan for nearly fifteen years to help my patients lose weight naturally and control their blood sugar without calorie counting. It is centered on good carbohydrates—those that provoke the smallest rise in blood sugar and insulin—and can be tailored to your individual needs.

The Good Carbohydrate Plan translates the latest scientific research about carbohydrates and other nutrients into a set of principles called The Five C's for finding good carbohydrates and a table I call the Carbohydrate Quotient to help you with your food choices. I've also included in this book recipes and tips on how you can make the most of good carbohydrates.

Let me emphasize that the Good Carbohydrate Plan is a flexible plan. It is not a one-diet-fits-all or an all-or-nothing plan. With the Good Carbohydrate Plan, you can tune up whatever diet you are on by replacing bad carbohydrates with good ones. Every good carbohydrate you add to your diet to replace a bad carbohydrate will be of benefit to you. Or you can try a complete version of the Good Carbohydrate Plan and obtain the maximum result of controlling blood sugar and cholesterol without medication. You'll begin with good carbohydrates as the core of the diet and add optional foods to create healthy diets such as vegetarian, Mediterranean, or Asian.

And here's the best part. The Good Carbohydrate Plan does not restrict the amount of food that you eat. It allows you to eat more carbohydrates while you control blood sugar, and helps bring your cholesterol levels to a safe range, i.e., below 170 mg/dl. You'll be able to eat whenever you feel hungry, and enjoy delicious, healthy foods for the rest of your life.

WHY A BOOK ABOUT CARBOHYDRATES?

I'm writing this book because there has been a lot of misinformation and confusion about carbohydrates over the last few years. Most of the popular literature on dieting these days touts the benefits of protein while bashing carbohydrates. They say that carbohydrates cause everything from obesity, diabetes, heart disease, to high blood pressure. Meanwhile, I have been reversing these same conditions with a high carbohydrate diet for over a decade using large amounts of the very foods that some have said would cause these diseases. Something is terribly wrong! The public is getting the wrong message.

Because of all the misinformation, many Americans are steering clear of exactly the foods they need to be healthy, trim, and fit. One popular protein diet book on its back cover indicates that carrots may be a food to avoid. Carrots unhealthy for you? No way! I want to set the record straight. Carbohydrates have been the cornerstone of health for the human race for thousands of years. Carbohydrates are also the center of the plan that I have been using for nearly fifteen years to get people to control their blood sugar, cholesterol, and weight, and regain their health as a result.

WHY THE GOOD CARBOHYDRATE PLAN?

I was born, raised, and still live in Hawaii where we have the advantage of being at the crossroads between East and West. Here, I am able to see firsthand the differences between a variety of diets and the health of the people on these diets. When I was studying medicine, I began to notice that the ancestors of the people who live in Hawaii— the people from Asia, Polynesia, Hawaii, the Mediterranean—all seemed to have quite good health. When their descendants moved to Hawaii, they began eating a Modern American Diet (MAD) and started to have high rates of obesity, cardiovascular disease, and diabetes like the majority of the United States population.

Modern people who base their diets on traditional eating patterns experience a fraction of the heart disease, obesity, diabetes, and other chronic diseases that have reached epidemic proportions in the United States. China and Japan are two obvious examples of cultures that eat very high carbohydrate diets and have populations with low rates of obesity, heart disease, breast cancer, prostate cancer, and diabetes.

Considering the grim statistics—nearly one-third of all Americans die of heart disease, nearly one quarter of all Americans die of cancer, 7 percent die of stroke, and diabetes has increased 33 percent in the last ten years—I thought this sharp contrast of the low rates of diseases in other countries compared to the United States was so important that I looked at this relationship more carefully. I began to realize that the populations with low rates of chronic diseases ate large amounts of what I call good carbohydrates. In fact, in ancient times over 80 percent of calories came from good carbohydrate foods. By sharp contrast, in modern times with our fast food, high fat, high animal product, high sugar diet, less than 15 percent of the American diet comes from good carbohydrates (see diagram, page 27). This is one of the fundamental reasons why our MAD diet is causing obesity and so many ill health effects.

To prevent and reverse some of the obesity and chronic diseases that plague so many of us, I developed the principles of the Good Carbohydrate Plan while studying nutrition at Harvard University. I launched my practice and a number of nutrition programs in Hawaii fourteen years ago based on the principles of the Good Carbohydrate Plan. Since then, I have been blessed to see thousands of people benefit from these principles, including, for many, life-changing improvements in their weight and health. I am writing this book to show you how you too can enjoy better health and natural weight control on the Good Carbohydrate Plan.

GETTING TO THE REAL PROBLEM

The reason the Good Carbohydrate Plan works so well is that it gets to the real problem. The problem is not that we are eating too many carbohydrates. The problem is that we are eating too many bad carbohydrates along with too much fat and animal products. Americans are eating more refined carbohydrates than ever. We now eat a record high of 33 teaspoons of sugar per person per day. We also consume an average of 149.7 pounds of flour products per person per year, with less than 2 percent of it coming from whole grain. The American diet is loaded with refined white flour and white sugar—bad carbohydrates—the very opposite of what we need for optimum health.

The American diet is also far too high in fat, cholesterol and animal products. Contrary to what some popular diet proponents have suggested, dietary fat intake continues to increase in this country. Objective data from the USDA for the years 1970–1999 shows that while sugar intake has increased dramatically, fat intake has gradually increased to record high levels, and we are eating more animal products than ever.

WHAT AMERICANS EAT
MEAT, SUGAR, AND FAT INTAKE HAVE
INCREASED WHILE OBESITY HAS INCREASED

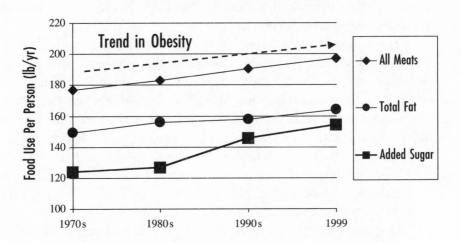

Data from U.S. Department of Agriculture, Agricultural Fact Book, 2000.

As you will see in the research I describe in Chapter 3, the solution to the American diet problem isn't replacing bad carbohydrates with protein and fat. The solution is in replacing bad carbohydrates with health-promoting good carbohydrates.

CARBOHYDRATES ARE NOT THE CULPRIT

In the age of so-called protein diets, carbohydrates have been labeled the guilty culprit. As a result, many Americans are afraid to chomp down on a nice crunchy carrot, eat a bowl of brown rice, or bite into a delicious slice of whole grain bread! Let's look at some of the reasons why all carbohydrates have been wrongly lumped together as bad.

Much of the recent evidence against carbohydrates is based on the actions of the hormone, insulin. Insulin is an important hormone in your body that is secreted into your bloodstream to process carbohydrates. While everyone needs the insulin their body makes, according to some recent research I describe in Chapter 3 on the relationship between insulin levels and health, having too much insulin circulating in your blood can be related to heart disease, obesity, and other health problems. There is also some evidence that in some people, high insulin levels may cause a cluster of health problems called Syndrome X, or Metabolic Syndrome. This syndrome includes high blood sugar, high blood pressure, and abnormal cholesterol levels.

Since carbohydrates have the potential for raising insulin levels, this has led some high-protein-diet proponents to proclaim that all carbohydrates are bad. However, what these diets and almost all other diets have ignored is that not all carbohydrates are the same. The research showing that carbohydrates may increase the risk of heart disease and diabetes is largely research using bad carbohydrates—flour products, white bread, juices, and refined sugar. When good carbohydrates are used as the basis of a diet, the results are very different. Good carbohydrates have been shown to help prevent, and even reverse, heart disease and diabetes.

For years, I have been working with high carbohydrate diets that are rich in good carbohydrates to reverse the very illnesses that high protein diet proponents claim are caused by high carbohydrates.

The program I have designed has been tested over a number of years and has helped thousands of people to naturally reduce their high blood sugar, cholesterol, and excess weight—all while going about their normal lives.

The Good Carbohydrate Plan has published research behind it, something that many programs lack. I have placed people on diets that are as high as 78 percent carbohydrate and published results showing consistent weight loss, substantial reduction in cholesterol (over 24 percent), and in people who have high blood sugar, a significant improvement in blood sugar control. More important, I know that this diet can be followed for a lifetime because it is based on the eating patterns that humanity has followed for hundreds and thousands of years while remaining slim and free of the diseases that plague us today.

DEBUNKING THE CARBOHYDRATE MYTHS

One of the biggest myths perpetrated by high-protein-diet advocates is that carbohydrates make you fat, and cause heart disease and diabetes. If high-protein-diet advocates are right, then populations eating lots of carbohydrates should have high rates of obesity, heart disease and diabetes. Let's examine this theory and apply it to one of the highest carbohydrate-eating countries in the world, China. People in China eat a diet that is about 75 percent carbohydrates, far more than we do in the United States. Yet, China has very little obesity, almost no heart disease in some areas, and very low rates of diabetes. Moreover, the most commonly eaten carbohydrate in China is rice, one of the very carbohydrates that the high-protein-diet advocates say is fattening and causes heart disease and diabetes.

You may say that China is not a good example because China has a largely rural population. So let's look at the consumption of carbohydrates and its relationship to health in a large industrialized population—the Japanese. The Japanese are similar to the Chinese in that they eat a very high carbohydrate diet centered on rice. Once again, according to the high-protein-diet advocates' theory, the Japanese should be fat, with lots of heart disease and diabetes. Contrary to this prediction, Japanese people living in Japan have very low rates of obesity, heart disease, and diabetes. In fact, they have the longest average life span of any country in the world.

If what high-protein-diet advocates are saying is true, then a decrease in carbohydrates should cause a decrease in obesity, heart disease, and diabetes. To test this hypothesis, let's look again at the Japanese population. What happens when the Japanese begin to adopt a lower carbohydrate, higher animal product diet? Their rates of obesity, heart disease, and diabetes increase dramatically.

If you think that this difference is because of race, and that these low rates of disease are simply because Asians are genetically less prone to obesity and diabetes, and handle carbohydrates better than other races, then think again. Just look at the Polynesian race. Polynesians are much more prone to obesity, diabetes, and glucose intolerance than Caucasians, Asians, or Africans. Yet they have been on a high carbohydrate diet (over 75 percent of calories) for centuries and remained slim and almost entirely free of diabetes and heart disease. They have suffered high rates of obesity and diabetes only after adopting a diet that is high in animal protein, high in animal fat, and high in refined carbohydrates.

In America, the same is true. Native Americans, Americans of European ancestry, Americans of African ancestry, and Americans of Asian ancestry were slim and healthy on their traditional diets high in good carbohydrates. When they began to adopt a MAD diet, they all saw an increase in their rates of obesity, diabetes, and heart disease with a *decrease* in carbohydrates and an *increase* in animal product intake.

Ten Carbohydrate Myths—Dispelled

From these examples, you can see that there is a lot of misinformation going around about carbohydrates. Here are ten common carbohydrate myths that I would like to dispel with some of the information in this book.

Myth 1. *All Carbohydrates Are the Same.*

No. Different carbohydrates can have very different effects. A diet high in bad carbohydrates (processed carbohydrates) can cause a rise in blood sugar. A diet high in good carbohydrates (whole carbo-hydrates) can bring blood sugar under control. Fructose raises blood sugar much less than glucose. Table sugar, which is half glucose and half fructose, is somewhere in between. Starches in the form of white bread raise blood sugar as much as twice as high as starches in the form of whole grains.

Myth 2. Carbohydrates Make You Fat.

Wrong. Calories and fat make you fat. Studies comparing the diets of different countries show that populations that eat the most carbohy-drate have the lowest rates of obesity. A study comparing diet and body fat indicates that those who eat the most carbohydrate tend to have the least fat percentage. It is possible that bad carbohydrates—white sugar and white bread—can contribute to obesity simply because they are highly concentrated in calories.

Myth 3. Carbohydrates Turn into Fat.

Generally wrong. Despite what you may hear, carbohydrates don't turn into fat except in unusual circumstances. Even when you eat a great deal of carbohydrate, almost none of it actually turns into fat. Only when your carbohydrate intake alone exceeds your total calo-rie expenditure does carbohydrate turn into fat in any appreciable amounts. This won't occur unless you are intentionally force-feeding yourself, or eating a large amount of refined carbohydrate.

Myth 4. High Carbohydrate Foods Raise Insulin Levels More than Meat.

Not always. For example, beef raises insulin levels 27 percent *more* than pasta.

Myth 5. High Carbohydrate Foods Raise Insulin Levels More than Dairy.

Not always. While dairy foods typically have a moderate effect on blood sugar, their impact on blood insulin levels is up to three times higher than its blood sugar effect might suggest. Most dairy products raise insulin levels 90 to 98 percent as high as white bread does.

Fruit-flavored yogurt raises insulin levels 15 percent higher than white bread and 85 percent higher than brown rice.

Myth 6. Complex Carbohydrates (Starches) Are Always Better than Simple Carbohydrates (Sugar).

Wrong. While complex carbohydrates from whole grains raise blood sugar moderately, complex carbohydrates from white bread actually raise blood sugar more than simple carbohydrates from white sugar.

Myth 7. Carbohydrates Are Less Satisfying than Fat.

Incorrect. Fats falsely appear to satisfy the most because they are so highly concentrated in calories; even a small amount seems to be very satisfying. In reality, even a small amount of fat provides a large amount of calories. Scientific studies comparing satisfaction levels confirm that calorie for calorie, carbohydrates are more satisfying than fat.

Myth 8. Carbohydrates Cause Diabetes.

No. Neither sugar nor starch causes diabetes. Carbohydrates are harder to handle when you have diabetes but they don't cause it. It's more likely that fat and obesity contribute to diabetes.

Myth 9. Carrots, Brown Rice, and Corn Are Bad for You.

Wrong. This myth is due to the mechanical reliance on a table called the Glycemic Index, without considering that these foods are moderate to low in calorie density. Because of the calorie density of these foods, an average person will tend to consume fewer calories from them over time than from higher calorie density foods. As a result the blood sugar and insulin responses to these foods are very moderate. The truth is that these are among the healthiest foods for you. (You can find more information on the Glycemic Index in Chapter 6.)

Myth 10. High Carbohydrate Diets Promote Diabetes and Heart Disease.

Wrong again. In general, a high carbohydrate diet can prevent diabetes and heart disease if it is low in fat and based on good carbohydrates. The Good Carbohydrate Plan can be very high in carbohydrates—as high as 78 percent—and causes a reduction in blood sugar, triglycerides, cholesterol, and the risk of coronary heart disease. Other research on high carbohydrate diets and their effect on blood sugar and cholesterol confirm this effect (see Chapter 3 on how the Good Carbohydrate Plan works).

CLEARING UP THE CONFUSION WITH THE GOOD CARBOHYDRATE PLAN

As you can see, there is a lot of confusion about carbohydrates and how to make them a healthy part of your diet. The Good Carbohydrate Plan is a step-by-step approach to reconstructing your diet and lifestyle so that good carbohydrates become the center of your diet, helping you automatically lose weight and control your blood sugar and cholesterol. From this good carbohydrate center, you can modify the diet to your own tastes and body type. In addition, the plan provides lifestyle guidelines to improve your health for a lifetime.

Since the day I started my medical practice, I have been using the principles of the Good Carbohydrate Plan to prevent and reverse health problems in my patients. High blood sugar, high cholesterol, obesity, and a whole litany of health problems can be corrected, or at least improved, by adopting the Good Carbohydrate Plan. Following are a few examples of individuals who have benefitted from the Good Carbohydrate Plan.

DIABETICS REDUCE NEED FOR INSULIN AND LOSE WEIGHT

Megan R. is a patient who came to me about nine years ago. At 206 pounds, she wanted to lose some weight and address her adult onset (Type II) diabetes. After six months on the diet, Megan lost 58 pounds, reaching a much healthier weight of 148 pounds for her 5'4" frame. Her diabetes also improved dramatically. When Megan began the diet, she was on 80 units of insulin per day. With my supervision, she was able to reduce her need for insulin to *zero* after just two weeks on the plan, and she hasn't needed insulin since. Best of all, learning and following the principles of the Good Carbohydrate Plan, Megan has kept the weight off to this day.

Another patient, Anne S., required 190 units of insulin when she first came to see me. By following the plan, she was able to stop taking insulin with the guidance of her doctor and required just one low dose of oral diabetes medication per day. These results should tell you that this plan could help you control your insulin even if your blood sugar is normal.

CHOLESTEROL DROPS BY 100 POINTS

Another one of my patients, a university professor named Jeff K., had a family history of heart disease and high cholesterol. He was concerned that his cholesterol level was high at 237 mg/dl—over 200 mg/dl is undesirable. By following the Good Carbohydrate Plan, within three weeks Jeff's cholesterol decreased to 134 mg/dl. His good cholesterol increased by 1 mg/dl and his triglycerides decreased by 143 mg/dl.

LOST WEIGHT WITH THE GOOD CARBOHYDRATE PLAN

Another woman, Jenny M., who at 29 years old lost 125 pounds, said that before she tried the plan she didn't think she could do it. However, once Jenny learned the principles, it became a part of her life. She explains:

> I saw the weight dropping. It was just coming off. It took about a year. I lost 100 pounds in a year, and I went down about 8 dress sizes. And then after that I continued going and I lost 25 pounds more, so that's a total of 125 pounds I lost and 10 dress sizes so far.

At 5'9" and 301 pounds to start, Jenny tired quickly and couldn't engage in much physical activity. Now she feels much better since she has lost the weight and is able to do a lot more with her friends, including vigorous sports such as jogging.

Leslie had less of a problem than Jenny but a familiar one to many of us. At 5'3" and 155 pounds, she had trouble losing weight after age 40. She decided to try the Good Carbohydrate Plan and lost 45 pounds, going from 155 all the way down to 110. Leslie admits, "Dr. Shintani said that I should exercise, but I never got around to it and I still lost the weight."

That was five years ago. Today, she maintains her weight to within five pounds of her lowest weight, even with her busy lifestyle.

These are just a few examples of how people have controlled their weight and improved their health, some of them in just three weeks, by using the Good Carbohydrate Plan. If you apply the principles of the Good Carbohydrate Plan, the same can happen for you.

CHAPTER 2

Carbohydrates and You

From the time we are infants, humans enjoy the flavor of carbohy-drates—the taste of sweet. In fact, of the four tastes that our tongue can sense—sweet, salty, sour, and bitter—only one of them, sweet, identifies a source of calories. There are no taste buds for protein or fat. Based on this fact, you might say that humans are designed to use carbohydrates. This is natural, as carbohydrates have been the chief source of human sustenance since the dawn of our existence.

WHAT ARE CARBOHYDRATES?

Most of us know of carbohydrates as sugar or starch—the granulated stuff that is put into coffee or the powdery white flour that is turned into bread. But carbohydrates are much more than that. Carbohydrates are actually some of the most important substances not only to humans but also to all organisms on Earth. They provide energy for us and can affect our bodies like a powerful drug. Used properly, they can cure illnesses. Used improperly, they can cause deadly diseases.

Let's look at some basic terminology about carbohydrates.

Carbohydrates: In this book, carbohydrates are defined in two ways. The first definition is the actual substances that are chemically called carbohydrates. These substances include simple carbohydrates, or sugar; and complex carbohydrates, or long chains of sugar molecules such as starches and fiber. Second, I also use the term carbo-hydrates to describe foods that contain carbohydrates such as fruit, vegetables, grains, and cereal products.

Simple Carbohydrates: These are also known as sugars. They can be made of one sugar molecule (monosaccharide) or two sugar mole-cules (disaccharide). See Appendix B.

Glucose: A one-molecule sugar that is one of the building blocks of two-molecule sugars and of starch. Glucose is the form in which sugar is most commonly found in the blood. The amount of glucose that is present in our blood is called serum glucose or blood sugar.

Fructose: Fruit sugar. A one-molecule sugar (with a slightly different chemical structure than glucose) that is found in substantial quanti-ties in fruit.

Sucrose: Table sugar. A two-molecule sugar made of one molecule of glucose and one molecule of fructose or fruit sugar.

Complex Carbohydrates: These are long chains of sugar molecules also known as polysaccharides. There can be dozens or hundreds of sugar molecules linked together in long chains and then branching chains (see Appendix B). The digestible forms are commonly known as starches. Starches are found in large concentrations in grains, beans, and root vegetables such as potatoes, taro, and yams. The nondigestible forms of complex carbohydrates in plants are also known as dietary fiber, such as cellulose, gums, and pectins.

Good Carbohydrates: In this book, good carbohydrates are defined in two ways. The first definition is a carbohydrate food that is absorbed slowly and causes a minimal rise in blood sugar. These are typically plant-based foods that are high in fiber and are whole and unprocessed. The second definition is what I call the other good carbohydrate, dietary fiber. Fiber is called a good carbohydrate because structurally, almost all dietary fiber is carbohydrate in a form that is not digestible. Fiber, found in most plants, forms the structural part of plants and also provides an important substance that helps to control how fast sugar is absorbed. This will be dis-cussed in greater detail in Chapter 4, Fiber: The Other Good Carbohydrate.

Bad Carbohydrates: A carbohydrate food that is absorbed quickly and causes a large rise in blood sugar. These are typically foods that are high in white sugar and refined white flour. In the Good Carbohydrate Plan, these foods are not necessarily excluded but rather may be used on occasion in small amounts in combination with large amounts of good carbohydrates.

THE BASIC COMPONENTS OF CARBOHYDRATES

Carbohydrates are literally formed from thin air. Their creation is one of the great miracles of life. Two of the simplest and most abundant substances on Earth, carbon dioxide and water, make up carbohydrates. Even the lowliest single-celled plant can produce them.

Carbohydrate, by definition, is carbon with water added to it. "Carbo" stands for carbon, and "hydrate" means to add water. The simple chemical reaction looks like this:

$$\text{Carbon dioxide } (CO_2) + \text{Water } (H_2O) = \\ \text{Carbohydrate } (HCOH) + \text{Oxygen } (O_2).$$

This process is repeated several times and the resulting product is a simple carbohydrate molecule also known as sugar. This chemical reaction is so simple and yet it is one of the most important building blocks of life. Not only does this process create carbohydrates, it traps energy from sunlight and it also releases oxygen (O_2) as a by-product.

Carbohydrates have been the cornerstone of fuel and energy storage throughout all of life. Because carbohydrates are made from key elements, carbon, hydrogen, and oxygen, when carbohydrate is burned, it releases its stored energy and burns completely and cleanly. The waste product is simply carbon dioxide and water—the very ingredients from which carbohydrate was created, forming a perfect nonpolluting fuel source in harmony with the great circle of life.

As energy (synonymous with calorie) sources, carbohydrates come in the form of sugars, as typically found in fruit, and starches, as typically found in grains, vegetables, potatoes, and bread. Carbohydrate is one of the four dietary sources from which you can get calories. The other three are protein, fat, and alcohol.

Carbohydrates in their pure form provide about four calories per gram. Proteins provide four calories per gram, fats nine calories per gram, and alcohol seven calories per gram. All of these forms of calories can provide energy for living.

Carbohydrates also form the basis of plant fiber, the major structural component of the plant kingdom. This includes cellulose, the most abundant organic molecule on Earth. In the form of fiber, carbohydrates are not digestible and therefore provide no calories. All whole, plant-based foods have carbohydrates in them, both digestible and nondigestible. In fact, they all contain carbohydrate, protein, fat, and fiber in different amounts. This is true for grains, vegetables, fruit, legumes, nuts, and whatever plant-based foods you can think of. Plant-based foods contain only carbohydrate when they are refined into white sugar. Plant-based foods contain no carbohydrate when they are refined into vegetable oil. Animal products have virtually no carbohydrates except for diary products, which contain milk sugar or lactose.

Knowing the structure of carbohydrates and the foods in which they are found allows you to understand why some sugars are absorbed so quickly and why it is important to know what type and form of carbohydrates you have in your diet. For a detailed description of the anatomy of good carbohydrates, see Chapter 5.

HOW YOUR BODY PROCESSES CARBOHYDRATES

When carbohydrates are absorbed, they cause a rise in blood sugar. Your body senses this rise in blood sugar and signals your pancreas, a small, elongated organ tucked below and behind your stomach, to secrete insulin into your bloodstream. The insulin regulates the amount of sugar in your bloodstream by helping to move sugar from the bloodstream into your body's cells. As the carbohydrate is gradually absorbed into the bloodstream and then moved into the cells, the blood sugar, after its initial rise, slowly comes down. Your body senses this decrease and signals the pancreas to stop secreting insulin.

If carbohydrates are absorbed very quickly, such as when you consume refined carbohydrates, your blood sugar rises quickly. In response insulin comes pouring into the bloodstream to process the blood sugar to keep the amount of sugar in the blood from rising too high. This could cause a number of potential problems. First, if there is not enough insulin in your body, or if your insulin is not working properly, your blood sugar may spike out of control. If this condition persists, the result is diabetes. Second, even if your blood sugar remains at a reasonable level, the high amounts of insulin in the bloodstream needed to control the repeated rapid rise in blood sugar can increase the risk of heart disease and other health problems. Third, after a while, the high insulin levels caused by this rapid influx of blood sugar may be too much, so that even after all the carbohydrate is absorbed, there are still high insulin levels in your blood, potentially causing your blood sugar to drop too low. This is sometimes called "hypoglycemia," or not enough sugar in your blood. Hypoglycemia may cause you to feel tired and irritable, and may cause unusual food cravings. I'll explain more about insulin and how your body handles carbohydrates more fully in Chapter 3, How the Good Carbohydrate Plan Works.

Do Carbohydrates Turn into Fat?

A popular myth that you may hear is that carbohydrates turn into fat. The reality is that carbohydrates don't turn into fat under ordinary circumstances. In an average individual eating an average amount of food, virtually none of the carbohydrate eaten turns into fat. This is confirmed in research with people eating a normal amount of calories on a high carbohydrate diet. In an experimental situation, one research team tried to see what would happen if an extra 1,000 calories of carbohydrates were added to a normal person's diet. Even during this overconsumption of carbohydrates, they found that only about 4 percent of the carbohydrates were converted to fat. Meanwhile, fat burning and carbohydrate burning increased, so there was little net gain in fat.

Another researcher found that carbohydrates turn into fat in substantial amounts only when carbohydrate intake alone (without counting fat or protein) exceeded total calorie expenditure. In all likelihood, this will never happen to you unless you try very hard. You would have to intentionally overeat and consume large amounts of bad carbohydrates to reach such a high number of calories. Thus, while it is remotely possible, carbohydrates generally don't turn into fat.

CARBOHYDRATES AS HUMANS' CHIEF FOOD

According to the Food and Agricultural Organization (FAO) of the United Nations, carbohydrates have been "the world's chief food throughout history." The importance of high carbohydrate foods to humanity is reflected by the fact that grains and other high carbohydrate staples are found in our words, economy, culture, religion, and many other aspects of our lives. As one expert points out, "All the early high civilizations . . . were based on seed-reproducing plants—wheat, maize, or rice. . . ."

Grains have been so important to humans' food supply that many different cultures use the word for grains to describe food in general. For example, the English word "meal" can describe a grain-based food such as cornmeal, or it can describe food in general, such as when we eat a meal. The Japanese word *gohan* can be used to describe their staple grain of rice, or it can also be used to describe a meal. Morning *gohan* means breakfast, evening *gohan* means dinner and so forth.

To gain some perspective on how carbohydrates affect you and the rest of the human race, let's step back and take a good look at the relationship between carbohydrates and humans. Early humans were almost completely vegetarian—in other words, their chief source of energy was carbohydrate. The nearest primate relatives of humans were also vegetarian or near vegetarian. This was true for millions of years. The use of meat as a substantial part of the human diet appeared around the time of the Ice Ages, when hunting was probably necessary for survival, as edible plant foods were chronically scarce. We see evidence of meat eating in Neanderthal humans (80,000 years ago) and Cro-Magnon humans (45,000 years ago).

The most recent Ice Ages occurred during the Old Stone Age— Paleolithic times. During this period, human beings subsisted by gathering wild plants such as fruits, root vegetables and beans, and they supplemented this diet by hunting for game. For this reason, gatherer-hunters is a better way to describe these humans than hunter-gatherers. With the primary source of their calories coming from plant foods, they still subsisted mainly on good carbohydrates, which probably gave them some protection from the ill effects of the high content of meat in their diet.

Some of the modern high-protein-diet advocates say that we should be eating like the hunter-gatherers of the Paleolithic era because humans as a species existed during this era for a longer evolutionary period of time than any other. I would hesitate to follow this advice, as the estimated life span of hunter-gatherers during this period was just 25 years. There is no way to use the diet of this era as a model for long-term health because they didn't live long enough, and the health status and causes of death of these people are unknown.

With the Cultivation of Grains, Humans Flourish

After the last Ice Age receded some 10,000 years ago, modern humans began to flourish, at first gradually and then much more rapidly. This period of time is known as the New Stone Age or the Neolithic period. What was the catalyst for this sudden growth in human population? It was the cultivation of good carbohydrates.

At this time, many different cultures around the world began to cultivate grains as their principal food. Humans also began to domesticate other plant foods such as fruits and vegetables. Agriculture started in the Near East, India, China, Guatemala, Andes, Sudanic-Abyssinian region, South American tropics, and Southeast Asia independently of each other. It is almost as if it were part of the natural development of humanity to adopt the use of grain and plant-based foods.

With the cultivation of grains, humans began to thrive and civilizations began to grow. Each flourishing society consumed grains as their staple foods:

Near East:	wheat and barley
Europe:	wheat, barley and rye
Asia:	rice, wheat, barley and millet
Africa:	barley and sorghum
Americas:	maize (corn), amaranth and quinoa

The food intake of the majority of people consisted mostly (if not entirely) of these staple grains, along with vegetables, legumes, and fruits.

While most civilizations began to blossom with the cultivation of grains, those that continued in the more primitive hunter-gatherer mode either died out or remained small in population. By contrast, the civilizations that utilized grains and other high carbohydrate foods as the main source of energy began to contribute to a population boom, the likes of which the Earth had never seen among the human race.

For hundreds of thousands of years, until human civilization began to cultivate and domesticate grains as their principal food, the Earth's human population remained at less than three million. With the advent of the use of grains, the world's human population is estimated to have reached between five and ten million by the Neolithic period, 8,000 to 9,000 years ago.

The use of agriculture and the cultivation of grains, which are inherently easy to store, continued to promote a population explosion. After the introduction of large-scale agriculture some 8,000 year ago, to the time of the Christian era, 2,000 years ago, the population had risen to an estimated 300 million people. By 1800, the world population reached one billion people. By 1930, the population was two billion and in just another 48 years the world's population doubled to four billion in 1978.

HUMAN POPULATION OVER TIME
POPULATION BOOMS WITH USE OF GRAINS

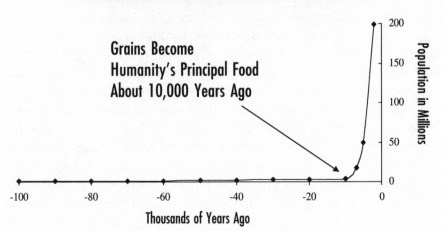

The advent of agriculture and the use of grains had a profound effect on the development of the human race. For the first time, humans had a reliable source of food and could settle in one place rather than roam around looking for food in the environment. This gave rise to many of the arts and trades of civilization, including: masonry and carpentry to construct permanent homes; metallurgy to build farming tools and implements to defend settlements (hence, the Bronze Age and the Iron Age); and pottery to store food and other supplies. The use of grains may have given rise to mathematics as a way of keeping track of the amounts of grain stored, and ultimately to an alphabet and a system of writing for a permanent record of transactions, events, and thoughts, in general. Some of the earliest writings in hieroglyphics in the Egyptian civilization and symbols in the Mayan civilization are records of grain harvests. Agriculture also gave rise to astronomy and the calendar in order to predict the best time of year for the planting of crops.

Certainly the development of human civilization suggests that humans should be eating carbohydrates as our main food. Our numbers suggest that at least as a population, humans do better on a high carbohydrate, Neolithic, agricultural diet than on a moderate animal-product, Paleolithic, hunter-gatherer diet. Some have argued that the chronic conditions associated with high animal-product intake, such as coronary heart disease and cancer, don't affect people until after their childbearing years are done, and thus should not affect evolution or natural selection. However, in terms of large populations, other characteristics, such as brain function and longevity of its elders, may be important to survival and propagation. An argument can clearly be made that the most intelligent cultures and those aided by elders were the ones that survived and thrived through the ages.

Because carbohydrates are the primary fuel for the brain, the increase in consumption of good carbohydrate foods may have promoted intellectual development that helps to preserve the health, safety, and food supply of the population. The survival of elders beyond childbearing age may have offered wisdom and experience to help ensure a culture's growth. We may speculate that a diet high in whole, natural carbohydrates tends to minimize aggressive behavior and promotes more stable societies. All of these factors could certainly help improve the survival and propagation of humans over time. In any case, it is clear that the cultivation and widespread use of high carbohydrate foods has played a central role in the advancement of human civilization.

DISEASES OF AFFLUENCE: WESTERN DISEASES

As human civilizations became more affluent, some health problems also became more prevalent—at least among the wealthy. Some cultures' success as a civilization allowed them to process food and also allowed the most affluent members to consume substantial amounts of animal products. Obesity, heart disease, and other chronic diseases were the inevitable result.

We see evidence of this as early as the times of the pyramids in Egypt. Evidence of obesity and coronary disease are present in some of the mummified remains found in their ancient burial sites.

The affluent members of Egypt—those affluent enough to be mummified—probably had easier access to richer foods, such as animal products, and suffered from obesity and related diseases in a similar way as the affluent members of other cultures around the world. For example, we find descriptions of chronic disease, obesity and diabetes among the royalty of Europe, and the Polynesian royalty, who ate large amounts of pig and were obese. The Polynesian commoners ate primarily good carbohydrates such as taro and sweet potato and were slim.

We could analyze endlessly what humans ate in the past and what that means to us today. We do know that records and anthropological evidence indicate that human societies that based their diet on good carbohydrates thrived, while the hunter-gatherer experienced little population growth. However, there is no way to know for sure how humans fared health-wise on a specific diet because the data to correlate health status and diet are not available. That's why the very best evidence for knowing what is the optimum human diet is to examine evidence we can see today. We can look at health effects of what people eat in modern times, and we can look at our anatomy, both of which provide modern-day clues to what nature intended for humans to eat.

HUMANS HAVE THE ANATOMY OF CARBOHYDRATE EATERS

Our anatomy gives us important clues to what we should be eating. There are three types of mammals: carnivores, who eat almost all meat; herbivores, who eat almost all plant foods; and omnivores, who eat both. By carefully looking at the human body structure and functions, it is clear that we are supposed to eat most, if not all, of our food from plant sources. Because most of the calories in plants are carbohydrate calories, we can conclude that humans are carbohydrate eaters.

Humans have 28 of 32 teeth clearly designed for eating grains and vegetables. Our eight front teeth (the incisors), four on the top and four on the bottom, are designed for cutting vegetables. The rear 20 teeth (10 molars and premolars on each jaw) are for grinding grains and vegetables. The remaining four canine teeth are questionably suitable for meat eating.

It is clear when observing our teeth that we are primarily intended to eat plant-based foods, but let's look at other anatomical features for further evidence. Humans are not equipped to catch game. We don't have the claws or the reflexes to pounce on prey and survive. We do, however, have hands suitable for collecting and gathering plant foods, just like our nearest vegetarian primate relatives.

What about the anatomy of our jaws? Carnivores have jaw joints that are rigid and allow for up and down shearing motion so that flesh is more efficiently torn. Their jaw joints are at the same level as the molar teeth. Herbivores have loose jaw joints that allow for side-to-side motion to chew and grind plant-based foods. Herbivores and humans have their jaw joints above the line of the molar teeth. Human jaws are of the herbivore type.

The intestines of carnivores are short because animal-based foods are compact and travel slowly through the intestinal tract. The small intestines are only three to six times the body length. Omnivores' intestinal lengths are slightly longer; four to six times the body length. Herbivores have intestinal lengths ten to twelve times the body length. Humans are similar to herbivores with intestinal lengths of ten to eleven times the body length.

One of the clearest indicators that humans are herbivores is the presence of the digestive enzyme in the saliva called salivary amylase. This enzyme is a starch-digesting enzyme; it is not present in the saliva of carnivores or even most omnivores. It is found uniquely in large amounts in the saliva of humans, suggesting that we should be primarily carbohydrate eaters.

And finally, perhaps the most convincing anatomical evidence that humans are herbivores is the fact that the human brain needs carbohydrates to function. When food is abundant, the brain uses only carbohydrates as its source of energy. When there is starvation, the brain switches its metabolism so it can use fat but it still needs at least 30 percent of its energy from carbohydrates. Where does it get the carbohydrates during starvation? The body tears down its own protein, such as muscle, and converts the protein into carbohydrates for the brain.

Objectively looking at the evidence of our anatomical and physiological structure, we have to conclude that humans are anatomical carbohydrate eaters and primarily or totally herbivorous. Behaviorally, it is true that humans were omnivores for thousands of years. However, this does not necessarily mean it was ideal. Based on the evidence of our anatomy, and based on the fact that studies show humans are healthiest on a good carbohydrate (plant-based) diet, it is clear that we should be eating mostly, if not exclusively, plant-based foods.

THE AMERICAN DIET: MORE ANIMAL PRODUCTS THAN EVER

You probably already know that the American diet is not a very healthy one, and very different from what our anatomy implies we should be eating. It is far too high in saturated fats, total fats, animal products, and refined carbohydrates. The American public has been told to reduce the intake of red meat by eating more chicken and fish, cut down on fat, and eat more vegetables and more complex carbohydrates.

The good news is that since the 1970s red meat consumption has decreased 12 percent, milk consumption has decreased 21 percent, and egg consumption has decreased 13 percent. The bad news is that poultry consumption has increased 94 percent.

Although Americans are eating leaner cuts of meat, we are now eating 197 pounds of meat (including poultry and seafood) per person per year—20 pounds more than in 1970. Cheese consumption has increased by 97 percent, and consumption of refined fats and oils has increased by 22 percent. The end result is that total fat consumption has gradually increased, although we are eating slightly less saturated fat.

AMERICANS EAT MORE FAT THAN EVER, MORE SUGAR AND MORE REFINED FLOUR

Americans consumed 45 percent more flour and cereal products in 1997 than in the 1970s. Of the 149.7 pounds of flour products, con- sumed per person per year, only *2 percent* of it was from whole grains—the equivalent of a pitiful one-tenth of a slice of bread per day. Making matters worse is the fact that sugar intake has also sky- rocketed. We now consume a record 154 pounds of added sugar (sucrose and corn sweeteners) per person per year. After adjusting for wastage, this is the equivalent of a whopping 33 teaspoons of sugar per day—25 percent more than in the 1970s.

What's the problem here? We are consuming way too much fast food, snack food, and sweetened beverages. Fast foods, besides being loaded with fat, always feature white flour in some form or another. Take your pick of white flour buns, white flour pizza crusts, and white flour tortillas.

Since 1970, we are eating 200 percent more refined-flour snack foods, such as crackers, corn chips, cookies, and pastries. Even low fat snack foods are loaded with sugar and white flour. Ready-to-eat cereals have increased by 60 percent. Twenty-two percent of our sweeteners are gobbled up in soft drinks, but sugar can be found practically everywhere: pizza, bread, hot dogs, soup, crackers, lunch meat, spaghetti sauce, canned vegetables, and flavored yogurt are a few of the unsuspected sources of refined sugar.

Americans are in trouble. Our diet has dramatically increased in refined bad carbohydrates, while at the same time remaining high in fat and animal products. If we compare our current diet to the eating patterns in ancient times, and in modern times where chronic disease rates are low, we see that these diets, made largely of whole food, contained roughly 80 percent or more good carbohydrates. Our cur- rent eating patterns are made up of less than 15 percent good carbo- hydrates (see graph opposite). This type of diet wreaks havoc on our metabolism over the long haul, and contributes to our epidemic of coronary heart disease, diabetes, and cancer.

FOOD CHANGES
CHANGE IN FOOD COMPONENTS OVER TIME

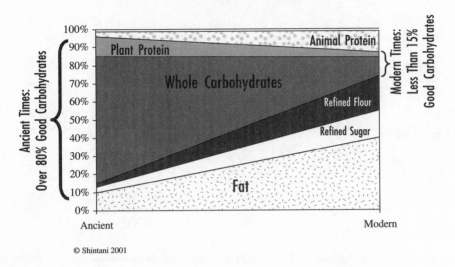

© Shintani 2001

REPLACING THE BAD WITH THE GOOD

I hope by now that you understand that we eat far too many refined carbohydrates, and we need to eat less of these foods to improve our health. Some of the latest high-protein-diet doctors have correctly pointed out this fact. But we shouldn't replace these refined carbohydrates with proteins and fats as they may recommend. We are already eating too much animal protein and fat as it is. We also know—from study after study—that it's not healthy to load our diet with fat and protein, especially from animal sources. (I'll explain why in Chapters 14 and 15 in greater detail.)

What we really need to do is replace the bad carbohydrates with good carbohydrates. We also need to replace the excess fat and animal products with good carbohydrates. Following this concept will bring you much closer to the diet that has kept humans healthy for generations. In fact, it is the very diet that facilitated the growth and development of human civilization.

CHAPTER 3

How the Good Carbohydrate Plan Works

The basic premise of the Good Carbohydrate Plan is to repair what's wrong with the modern American diet—too many bad carbohydrates, too much fat, and too many animal products. The Good Carbohydrate Plan induces weight loss and an improvement in blood sugar and cholesterol control by replacing excess bad carbohydrates, fats, and animal products with good carbohydrates. By doing this, it provides you with the right kinds of foods that allow your body's metabolism of carbohydrates and fat to normalize. As a result, weight loss and health come naturally. My patients see it happen all the time.

There are three main ways the Good Carbohydrate Plan works: (1) Insulin control (2) fat control and (3) automatic calorie control. The new science behind the Good Carbohydrate Plan is centered on how carbohydrate foods affect your blood sugar and insulin. This is important because we are now discovering that high levels of insulin in the blood can cause a number of health problems such as atherosclerosis, diabetes, high cholesterol, and possibly obesity. The Good Carbohydrate Plan helps you to control insulin and minimize your risk of these health problems while maintaining long-term weight control.

There are four terms that I want to define for you here to help you understand how the Plan works:

Glycemic Index: Glycemic is pronounced gly-see-mick, which means pertaining to sugar in the blood. This is an index that measures how high blood sugar rises in response to 50 grams of carbohydrates from a specific food.

Glycemic Load: This means how much blood sugar a body has to handle over time. It is represented by a number calculated by multiplying the Glycemic Index of a food times the quantity of that food.

Calorie Density: How many calories there are per weight of food. Usually calorie density is measured as calories per gram. The higher the calorie density, the more calories from that food you are likely to consume. To make calorie density a little easier to grasp, I created another set of numbers that represent calorie density that I call the Mass Index of food. This is described in Chapter 8 and is found in Appendix A in the Carbohydrate Quotient table.

Insulin Resistance: This is a term that describes a condition in which the body resists the effect of insulin. It is the opposite of the term Insulin Sensitivity, which describes how effective insulin is. When Insulin Sensitivity is high, Insulin Resistance is low.

THE INSULIN STORY

In some ways, carbohydrates act like powerful drugs. When we eat carbohydrates, they not only provide us with our most important source of energy, they trigger a series of metabolic processes in the body that allow it to absorb, burn, and store carbohydrates. The most important hormone in this process is insulin. Insulin helps to control blood sugar. You've undoubtedly heard of insulin in relation to people who have diabetes. When people have adult onset Type II diabetes, their blood sugar runs high because their insulin isn't working effectively, and they sometimes have to take medication or inject insulin to help control their blood sugar.

"If my blood sugar is normal, should I be concerned about controlling blood sugar and insulin?" This is a question my patients ask me these days. Today, the answer to this question is yes. I can remember a time in my medical practice, as recently as ten years ago, when we really didn't pay much attention to blood sugar and insulin in someone who didn't have abnormal blood sugar level. We were concerned about more obvious conditions like cholesterol levels, obesity, and hypertension. As for blood sugar and insulin, these were only of concern in people who had diabetes. Now we know better.

High Insulin Levels Can Be Harmful

There is increasing awareness among medical researchers that insulin levels are important even when blood sugar is normal. Why should we be concerned? A number of recent studies have shown that blood insulin levels, even in normal individuals, are a good predictor of heart disease. For example, one study involving 5,550 men compared insulin levels and heart disease in nondiabetic men. After 11.5 years of observation, they found that those who had the highest insulin levels had almost double (1.9 times) the rate of heart disease as those who had the lowest insulin levels. This is important because even if blood sugar levels are normal, in some people, it may take a great deal of insulin to keep their blood sugar levels within a normal range. While no problem shows up on a blood sugar test, the high level of insulin may be contributing to health problems in the long run.

There is also a condition that may be caused by high insulin levels called Syndrome X, or Metabolic Syndrome, in which a person has high blood sugar, high cholesterol, and high blood pressure at the same time. Some studies even suggest that blood insulin levels may be a better predictor of heart disease than blood cholesterol. Don't jump to the conclusion that blood cholesterol levels are not important. They are still of primary importance, but we now know that insulin levels provide additional information about our risk for heart disease. How is this possible? How does insulin affect heart disease risk? The prevailing theory about the relationship between insulin and heart disease has to do with what insulin does in the body.

What Does Insulin Do?

Insulin is a hormone that is secreted by the pancreas, an organ that is found below and slightly behind the stomach. Insulin is produced and secreted by groups of cells called beta cells, which are scattered throughout the pancreas in areas called islets of Langerhans. When the body requires it, insulin is secreted into the bloodstream. The secretion of insulin is usually triggered by the presence of sugar or amino acids (the building blocks of protein) in the bloodstream. The insulin then acts to move the blood sugar and the amino acids from the bloodstream into cells to be used for energy and other metabolic processes.

Insulin is known as a hormone of abundance because it is secreted when there is an abundance of nutrition available to the body. When a person consumes a lot of carbohydrates, and to a lesser extent, protein, insulin is secreted and circulates in the bloodstream at higher levels. Insulin does many things in the body to help store energy and build up tissues when there is an abundance of carbohydrates and protein. I'll describe the top seven of them here:

- The most familiar action of insulin is to assist **in moving blood sugar from the bloodstream into the body's cells for use and storage.** Insulin is like a key that unlocks the door in the body's cells for sugar to enter them. When a person has adult onset diabetes, sugar builds up in the bloodstream because that person's insulin doesn't work well and is not moving blood sugar into the cells quickly enough.

- **Insulin stimulates the production and storage of fat.** It may contribute to a rise in triglycerides (blood fats) in the process. Whether insulin by itself causes obesity is in question because insulin also helps to stop hunger, as described below.

- **Insulin increases the production of cholesterol in the liver.** Insulin is known to stimulate HMG CoA reductase, the enzyme that triggers the production of cholesterol. This may not increase total cholesterol but may have a role in increasing bad cholesterol (LDL) and decreasing good cholesterol (HDL).

- **Insulin helps to move amino acids, which are the building blocks of protein, into the body's cells.** This is important to know in order to understand why protein causes a rise in blood insulin levels just as carbohydrates do.

- **Insulin causes the kidneys to hold sodium.** This effect may be responsible for the association between high insulin levels and high blood pressure in individuals with Syndrome X or Metabolic Syndrome, which I described earlier as a cluster of diseases—abnormal lipids (cholesterol and triglycerides), high blood sugar, and high blood pressure.

- **Insulin stimulates the production of hormones called eicosanoids.** These are microhormones that regulate a number of functions in cells and in the circulatory system. For example, insulin stimulates the production of a class of eicosanoids that simulate clotting, inflammation, and constriction of blood vessels. These may also contribute to high blood pressure and heart disease.

- **Insulin also suppresses hunger.** The hunger suppression is similar to a feedback system where the body senses that it is getting enough nutrients and tells the brain that it has enough and helps to shut off the hunger. However, this is a controversial point because in practice, when insulin is injected into individuals with diabetes, it appears to contribute to hunger and obesity.

When the body has to process an overabundance of blood sugar over a long period of time, two things can happen. You can have a chronically high level of insulin in your blood simply because your body needs the insulin to process the blood sugar. Also, insulin resistance can set in. Insulin resistance describes a situation in which the body resists the action of insulin. It is often associated with obesity, a high-fat diet and lack of exercise, coupled with genetic predisposition.

Insulin is like a key to open the lock that lets blood sugar into the body's cells. When there is insulin resistance, the keys don't work properly and the body has difficulty getting the sugar into the blood cells. This causes sugar levels in the blood to rise. When the body senses the blood sugar rise, it produces more insulin. This cycle continues and the body is exposed to high levels of insulin because it is trying to secrete more insulin to make up for the ineffectiveness of the insulin due to the "insulin resistance."

Whether you have high insulin levels because of a high exposure to blood sugar or because you have insulin resistance, it becomes a problem even if you don't have diabetes. High levels of insulin are implicated in a number of health problems, such as high blood pressure, high cholesterol, and possibly obesity. When these conditions are severe enough, it may be considered to be Syndrome X or Metabolic Syndrome, because the common link among these health problems may be high insulin levels.

Elevated Levels of Insulin May Promote Cholesterol Deposits

In the process of producing more fat, and more tissue, insulin may contribute to a derangement in blood cholesterol and an increase in triglyceride levels. Triglycerides are the most common form of fat storage in the body. What may be detrimental to the body is that insulin may also promote deposits of fats into the arteries. High insulin levels are associated with higher levels of bad cholesterol or LDL, the type of cholesterol that is deposited into the arteries. High insulin levels are also associated with low levels of HDL cholesterol, the good type of cholesterol that takes cholesterol away from the arteries and back to the liver.

Insulin may well be one of the most important factors in producing coronary heart disease and other forms of arteriosclerosis. Evidence of the relationship between insulin and heart disease, in part, is the association between insulin and high levels of LDL, the bad cholesterol; low levels of HDL, the good cholesterol; and high levels of triglycerides or blood fats.

Insulin May Cause Obesity

Nowadays you might hear the claim that "Fats don't cause obesity—insulin does." Scientifically, fats have never gotten off the hook, but now, we're finding out that insulin may be important in causing obesity. While the relationship between insulin and heart disease is becoming quite clear, the relationship between insulin levels and obesity is controversial. Theoretically, insulin should cause obesity because of insulin's role in stimulating the production of fat. Insulin does stimulate the body to produce and store fat.

Clinically, it make sense that insulin has a role in causing obesity because people who have juvenile onset Type I diabetes produce no insulin and are typically slim. People who have adult onset Type II diabetes may have a lot of insulin in their bloodstream because their insulin doesn't work very well and the body demands more insulin. These types of patients with Type II diabetes are typically obese. In addition, when insulin is administered to either type of patient, appetite increases and weight gain is often one of the side effects of insulin injections.

However, Dr. Gerald Reaven of Stanford University, who coined the term "Syndrome X," researched the effects of insulin resistance quite extensively and flatly states that insulin does not cause obesity. He cites his studies, which demonstrated that individuals with high insulin levels don't gain weight any faster or slower than those who have lower insulin levels. Other recent research shows contrary results, indicating that insulin levels are indeed associated with obesity. These findings are difficult to interpret because this shows an association between insulin and obesity and not necessarily causation. Part of the dilemma is that it is difficult to tell whether high insulin levels cause obesity or whether obesity causes high insulin levels. Obesity has long been believed to cause insulin resistance.

One important fact that I should add is that while insulin may be implicated in causing obesity, scientifically, carbohydrates are not. A popular myth holds that carbohydrates cause obesity because they tend to cause a rise in insulin and therefore should be associated with an increase in obesity. However, in scientific study after study, the opposite is true. Studies have shown that when people eat more carbohydrates, especially good carbohydrates, they tend to be less obese. This is why it is important to use carbohydrates to control obesity.

INSULIN CONTROL

One of the main reasons that the Good Carbohydrate Plan works in restoring health is insulin control. The most important factor in controlling your insulin levels is eating the right carbohydrates. The Good Carbohydrate Plan uses carbohydrates that minimize the impact on your insulin levels, which in turn helps your metabolism to function properly. Along with a foundation of good carbohydrates, other foods are added that provide a full complement of nutrients; this is an eating plan that you can stay with for the rest of your life.

The keys to the selection of good carbohydrates—carbohydrates that have a modest impact on insulin levels—are the Five C's method of evaluating carbohydrates and a table called the Carbohydrate Quotient. I'll describe how to find good carbohydrates in more detail in Chapter 6. In this chapter, I'll describe why the Carbohydrate Quotient helps you identify good carbohydrates.

One of the main factors in controlling your insulin levels is to keep your Glycemic Load at a moderate level. The word glycemic literally means blood sugar. Glycemic Load is the amount of sugar entering your bloodstream that your body has to process over time. It is a major factor in making your body demand insulin. Glycemic Load is determined by two main factors:

- Rate: How fast a carbohydrate is absorbed

- Quantity: How much of a carbohydrate you consume

If you multiply these two factors together you have a number that is called Glycemic Load. Basically it is a number that estimates rate of absorption of carbohydrate and how much total carbohydrate is absorbed.

Because some carbohydrates are absorbed more quickly than others, diets that are primarily made up of bad carbohydrates can create a very high Glycemic Load even with a small number of calories. This can cause an increase in blood sugar and/or a heavy demand for insulin. Your body tries to process blood sugar that is being absorbed quickly by pouring insulin into the bloodstream. By contrast, good carbohydrates are absorbed much more slowly and require much less insulin to control blood sugar levels. See the following chart for examples.

CARBOHYDRATES, INSULIN AND BLOOD SUGAR

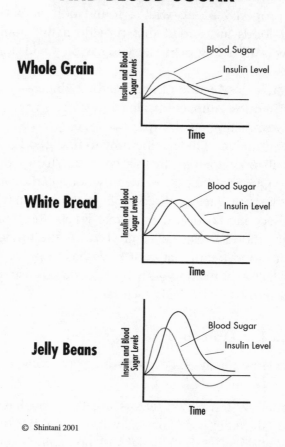

© Shintani 2001

Notice that the insulin response is not necessarily proportional to the blood sugar response. In some instances insulin response is greater or less than the blood sugar response to eating a specific food.

The rate of absorption of carbohydrate is represented fairly well by an index called the Glycemic Index. The Glycemic Index is a table that assigns a number to each food that is tested to compare how high blood sugar rises in response to that food. The higher the Glycemic Index number, the higher a food raises blood sugar.

The amount of a carbohydrate you are likely to eat is to a large extent determined by the calorie density of a food, that is, how many calories there are per gram of the food. For example, there is about 1.1 calorie per gram of cooked whole grain, 2.7 calories per gram of white bread, and 4.0 calories per gram of sugar. Because there are more calories packed into white bread than whole grain, it is more likely that you will consume more calories of the white bread. Thus, the potential impact on your Glycemic Load of white bread is greater than cooked whole grain because the amount of calories you eat of white bread is likely to be greater.

The Carbohydrate Quotient Helps to Predict Glycemic Load

Because Glycemic Load is determined by two factors, rate of absorption and quantity of carbohydrate, I created a table I call the Carbohydrate Quotient; this would incorporate figures that could predict rate and quantity. I created it for people who want a specific number assigned to each food. This number takes into account the rate of absorption and the quantity of carbohydrate from a food you are likely to consume, and helps to predict the Glycemic Load of specific foods and how they will influence your insulin levels.

In other words, the Carbohydrate Quotient is a modified version of the standard table called the Glycemic Index, which is one factor in estimating Glycemic Load. The Carbohydrate Quotient goes a step further and incorporates the calorie density into the table to adjust for the quantity of the food you are likely to eat, which is the second factor in determining Glycemic Load. Together, the Carbohydrate Quotient is not only better than the Glycemic Index alone in estimating Glycemic Load, it is a better predictor of the foods' impact on insulin levels than the Glycemic Index alone.

While the Carbohydrate Quotient is useful, no table describing foods tells the whole story. In order to make it easy for you to choose the best carbohydrates, I also developed a simple five-point method (Five C's) for finding good carbohydrates. Using this method along with the Carbohydrate Quotient, the Good Carbohydrate Plan uses foods that help you keep your insulin under control. In doing so, it improves your ability to control weight, blood sugar and cholesterol, and optimize your health. This will be explained further in Chapter 6 and the Appendix on the Carbohydrate Quotient.

FAT CONTROL

The Good Carbohydrate Plan also works because one of the important steps in implementing the Plan is to replace added fats with good carbohydrates. Replacing fat with good carbohydrates aids insulin control by helping to maximize insulin sensitivity.

Dietary fat plays more of a role in blood sugar control than you might think. Dietary fat, by itself, doesn't raise blood sugar. However, it has a role in controlling how well your body processes blood sugar. Fat apparently interferes with the action of insulin and makes it less effective. In a study comparing blood sugar response with increasing amounts of fat, researchers found that blood sugar control for those on high fat diets was worse than for those on low fat diets.

In that study, researchers compared the effect of a low fat diet, a high fat diet and a very high fat diet on blood sugar control. They found that on a low fat diet (13 percent fat), blood sugar control was very good. When a test dose of pure sugar was given during the low fat diet, the blood sugar response was very modest. Then, they administered a high fat diet (47 percent fat) for a period of several weeks. At the end of this period, blood sugar control was worse. The same test was conducted with an 80 percent-fat diet and blood sugar response to the test dose of sugar was even worse.

BLOOD SUGAR RESPONSE TO HIGH FAT DIET

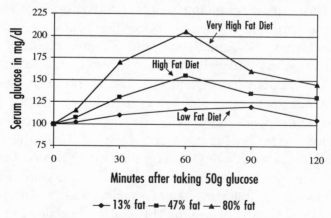

Adapted from: Himsworth, H. P. *Clin Sci* (1935) 2:67-94.

The researchers concluded that blood sugar control was better on a low fat diet than on a high fat diet. Researchers believe that this is a result of the effect of fat on the effectiveness of insulin or insulin sensitivity. Because of the effect that fat has on insulin sensitivity, one important aspect of the Good Carbohydrate Plan is to maximize insulin sensitivity by keeping fat in the diet at a low level. Keeping fat intake low must be done properly, however, because you have to replace the fat with something. If you replace the fat calories with bad carbohydrates, you may be defeating yourself. This is one reason why knowing how to choose good carbohydrates is so important.

Replacing fat with good carbohydrates also helps with weight loss because fats make you fat. Removing fat from the diet helps with weight control. Population studies, animal studies, and clinical trials all point to this fact. When populations begin consuming a higher fat diet, obesity increases. When animals are fed more fat, obesity increases. In clinical trials, when people are fed very low fat diets they consistently lose weight when the fats are replaced by good carbohydrates. Even those who believe that there is nothing special about fat that makes people fat agree that fat has more than twice the calories of the most refined sugar. Replacing fats with good carbohydrates also helps with cholesterol control. These effects are described in detail in Chapter 8 on weight loss and Chapter 15 on fats and cholesterol.

NATURAL CALORIE CONTROL

The Good Carbohydrate Plan, if done properly, is an all-you-can-eat program. The reason for this is that good carbohydrates satisfy your hunger naturally. This occurs because good carbohydrates tend to be low in calorie density. This means that there is a small number of calories per weight of the food. In other words, there is a lot of food for the number of calories in it. If good carbohydrates are chosen properly, calorie density will work in your favor and fill you up before you can consume too many calories. It is this characteristic of good carbohydrates that explains why the Good Carbohydrate Plan helps you to lose weight without limiting quantity or portion sizes.

For example, an average active woman or inactive man uses about 2,500 calories per day. Any more intake than that and they gain weight. Any less intake and they lose weight. In order to obtain 2,500 calories from corn, a person would have to eat approximately six pounds of corn kernels or about 27 ears of corn in a day. How is anyone going to eat that much of anything in one day? They won't. If it takes that much corn to provide a day's worth of calories, how can corn make you fat? It can't. Studies show that an average person will probably feel full after about three to four pounds of food per day. If that person were eating just corn, she/he would lose weight. In order to gain weight, that person would also have to eat some other food—a high calorie density food that takes fewer pounds to provide that many calories—such as a bad carbohydrate or something that has a lot of fat in it, like the butter you may put on your corn.

In other words, you will tend to eat fewer calories of foods that are low in calorie density than foods that are high in calorie density. You will also tend to eat fewer carbohydrates from foods that are low in calorie density than foods that are high in calorie density. Using calorie density, you can predict which foods will contribute to weight gain and which will contribute to weight loss. The lower the calorie density, the more likely it is to induce weight loss. It turns out that almost all good carbohydrates are moderate to low in calorie density.

In 1991, my research demonstrated that this characteristic induced a natural reduction in calorie intake. In 1999, a research team at Pennsylvania State University published results demonstrating that calorie density is more important than fat content in the control of obesity. They found that calorie density of food was a better predictor of how many calories participants would consume than the fat content of the food. In Chapter 8, I elaborate more on the concept of the calorie density of food and how to apply this principle to enhance your weight loss efforts with good carbohydrates.

GOOD CARBOHYDRATES IN ACTION

How well does the Good Carbohydrate Plan work in practice? Everyone should question the science behind any diet program. Most diets make claims of effectiveness and give testimonials of people who have lost weight but provide no published studies. I have tested the Good Carbohydrate Plan in Hawaii under formal research conditions and the results speak for themselves.

There is a consistent drop in cholesterol and an improvement in risk factors for coronary heart disease and diabetes. What you'll probably like even more is that people spontaneously lose excess weight on this program without counting calories. We have even documented that people tend to eat more food on this program but they eat fewer calories. This makes the diet easier to stay on than a diet that simply restricts your calories or portion sizes.

In Hawaii, we have a very serious problem among our Native Hawaiian people. They experience very high rates of obesity, heart disease, cancer, and diabetes. In ancient times, this was not so. Just over 100 years ago, photographs and drawings depict Native Hawaiians as a trim, athletic, and healthy population. The key to their health was their diet. Hawaiians, over the last several decades, have abandoned their traditional diet high in good carbohydrates and have adopted a modern American diet high in meats, fats, sugars, and white flour. I felt that the way to restore health was to restore people to a traditional diet.

To demonstrate the effectiveness of this approach, I placed 20 people on a traditional Hawaiian diet for 21 days. The results were dramatic. Weight came off, blood sugars improved, cholesterol decreased, and people felt an improvement in their energy level and overall well-being. The diet was largely made up of carbohydrates (78 percent of calories). I believe that one of the reasons participants in this diet did so well is because the main staple of the Native Hawaiian people was taro, an excellent example of a good carbohydrate food.

I then applied the principle of using good carbohydrates to the general population with another high carbohydrate diet. I wanted to show that I could obtain the same good results with foods from many cultures, and varieties of foods that were delicious, available, and familiar enough that people could continue this diet for the rest of their lives. I chose foods based on the principles of good carbohydrates. Again, I found that weight was reduced and blood sugar levels improved. This occurred despite the fact that participants were allowed to eat as much as they wanted. Cholesterol, triglycerides, blood pressure, and blood sugar all improved in just 21 days on this diet.

RESULTS AFTER 21 DAYS ON A DIET HIGH IN "GOOD CARBOHYDRATES"

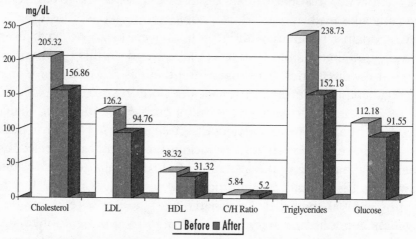

Shintani, T.T., et al. *Hawaii Med J* (2001) 60:69-73.

In my project, I have repeatedly validated the effectiveness of the Good Carbohydrate Plan in my medical clinic as well as in strictly monitored research settings. I have conducted studies of groups of 19 to 32 people at a time who followed our diet for a period of 21 days. Remember that this is without calorie restriction or portion size control. We let participants eat as much as they want on the diet and they still lose weight, improve their blood sugar control, cholesterol, and triglycerides.

Other scientists have done research on high carbohydrate diets similar to the Good Carbohydrate Plan and show that our results are not accidental. Studies dating back to 1926 demonstrate the effectiveness of high carbohydrate, high fiber diets to control blood sugar and weight and have been confirmed in studies dating from the 1960s to the present.

The Good Carbohydrate Plan Helps to Control Blood Sugar

One of the best ways to tell how blood sugar and insulin respond to a diet is by measuring what happens in someone with diabetes or borderline diabetes. Remember that I am talking about adult onset

Type II diabetes. These people must be extra careful because diet will affect their blood sugar, sometimes dramatically. For this reason I repeatedly remind you that if you have any health problems and are going to try this diet, you must do so under the supervision of a physician, especially if you are on medications.

In my closely monitored studies in Hawaii, those who had high blood sugar saw their blood sugar decrease. In some cases, blood sugar decreased even in patients who reduced their medication (under their doctor's supervision). In one of my groups, for example, the average blood sugar level of the 24 participants before going on the diet was 112 mg/dl. (Normal blood sugar ranges between 70 to 110 mg/dl.) When blood sugar was tested after three weeks on the program, the average blood sugar was 20.5 mg/dl less than when they started the program, and perfectly normal.

In groups that started the program with abnormally high blood sugars, the results are even more dramatic. In one group the average blood sugar level before going on the program was 177 mg/dl. At the end of three weeks on the Good Carbohydrate Plan, the average blood sugar was 122 mg/dl—a decrease of 55 mg/dl. All of the individuals who had high blood sugar levels found that their levels were lower on the program than before the program. Some of them had a drop in blood sugar that was small and some were so dramatic that their diabetes medication had to be reduced.

The Good Carbohydrate Plan Helps to Control Insulin

Looking at people with Type II diabetes who are on insulin to control their blood sugar is an important way to tell whether the Good Carbohydrate Plan controls insulin levels. In the course of conducting my research for the Good Carbohydrate Plan, a number of individuals with Type II diabetes reduced their insulin requirement to zero. I want to be clear that not everyone did this well. There are individual differences in blood sugar responses to dietary changes. Still, the fact that some eliminated their requirement for insulin with the Good Carbohydrate Plan (and under supervision of their doctor) is quite remarkable. (Type I diabetics will always need insulin.)

One participant who had Type II diabetes needed 188 units of insulin when she started the program. Her insulin doses had to be adjusted during the program because her blood sugar levels fell. At one point, her blood sugar levels were as low as 74 mg/dl. By the end of three weeks, she required no insulin and just one oral pill for diabetes. Another patient was on 50 units of insulin. After following the plan for a period of four months, he was able to reduce his insulin requirement to zero. Yet another patient following the plan was on 80 units of insulin for many years. Within two weeks of starting the plan, she required no insulin to keep her blood sugar in check and still requires no insulin and has normal blood sugars.

Perhaps the ultimate test of a diet's ability to influence insulin resistance is with someone who has full-blown Metabolic Syndrome—complete with high blood sugar, high blood pressure, high triglycerides, high cholesterol, and obesity. One of my patients with Metabolic Syndrome had a blood sugar of 202 mg/dl while on two medications for blood sugar, a blood pressure of 180/102 with one medication, a triglyceride level of 988 mg/dl, and a cholesterol level of 239 mg/dl. After three weeks of following the guidelines of the Good Carbohydrate Plan, I took him off one blood sugar medication and his blood sugar was in the low 100's, sometimes dropping below 100 mg/dl. His blood pressure was 124/80, his cholesterol dropped to 123 mg/dl, and his triglycerides decreased by an astonishing 863 mg/dl to 125 mg/dl. Meanwhile, he lost about 18 pounds. Remember that this is while eating as much as he wanted.

These results should convince you that the Good Carbohydrate Plan helps to control blood sugar and insulin whether you have diabetes or not. This improvement in blood sugar control occurs despite the high carbohydrate content of the diet. Even if you don't have high blood sugar, this is important for you especially if you are at risk for coronary heart disease—and most of us in America are at risk.

The Good Carbohydrate Plan Induces and Sustains Weight Loss

People who follow the Good Carbohydrate Plan lose weight without counting or restricting calories. My studies have demonstrated an average weight loss of roughly 11 to 17 pounds in three weeks. This varies among individuals and is related to the amount of excess weight carried. The more excess weight you have, the more weight you are likely to lose on the Good Carbohydrate Plan. Long-term follow-up data shows that participants tend to keep their weight off. In a seven-year follow-up study of original participants, the average retained weight loss was approximately 15 pounds. Many participants continued to lose weight by following the principles of the diet even after they lost contact with us. While some participants gained their weight back, the number was far less than the number who gained their weight back on other diet programs.

The Good Carbohydrate Plan Helps to Control Cholesterol and Risk of Heart Disease

The Good Carbohydrate Plan reduces cholesterol and the risk of coronary heart disease in three ways:

- It helps to control blood sugar, which helps to control the release of insulin.

- It is high in fiber, which helps to bind cholesterol in the digestive tract and reduce the absorption of cholesterol.

- It is low in total fat, saturated fat, and cholesterol, so blood cholesterol levels are likely to be reduced.

Please note that the Good Carbohydrate Plan, like other low fat, high carbohydrate diets, is associated with a reduction in HDL, the good cholesterol. However, it is important to understand that when total cholesterol decreases substantially, good cholesterol (HDL), which is a part of the total, also has to decrease. Of course, LDL, the bad cholesterol, decreases even more. When total cholesterol levels are reduced to the low levels seen with the Good Carbohydrate Plan, HDL and even triglycerides become irrelevant. I say this with confidence because according to the great Framingham Study on cholesterol and heart disease virtually no one with cholesterol below 150 mg/dl ever has a heart attack. This is despite low HDL levels. In addition, some of the Framingham Study researchers also studied a high carbohydrate, low fat diet based on brown rice. They found that cholesterol levels averaged 127 mg/dl and cholesterol: HDL ratio was better than in those on a modern American diet. Clinical results of the Good Carbohydrate Plan are similar to the landmark Lifestyle Heart Trial study, in which heart artery plaques were reversed. The results of my study after three weeks showed a similar dramatic improvement in total cholesterol. Our average cholesterol decreased from 205 mg/dl down to 157 mg/dl. The average HDL decreased from 38 mg/dl down to 31 mg/dl, however the cholesterol:HDL ratio improved with a drop of 0.6 points. Our average triglyceride levels decreased from 239 mg/dl to 152 mg/dl. This positive result may be due to our emphasis on good carbohydrates.

The Good Carbohydrate Plan Reduces Blood Pressure

Good carbohydrates may be very important in the control of blood pressure because researchers have found that high insulin levels may be related to high blood pressure. In a study of 5,221 middle-aged individuals in England, those who had the highest insulin levels were twice as likely to get hypertension than those who had the lowest insulin levels. In the United States, African Americans with elevated insulin levels had 2.77 times the risk of hypertension and European Americans had 1.69 times the risk of hypertension. The fact that insulin may induce the kidneys to hold on to additional sodium may play a part in causing hypertension.

High blood pressure was of great concern to one of our participants who had high blood pressure and had a relative who had high blood pressure and died of a stroke at age 57. At the beginning of the plan, this participant told me that one of his goals was to control his blood pressure, for which he was already taking oral medication. After just three days on the Good Carbohydrate Plan, he reported feeling a little lightheaded. I checked his blood pressure and found that it was low, so I recommended that he stop his medication until he could check with his own doctor the next day. His doctor confirmed that his blood pressure was reduced so greatly that he no longer needed blood pressure medication.

The Good Carbohydrate Plan Helps to Control Arthritis

One day I received a call from a rheumatologist who was treating two patients of mine who had been following the principles of the Good Carbohydrate Plan for one month. She asked me what type of diet I was using because the two patients' arthritis was improving dramatically. Both patients required medication for inflammatory arthritis. After following the Good Carbohydrate Plan, both patients showed a substantial reduction in symptoms, sedimentation rate (an indicator of inflammation) and a reduction in need for medication. The rheumatologist and I compared notes and we published objective data on these two cases in a medical journal.

The Good Carbohydrate Plan Helps to Control Blood Fats

Another individual following the Good Carbohydrate Plan who had trouble with blood fats (triglycerides) provides another excellent example of the healing power of the good carbohydrates. He started with blood triglyceride levels of 617 mg/dl. After following the Good Carbohydrate Plan for three weeks his triglycerides had decreased to 83 mg/dl. His cholesterol decreased from 234 mg/dl to 162 mg/dl while his HDL increased by 6 mg/dl. While this is an extraordinary case and every individual is different, the average participant in my studies saw a dramatic improvement in blood fats and cholesterol levels.

The Good Carbohydrate Plan Helps to Control Fatigue and Hypoglycemia

A number of patients came to see me with symptoms of fatigue and depression. In some of them these symptoms are caused by chronic hypoglycemia or low blood sugar. The symptoms are varied, such as headache, fatigue, hunger, irritability, sleepiness, and inability to concentrate. Hypoglycemia is common in people with diabetes who are on medication, because the side effects of many medications for insulin include low blood sugar.

In those who don't have diabetes, it is difficult to diagnose because unlike those with diabetes, most of us don't check our blood sugar regularly. It may occur as a result of overconsumption of bad carbohydrates. If you look at the previous diagram on blood sugar curves, you'll see that the blood sugar curve for jelly beans dips below the starting blood sugar level. This is because the high rate of absorption of sugar causes a large increase in insulin.

Because the sugar is digested and absorbed so quickly, the stomach runs out of sugar after a short time. Meanwhile, the high level of insulin that is pushing the blood sugar levels down suddenly has no incoming blood sugar to oppose it. The result is that the insulin on board causes an over-control of the blood sugar levels to below the starting point, causing low blood sugar.

Good carbohydrates prevent this from happening for two reasons. First, they do not cause a high insulin level. Thus, there is not enough insulin to cause a significant decrease in blood sugar. Second, because the absorption of sugar is slow, it is spread out evenly over time. As a result, the amount of sugar in the stomach doesn't run out immediately and the absorption of sugar doesn't shut off suddenly as it might with a refined carbohydrate.

There isn't room in this book to discuss the many patients and the many different health problems that have improved after my patients began eating good carbohydrates. I have seen patients who have gotten rid of headaches, irritable bowel syndrome, indigestion, acne, asthma, fibromyalgia, chronic fatigue, gout, menstrual problems, and numerous other conditions by following my dietary recommendations. Will it work for you? The best way to find out is to try it and see.

CHAPTER 4

Fiber: The Other Good Carbohydrate

With the emphasis on refined, processed, and depleted foods in the American diet, our intake of fiber has diminished to an unhealthy level. The average fiber intake for women in America is about 12 grams per day. The recommended minimum amount is 20 to 30 grams per day. Though it cannot be digested, fiber is actually one of the healthiest substances in food. Dietary fiber acts as a:

- **Carbohydrate Blocker** and naturally slows down the absorption of digestible carbohydrates
- **Calorie Blocker** by limiting the intake of calories
- **Cholesterol Blocker** by binding cholesterol
- **Natural food substance** that improves digestion

WHAT IS DIETARY FIBER?

What most people don't realize is that most of what is called dietary fiber is actually nondigestible carbohydrate. That's why I call fiber the other good carbohydrate. Like starches, fiber is made up of long chains of sugar molecules. The difference is that fiber cannot be digested, so it stays in the digestive tract.

There are two main types of dietary fiber: soluble fiber, which can be dissolved in water; and insoluble fiber, which cannot be dissolved in water. Cellulose is an example of insoluble fiber. Soluble fiber, when it is dissolved in water, turns into a jellylike substance. Pectin, a powdered substance used to give jelly its gel-like consistency, is an example of soluble fiber.

Insoluble fiber is what we sometimes refer to as "roughage." It is one of the most abundant organic substances found on Earth. Insoluble fiber forms the structural parts of plants, trees, leaves, fruit, seeds, and grains. It can be found in the skin and fibrous parts of fruits and vegetables, such as the fibrous parts of broccoli, the husks of grain, and in beans and legumes, and helps to give rounded form to these plants. Soluble fiber helps to thicken the consistency of the fluid part of plants and can give the liquid part of plants a gooey or sticky feel. Oat bran, wheat bran, and rice bran are the shavings from the outer coat of whole grains. These are a mixture of both soluble and insoluble fiber.

Fiber forms the structural elements of just about all plants, including the plants we use for food. If there is a yin and yang of carbohydrate foods, sugar and starch are the yin and dietary fibers are the yang. Without the fiber, digestible carbohydrates (sugar and starch) become bad carbohydrates that can make you sick. With fiber in its natural form, digestible carbohydrates are balanced and they become good carbohydrates that can make you well.

A good analogy is a nuclear reactor. Dietary fiber slows the digestive process of carbohydrates in much the same way that control rods slow the nuclear fission process in a nuclear reactor. A typical nuclear reactor has radioactive rods used as nuclear fuel and inactive control rods made of cadmium or boron. Control rods are inserted between the radioactive rods to block some of the nuclear reaction and produce heat in a slow, manageable fashion. If there are enough control rods in a nuclear reactor, the nuclear reaction produces steady, useful energy. If the control rods are taken away, nuclear fission occurs too rapidly and a dangerous meltdown results. This is similar to the way fiber works in our body. Fiber, or nondigestible carbohydrate, helps to slow the absorption of the digestible carbohydrate, fat, and total calories to a manageable and healthy level.

One of the reasons the Good Carbohydrate Plan works so well is that it is high in fiber content. We use foods that are, in general, whole, plant-based, and unprocessed. As a result, almost all the foods in the plan are high in natural fiber.

Here is an example of a comparison between a Good Carbohydrate Plan meal and a typical modern American meal. The Good Carbohydrate Plan meal consists of two whole wheat burritos filled with nonfat refried beans, salsa, lettuce, and tomato; a salad; and an orange. The modern American fast food meal is a double burger, large fries, and a shake. Notice that the Good Carbohydrate Plan meal has over four times the fiber with less than half the calories.

Good Carbohydrate Plan Meal	Amount	Fiber (gm)	Calories
Whole wheat tortilla	2 tortillas	7.2	228
Non-fat refried beans	6 ounces	8.7	145
Tomatoes	½ cup	1.0	19
Lettuce	2 cups	1.5	13
Salsa	6 tablespoons	0.5	28
Orange	1 large	4.4	87
	Total	23.3	520

American Fast Food Meal			
Double burger	1 sandwich	1.0	560
French fries	1 large	4.0	400
Milkshake	1 serving	0.0	356
	Total	5.0	1,316

Calculated from: USDA Nutrient Database for Standard Reference, Release 12.

The removal of dietary fiber is one of the worst things you can do to high carbohydrate foods. Removing the fiber is one of the ways that modern processing of food turns good carbohydrates into bad carbohydrates. For example, brown rice is a very healthy food. It is full of B vitamins, vitamin E, selenium, and fiber. By milling brown rice and removing the outer bran layers, you get white rice. In doing so, you lose 60 percent of its fiber, nearly 90 percent of its vitamin E, and so much thiamin (vitamin B1) that white rice has to be enriched with thiamin in order to avoid the risk of beriberi, a disease of thiamin deficiency. In addition, the blood sugar curve for white rice can be 50 percent higher than that of brown rice.

If there is adequate fiber in its intact form, digestion of carbohydrates is slowed to a healthy rate. If there is not enough fiber, or if the fiber is processed excessively into a fine powder, then the digestible carbohydrates are absorbed too quickly, insulin levels rise and health problems result. Fiber helps to keep the absorption of carbohydrates at a manageable and healthy level. It is as if nature intended us to eat digestible carbohydrates only when mixed with a healthy dose of nondigestible carbohydrates (fiber).

FIBER AS A CARBOHYDRATE BLOCKER

Fiber is a carbohydrate and is also a carbohydrate blocker. In other words, it slows down the absorption of digestible carbohydrates. One reason dietary fiber is a carbohydrate blocker is in its action during the digestive process. Dietary fiber cannot be absorbed in the digestive process. Instead, it absorbs water and occupies a fair amount of space in the stomach and intestines. When this happens, the fiber gives us a sensation of fullness. It expands with the absorption of water, and begins to press on the sides of our stomach. The stretching of the stomach sends nerve signals through the vagus nerves to the brain. The brain signals the hypothalamus, where the central satiety system (the system that tells us whether we are hungry or satisfied) is located, and tells us we are full and satisfied. This helps to turn off our hunger drive.

Because foods high in fiber fill up the stomach more quickly, this helps to reduce or minimize the number of calories we need to feel satisfied. Thus, dietary fiber can be considered a calorie blocker nutrient because it creates a natural barrier to the overconsumption of calories by making us feel satisfied.

Another way in which dietary fiber is a carbohydrate blocker is that the number of grams of digestible carbohydrate consumed is generally reduced on a high fiber diet. This is because fiber provides bulk and dilutes the amount of digestible carbohydrate in a food. For example, a pound of white bread contains 225 grams of digestible carbohydrate but only a few grams of fiber. A pound of cooked pinto beans contains over 33 grams of fiber, but just over half the digestible carbohydrate—116 grams. Thus, on a pound-for-pound basis, there are fewer digestible carbohydrates in high fiber foods. This decreases the glucose load by reducing the total amount of carbohydrates consumed. Thus, fiber serves as a carbohydrate blocker and helps to reduce the blood sugar impact of a high carbohydrate food. In doing so, it reduces the insulin response, and in turn, reduces the risk of a number of health problems.

FIBER REDUCES RISK OF DIABETES

My research and that of other scientists around the world show that fiber intake seems to protect people against diabetes. This is a good indication that fiber helps to control blood sugar even to the point of preventing diabetes, the ultimate disease of poor blood sugar control. Studies conducted around the world—in Africa, America, Europe, Asia, and the Pacific islands—all show that people eating high fiber diets have low rates of diabetes.

In my research in Hawaii, I found evidence that in ancient times, Hawaiians, who also ate a diet full of good carbohydrates that are naturally high in fiber such as taro, poi, breadfruit, yams, greens, sea vegetables and fruit, had very low rates of diabetes. Today, while eating a modern American diet, high in animal products and refined carbohydrates that are depleted of fiber, Native Hawaiians have a diabetes rate that is among the highest in the world, with a mortality rate nearly six times as high as the United States' national average.

When we conducted a study in Hawaii putting Native Hawaiians back on traditional Hawaiian food, participants saw their blood sugar levels improve and some of them were able to eliminate their need for insulin in as little as three weeks. This occurred despite the fact that the carbohydrate content was 78 percent of the diet! One of the main reasons for this improvement in blood sugar in the presence of a high carbohydrate diet was the high fiber content that slowed the absorption of carbohydrate, which is always absorbed as sugar. This reduced the amount of sugar the body had to handle over time and made it easier for the body to maintain a reasonable blood sugar level at all times.

FIBER AS A CALORIE BLOCKER

Dietary fiber is also associated with lower rates of obesity. One reason for this is the fact that dietary fiber provides more bulk and induces an increased feeling of satiety without increasing calorie consumption. In fact, dietary fiber can reduce the total amount of calories consumed, even though it adds to the weight of the food consumed. In my studies, I found that on a high fiber, high carbohydrate diet, calorie consumption decreased by as much as 20 percent while satiety levels (satisfaction from the amount of food consumed) remained adequate to high.

In fact, when I first started testing the Good Carbohydrate Plan, some participants told me that they were not accustomed to eating so much food. I found that some of them had calorie intakes as low as 1,200 calories per day. I had to tell them to eat more food! Meanwhile, they kept telling me they felt full! Long-term follow-up of these patients has confirmed for me that long-term weight control is achievable using the Good Carbohydrate Plan.

It's important to understand that the human digestive tract was intended to handle a great deal of dietary fiber. This can be inferred from the fact that we have a long digestive tract similar to that of herbivores who consume very large amounts of plant material. While current recommendations are at 20 to 30 grams of fiber per day with a caution of going above 35 to 50 grams of fiber, estimates of human consumption of dietary fiber in ancient times suggest that humans ate an average of up to 100 grams of fiber per day. (Again, remember that this was in the form of whole food and not as a supplement.) This is in very sharp contrast to the estimated 12 grams of fiber consumed today. It is very possible that this great difference in dietary fiber intake contributes to many of the diseases and health problems prevalent today, including obesity, heart disease, cancer, and diabetes.

FIBER AS A CHOLESTEROL BLOCKER

Dietary fiber helps to prevent heart disease by aiding in the control of obesity and blood sugar, but it also directly helps to reduce cholesterol levels. Of the two types of fiber, it is the water-soluble type that produces the direct cholesterol-lowering effect. Soluble fiber, when dissolved in water, turns into a gel-like substance in the intestinal tract and binds onto cholesterol. It holds on to cholesterol that you eat, and it also binds cholesterol that is found in bile.

Bile is a substance that is produced in the liver, stored in the gallbladder, and secreted into the intestinal tract to help in digestion. Bile is made from a cholesterol nucleus. Thus, a substantial amount of cholesterol circulates from the liver through the gallbladder into the digestive tract. In the process of digestion, bile is typically absorbed and recirculated into the bloodstream. It is broken down, and cholesterol is retained for reuse. If, however, there is a large amount of soluble fiber in the digestive tract during the digestive process, the soluble fiber holds onto the bile and it is eliminated from the body with the passing of stool. In this way, the soluble fiber helps rid the body not only of dietary cholesterol, but also cholesterol from the bile that is involved in the digestive process.

This is how soluble fiber seems to help in the control of cholesterol. Studies that confirm this result have been conducted over the years. Probably the best-known studies on the cholesterol-lowering effect of dietary fiber are those that involve the use of oat bran as a source of soluble fiber. Similar reductions in cholesterol were found with other grain-based fiber; in other words, fiber from good carbohydrates. In my research, using diets made up primarily of good carbohydrates, cholesterol was decreased somewhere between 14 to 24 percent. This translates to a reduction in coronary risk of 28 to 48 percent. One of the main reasons for this reduction is the high fiber content of the diet.

FIBER AS A NATURAL SUBSTANCE THAT IMPROVES DIGESTION

Dietary fiber intake is associated with lower rates of a variety of digestive diseases including ulcers, appendicitis, gallbladder disease, constipation, diverticular disease, and colon cancer. The bulkiness of fiber appears to be part of the reason for its protective effect. Because fiber is indigestible, it remains in the digestive tract throughout the process of digestion until the body eliminates the digestive waste.

Fiber's bulkiness within the digestive system provides a number of benefits. First, the bulk effect of fiber allows the walls of the intestines to push the contents of digestion along in an efficient manner. This means that the stool is easily moved through the digestive system and constipation becomes virtually nonexistent. Also, since the digestive contents are able to move along more quickly, this makes it less likely that cancer-causing substances will be created or will be in contact with the intestinal walls for a significant period of time.

An example of a cancer-causing substance in the intestines is nitrosamines, which are created from nitrates found in food. If the bowel transit time is short, there is little time for nitrates to turn into nitrosamines or for the intestines to be exposed to these cancer-causing substances, making cancer of the colon less likely. When the bowels are moving smoothly, there is less time for any carcinogen in the digestive tract to cause damage that may trigger cancer.

Fiber's bulk effect in the stool makes diverticular disease and appendicitis less likely, too. Diverticular disease is caused by increased pressure in the bowel (usually caused by straining at the stool) that causes weak spots in the large intestine to be pushed out in tiny balloon-like pouches called diverticuli. The diverticuli can become blocked, bacteria can be trapped within, and infection may result. The diverticuli can then burst and result in a life-threatening infection.

A similar process can happen in the appendix. Increased pressure in the stool can cause the appendix to become blocked and infected, causing what is commonly known as appendicitis. In countries that consume large amounts of dietary fiber, appendicitis, gallstones, and diverticulitis are rare conditions.

Gastric ulcers are also less common in countries that consume more dietary fiber. Exactly how fiber helps to protect against ulcers is unclear, especially since the discovery that antibiotics can help to remedy ulcers by dealing with the bacteria, *Helicobacter pylori,* which is found in most gastric ulcers. Nonetheless, the important thing to know is that high fiber diets seem to prevent ulcers and help in healing them. Most of the patients I have seen who had gastritis or gastric ulcers found that these problems improved or resolved by eating a diet high in fiber from good carbohydrates even before the use of antibiotics for ulcers was recommended.

Gallbladder disease is a complex problem usually involving gallstones. While gallstones are more a result of a high fat diet and obesity than a lack of fiber, high fiber diets help to prevent gallstones in a number of ways. Gallstones are usually made up of cholesterol and found most often in people who are obese. Fiber helps to reduce both cholesterol and obesity and thus reduces the likelihood of gallstone production. In addition, people eating a lot of fiber are less likely to be eating the high fat animal products that contribute to high cholesterol levels, which ultimately contribute to the production of gallstones.

FIBER CAN BE A REMEDY FOR DIGESTIVE PROBLEMS

Dietary fiber is easily forgotten because it does not provide any nutrition. However, as we have seen, dietary fiber is of primary importance to digestive health. In the absence of dietary fiber, the remnants of digestion can harden and become compacted. If this occurs, the intestines have a difficult time moving along the digested food, resulting in constipation. Constipation, as you may know, is a potential setup for a number of digestive problems.

In 14 years of private practice, I have never prescribed stool softeners or laxatives. I simply ask my patients to consume 50 to 60 percent of their diet as whole grain, that is, a good carbohydrate. Constipation disappears within one to two days, without fail. If you are going to try this on your own, be sure you don't have any health problems that may contraindicate eating that much dietary fiber. If you have any questions or if you have any health problems, please check with your doctor first. However, for most people who have no health problems, dietary fiber, especially in the form of good carbohydrates, is an excellent way to alleviate constipation.

WHAT ABOUT FIBER SUPPLEMENTS?

As for using fiber supplements to achieve these effects, the scientific literature suggests that there is some benefit but not as much as if you obtain fiber from whole foods. Some studies indicate that dietary fiber can induce a reduction in calorie intake and obesity while other studies, especially those using fiber supplements, do not show the same result. So the use of dietary fiber as a supplement to induce weight loss is somewhat controversial. There is also some concern that excessive amounts of fiber as a supplement (not as whole food) taken all at once can cause intestinal blockage.

However, there are good studies that suggest that dietary fiber supplements can improve blood sugar control, help with cholesterol control and reduce constipation. For example, researchers at the Cleveland Clinic also found that fiber supplements can achieve a significant reduction in cholesterol and risk of coronary heart disease. In a double-blind study, a fiber supplement containing guar gum, locust bean gum, pectin, oat fiber, acacia fiber and barley fiber—in other words, a supplement high in soluble fiber—was tested against a placebo. The researchers found that after two months on a fiber supplement, participants' LDL cholesterol was nearly 10 percent lower than the LDL of those on a placebo.

On balance, looking at the various studies, a reasonable daily fiber supplementation is a good idea for people who aren't getting adequate fiber through their food. As for weight control, while the effectiveness of fiber supplements is not certain, it is quite clear that consuming more whole foods that are high in fiber such as whole grains, vegetables, and fruits appears to help in long-term weight management.

GOOD CARBOHYDRATES ARE HIGH IN DIETARY FIBER: THE OTHER GOOD CARBOHYDRATE

Considering all the facts about the healthfulness of dietary fiber, it is clear that this nondigestible carbohydrate was intended by nature to go along with digestible carbohydrates. All sugars and starches should be eaten with an adequate amount of dietary fiber.

Fiber is important in the healthful consumption of not only carbohydrates, but also fats, cholesterol and any food that you might consume. This is because fiber helps to slow down the intake and absorption of all these nutrients to a manageable level so that it is less likely that we will absorb sugar, fat, or cholesterol too quickly. Dietary fiber, the other good carbohydrate, is abundant in foods that are considered good carbohydrates. Consuming fiber naturally decreases the rate of absorption and quantity of bad carbohydrates consumed. This reduces insulin requirement, which automatically helps you control blood sugar, cholesterol, and weight. I'll provide more detail about fiber in different types of food in the next chapter, The Anatomy of Good and Bad Carbohydrates.

CHAPTER 5

The Anatomy of Good and Bad Carbohydrates

GOOD CARBOHYDRATES: A HEALTHY BALANCE OF FIBER AND CARBOHYDRATE

Think of the last time you ate an apple, some corn on the cob, or a nice bowl of lentil soup. Did you notice a big blood sugar rush, or feel drowsy after eating these foods? Most likely not, because these foods are examples of good carbohydrates.

Good carbohydrates are high carbohydrate foods that are absorbed slowly and have a minimal impact on blood sugar. They are also foods that have a lot of fiber (nondigestible carbohydrate) compared to the amount of sugars or starch (digestible carbohydrate). In general, good carbohydrates are foods that are bulky for the number of calories they contain. In other words, they are low in calorie density. They are bulky because they contain other nutrients and food components besides carbohydrates and calories—the way nature intended.

Good carbohydrates include whole, plant-based foods such as vegetables, beans and legumes, fruit, and whole grains. As you can see in the table opposite, vegetables have the highest proportion of fiber, followed by beans and legumes, then fruit, and then whole grains. A bad carbohydrate such as white bread has just one gram of fiber per 50 grams of carbohydrate (50 grams is about 1.75 ounces). Sugar, of course, has no fiber at all.

FIBER CONTENT OF 50 GM. OF DIGESTIBLE CARBOHYDRATE

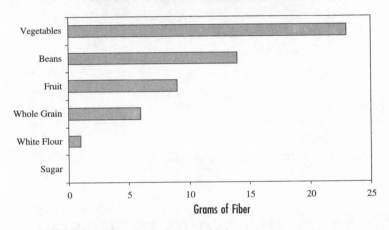

Calculated from: USDA Nutrient Database for Standard Reference, Release 12.

Good carbohydrates typically have four or more grams of fiber per 50 grams of digestible carbohydrate. You can find the fiber content of various foods in the Carbohydrate Quotient table in Appendix A.

Good Carbohydrates	
Vegetables	10 to 33 grams of fiber
Beans and legumes	13 to 19 grams of fiber
Fruit	4 to 11 grams of fiber
Whole grains	4 to 8 grams of fiber

Bad Carbohydrates	
White bread	1 gram of fiber
Sugar	0 gram of fiber

Good Carbohydrates Can Have the Opposite Effect of Bad Carbohydrates

A high carbohydrate diet based on bad carbohydrates such as white bread, white flour muffins, and sugars can cause an increase in blood sugar and triglycerides (blood fats). A high carbohydrate diet based on the Good Carbohydrate Plan has the opposite effect. Blood sugar and blood fats levels both improved substantially. My studies show that the effect of carbohydrates on blood sugar and health can be different, even opposite, based on a number of factors, including the type of carbohydrate.

Type of Diet	Blood Sugar Effect	Blood Fat (Triglyceride) Response
Bad Carbohydrate Diet	+19	+37
Good Carbohydrate Diet	−21	−87

BLOOD SUGAR RESPONSE TO DIFFERENT HIGH CARBOHYDRATE DIETS

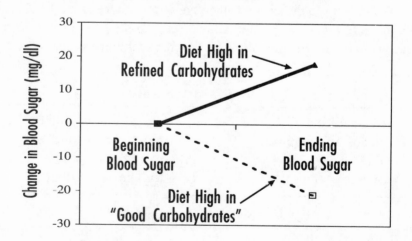

Shintani , T.T., et al. *Hawaii Med J* (2001) 60:69-73.
Coulstan, A.M., et al. *Diabetes Care* (1989) 12:94.

ANATOMY OF GOOD CARBOHYDRATES

Let's look at what makes up good carbohydrates. This will help you to understand what's so good about good carbohydrates and why processing these whole foods into refined products creates health problems.

Good carbohydrates are whole foods. They are much more than just carbohydrates and fiber. They all contain some protein and some fat, along with a whole array of vitamins and minerals. It is a common misconception that plant-based foods contain only carbohydrates and no protein or essential fats. Actually, all good carbohydrates (all whole vegetables, fruit, legumes, and grains) contain both protein and essential fats. Even lettuce contains some protein and essential fats. It is virtually impossible to design a varied diet based on whole, plant-based food that is inadequate in protein or essential fats.

Vegetables

Good carbohydrates that have the smallest impact on blood sugar are vegetables. There are hundreds of different vegetables, and they can be classified into three main types: leaf and stem vegetables, such as lettuce and broccoli; root vegetables, such as carrots and potatoes; and fruit-type vegetables, such as squash and tomatoes.

Leaf and Stem Vegetables

Leaf and stem vegetables typically have the highest nutrient density, that is, they have the most nutrition per calorie. These vegetables have a large amount of nondigestible carbohydrates (fiber) in them because they are the structural and manufacturing components of the plant. Leaves and stems have a small amount of digestible carbohydrate because those parts of the plant are not the structures that store energy calories. The leaves are where carbon dioxide is exchanged and where the miracle of the creation of carbohydrates takes place through photosynthesis. Because the manufacturing of plant material is happening in the leaves, there is a great deal of noncaloric nutrition in this part of the plant. For example, there is chlorophyll, carotenoids (powerful antioxidants), vitamin K, minerals, and a vast array of vitamins, minerals, and phytonutrients necessary for producing nutrients and structural components for the plant.

To more clearly illustrate this point, here is the nutrient content of four ounces of broccoli in terms of daily U.S. requirements.

Vitamin C	174 percent
Fiber	17 percent
Folic acid	44 percent
Beta carotene	21 percent
Potassium	18 percent
Pantothenic acid	14 percent
Magnesium	10 percent
Riboflavin	10 percent
Protein	6 percent

Broccoli also has many other vitamins and minerals, including the rest of the B complex vitamins (except B12) and other minerals. This is a large amount of healthy nutrients and yet four ounces of broccoli contains just 31 calories, six grams of carbohydrate, and 0.4 grams of fat. Because of the high content of fiber compared to the digestible carbohydrate, the effect of four ounces of broccoli on blood sugar is very small.

Root Vegetables

Root vegetables tend to be higher in carbohydrate because in some plants, roots are a structure that stores energy for the plant for times of water and nutrient shortage. Usually it is this type of storage root that humans have chosen as a food source. Examples of root vegetables include carrots, beets, potatoes, sweet potatoes, turnips, and lotus root. All the root vegetables are a good source of fiber with about 2.3 grams to 3.5 grams per four-ounce serving.

Turnips are low in digestible carbohydrate with 5.5 grams per four ounces and low in sugar content (2.2 grams of the carbohydrate is sugar). Carrots are slightly higher in carbohydrate content, with 11.5 grams per four ounces, and have a larger amount of sugar, with 7.5 grams of the carbohydrate being sugar. Potatoes and sweet potatoes have even more carbohydrate, with about 24 to 27.5 grams of carbohydrate per four ounces of these foods. However, when you compare the carbohydrate content of root vegetables to processed foods such as white bread and sugar, you can see how much more carbohydrate there are per a four-ounce portion of white bread and sugar. White bread has about 55 grams of carbohydrate in every four ounces and sugar has 112 grams of carbohydrate per four-ounce portion. See the chart below.

CARBOHYDRATE CONTENT OF HIGH CARBOHYDRATE FOODS
GRAMS OF DIGESTIBLE CARBOHYDRATE IN 4 OUNCES OF FOOD

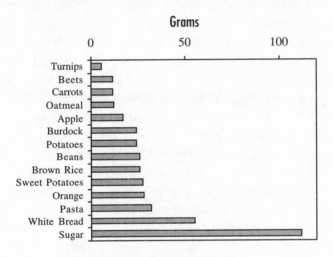

Calculated from: USDA Nutrient Database for Standard Reference, Release 12.

Fruit-Type Vegetables

Fruit-type vegetables include cucumbers, squash, peppers, and tomatoes. While these foods are not considered to be fruits from a nutritional standpoint—mainly because they are not very sweet—structurally, they are the fruits of their respective plants. Because these vegetables are not very sweet, it means that there is not much sugar in them. All of the fruit vegetables have about 1.5 to 2.5 grams of fiber per four-ounce portion. Cucumbers contain a very small amount of carbohydrate (3.1 grams per four ounces) and calories. Pumpkins have somewhat more calories and are slightly sweeter, with 7.1 grams of carbohydrate and of that, about five grams is simple carbohydrate or sugar.

Fruit

Fruits as we commonly know them are high in sugar content and are naturally sweet. In general, almost all fruits can be considered good carbohydrates. There are hundreds of fruits to choose from and almost all of them are desirable foods that are high in carbohydrates and low in fat. One of the reasons fruit suits our taste buds is that nature intentionally made fruit tasty as a means of distributing seeds and propagating plants. In the same way that nature made flowers fragrant to attract bees in order to scatter pollen, nature made fruit sweet in order to attract animals and humans to eat the fruit of a plant so that its seeds would be carried to distant locations in order to propagate its species. Those plants that had the tastiest fruit would have its fruit eaten more widely and its seeds scattered more widely than plants that had less sweet fruit. Thus, nature selected in favor of plants that had a lot of sweet carbohydrates. This is one reason why fruit has more carbohydrate than vegetables and why more of it is in the form of sugar.

Even though fruit contains a lot of sugar, the surprising fact about fruit is that it is generally gentle in its effect on blood sugar. There are three reasons for this. First, as with vegetables, there is a lot of fiber that comes along with whole fruit. Second, unlike vegetables, much of the carbohydrate in fruit comes from fructose or fruit sugar. On a gram-for-gram basis, fruit sugar actually raises blood sugar less than white sugar or even pure starch. Third, fruit is very bulky for the amount of calories in it.

Don't forget that whole fruit contains a wealth of nutrients in addition to fiber. For example, citrus fruit has loads of vitamin C, yellow and orange fruit is high in beta carotene and other retinoids, and grapes and blueberries are full of antioxidants. Fruits are typically low in protein and fat. Apples, for example, are 94 percent carbohydrate, five percent fat and one percent protein. One medium-size apple is about 4.9 ounces and contains 21 grams of carbohydrate and about three grams of fiber. Oranges are 91 percent carbohydrate, two percent fat and seven percent protein, with 21.7 grams of carbohydrate and 4.4 grams of fiber in one orange. Of the

21.7 grams of carbohydrate, 16.9 grams are simple carbohydrates or sugar, and most of the sugar is fructose.

Legumes

Among the good carbohydrate foods, beans and legumes have the highest concentration of protein. In this book, the terms legumes and beans are interchangeable. Examples of these foods include kidney beans, pinto beans, garbanzos (chickpeas), lentils, soybeans, peas, black-eyed peas, and navy beans, to name a few. While these foods contain a lot of protein, they are still mainly carbohydrate. For example, in every four ounces of pinto beans there are nine grams of protein, 29 grams of carbohydrate, and less than half a gram of fat—that's 23 percent of calories from protein, 73 percent of calories from carbohydrate, and three percent of calories from fat. In addition, the fiber content is substantial, with 8.4 grams of fiber in this small portion of beans. This high content of fiber is reflected in the modest impact on blood sugar produced by beans. The high protein, high carbohydrate, low fat profile of pinto beans is fairly typical of almost all legumes.

Contrary to what has been taught in nutrition classes for many years, the protein found in legumes is complete by itself. It is not incomplete or inferior. If you have any doubt about this, look at the table in Chapter 14, What About Protein?. You will see that by eating legumes (even if that's all you ate), you'd get well in excess of the minimum requirements for total protein, as well as all of the essential amino acids.

Grains

Grain products provide more calories for humans throughout the world than any other food product. They are also the most often adulterated and processed carbohydrate food that we eat. Let's look at the physical structure of grains to help us to understand why processing grains can turn a good carbohydrate into a bad carbohydrate. Whole, intact wheat is the most commonly used grain staple in the world, so we'll use that as our example. All grains (except for buckwheat, which is not truly a grain) have the same basic structure as wheat.

There are three main parts to a kernel of wheat or grain: *endosperm, bran,* and *germ.*

The endosperm, the creamy white inner part of the grain, provides all the starch and almost all of the calories. It might surprise you to learn that the endosperm is also where most of the protein resides. The intact inner starchy endosperm is what remains when the outer bran and germ are milled off in processing. This refined product has the pure white appearance that we are all familiar with in pastries and breads made of white flour.

The bran is the outer layer of the whole kernel of grain. There are multiple layers of bran that are largely made of cellulose or hemicellulose—both are insoluble fibers. There are also soluble fibers in the bran coatings. The bran contains most of the fiber and also most of the minerals, such as calcium, potassium, phosphorus, and magnesium. Bran also contains a small amount of iron and zinc. Bran gives whole grains their distinctive brownish color, and also provides roughage. The bulk effect of bran in the human digestive system helps to prevent constipation and provides a number of related benefits. Bran holds onto water as well as some fat and cholesterol in the digestive tract and helps to eliminate them through bowel movements. It also helps you to feel full so that you are satisfied with fewer calories and thus less likely to eat more calories than you should.

THE ANATOMY OF A WHOLE GRAIN

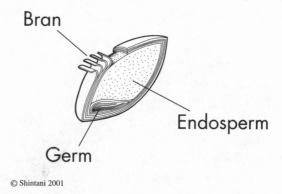

Bran

Endosperm

Germ

© Shintani 2001

NUTRIENT CONTENT OF WHEAT KERNEL

	Percent of Total		
	Bran	Germ	Endosperm
Protein	19.0	8.0	73.0
Carbohydrate	7.0	4.0	89.0
Fat (oils)	59.0	6.0	35.0
Minerals	77.0	0.3	22.0
Thiamin	13.0	64.0	3.0
Riboflavin	42.0	26.0	32.0
Niacin	86.0	2.0	12.0
Pyridoxine	73.0	21.0	6.0

Data from: Wheat Flour Institute, Educational Division of Miller's National Federation, 1974,Washington, D.C.

The germ is the live embryo of the whole grain. Whole grains are, of course, also seeds. The germ contains the genetic information and the beginnings of a new grain plant. The germ contains 64 percent of vitamin B1 and has almost all of the vitamin E present in a whole grain. Vitamin E, incidentally, may help prevent heart disease.

Whole Grains Provide Whole Protein

As we have seen, whole grains are a good supply of complex carbohydrates. Grains also provide a fairly good source of protein. For example, brown rice is 85 percent carbohydrate, 8 percent protein, and 7 percent fat. Whole wheat is somewhat higher in protein with 14 percent of its calories coming from protein, 80 percent from carbohydrate, and 5 percent from fat. As with legumes, the protein from whole grain is also complete. If you again look at the protein table in Chapter 14, you will see that by eating whole grains (even if that's all you ate) you'd get more than the minimum requirements for total protein, as well as all of the essential amino acids. Also note that even from the grain that is polished, such as white rice, you would still get nearly the required amount of protein in one day's worth of calories. Even an inferior form of grain has almost enough protein and essential amino acids for our daily needs.

Vitamins

Another excellent health benefit of whole grains is their micronutrient content. Whole grains are abundant in vitamin E, which is a powerful fat-soluble antioxidant, and is associated with a lower risk of heart disease and certain cancers. Whole grains are also an excellent supply of B complex vitamins, including vitamin B1 (thiamin), vitamin B2 (riboflavin), vitamin B3 (niacin), and vitamin B6 (pyridoxine). Grains also provide some calcium, magnesium, potassium, phosphorus, and trace amounts of iron and zinc.

Whole Grains Provide Whole Fiber

As we discussed in Chapter 4, fiber is very important to our health. Along with the many other benefits, whole grains are a good source of fiber. Whole grains such as brown rice provide about four grams of fiber for every 50 grams of carbohydrate (this is little more than a bowl of rice). Whole wheat provides about the same.

BAD CARBOHYDRATES: TOO MUCH, TOO FAST

Bad Carbohydrates are refined in such a way that either most of the natural fiber is removed, or the whole food is processed into a very fine flour, allowing the carbohydrates to be absorbed very quickly. Some bad carbohydrates, such as white sugar and white flour, have been processed in both ways at the same time. The fiber is stripped away from the food and the refined product is ground up into fine granules or powder.

Another problem caused by this processing is that the calorie density drastically changes so that you have more calories for less food. For example, four ounces of brown rice contains 126 calories, four ounces of white bread contains 303 calories, and four ounces of sugar contains 438 calories. Thus, it is much easier to consume an excessive amount of calories from sugar or white bread than it is from brown rice.

Carbohydrates in the form of white bread or sugar, that is, bad carbohydrates, tend to wreak havoc on our blood sugar and insulin in two ways. First, they are absorbed too quickly. Your blood sugar rises rapidly and your body has to throw insulin at it to keep it under control. Your body goes through a roller coaster of high blood sugar, high insulin, and then, in some people, periods of low blood sugar. Second, bad carbohydrates are high in calorie density and you are likely to consume more calories from this source, thus magnifying their negative effects. In these ways, bad carbohydrates produce negative effects, such as increasing the risk of cardiovascular disease as well as possibly contributing to obesity.

THE ANATOMY OF A BAD CARBOHYDRATE: HOW GOOD CARBOHYDRATES TURN BAD

Rice, wheat, and virtually all carbohydrate foods are good for you—when you eat them in their whole, natural form. Unfortunately, in today's world, most of these healthy foods are turned into bad carbohydrates. Let's look at how this happens.

Whole grains can be processed in different ways to produce the foods that are familiar to us. Processing may involve polishing the grain to create white rice or pearled barley, for example, or it may involve grinding the grain into a flour product.

When the outer layers of brown rice are removed, it becomes white rice or polished rice. In order to produce white rice, one has to harvest the whole grain, remove the grain from the stalks, and remove the hull, which is a very thick, woody outer covering of the grain. This leaves the whole, intact grain. The outer bran and germ of the grain are then polished off. By getting rid of both the bran and the germ, the polishing process eliminates nearly all of the fiber, minerals, and vitamin B complex, and completely removes the vitamin E, which is known to help heart disease.

Polishing or milling whole grains also has a negative effect on the way the remaining starchy part of the grain, the endosperm, is absorbed and affects blood sugar. Because most of the fiber is removed, the remaining carbohydrate is rapidly broken down in the digestive tract. Although this carbohydrate is mostly complex, the blood sugar response is much worse than if the whole, unprocessed kernel is eaten.

When whole grains are milled into flour, they are crushed into coarse particles and then ground up again into finer particles. The second step, which is optional, is to sift out the bran and the germ, leaving just the starchy endosperm. A third step in processing is to bleach the grain using a chemical agent. Some of the chemical agents are benzyl peroxide, chlorine, chlorine dioxide, nitrosyl chloride, and other agents.

In the process of milling the flour, the manufacturer can opt to grind the flour into finer and finer particles. This creates different degrees of coarseness and fineness and different types of flour. The finer the flour, the more it will affect your blood sugar.

Grinding whole grains into flour has been done throughout the history of mankind's use of grain. If you simply grind the whole kernel, it is whole-grain flour. This is probably the most acceptable form of processing *if* the flour is not too finely ground. A very nice, coarse, rich whole-grain bread can be produced using coarsely ground whole grain flour. If the flour is fresh, it has virtually all the nutrients and almost all the good qualities of the whole, intact grain.

Probably the worst thing that can be done to grain is to use a combination of milling and polishing: the grain is ground into flour, and the fiber and nutrient-rich germ are discarded. This is what happens with white flour.

Here is a summary of the different types of processing, resulting in four forms of grain:

1. The unprocessed grain is whole, intact, and unadulterated with all of its natural nutrients preserved. Because it retains its natural form, as intact kernels, it is absorbed at a manageable rate and it affects blood sugar and insulin modestly.

2. You have whole grain flour if the grain is simply ground into flour without discarding the bran and germ. In whole grain flour, all the vitamins and fiber are present. However, grinding the grain into flour causes it to induce a sharper rise in blood sugar than it would in its intact, whole-grain form. The finer the flour, the higher the blood sugar response. For example, bread made from mixed grains raises blood sugar only 64 percent as high as white bread does.

3. When the grain is polished, such as with white rice, it is stripped of many of its healthful nutrients, such as the bran, vitamin B complex, and vitamin E. Because it has lost most of its fiber, it is absorbed more quickly than a whole grain. However, because it is in the form of rice kernels, it is not absorbed as fast as if it were ground into flour.

4. If the grain is refined in both ways, the grain is milled into flour and the bran and germ are sifted out and discarded. The resulting white

flour will produce a sharp rise in blood sugar. The finer the flour, the sharper the rise. In the form of commercially prepared white bread, the blood sugar response is higher than that of table sugar.

The following is a comparison of the nutrient content of whole brown rice compared to polished unenriched white rice. Notice the percentage of each nutrient lost in the process.

Nutrient	Brown Rice	White Rice	Percent Loss by Polishing
Fiber	3.40 gm	1.30 gm	62%
Vitamin E	0.66 mg	0.13 mg	80%
Thiamin (B1)	0.41 mg	0.07 mg	83%
Niacin (B3)	4.30 mg	1.60 mg	63%
Pyridoxine (B6)	0.51 mg	0.14 mg	71%
Folic acid	20.00 mcg	9.00 mcg	55%

Calculated from: USDA Nutrient Database for Standard Reference, Release 12.

REFINING OF A GRAIN

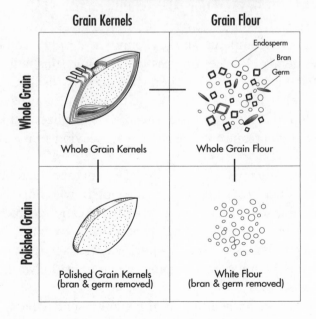

The following table shows how much is lost when one cup of whole wheat flour is converted to unenriched white flour.

Nutrients	Whole Wheat Flour	White Flour	Percent Loss
Fiber	12.2 gm	2.70 gm	78%
Vitamin E	1.23 mg	0.06 mg	95%
Thiamin (B1)	0.45 mg	0.12 mg	73%
Niacin (B3)	6.30 mg	1.25 mg	80%
Pyridoxine (B6)	0.34 mg	0.04 mg	87%
Folic acid	44.00 mcg	26.00 mcg	41%

Calculated from: USDA Nutrient Database for Standard Reference, Release 12.

SUGAR: THE MOST HIGHLY REFINED CARBOHYDRATE

Even more processed and adulterated from its natural form is table sugar. Sugar, that staple of the American diet, is the other primary bad carbohydrate. I'm not referring to the kind of sugar you find in its natural form, as in fruit, but pure white granulated sugar.

Sugar originally comes from a tall, tropical grass, which is mostly fiber and water, accompanied by an abundant supply of other nutrients and minerals. In the process of refining, this tall grass is burned, crushed, and heated. Then, the juice is distilled, and the syrup that forms is filtered a number of times until you have a relatively clear liquid. This liquid is allowed to crystallize and the remnants of the sugar plant are washed away, leaving pure crystalline sugar.

White cane sugar is an example of an extremely refined and processed product. To give you an idea of how refined sugar is, consider that it takes about three feet of sugar cane to produce one teaspoon of sugar. After the final processing to white granulated sugar, all that is left is essentially pure calories. To get sugar, we throw away the natural plant, keeping only the dead crystalline-pure carbohydrate calories.

Sugar, as sweet as it tastes, is the quintessential bad carbohydrate because it is pure digestible carbohydrate. It carries with it no other nutrients other than the calories it contains and those calories can be absorbed very quickly with no fiber to slow it down. It is not only its lack of fiber or redeeming nutrients that is a problem. Another reason why sugar can be a problem is that it is high in calorie density. At four calories per gram, it is four times more concentrated in calories than most whole grains and nearly seven times more concentrated in calories than most fruit. Because of this high calorie density, it is easy to overconsume sugar. One serving of it occupies so little space in your stomach, making it easy to consume many servings of the pure carbohydrate. With this high calorie density and the lack of fiber, you have a food that can easily increase your Glycemic Load. (Remember that Glycemic Load is determined by Glycemic Index *times quantity*.)

Later, you will see that pure fruit sugar or fructose has a lower Glycemic Index and raises blood sugar less than other sugars or even some forms of complex carbohydrates. However, it is still not considered a good carbohydrate because it is still just as high in calorie density as other sugars and can easily be overconsumed. In addition, fructose actually raises bad cholesterol as much as or more than other sugars and also has no other redeeming nutrients that come with it.

This doesn't mean that we can't eat sugar at all. It means, however, that we need to be careful about how much we eat, in what form, and with what other food. In fact, one of the most surprising facts about bad carbohydrates is that the most common complex carbohydrate, white bread, may be worse than the most common simple carbohydrate, white sugar. In either case, eating too much white sugar or white flour is sure to cause fluctuations in blood sugar and to increase insulin levels. So what do we eat in place of these foods? In the next chapter I'll describe how you can make healthy adjustments in your diet by choosing good carbohydrates.

CHAPTER 6

How to Find Good Carbohydrates

Finding good carbohydrates is easy when you understand some basic principles. The overriding principle in choosing good carbohydrates is to select carbohydrates that are in their whole, natural form—as unprocessed as possible. When you stick to this fundamental principle, you will greatly improve your diet and reduce your risk of disease.

Within the family of good carbohydrates, there is a range of different types of carbohydrates and their characteristics, such as how they affect your blood sugar, how high in calories they are, etc. The principles that I outline in this chapter will help you to understand how to select the very best good carbohydrates for your needs.

Our modern diet is so loaded with processed food that we seem to have lost, to a large degree, our natural ability to make healthy food choices. Because of this, we tend to rely heavily on tables, indexes, and various other numerical measures of food. While these tools may be helpful as you adjust to your new way of eating, it is important to understand that a single table such as a fat gram table or a carbohydrate counter or the Glycemic Index, while useful in many ways, is also bound to be misleading at times because it usually only evaluates one particular aspect of a food.

TO CHOOSE YOUR GOOD CARBOHYDRATES, JUST STICK WITH THE FIVE C'S (NO NEED TO ADD, SUBTRACT, OR MULTIPLY)

Everyone wants to enjoy their food. This is natural—and it's hard to do if you have to start adding and subtracting and calculating all kinds of numbers in your head every time you would like to have something to eat. That's why I've boiled down the process of selecting good carbohydrates to looking at five simple characteristics that you can easily remember and understand. They are embodied in the Five C's, which I describe a little later in this chapter. (If you like, you can post these Five C's for Choosing Good Carbohydrates on your refrigerator. This will help to keep the information fresh in your head and will be particularly useful as you make the transition to your lifelong, healthy Good Carbohydrate Plan.)

While these principles will be your main guiding tool, numerical evaluations of food may sometimes be helpful for you to make your food choices, especially as you are learning about the different types of carbohydrates. Many health professionals use the Glycemic Index to determine what carbohydrates are better for blood sugar control. My experience is that the Glycemic Index is useful, but for the average person, it is prone to provide misleading information if it is used without taking into account other aspects of foods.

In order to provide you with a table that helps you to find good carbohydrates, I developed the Carbohydrate Quotient. The Carbohydrate Quotient is an adjusted Glycemic Index number, which accounts for other properties of food in addition to a food's effect on blood sugar. This adjustment makes it a better predictor of how your blood sugar and insulin levels will be affected by that food. In other words, the Carbohydrate Quotient helps to compensate for some of the limitations of the Glycemic Index in helping you to find good carbohydrates.

THE GLYCEMIC INDEX

To describe how the Carbohydrate Quotient works, I'll first explain the main part of the Carbohydrate Quotient, the Glycemic Index. The Glycemic Index was developed by scientists for the purpose of measuring how a set amount of carbohydrate from a food will affect your blood sugar. This is done under strictly controlled laboratory conditions.

It was designed to help health professionals in counseling people with diabetes on how to plan meals that will have the least impact on blood sugar. A number of popular books rely on this table to evaluate foods.

The Glycemic Index number of a food is calculated by using measurements of how high blood sugar levels rise over time in response to eating 50 grams of carbohydrate from that food. A number is assigned to a food based on how high blood sugar levels rise as a result of the food compared to the blood sugar rise of white bread. The Glycemic Index number for bread is set at 100, and used as the standard. If a food raises blood sugar 63 percent as high as bread does, that food is assigned a Glycemic Index number of 63. For example, sweet potatoes raise blood sugar 77 percent as high as white bread does, so the Glycemic Index number for sweet potatoes is 77. The Glycemic Index is useful in comparing apples with apples—or even comparing apples with oranges, because they are similar types of foods with similar amounts of calories, fat, and carbohydrate.

But things go wrong when you compare foods that have different characteristics such as calorie densities. If you use the Glycemic Index without understanding its limitations, you might mistakenly come to the conclusion that carrots, brown rice, and pumpkins are bad for you

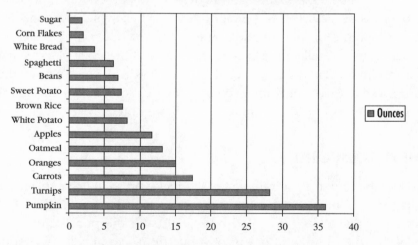

AMOUNT OF FOOD REQUIRED TO PROVIDE 50 GRAMS OF CARBOHYDRATE

Data from: USDA Nutrient Database for Standard Reference, Release 12.

(with Glycemic Indexes of 101, 79, and 107, respectively). The reality is that these are three of the healthiest foods you can eat.

One of the limitations of the Glycemic Index is that it doesn't take into account the calorie density or the bulk effect of a food. As a result, it may over or underestimate how much a food will affect blood sugar in real life. For example, there are 50 grams of sugar in about one-fourth cup of sugar or a little more than a can of soft drink. Anyone can easily eat that much sugar. In contrast, carrots are high in bulk and fiber and low in calorie density. It takes almost seven carrots to provide 50 grams of carbohydrates.

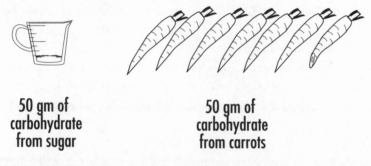

50 gm of carbohydrate from sugar   **50 gm of carbohydrate from carrots**

Calculated from: USDA Nutrient Database for Standard Reference, Release 12.

In a real situation, a person will not eat the same amount of calories from carrots as he or she would of sugar. While it's highly unlikely for a person to gulp down seven carrots at one sitting, most people can gulp a can of soda in no time, and crave even more. Because you tend to eat far less carbohydrates from carrots in real life, the laboratory-based Glycemic Index greatly overestimates how much eating carrots will affect your blood sugar. This is because the Glycemic Index doesn't account for the bulkiness of carrots compared to that of sugar. So even though carrots don't appear very healthy on the Glycemic Index, with a value of 101, carrots are actually a very healthy food. Despite its high Glycemic Index number, it will have a very modest impact on your blood sugar in a real life situation because there are only seven grams of carbohydrates in a whole carrot. Remember that it is the Glycemic Load (Glycemic Index value times amount of food) that is more important than just the Glycemic Index of a food alone.

THE CARBOHYDRATE QUOTIENT IS A BETTER MEASURE OF GOOD CARBOHYDRATES

To improve on the Glycemic Index as a way to find good carbohydrates, I created the Carbohydrate Quotient to account for the different calorie densities of different foods. The Carbohydrate Quotient describes how high a particular food is likely to raise blood sugar over time. The higher the Carbohydrate Quotient, the higher your blood sugar and insulin is likely to rise in response to that food. The Carbohydrate Quotient is essentially an adjusted Glycemic Index table that incorporates the calorie density of a food.

As with the Glycemic Index, the Carbohydrate Quotient compares blood sugar response of different foods using white bread as its standard. What is different about the Carbohydrate Quotient is that it is adjusted downward if a food has a low calorie density. Thus, the Carbohydrate Quotient is a number that is based on the Glycemic Index but is adjusted by dividing the Glycemic Index by a factor determined by the calorie density. This is why it is called a quotient.

By incorporating the calorie density, the Carbohydrate Quotient provides a more accurate measure of how a food will affect your blood sugar in real life. When compared to insulin response studies, the Carbohydrate Quotient is a better predictor of insulin response than the Glycemic Index for most foods, and a better predictor of the overall healthfulness of foods in general. If you examine the explanation of the Carbohydrate Quotient in Appendix A, you will see that Carbohydrate Quotient numbers correlate more closely to insulin response than the Glycemic Index.

THE SIMPLE FIVE C'S METHOD FOR CHOOSING GOOD CARBOHYDRATES

If this seems a little complex, relax. The numbers game is not what the Good Carbohydrate Plan is about. The Carbohydrate Quotient numbers that I provide are simply an added tool that can help to reinforce for you the principles that are outlined in this chapter. Just try to understand the basic good carbohydrate principles that are revealed in this chapter. You'll quickly find it easy and natural to select good carbohydrates. In a few weeks' time you will probably rarely need to consult the charts that I provide, except for occasional reference.

To make your food choices easy as you learn the principles of the Good Carbohydrate Plan, I've boiled down the characteristics of carbohydrates to Five C's. These are the characteristics you should look at in choosing your good carbohydrates.

- **Character (or Form) of the Carbohydrate**: Whole and natural is best.

- **Carbohydrate Type**: Some specific types of carbohydrates raise blood sugar more than others.

- **Content of Fiber**: In general, more is better.

- **Calorie Density**: Lower calorie density foods are good choices.

- **Composition of the Food**: Consider other factors in the food, such as fat, protein, and vitamins.

In all the discussion about the Five C's, you'll see that there are twelve insights that are useful in fine-tuning your food choices. Let's look at these Five C's and twelve insights in more detail.

First C: Character (or Form) of the Carbohydrate: Whole and Natural Is Best

Is your carbohydrate good, bad, or something in between? To find out, the first C to consider is the *character* of the carbohydrate. Is the carbohydrate in its whole, natural form? Or is it stripped of its fiber or ground up? In general, carbohydrate foods that are whole and are in their natural, intact, unprocessed form are best.

Insight (i): Whole, Intact, Plant-Based Foods Are Always the Best Source of Good Carbohydrates.

A diet based on whole, intact, plant-based foods is ideal for reducing your risk of coronary heart disease, certain cancers, strokes, diabetes, and other prevalent modern diseases. These natural plant foods have the least impact on blood sugar and insulin. Whole grains, vegetables, legumes, and fruit provide carbohydrates in a form that is ideal for slow, easy digestion and assimilation.

These foods also tend to have a very low calorie density. This means that you can eat a lot of them without gaining weight. The natural bulk effect of foods with a low calorie density makes them filling and satisfying. Because you tend to eat less of these bulky-type foods, they have less impact on your blood sugar. This is why the bulk effect is incorporated into the Carbohydrate Quotient, to help you have a more realistic appraisal of how different foods will affect your blood sugar.

Besides being ideal for controlling your blood sugar and insulin levels, plant-based carbohydrates in their *whole, natural form* are also excellent sources of vitamins, minerals, antioxidants, and other phytonutrients (plant-based nutrients) that help to protect us against the cell damage that is associated with heart disease and cancer. The high fiber content of whole, natural plant foods helps to reduce cholesterol and lower the risk for coronary heart disease.

Based on the Character/Form principle, whole, intact grains are the best choice for your grain products. When I say whole grain, this means literally the whole grain, such as a brown rice kernel or a whole wheat kernel. There are hundreds of whole grain products that may actually be from whole grains, but the grains are ground up into a fine flour. (These are also good, but they are not as good as whole, intact grains.)

Insight (ii): The Greater the Processing or Refining of a Food, the Greater the Impact on Blood Sugar and Insulin.

In general, the more processed a food, the greater its impact on blood sugar and insulin. This is true whether you process grains, fruits, or vegetables. When any of these foods are stripped of their fiber and ground up into a fine powder, what was formerly a healthy food can be detrimental to your health. In other words, these carbohydrates have lost some integrity—they have an impaired character. When you disrupt a food's natural form, you amplify its effect on blood sugar and insulin.

Insight (ii a): Grains That Are Ground Up into Flour Have a Greater Impact on Your Blood Sugar and Insulin than Whole, Unprocessed Grains.

Unfortunately, in modern America, the largest source of carbohydrates is highly refined flour products. Whole, intact grains have the least impact on your blood sugar and insulin of any form of grain. The more ground up your grains are, the more quickly they are digested and the more rapidly they will raise your blood sugar and insulin. For example, cracked wheat raises blood sugar more than whole wheat berries. Wheat flour raises blood sugar more than cracked wheat.

Because intact grains are better, white rice is a better selection than white bread—if you were to eat a processed carbohydrate. Even though the bran and germ are polished off the rice, the inner starchy white portion of the grain is still intact, so there is somewhat less impact on your blood sugar than with a finely ground flour product. Of course, brown rice or another whole grain would be a superior choice, but the example of white rice versus white bread illustrates the importance of eating your carbohydrates in their whole, intact form.

We can further see how important the natural form of the grain is when we compare white rice or brown rice flour. White rice has less impact on blood sugar and insulin than brown rice flour—even though the brown rice flour has more fiber. It appears that the grinding of the kernel into flour has a greater impact on blood sugar than the fiber content.

BLOOD SUGAR RESPONSE TO RICE AND RICE FLOUR

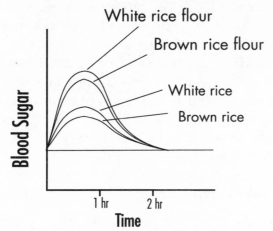

Adapted from: O'Dea, K. *Am J Clin Nutr* (1980) 33:760.

Insight (ii b): Breads Made from Coarse, Stone-Ground Flour or Cracked Grains Raises Blood Sugar Less Than Bread Made from Finely Ground Flour.

Everyone loves bread. As we see, though, the typical breads we buy in the grocery store are very refined and are not good for our health. So when you're selecting bread, just remember: the more intact the form of the grain, the better. That's why bread made from coarse, stone-ground flour or cracked grains is better for you. With these types of bread, the grains are not so finely ground. Therefore, they are more slowly digested and have less impact on your blood sugar and insulin.

There's a big difference between the different types of bread and how they will affect your blood sugar. The more finely ground the flour is, the more it raises your blood sugar. For example, the processing of wheat into fine white flour affects digestion and absorption so much that white flour raises your blood sugar a little more than even pure white sugar.

When the flour is so finely ground, there is a great deal of surface area for your digestive enzymes to quickly break the starches down into simple sugars. These sugars are then rapidly absorbed, which is why we see a dramatic rise in blood sugar and insulin with finely ground flours.

To find cracked-grain or stone-ground products, check out your local health food store; you may also find these products in some local bakeries. To make your own bread, shop for the more coarse stone-ground flour in a health food store. Stone-ground whole wheat bread has a significantly lower impact on blood sugar than regular whole wheat bread, which is reflected in their Carbohydrate Quotient values (61 for stone-ground as compared to 96 for regular whole wheat).

Besides being better for your blood sugar and insulin, breads made from coarsely ground whole grains also provide more fiber, vitamins, and minerals. As an added bonus, coarsely ground whole grain products also have a lower calorie density, making them beneficial for reaching or maintaining a healthy weight.

Insight (ii c): Whole Fruit Is a Better Choice than Fruit Juice.

When we eat foods in their whole, intact form, there are natural controls in place that help digestion to proceed at a slow, steady pace, providing us with sustained energy. The more refined the food is, the greater the impact on blood sugar and insulin. For this reason, whole fruit is a better choice than fruit juice.

Sweet, natural, whole fruit is the best way to satisfy our natural craving for the taste of sugar. The blood sugar response to fruit can be quite moderate depending on the fruit. The fiber that is present in fruit helps to slow the absorption of the natural fruit sugars. Fruit juice is devoid of fruits' natural fiber, so juice can cause a steep rise in blood sugar.

To illustrate this principle, let's compare apples with apples. In this case, let's look at whole apples, applesauce, and apple juice. Blood sugar response studies have demonstrated that carbohydrate from whole apples provoked a very modest rise in blood sugar. The same amount of carbohydrate from applesauce provoked a steeper blood sugar curve. As you might imagine, apple juice, the most processed of the three sources of carbohydrate, had the steepest and highest blood sugar curve of the three.

BLOOD SUGAR RESPONSE TO DIFFERENT FORMS OF THE SAME FOOD

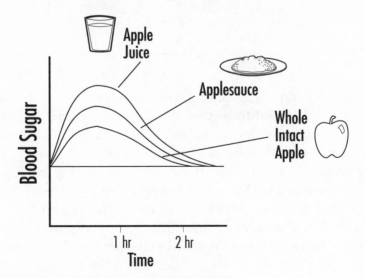

Adapted from: Haber, G.B. *Lancet* (Oct. 1977) 2(8040):679-82.

Insight (iii): The Character (or Form) of the Carbohydrate Is More
Important than Whether It Is Simple or Complex.

We should stop thinking of carbohydrates in terms of whether they are simple or complex and start thinking about the character or form of the carbohydrate. One of the most common misconceptions that I hear is that complex carbohydrates (starches) are always better than simple carbohydrates (sugars). Yet this doesn't make much sense when you look at their effect on blood sugar. If you review the table below, you will see that some refined white flour products, which are mostly complex carbohydrates, are as bad as pure table sugar in terms of their effects on blood sugar. Refined complex carbohydrates are actually worse than fruit sugar either in the form of pure fructose or in the form of whole fruit.

Food	Glycemic Index	Carbohydrate Quotient
White bread	100	100
Soda crackers	103	131
White sugar	93	115
Oatmeal	84	41
Fructose	33	41
Orange	61	48
Apple	51	42

It's actually more important to consider whether a carbohydrate is in its whole, natural form than whether it is simple or complex. Whether the carbohydrate is simple or complex is actually not very important and can be misleading in some cases.

For example, the carbohydrates in fruit come primarily from fructose, which is a natural sugar. However, when we eat fruit in its whole form, the natural fiber content, water, etc., help the sugars to be absorbed at a healthy, comfortable pace. Eating a simple—but natural—carbohydrate such as fruit would certainly be a much better choice than eating a slice of white bread, which is made of complex—but highly refined—carbohydrates.

Second C: Carbohydrate Type

The Carbohydrate Type refers to that fact that some carbohydrates have very specific effects on blood sugar and insulin. We should keep these in mind when selecting the best carbohydrates.

Insight (iv): Among Refined Flour Products, Pasta Is Better than Bread for Both Blood Sugar and Insulin Response.

Sometimes there are circumstances where the ideal good carbohydrate choices perhaps are not available to you. So if it comes down to white bread or white pasta, pasta is definitely the better choice.

Most pasta is made from refined flour. However, in terms of insulin and blood sugar response, pasta is comparable to whole grains. Certainly pasta such as spaghetti is far better for you than white bread. (Pasta has a Carbohydrate Quotient of 40, whereas white bread has a Carbohydrate Quotient of 100.) White bread raises your blood sugar and insulin a great deal more than pasta. The reason for this difference is probably because of the type and mechanics of cooked pasta. The cohesion and water retention of the cooked pasta apparently makes it digest more slowly than bread.

Of course, white flour pasta is not an ideal carbohydrate because of its character. Made from refined flour, it is deficient in natural vitamins, minerals, protein, and fiber. The best pastas to eat are those made from whole grains, such as whole wheat pastas. In either case, pasta is a pretty good choice that is better for your health than white bread products.

Insight (v): Among Starchy Vegetables, White Potatoes Induce a Moderately High Insulin Response.

White potatoes represent sort of a peculiar case in the sense that they are a natural carbohydrate in its whole form, yet they induce a relatively high glycemic and insulin response. (This does not hold true for sweet potatoes, by the way. Sweet potatoes are very moderate in their impact on blood sugar, despite their pleasant sweet taste.)

The fact that potatoes rank high on the Glycemic Index does not necessarily mean that potatoes should be considered a bad food.

Rather, we should look at all of their C's. One of the redeeming qualities of the potato is that it has a low calorie density. This means that potatoes are very bulky compared to the amount of calories and carbohydrates in them. It would take somewhere between 5.9 to 9.1 pounds of potatoes to provide one day's worth of calories—versus just 2.1 pounds of bread.

Because potatoes have a low calorie density, they satisfy your hunger more than other refined carbohydrates, such as bread. Studies on hunger satisfaction show that potatoes are more than twice as satisfying as bread. So if you eat potatoes, you will tend to eat fewer calories of them than from other foods that you might choose, such as bread or meat. Thus, the overall effect of potatoes on blood sugar and insulin will be less than what their Glycemic Index numbers suggest.

In the table below you'll notice that the Carbohydrate Quotient values for potatoes are much lower than the Glycemic Index values because of the fact that they have a low calorie density. Potato chips and French fries, of course, are exceptions because of their high fat and calorie content.

Food	Glycemic Index	Carbohydrate Quotient
Potato, new	89	43
Potato, white, baked	86	51
Potato, boiled, mashed	100	58
Potato, instant	119	65
Potato, baked (russet)	121	72
Potato, French fried	107	98
Potato, chips	77	112

Overall, the best approach to potatoes is to use them occasionally rather than on an unlimited basis. Also, different types of potatoes will have somewhat different effects on your blood sugar. The type of potatoes called new potatoes has the least effect on blood sugar. So if you choose to use potatoes frequently, try to use new potatoes.

Insight (vi): Among Different Types of White Rice, Long-grain and Basmati Rice Have Less Impact on Blood Sugar and Insulin.

Long-grain and basmati white rice are almost as good as brown rice in terms of the effects on your blood sugar (they both have Glycemic Index values of about 80). This is much better than some other varieties of white rice, which may have Glycemic Index values as high as 119. Researchers have discovered that the reason why long-grain and basmati rice are so much better than other varieties of white rice is due to its high content of a particular type of starch called amylose. Amylose is digested more slowly than other rice starches, causing less impact on blood sugar.

Most types of rice have a different starch, called amylopectin, as the primary carbohydrate. Amylopectin is a complex carbohydrate that has many branches. When you eat regular white rice, the digestive enzyme amylase goes to work on each end of the many branches of amylopectin. This causes the carbohydrate to be digested relatively quickly. With basmati rice, however, the situation is different because of its high levels of amylose. Amylose is a straight-chained carbohydrate, so the digestive enzyme amylase can only work at one end, digesting one sugar at a time. Therefore the sugars are digested more slowly, and there is less impact on blood sugar. (See Carbohydrate Family Tree Chart in Appendix B.)

Long-grain or basmati white rice, therefore, are a better choice for white rice. However, the principle of choosing grains in their whole, natural form still holds true. Any type of brown rice is still better for you because it contains valuable fiber, vitamins, and minerals.

Insight (vii): If You Do Eat Refined Sugars, You Should Eat Them with Large Amounts of Good Carbohydrates. Fructose (Fruit Sugar) Is Better for Blood Sugar and Insulin but Worse for Heart Disease.

Refined sugars are the quintessential bad carbohydrates. Refined sugar is found in table sugar and other sweeteners, as well as in all kinds of candies, soda, pastries, etc. Refined sugar is pure carbohydrate, which has had all of the other natural elements of the plant stripped away. Sugar provides only calories and is completely devoid of fiber, protein, vitamins, or any other redeeming qualities.

This is in contrast to white flour, which contains some protein and does retain a small amount of vitamins and fiber. Because sugar is pure calories, it tends to be absorbed very quickly and has the lowest calorie density of all carbohydrates.

The best way to eat refined sugar, if you are going to eat it, is to consume small amounts of sugar along with large amounts of good carbohydrates. For example, a little sugar in a salad dressing to go on a big good carbohydrate salad is a good choice for using sugar. The presence of the good carbohydrates helps to blunt the effects of the refined sugar on your blood sugar and insulin. Also, it is good to choose sweeteners that are only partially refined, such as rice syrup, barley malt, or honey. For optimal health, limit your consumption of refined sugars. Sweet whole fruit is the best choice for satisfying our desire to enjoy sweet-tasting food.

Also, be aware that different types of refined sugars can have surprisingly different effects on your blood sugar and insulin. For example, fructose (refined fruit sugar) has a Glycemic Index value of just 33. This is quite low compared to table sugar, which has a Glycemic Index value of 93.

Why such a difference? One of the reasons is that fructose must be passed through the liver before it appears in the bloodstream as serum glucose.

The downside of fructose is that despite its lower impact on blood sugar and insulin, there is good evidence that fructose causes LDL (bad cholesterol) to rise and increases the risk of coronary heart disease more than sucrose (table sugar). Thus, fructose is better than sucrose for someone with diabetes who is trying to control their blood sugar, but is worse than sucrose for someone who is having difficulty controlling cholesterol.

Third C: Content of Fiber

Insight (viii): High Fiber Foods Tend to Have Less Impact on Your Blood Sugar and Insulin.

The higher the fiber content, the less a food will impact your blood sugar and insulin. This fact holds true for grains, flour products, vegetables, and whole meals. Vegetables have the most fiber per gram of carbohydrate, so they also have the least effect on your blood sugar. Beans and fruits are the next highest fiber foods, followed by grains. These are all excellent high fiber foods to choose for your good carbohydrates.

There are comparisons that show that the fiber content only affects the blood sugar response a little bit. We see this in comparing white rice to brown rice, or white bread to whole wheat bread. The difference in blood sugar and insulin response is fairly small but is always in favor of the food that has more fiber in it. This is because the fiber helps to slow the absorption of the carbohydrates.

Food	Carbohydrate Quotient
White bread	100
Whole wheat bread	96
Oat bran bread	73
White rice	80
Long-grain white rice	52
Basmati white rice	52
Brown rice	51

Even though the difference in effects on your blood sugar are fairly small between whole grain flour products and refined flour products, you are still far better off choosing the whole grain product. Whole grain products provide more vitamin B complex, vitamin E, and other nutrients that come along with the fiber in grains. In addition, high fiber foods hold on to water in the digestive tract better than low fiber food. The presence of fiber improves digestion and increases your feeling of satiety. In this way, high fiber foods help to curb your appetite, which in turn helps you to naturally control your blood sugar and weight.

Fourth C: Calorie Density

Insight (ix): Foods with a Lower Calorie Density Are Better for Controlling Blood Sugar and Insulin.

As we mentioned earlier in this chapter, calorie density simply refers to how many calories are present compared to the weight of the food. If a food has a lot of calories compared to its weight, then it is a high calorie density food. Pure oil is the highest calorie density food you could eat. In other words, fat or oil with nine calories per gram has more calories per weight of food than any other food, with nine calories in every gram. Pure sugar is another food that is very dense in calories, with four calories in every gram.

The calorie density of foods is important because if a food is bulky but has few calories, you will tend to eat fewer calories from that food. After all, your stomach can only hold so much food, so if you fill it up with low calorie density foods, you will have taken in fewer calories and fewer carbohydrates, and there will be less impact on your blood sugar and insulin.

For example, sweet potatoes have a much lower calorie density with just one calorie per gram than say, a candy bar that has about five calories per gram. Because sweet potatoes are rather bulky for the number of calories in them, naturally you will eat fewer calories and carbohydrates from a sweet potato than from a candy bar. Because the calorie density affects how many carbohydrates you will consume from a particular food in a real life situation, low calorie density foods tend to have less of an impact on your blood sugar. This is why calorie density is factored into the Carbohydrate Quotient.

The calorie density principle is easy to remember if you realize that it simply reinforces the other principles you have already learned. Whole, natural plant foods, such as vegetables, beans, fruits, and grains are all low calorie density foods. A rule of thumb is to look for foods that are less than 130 calories per 100 grams (3.5 ounces). Another way of looking at this is through the concept of Mass Index of food. This is explained further in Chapter 8, where I discuss how low calorie density foods help to induce natural weight loss.

Fifth C: Composition of the Food

Insight (x): High Protein Foods Raise Insulin Levels Even Though They Don't Raise Blood Sugar.

One of the biggest myths that has come out of the high protein diet books is that protein doesn't affect your insulin. The popular trend is to tell people to eat meat instead of carbohydrates, because carbohydrates cause a rise in insulin. This is a half-baked recommendation that can easily mislead you into making misguided food choices.

The idea that protein foods don't affect insulin is based on a simplistic view of only looking at how a food measures on the Glycemic Index, rather than looking at the whole effect of the food. For example, since meats consist almost exclusively of protein and fat, they don't cause much of a rise in blood sugar. However, meats do cause a distinct rise in blood insulin—even more than some carbohydrates, including pasta. The insulin response index shows that *beef raises insulin 27 percent more than pasta does for the same number of calories*. This is because protein stimulates the release of insulin even though it doesn't raise blood sugar.

To conclude that beef doesn't affect insulin levels just because it doesn't have any carbohydrates, is simply wrong. Furthermore, beef has a high calorie density, which means you are likely to eat more calories from beef at one sitting. This makes beef's likely effects on insulin even worse. Of course, animal products also add a lot of cholesterol and saturated fat to the diet, increasing your risk of heart disease.

Insight (xi): Foods with a Sour Flavor (a High Acid Content) Are Absorbed More Slowly and Induce a Lower Blood Sugar and Insulin Response.

The acid content of food is useful in considering its effects on blood sugar. Acid in food is what gives it a sour or tart flavor. Sourdough bread, vinegar, and lemons are examples of acidic foods. Foods that are acidic tend to be absorbed more slowly and have less impact on your blood sugar and insulin. This is probably because acid in the stomach slows the emptying of the stomach's contents into the small intestine. The small intestine is where most of the digestion and absorption of food takes place. So when food is more acidic, the digestion of its carbohydrates is delayed.

Because of its acidity, sourdough is a good choice for bread. It has a surprisingly moderate impact on blood sugar and insulin. The Carbohydrate Quotient for sourdough bread is 74, which is better than most breads, including white bread and commercially processed whole wheat bread. The acidity of sourdough bread comes from the propionic acid and lactic acid that is produced during the fermenting process. These acids are also what make the bread taste sour.

If you're choosing between two similar foods, it's useful to know that the food that has more of a tart or sour flavor will probably have less of an impact on your blood sugar. (You can also take advantage of this fact by adding sour flavoring to your food, such as lemon juice or a vinegar-based dressing.)

Insight (xii): High Fat Foods Induce a Lower Blood Sugar Response but Raise Cholesterol Levels, Insulin Resistance, and Calorie Intake.

This fact is another reason why relying exclusively on the Glycemic Index can really lead you astray in your attempts to select healthy foods. Fats tend to slow blood sugar absorption, so fatty foods tend to score lower on the Glycemic Index. Of course, this doesn't mean that those foods are necessarily good for you. In fact, these low Glycemic Index foods are sometimes anything but healthy.

For example, a chocolate candy bar (because of its high fat content) has a lower Glycemic Index than brown rice. If you abandoned your common sense and followed the Glycemic Index—as suggested in some diet books—you would conclude that the candy bar is a better choice.

Of course, fatty foods are also high in calorie density. They don't fill you up very much for the amount of calories they contain, so you tend to eat a lot more calories from them. You can easily get a lot of calories—both carbohydrates and fat—by filling up your stomach with candy bars. Obviously, candy bars, cookies, ice cream, and other fatty foods with fairly low Glycemic Indexes are not good carbohydrate choices.

Since my Carbohydrate Quotient takes the calorie density of foods into account, the numbers more accurately reflect the foods' healthfulness. However, even the Carbohydrate Quotient is limited in its application—there are foods that have a good Carbohydrate Quotient value, such as soybeans, that you should eat only occasionally due to their high fat content. Overall, if you stick to plant-based foods in their whole, natural form, you will be well on your way to choosing from the many delicious varieties of good carbohydrates.

Just Remember the Five C's

When selecting good carbohydrates, the most important principle to remember is the first: choose whole carbohydrate foods in their natural, unprocessed form. Then use the rest of the Five C's along with

the twelve insights that go along with them to make a quick evaluation of any food you choose. When necessary, you can refer to the
Carbohydrate Quotient at the back of the book. These tools will
help you to choose the good carbohydrates that you can use to
replace the bad carbohydrates and the rest of the junk foods in your
diet. In doing so, you can begin to create a delicious Good
Carbohydrate Plan with the wide variety that suits your taste.

CHAPTER 7

The Good Carbohydrate Plan Pyramid

Good carbohydrates are the foundation of the healthy diet that has sustained humanity for millennia. In modern times, the scientific and medical literature has simply rediscovered what ancient cultures have known all along. Among the medicine men of the ancient Native American tribes there is a wise saying that states: If you want to regain health, "return to the arms of Mother Corn." In other words, for good health, choose the whole, natural foods that Mother Nature provides. By choosing good carbohydrates as the primary source of your calories, and supplementing these with other health-promoting foods, you will be sure to supply your body with a nutritious array of vitamins, minerals, phytonutrients, and fiber.

Both national and international organizations use the pyramid as a way to convey dietary recommendations in the United States. Because the concept of the pyramid as a guide to eating was widely recognized as useful, I started with this concept as well. For the Good Carbohydrate Plan, I created a pyramid that will make it easy for you to get started based on the latest nutritional science. The Good Carbohydrate Plan Pyramid reflects as closely as possible an optimally healthy diet.

THE GOOD CARBOHYDRATE PYRAMID

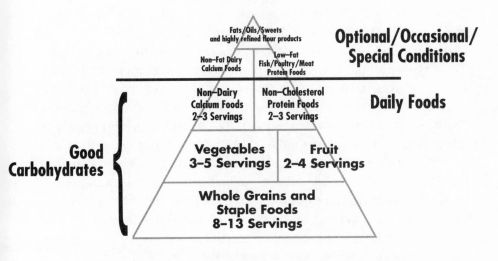

© Shintani 1993, 2001

THE FIVE C'S AND THE CARBOHYDRATE QUOTIENT

The Five C's of Good Carbohydrates and the Carbohydrate Quotient make it easy for you to identify good carbohydrates within each category of food. In the description below, I have evaluated foods for liberal use, moderate use, and rare use based on the Five C's and the Carbohydrate Quotient. The Carbohydrate Quotient numbers are listed for those foods that have these numbers available.

Remember that the numbers are not the last word and that the Five C's and your common sense are a better way to evaluate foods individually. This is why the foods may not be ranked in order of their Carbohydrate Quotient in the tables in this chapter. A food that has a low Carbohydrate Quotient may be considered less desirable because of its fat content, its low fiber content, its degree of refinement, or other considerations based on the Five C's method of evaluation.

WHOLE GRAINS AND STAPLE FOODS ARE THE PRIMARY SOURCE OF CALORIES

The Whole Grains and Staple Foods Group forms the base of the Good Carbohydrate Plan Pyramid. I recommend eating 8 to 13 servings from this group every day. A serving in this group is one-half cup of cooked grain, one ounce of dry cereal, or one slice of bread. The largest number of servings are in this group because the foods in the other groups, such as fruit and vegetables, don't provide enough calories. Also, on the Good Carbohydrate Plan, many high calorie foods, such as high-fat animal products, cheeses, oils, and sugars are minimized. Our primary source of calories, as reflected in the Good Carbohydrate Plan Pyramid, should come from the Whole Grains and Staple Foods Group. This reflects scientific recommendations as well as the dietary patterns of people who have remained free of heart disease for generations on a traditional high carbohydrate diet.

A serving size in this category is one-half cup of cooked grain or pasta, one slice of whole grain bread, or two ounces of a starchy staple food such as sweet potato. This is just a measurement and not meant as a limitation. For instance, you may choose to eat three to four servings of brown rice at one meal, and this is okay. The good carbohydrates are the whole foods that are healthiest for you to choose. The Intermediate Carbohydrate foods are somewhat more refined or have a likelihood of raising blood sugar and insulin higher than good carbohydrates, so they should be used less often. Here are some foods for you to choose:

Whole Grains

Good Carbohydrates (Liberal Use)		Intermediate Carbohydrates (Moderate Use)		Bad Carbohydrates (Rare Use)	
	CQ		CQ		CQ
Whole barley	24	Whole wheat pasta	37	French baguette	96
Bulgur wheat	39				
Whole oats (oatmeal)	41	Wheat (white) pasta	44	White bread	100

Good Carbohydrates (Liberal Use)		Intermediate Carbohydrates (Moderate Use)		Bad Carbohydrates (Rare Use)	
	CQ		CQ		CQ
Buckwheat (Kasha)	46	Cream of wheat cereal	48	White flour bagels	105
Corn	49	Basmati white rice	52	Cornflakes	124
Whole wheat cereal	48	Long-grain white rice	52	Soda crackers	131
Brown rice	51	Stone ground whole wheat bread	61	Doughnut	138
		Whole wheat flat bread	72		
		Sourdough bread	74		
		White rice	77		
		Pita bread	78		

Other Grains Without a Carbohydrate Quotient Rating (categorized based on the 5 C's)

Amaranth	Buckwheat pasta (soba)	White flour baked goods
Basmati brown rice	Whole wheat bagels	White flour rolls
Quinoa	Whole wheat chapati	White flour tortillas
Rye	Whole wheat tortillas	Corn tortillas
Wheat berries		

Good Whole Grains

Barley has the lowest Carbohydrate Quotient number among all the grains for which information is available. All whole grains qualify as good carbohydrates such as brown rice, whole wheat berries, whole oats, bulgur wheat, kasha (buckwheat), amaranth, and quinoa. Remember that pressure cooking reduces the Glycemic Index numbers for rice and presumably could do the same for all whole grains.

Good Rice

Of course, brown rice is better than white rice because of its whole, intact character (the First C). However, if you are going to choose white rice, the best rice is basmati rice and other long-grain white rice, apparently because of the type of carbohydrate in them (the Second C). Long-grain brown rice would be even better. Surprisingly, converted rice (parboiled) has a lower blood sugar response than regular cooked rice. This may be because parboiling involves pressure cooking prior to milling into white rice. Asian-style rice is typified by Calrose® rice, which has a relatively high Glycemic Index. However, its Carbohydrate Quotient is moderate at 77 because of its calorie density.

Good Pasta

If you have a choice between white bread, white rice, and white pasta, the pasta is the preferred choice because of its moderate blood sugar effects. Whole wheat pasta is even better. However, whole wheat pastas must be purchased fresh because the oil from the germ of the wheat in the pasta can go rancid if it sits on a shelf for too long.

Good Bread

None of the breads are considered ideal. However, if you do use them, the best breads are those that are made up of minimally ground grains or flour. Some examples of healthier breads and their Carbohydrate Quotient numbers are stone ground whole wheat bread (61), mixed grain bread (68), whole grain pumpernickel (71), and oat bran bread (73). If you are going to use white flour breads, consider using pita bread (78), or sourdough bread (74). Flatbreads (chapatis or tortillas) are also a good choice, but be aware that tortillas may contain a lot of fat if they are prepared with lard or oil, so choose tortillas that have less than three grams of fat per tortilla.

Good Cereals

The best breakfast cereals are cooked whole grains such as oatmeal, cream of wheat, kasha, barley, and brown rice. Instant cooked cereals are a mixed bag. Some are almost as good as whole-grain cereals, others quite a bit worse. For example, instant oatmeal is almost as good as cooked whole oats. However, instant rice raises blood sugar nearly twice as high as brown rice.

As for ready-to-eat cereals, most of them are made of white flour and loaded with sugar and are poor choices for any meal. The ready-to-eat cereals that are moderate in their effect on blood sugar are the bran cereals such as "All Bran." There is also some redeeming value in using vitamin fortified cereals despite their relatively high Carbohydrate Quotient numbers.

Staple Root Vegetables

Good Carbohydrates (Liberal Use)				Intermediate Carbohydrates (Moderate Use)	
	CQ		CQ		CQ
New potato	49	Taro	50	Baking Potato	74
Sweet potato	49	White potato	51		
Yams	49				

Of the staple root vegetables, potatoes have a fairly wide range of Carbohydrate Quotient values. Surprisingly, sweet potatoes have slightly less of an impact on blood sugar than regular potatoes. New potatoes are the preferred potato for regular use. The firmer white potato is better than the baking potatoes such as russet potatoes.

THE VEGETABLE GROUP IS FOR GREAT HEALTH

The next largest group in the Good Carbohydrate Plan Pyramid is the Vegetable Group. I recommend eating three to five servings from this group every day. A serving is one cup of raw leafy vegetable or a half cup of cooked greens or other vegetables. These serving sizes are a measurement and not meant as a limitation. For instance, eating a cup of green beans at one meal would be okay—it's two of your five servings. Eating more than five servings of vegetables in a day is also okay.

The Vegetable Group includes vegetables of all kinds, such as lettuce, squash, onions, green beans, radishes, zucchini, and tomatoes, as well as others. (Tomatoes are technically a fruit, but are placed in this section because of their low sugar content.) High starch vegetables such as corn and potatoes are included in the Whole Grain and Staple Root Vegetables Group because they have traditionally been used as staple foods. Vegetables such as broccoli, cabbage, green leaf lettuce, and spinach are also listed with the Non-Dairy Calcium Foods Group.

Vegetables are very high in fiber and relatively low in calorie content. Vegetables also provide a wide range of nutrients that are required for great health, such as vitamins, minerals, antioxidants, and a wide array of phytochemicals that fight heart disease, diabetes, certain cancers, and a number of other chronic diseases. Some of your choices are:

Good Carbohydrates (Liberal Use)			Intermediate Carbohydrates (Moderate Use)
Artichokes	Garlic	Radishes	Parsnips
Asparagus	Ginger root	Shallots	
Bamboo shoots	Green beans	Spinach	
Burdock root	Green leaf lettuce	Summer squash	
Broccoli	Kale	Sweet peppers	
Cabbage	Kohlrabi	Seaweed	
Carrots	Leeks	Tomatoes	
Cauliflower	Lotus root	Turnips	
Celery	Mushrooms	Water chestnuts	
Chinese	Mustard greens	Watercress	
cabbage	Okra	Winter squash	
Cilantro	Onions	Zucchini	
Collard greens	Parsley		
Cucumber	Pumpkin		

THE FRUIT GROUP: FIBER, VITAMINS, AND ANTIOXIDANTS

I recommend two to four servings of fruit per day, preferably in season and from your locality. One serving would be one medium fruit or a half cup of chopped, cooked, or canned fruit. Whole fruits provide vitamins and antioxidants and they are also a good source of fiber. If you are sensitive to carbohydrates, you should choose fruits that have lower (i.e., better) numbers on the Carbohydrate Quotient, otherwise you might see a rise in your triglyceride levels. This section recommends whole fruit and does not include fruit juices because fruit juice carbohydrates, devoid of the natural buffer of fiber, are absorbed more quickly. Here are some of the fruit choices:

Good Carbohydrates (Liberal Use)				Intermediate Carbohydrates (Moderate Use)	
	CQ		CQ		CQ
Grapefruit	25	Blueberries	unavailable	Kiwi	62
Cherries	27	Lemons	unavailable	Papaya	62
Plums	28	Melons	unavailable	Apricots	66
Peaches	31	Nectarines	unavailable	Mangoes	67
Apples	42	Raspberries	unavailable	Cantaloupes	68
Pears	43	Strawberries	unavailable	Bananas	70
Oranges	48	Tangerines	unavailable	Watermelons	73
Grapes	53			Pineapple	75

THE NON-DAIRY CALCIUM GROUP PROVIDES ABUNDANT CALCIUM

The Non-Dairy Calcium Group overlaps with the Vegetable Group. As with the Vegetable Group, a serving is a half cup of cooked or one cup of raw vegetable. It is an important part of the Good Carbohydrate Plan Pyramid because it ensures a good supply of calcium. For those who want to include dairy, I suggest it as an optional or occasional food. The Non-Dairy Calcium Group is important in preventing osteoporosis, which has become all too common in this country.

High Dairy Intake Associated with More Osteoporosis

When we talk about the importance of calcium and the prevention of osteoporosis, many people ask, why a Non-Dairy Calcium Group? Aren't we supposed to eat more dairy to get plenty of calcium?

Considering all the research on osteoporosis, the answer is that there is still a serious question as to whether dairy actually helps to prevent osteoporosis.

DAIRY VS. OSTEOPOROSIS

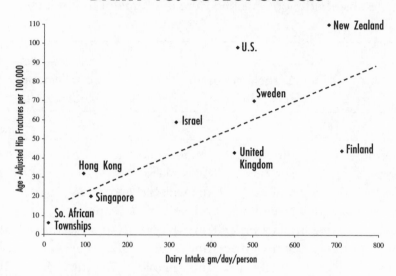

Cummings, Kelwey, Nevitt, O'Dowd. *Epidemiologic Reviews* (1985) 7:178.

It is of considerable concern that the populations who consume the most dairy actually have the most osteoporosis. A thorough review of scientific literature conducted at Harvard University and published in the *American Journal of Clinical Nutrition* concludes: "Studies have not supported a protective role of dairy product consumption against fracture." They hasten to point out that calcium may prevent osteoporosis but that the evidence did not support the protective effect of dairy. A number of studies suggest that the high animal protein content of dairy actually causes a loss of calcium in the urine, which may negate the positive effect of the calcium present.

The other important reason for limiting dairy intake in the Good Carbohydrate Plan Pyramid is that dairy, with the exception of skim milk products, can be very high in fat. Cheddar cheese, for example, derives 74 percent of its calories from fat. It is also high in saturated fats. Even dairy that is 2 percent fat is not actually a low fat product, with 35 percent of its calories coming from fat (and much of it is saturated fat).

Another reason for being cautious about dairy is its potential for causing allergies. Numerous studies suggest that dairy is one of the most common causes of allergies in this country. There is even some concern that dairy protein may be associated with Type I diabetes because of the autoimmune response to dairy protein.

Finally, most people in this world are lactose intolerant as adults. In other words, they cannot handle milk sugar after childhood. Lactose intolerance leads to stomach discomfort, gas, and in some individuals, diarrhea. Estimates suggest that it is less common in Caucasians and very common among all other ethnic groups. One survey indicates that in North America, it affects 21 percent of Caucasian Americans, 51 percent of Hispanic Americans, 75 percent of African Americans, and 79 percent of Native Americans. Estimates in Asia, South America, and Africa vary widely with a range of up to 100 percent of people, depending on the group.

In order to avoid these potential problems with dairy that I have described, I have replaced the dairy group with a group of foods that are non-dairy sources of calcium. But, be realistic with yourself. Eating a large amount of dark leafy greens on a daily basis is not always practical. If you know you won't be eating enough greens for your calcium, consider taking a calcium supplement with the advice of your physician.

Dark Leafy Greens Are the Best Source of Calcium

Dark leafy greens such as kale, broccoli, collard greens, watercress, Chinese cabbage, and sea vegetables (seaweed) are actually better sources of calcium than dairy if you factor in absorption. Only 32 percent of the calcium from milk is absorbed whereas 67 percent of the calcium from these vegetable products is absorbed. The result is more calcium actually gets to your cells from one serving of dark leafy greens than from one serving of milk.

Sea vegetables, which are an excellent source of calcium, are probably one of the most underrated, underutilized foods in the United States. Sea vegetables were part of the traditional diets, not only in Asia and the Pacific, but also in Ireland and in the Americas (for the Native

Americans living on the coasts). The Calcium Table below gives examples of high calcium greens, including sea vegetables.

THE CALCIUM TABLE*
Comparison of calcium from one cup of selected foods[a]

Food	Portion 1 cup (gm)	Calcium (mg)	Fraction Absorbed[b]	Estimated Absorption (mg)	Loss Due to Protein
Kelp (konbu)	144	242	0.59[c]	142.8	
Wakame (seaweed)	144	216	0.59[c]	127.4	
Watercress	144	169	0.67	113.2	
Kale (from frozen)	130	178	0.588	104.7	
Turnip greens	144	198	0.516	102.2	
2% Milk	244	297	0.321	95.3[d]	Significant[d]
Broccoli	155	178	0.526	93.6	
Tofu	126	258	0.310	80.9[d]	Significant[d]
Mustard greens	144	128	0.578	74.0	
Spinach	180	244	0.051	12.4[e]	

[a]Greens are cooked and seaweed is raw in this table.

[b]Absorption figures from Weaver and Plawecki. Some of this comes from animal data.

[c]Seaweed absorbability estimated from an average of figures for land greens.

[d]Calcium balance is less than absorption figure due to calcium loss resulting from high protein content in this food.

[e]This figure is low due to high oxalate content of the food.

*From Dr. Shintani's Eat More, Weigh Less® Cookbook, 1995, p. 263.

All the high calcium vegetables may be used liberally. I recommend you eat at least two to three one cup servings per day. Some examples of high calcium vegetables are listed below.

Good Carbohydrates
(Liberal Use)

		Sea Vegetables
Broccoli	Green onions	Dulse
Brussels sprouts	Kale	Hijiki
Cabbage	Mustard greens	Kelp
Choi sum (Chinese greens)	Spinach	Konbu
Collard greens	Swiss chard	Wakame
Edible Hibiscus leaves	Turnip greens	
Endive	Watercress	
Green leaf lettuce		

THE NON-CHOLESTEROL PROTEIN GROUP MINIMIZES FAT AND CHOLESTEROL

The purpose of this food group is to ensure an adequate amount of good quality protein while minimizing the risk of coronary heart disease. A serving in this group is a half cup of cooked legumes. One of the most damaging components of the modern American diet is the high consumption of protein from animal sources. In Chapter 14, I describe the Thirteen Perils of Protein, explaining why animal protein should be minimized.

The most important reason for limiting animal protein intake is the potential risk of coronary heart disease that comes with eating it. If protein comes from animal sources, it typically comes along with a lot of cholesterol and saturated fat. Remember that all animal flesh (including poultry and seafood) has cholesterol in it, while plants have none. For example, a 3.5-ounce portion of beef contains about 90 mg of cholesterol, with 65 percent of its calories coming from fat (much of it saturated fat).

When you hear that you should eat more chicken and fish, they never tell you that 3.5 ounces of chicken has 88 mg of cholesterol and the same portion of fish has 70 to 80 mg of cholesterol. Although most cuts of chicken have less fat than beef, chicken is still high in fat. For example, a chicken thigh derives 58 percent of its calories from fat. Even if you take the skin off, the remaining skinless chicken thigh is still 49 percent fat.

For optimal health, I have moved meat, poultry, fish, and eggs to the apex of the pyramid, indicating that these foods are optional and should be minimized. Since all flesh and animal products have cholesterol, and most meats and poultry have large amounts of fat and saturated fat, these foods should be eaten in small amounts, if at all.

Plant Sources Provide an Abundant Supply of Healthy Protein

The Good Carbohydrate Plan Pyramid emphasizes the use of non-cholesterol proteins. This reflects the traditional diet of healthy cultures as well as the latest nutritional science. Non-cholesterol sources of protein include beans and legumes, as well as nuts and seeds.

Is vegetable protein adequate? This is a question that people commonly ask. For years you have been told that plant protein is inferior to animal protein because of the mix of amino acids. However, the American Dietetic Association confirmed many years ago that plant protein is every bit as good as animal protein. Unfortunately, their finding has received little press.

Protein from plant sources is not only adequate in total grams, but also provides all the essential amino acids in sufficient quantity if you take in enough of these foods to sustain you for a day. The only way to be protein deficient while eating a plant-based diet is to severely restrict the amount of food you eat. If you have any question about the adequacy of plant-based protein, please see the chart on proteins and amino acids in Chapter 14, page 325.

Healthy Protein Choices

I recommend that you eat two to three half cup servings of non-cholesterol protein, cooked beans and legumes, every day to replace meat or flesh foods. You may eat as much as you want of the foods that fall in this Non-Cholesterol Protein Foods Group. Here are some examples of good carbohydrate, non-cholesterol protein choices:

Good Carbohydrates (Liberal Use)		Intermediate Carbohydrates (Moderate Use)		High Fat Protein Foods (Rare Use)	
	CQ		CQ		CQ
Butter beans	25	Soybeans	19	Peanuts	31
Kidney beans	27	Broad beans	59		
Lentils	28	Fava beans	62		
Lima beans	29				
Chickpeas (garbanzo beans)	30				
Black beans	30				
Split peas	31				
Green peas	38				
Black-eyed peas	39				
Navy beans	40				
Pinto beans	40				
CQ Unavailable		CQ Unavailable		CQ Unavailable	
Azuki beans, cranberry beans, great northern beans, mung beans, pigeon peas, pink beans, red beans, and white beans		Tofu		Cashews, pumpkin seeds, sesame seeds, sunflower seeds	

THE TIP OF THE PYRAMID: OPTIONAL FOODS

I have divided the smallest group in the Good Carbohydrate Plan Pyramid, the Optional Foods, into three sections: Non-Fat Dairy Calcium Foods, Low Fat Fish/Poultry/Meat Protein Foods, and Fats/Oils/Sweets and Highly Refined Flour Products.

Low Fat Fish/Poultry/Meat Protein Foods

The traditional cultures around the world who eat no animal products or very small amounts of animal products have low rates of the
chronic diseases that we suffer from today in America. The Asian-
style diets include about an ounce of animal products per day.
Similarly, the ideal Mediterranean-style diet is very low in animal
flesh intake, limited to roughly one ounce per day. This low intake
of animal products is associated with lower rates of chronic diseases
and longer life spans.

Animal products are generally high in cholesterol. All animal
flesh has cholesterol whether it is lean or fatty. For those who think
the best diet is the Paleolithic-style diet—the diet of the Stone Age
cave man—please realize that even the Stone Age cave man's diet
was primarily plant-based and derived most of its calories from
good carbohydrates. Also, the cave man's intake of animal product
was up to 30 percent of calories, but the fat profile of the animals
was quite different than today. We can estimate the fat of wild game
in ancient times by looking at the fat content of modern wild animals. Modern wild game has a fat content ranging from 7 percent fat
in moose, and 18 percent fat in deer to 24 percent fat in wild boar.
An average cut of commercially raised beef or pork is about 65 percent fat. In addition, wild game contains a reasonable amount of
Omega 3 fatty acids while commercially-raised animals have virtually none.

If you are interested in animal protein, you should find animal
products that are low in total fat and low in saturated fat, but which
have some Omega 3 fatty acids, as are found in wild game. If you
must eat animal flesh, seafood is likely to be the least harmful
because, typically, it has a relatively low fat profile and does have
the less harmful Omega 3 fatty acids in them. You might look at animal products in this way. The animals that feed in the wild tend to
be less harmful as food because they have less fat and a better profile of fatty acids, probably because they eat more plant material.
Precursors to Omega 3 fatty acids are found in chloroplast membranes of plants. The animals that are fed artificially in commercial
settings have less access to plants, don't exercise as much, may be
injected with hormones, and wind up being obese animals. When

you eat such animals, you risk being obese yourself. Thus, to minimize the potential risk from the consumption of animal flesh, seafood is better than commercially fed animals.

If you choose to use animal products, I recommend no more than seven ounces of animal flesh per week. Again, choose those that are low in fat and saturated fat, and have the least chance of contamination with pesticides. It is also preferable that the meat be broiled, roasted, steamed, grilled or stir-fried in vegetable broth, but not in oil.

Non-Fat Dairy Calcium Foods

Despite the wide promotion of dairy in this country, I do not believe that cow's milk is a natural food for adult humans. For this reason I list dairy as an optional food. About 70 percent of the world does not use dairy. In addition, looking at nature, no other species on Earth consumes dairy as adults, nor regularly consumes the milk of another species.

As I have described in the Non-Dairy Calcium section of the pyramid, plant sources of calcium such as dark leafy greens and sea vegetables are actually a superior source of calcium. Consider where the cow gets her calcium. She gets it from eating greens, not from drinking milk.

However, the use of dairy is very common in the United States. It has been part of the traditional diet of a number of cultures, and it is difficult to avoid in modern diets. I suggest that dairy be considered a food to be used on occasion, if desired. In the healthy Asian-style diet, no dairy is included. In the healthy Mediterranean-style diet, dairy is included in small amounts.

If you use dairy, choose non-fat dairy products made from skim milk. Whole milk contains almost as much fat (55 percent) and saturated fat as meat, and contains slightly more cholesterol. Cheese, for example, is typically around 70 percent fat. Cheddar cheese is 74 percent fat and American cheese is slightly higher. Even 2 percent milk derives 35 percent of its calories from fat (much of it saturated fat). And remember, if you are not getting calcium somewhere in your diet, consult your physician and consider taking a calcium supplement.

Fats and Oils: Weighing the Evidence

Fats/Oils/Sweets and Highly Refined Flour Products are the last category of optional foods. Fats and oils include lard, vegetable oil, olive oil, shortening, butter, margarine, mayonnaise, and salad dressings (except fat free dressings). The use of these products is one of the more controversial debates regarding a healthy diet. The general consensus is that saturated fats promote heart disease. The role of polyunsaturated and monounsaturated fats is less clear; it is debated whether these oils promote heart disease (although less than saturated fat), have no effect on heart disease, or are protective against heart disease. Heart disease is not the only issue, however. Epidemiological evidence, as well as some clinical evidence, suggests that fats and oils increase the risk of obesity and certain cancers. Animal studies suggest that polyunsaturated fats are more likely to promote cancer than other types of fat.

Some experts advocate a very low fat diet such as an Asian-style diet, which is demonstrated in clinical trials to actually reverse heart disease. Other experts suggest that a Mediterranean-style diet is better, with moderate use of monounsaturated fats, especially those from olive oil. The Good Carbohydrate Plan takes the view that this is a point of individualization. Some individuals can handle the higher fat intake and have no trouble with weight. Still others fare better on a very low fat diet and see a better cholesterol profile, as well as better weight control. How to individualize the Good Carbohydrate Plan to fit your needs is described in Chapter 13.

Avoid Added Fats and Oils for Better Health

Fats and oils have the highest concentration of calories of any food and, in general, fats contribute to weight gain. Fats and oils all have nine calories per gram—the highest caloric density of any food. This includes the so-called healthy oils, such as olive oil and macadamia nut oil. Thus, any fats or oils, whether they are good fats or bad fats, all tend to contribute to obesity. It is also important to remember that fats and oils may contribute to insulin resistance. It's wise to avoid added fats and oils for the purpose of controlling your weight, blood sugar, and insulin.

To stay clear of added fats, you should also avoid butter, margarine, cream sauces, salad dressings with oil, nut butters, mayonnaise, deep-fried foods, frostings made with partially hydrogenated fats, pastries that have oil or lard in them, and other refined oils.

If you're in the category of people who don't have a weight problem, then you may do reasonably well using what I call good fats or good oils in moderate amounts. If you use oil at all, I recommend extra virgin olive oil, macadamia nut oil or canola oil. These oils are considered healthier because they are high in monounsaturated fat. For more detail about fats and oils, see Chapter 15.

Sugar: A Little Goes a Long Way

Sugar, used in small amounts, can be part of a healthy Good Carbohydrate Plan. Although refined sugars are bad carbohydrates, when consumed along with plenty of good carbohydrates, the effects of sugar are diluted. Sugar can be used to help enhance the taste of a good carbohydrate meal. For example, a little sugar in a non-fat dressing is a good trade-off to make good carbohydrates more tasty. It's okay to eat a little sugar along with other foods that are high in fiber.

When choosing the type of sugar you use, remember that the best source of sweet taste is whole fruit. When using whole fruit isn't practical, consider using pureed fruit or fruit preserves with no added sugar. As with flour, the greater the processing, the higher the insulin response becomes. Rice syrup and maple syrup, for example, are healthier alternatives to white sugar because they are not as processed.

When using pure sugar, remember that it takes less fructose for the same sweetness as table sugar. Whether this translates into a reduction in risk of obesity or coronary disease remains to be seen. However, there seems to be some justification to prefer fructose to table sugar when given a choice. See Chapter 11 for more details on using sweeteners.

Enjoy!

CHAPTER 8

Losing Weight the Good Carbohydrate Way

If you are overweight, you are not alone. Obesity has reached epidemic proportions in the United States. According to the Centers for Disease Control (CDC) in Atlanta, Georgia, obesity rates have risen every year for the past 15 years. The Good Carbohydrate Plan can help you to lose excess weight—you don't need to be one of the obesity statistics.

Today, obesity is defined by using a number called the Body Mass Index or BMI. To find out your BMI, simply look for your height and weight on the BMI table in this chapter. BMI is calculated by taking your weight in kilograms divided by your height in meters squared. To find your weight in kilograms, just take your weight in pounds and divide by 2.2. To find your height in meters, take your height in inches, multiply by 2.54 and then divide by 100. The BMI makes it possible to set single numbers as the standard for what is obese, overweight, and healthy, rather than having to set a different standard for every height.

A BMI of 25 or higher is considered overweight and a BMI of 30 or higher is considered obese. These numbers are based on statistics, which show an increased risk for chronic diseases such as heart disease and diabetes in people who have BMI numbers in these ranges. Based on your own BMI, you can determine what your weight loss goals should be.

WEIGH YOUR RISK WITH BMI

BMI	20	24	25	26	27	28	29	30	31	32	33	34	35	36	37	38	39	40
Height	Desirable		Overweight					Obese										
4'10"	95	115	119	124	129	134	138	143	149	153	158	163	167	173	176	182	187	191
4'11"	99	119	124	128	133	138	143	148	154	158	164	169	173	179	184	189	194	198
5'0"	102	123	128	133	138	143	148	153	159	164	169	175	179	185	190	195	200	204
5'1"	106	127	132	137	143	148	153	158	165	169	175	180	185	191	196	202	207	217
5'2"	109	131	136	142	147	153	158	164	170	175	181	186	191	197	203	209	214	218
5'3"	113	135	141	146	152	158	163	169	175	181	187	192	197	204	209	215	221	225
5'4"	116	140	145	151	157	163	169	174	181	187	193	199	204	210	216	222	228	232
5'5"	120	144	150	156	162	168	174	180	187	193	199	205	210	217	223	229	235	240
5'6"	124	148	155	161	167	173	179	186	192	199	205	211	216	224	230	236	242	247
5'7"	127	153	159	166	172	178	185	191	198	205	211	218	223	230	237	243	249	255
5'8"	131	158	164	171	177	184	190	197	204	211	218	224	230	237	244	250	257	262
5'9"	135	162	169	176	182	189	196	203	210	217	224	231	236	244	251	258	265	270
5'10"	139	167	174	181	188	195	202	207	216	223	230	237	243	251	259	265	272	278
5'11"	143	172	179	186	193	200	208	215	222	230	237	244	250	259	266	272	280	286
6'0"	147	177	184	191	199	206	213	221	228	236	244	251	258	266	273	281	288	294
6'1"	151	182	189	197	204	212	219	227	236	243	251	258	265	273	281	289	296	302
6'2"	155	187	194	202	210	218	225	233	241	250	258	265	272	281	289	297	304	311
6'3"	160	192	200	208	216	224	232	240	248	256	264	272	279	289	297	305	313	319
6'4"	164	197	205	213	221	230	238	246	254	263	271	280	287	296	304	313	321	328

*Weight in pounds.

THE AMERICAN PARADOX

The relationship between obesity and fat intake is well documented. Health organizations such as the American Heart Association, the National Cancer Institute, the National Heart, Lung and Blood Institute, and the Surgeon General's office have all recommended a reduction in fat intake. Recently, some have questioned the effectiveness of this recommendation, because obesity continues to increase in America, while paradoxically, the percentage of dietary fat intake in America has been decreasing. Some lay and scientific writers have dubbed this phenomenon the American Paradox.

The reality, however, is that dietary fat consumption is not decreasing at all. The appearance of decreased fat intake is an illusion. USDA data clearly shows that we are eating more fat than ever. Daily fat intake per capita, after adjusting for wastage, has drifted upward from an average of 107 grams in the 1970s to 110 grams in the 80s to 111 grams in the 90s. In 1999, the fat intake level inched up to a record high of 116 grams per day. However, while we continue to eat the same excessive amount of fat, we have increased our total calories by eating more meat and more carbohydrates, with an explosive increase in consumption of bad carbohydrates. Because this increase in bad carbohydrate intake has increased so quickly, total carbohydrate and total calorie intake have risen so much that the *percentage* of calories from carbohydrate has increased while the *percentage* of calories from fat has decreased. This is despite the fact that the *amount* of fat has gradually increased as well.

The Carbohydrate Confusion

Since an increase in the percentage of carbohydrate calories has been associated with an increase in obesity, this "American Paradox" has led some promoters of high protein diets to conclude that carbohydrates are the cause of obesity. They claim that since carbohydrates cause insulin levels to rise, and since insulin can promote lipogenesis (body fat production), carbohydrates cause obesity. However, the reality is that proteins also cause insulin levels to rise, and that meat raises insulin levels more than pasta. In addition, while fats raise insulin the least, fats are most likely to make you fat.

Thus, while insulin may play a role in causing weight gain, there are a number of factors that affect insulin levels—not just carbohydrates. In addition, insulin is not the only factor in causing obesity. The truth is, it's not the carbohydrates. There are a number of factors that contribute to obesity. Total calories, the low calorie density of food, the high fat consumption, the overconsumption of animal products, the lack of exercise, the overconsumption of bad carbohydrates and the underconsumption of good carbohydrates all help to add up to the current epidemic of obesity.

Scientific Studies Show That Carbohydrates Correlate to Leanness

The idea that carbohydrates make you fat goes against scientific research. I know that there are a lot of theories about carbohydrates causing craving and carbohydrates causing an over-consumption of calories. However, the proof is in the bottom line; that is, what happens to people and their health while eating a lot of carbohydrates. As we have seen, population studies indicate that high carbohydrate diets are associated with slim populations. Additionally, a number of very good scientists have researched this issue and have not been able to find a relationship between carbohydrates and obesity.

It is even difficult to find studies that show that sugar causes obesity. One review of the scientific literature published in 1996 concluded that there is "no basis for a causative association between sugar intake and obesity." Another review of dozens of scientific articles concluded that: ". . . although high intake of dietary fat is positively associated with indexes of obesity, high intake of sugar is negatively associated with indexes of obesity." In other words, the people who eat the most carbohydrates tend to be the slimmest people.

In fact, other researchers consistently find that the more carbohydrates one consumes, the less likely a person is to be overweight. In a study done at Stanford University, the food consumption of a group of middle-aged men was surveyed. Their height, weight, body fat and other measures of obesity were recorded, and the researchers looked for correlations between diet and levels of obesity in these participants. The researchers found that carbohydrate consumption was inversely correlated with obesity. That means that when researchers looked at total carbohydrates, complex carbohydrates and even simple carbohydrates, they found that the more carbohydrates the men ate, the less likely they were to be obese. Now, I'm not saying that sugar will make you slim. I'm saying that fat is more likely to make you fat.

It does seem contradictory that nationally, carbohydrates are associated with obesity and yet scientific studies show that carbohydrates are associated with leanness. Why the discrepancy? What's happening is this: When researchers look at what people eat in a dietary survey, most people eating more carbohydrates are eating less fat. So what you have is data that shows that people who eat more carbohydrates *and* less fat are leaner.

What's happening nationally is very different. America, in general, is eating a lot more carbohydrates but also more fat. In this situation, if people eat more carbohydrate *and* more fat, of course, people are getting fatter because the total calorie intake has increased. Fat percentage is decreasing only because carbohydrate intake is growing at a faster rate. Fat intake is actually increasing as well. The Good Carbohydrate Plan helps to remedy this problem in the most effective way by replacing the fat with good carbohydrates.

We Eat Too Much Fat

Fats are probably the most important factor in weight gain. In the study described above that found a correlation between carbohydrates and leanness, researchers found that dietary fat was directly correlated with obesity. It's also important to note that this correlation was consistent regardless of whether it was saturated fat, monounsaturated fat, polyunsaturated fat, or total fat intake. The amount of fat consumed was directly correlated to how obese these individuals became.

Fat has the highest concentration of calories of any food; it provides a lot of calories without filling up your stomach. Fat is 9 calories per gram, which is more than twice as concentrated as sugar at 4 calories per gram. Let me give you some examples. A cup of oil has 1,927 calories, while a cup of orange juice has 110 calories. In other words, a tablespoon of oil, with 119 calories, has as many calories as 1½ apples (76 calories per apple).

Consider an example of how adding fat piles on the calories. A medium baked potato is about 156 grams, or about one-third of a pound, and contains 145 calories. By frying this potato in cooking oil and turning it into French fries, you now have a food that has 511 calories. By deep frying, you more than triple the calories.

Data from 1996 show that the largest source of fat in the average American woman's diet is salad oil in salad dressing. Let's look at what happens to salad when you add dressing. Most salad dressings are 80 to 90 percent fat; French dressing, for example, contains 6.2 grams of fat and has 62 calories per tablespoon. Without dressing, a generous salad of six cups of lettuce contains 43 calories. By adding three tablespoons of dressing, the same salad has 229 calories with 19 grams of fat.

Fat, Not Carbohydrate, Is Associated with Overeating and Obesity

More fat means more calories with less satisfaction. Because fat is so concentrated in calories, it's very easy to eat too many calories from fat—despite the fact that we are not eating much more food. Because of the high calorie concentration of fat, and possibly other factors, fat satisfies hunger the least. If you have heard that fat is the most satisfying food, don't believe it. When fat is compared with carbohydrates or protein on a calorie-for-calorie basis, it is the least satisfying type of food.

In 1994, researchers at the University of Sydney published a study designed to measure how well different foods satisfy hunger. The researchers fed participants 38 different foods and measured hunger satisfaction over time, to account for the total satisfaction produced by the foods. They found that on a calorie-for-calorie basis, the higher the fat content, the less satisfying the food. Other research suggests people tend to overconsume calories from high fat meals compared to low fat meals because high fat meals are less satisfying. One scientific review of a number of studies concluded that: "Metabolic studies show that diets high in fat are more likely to result in body fat accumulation than are diets high in carbohydrate." Another researcher reviewed 55 articles on the subject of carbohydrates, fat, and obesity. This review, published in the *American*

Journal of Clinical Nutrition, concluded, "Fat, not carbohydrate, is the macronutrient associated with overeating and obesity."

The Calorie Density of Food Is a Better Answer

Looking just at carbohydrates, or looking just at fat, doesn't really give the full answer to the question of why obesity continues to get worse in this country. The missing piece lies in an important factor related to the difference between good and bad carbohydrates. This crucial, but often overlooked factor is the calorie density of food, or what I call the Mass Index of food.

I designed the Mass Index of food in the early 1990s to make the concept of calorie density easier to understand. Calorie density is an important aspect of food; it is usually reported as calories per gram. But, who knows what a calorie per gram means? I found that most of my patients don't understand grams. They do understand pounds, however. So in order to make it more friendly for most people, I converted it to pounds of food per daily calories. Thus, the Mass Index is a number that represents how many pounds of food it takes to provide one day's worth of calories. It is based on 2,500 calories, which is the average daily calorie requirement for an active woman or an inactive man, and also about halfway between the RDA for adult women (2,200 calories) and the RDA for adult men (2,900 calories). The Mass Index is derived from what is known as a food's calorie density. In other words, if a food is high in calories for a certain weight of food, it is called a high calorie density food. If a food is low in calories for a certain weight of food, it is called a low calorie density food.

For hunger satisfaction, I believe the mass or weight of the food is more important than the calories. For these reasons I created the Mass Index of food, which is essentially the calorie density table turned upside down and converted to pounds. The Mass Index helps you to find foods that will help you to lose weight by filling up your stomach before you've had a chance to eat too many calories.

Using the Mass Index, it's easy to see why Americans are getting more and more obese as a nation. Fats have a very low Mass Index, hence a very high calorie density. It takes just 0.6 pounds of fat to provide 2,500 calories, so the Mass Index for fat is 0.6. Sugar and white flour also have a very low Mass Index and high calorie density. It takes just 1.4 pounds of sugar and 1.7 pounds of white flour to provide 2,500 calories. By contrast, it takes over 6 pounds of corn kernels to provide the same 2,500 calories.

Clearly, if dietary fat is causing obesity, adding refined carbohydrates such as sugar and white flour products will not prevent obesity from occurring. The high calorie density of these bad carbohydrates will only intensify the weight gain.

MASS INDEX OF FOOD

NUMBER OF POUNDS REQUIRED FOR 2,500 CALORIES

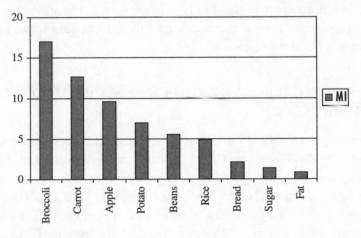

Dr. Shintani's Eat More, Weigh Less® Diet, 1993.

The Mass Index helps us to look at a much broader range of food in the context of whether these foods will have a negative or positive effect on weight loss. The Mass Index helps us to evaluate how different foods affect us in real life. By understanding the importance of the number of calories of a food compared to the bulk or weight of the food, we can easily understand the American Paradox. In America, in our effort to reduce fat, we are largely replacing it with sugar and white flour. By using the Mass Index, you can predict that if you replace fat, a low Mass Index/high calorie density food, with another low Mass Index/high calorie density food, such as sugar or white flour, then logically, you will continue to see an increase in weight.

In fact, if we sit back and look at the whole obesity problem in this country, we can deduce that we actually weigh too much because we eat too little. This may be one of the most important aspects of dieting that is neglected by almost all other diets. In this country, we have moved away from traditional foods—those high in unprocessed good carbohydrates. Meanwhile, we have continued to eat more and more high fat and bad carbohydrate foods over the years.

When we consume large amounts of refined carbohydrates and fat, our stomachs are not as full as they would be with higher Mass Index foods, such as good carbohydrates. The result is we feel hungrier and eat more of the same low Mass Index/high calorie density foods. Weight gain is the likely consequence, because despite the fact that we are eating less food than in ancient times, we are actually consuming more calories.

THE GOOD CARBOHYDRATE PLAN NATURALLY CONTROLS CALORIE INTAKE

Fortunately, the Good Carbohydrate Plan takes into account calorie density. In doing so, the Good Carbohydrate Plan naturally induces weight loss by automatically limiting the amount of calories consumed. At the same time, insulin levels are kept at a moderate level because good carbohydrates have less of an impact on insulin levels than bad carbohydrates. With the Good Carbohydrate Plan, you will be using low calorie density foods because the Mass Index is incorporated in the Carbohydrate Quotient. These foods fill you up before you eat too many calories. In other words, you will eat more food on the Good Carbohydrate Plan than on the standard American diet. Yet you will lose weight because your calorie intake will be naturally less.

Using the Mass Index, you can find foods that will help you to lose (or gain) weight if you want. The higher the Mass Index, the more likely you will eat less calories from this food. The lower the Mass Index, the more likely you will eat more calories from this food.

Besides creating more bulk and the feeling of fullness, high Mass Index foods also tend to be low Carbohydrate Quotient foods.

Low Carbohydrate Quotient foods are healthier because they do not provoke a sharp rise in blood sugar, and therefore the body doesn't have to produce as much insulin. The Mass Index is incorporated in the Carbohydrate Quotient. You can use either the Carbohydrate Quotient or the Mass Index to choose foods that will cause a minimal rise in insulin.

THE GOOD CARBOHYDRATE PLAN'S EIGHT PRINCIPLES OF WEIGHT LOSS

The Good Carbohydrate Plan provides a set of principles to optimize weight loss.

Weight Loss Principle One. Use the Five C's and the Carbohydrate Quotient to Choose Good Carbohydrate Foods.

Simply follow the Five C's method of evaluating carbohydrates and the twelve good carbohydrate insights, as outlined in Chapter 6. This helps to minimize any potential fat producing effects of insulin.

Weight Loss Principle Two. Choose Foods Based on the Carbohydrate Quotient Table. Use the Mass Index If They Are Not on the Table.

When in doubt, use the Carbohydrate Quotient table. The lower the Carbohydrate Quotient, the better. If it is not on the table, use the Mass Index or calorie density as your basis for food choices. The basic rule is that higher Mass Index numbers mean they are better for helping you to control your weight. The cutoff point is 4.1. Foods with a Mass Index of 4.1 or higher are foods that contribute to weight loss. (See the Carbohydrate Quotient table in Appendix A for Mass Index numbers.)

Weight Loss Principle Three. Minimize White Sugar and White Sugar Products.

While sugar is not associated with obesity, calories are. Sugar is very high in calorie density and has a low Mass Index. Sugar also provokes a substantial insulin response, which is undesirable. So use sugar sparingly and with large amounts of good carbohydrates.

Weight Loss Principle Four. Avoid Calorie-Containing Beverages. Drink Water or Herbal Tea Instead.

There are about ten teaspoons of sugar in a 12-ounce soft drink. This applies to carbonated beverages as well as fruit drinks. If you want a sweet beverage, 100 percent fruit juices are better. However, remember that it is even better to use whole fruit instead. The best beverages are water and herbal teas, which contain no calories or sugar.

Weight Loss Principle Five. Minimize White Flour and White Flour Products.

In many ways white flour acts just like sugar in the body and is almost as low in Mass Index as white sugar. In addition, white bread actually raises insulin slightly more than white sugar. Pasta is the exception. Its blood sugar response and therefore Carbohydrate Quotient rating is moderate so pasta may be used moderately.

Weight Loss Principle Six. Minimize Added Fat in All Forms.

Limiting fat intake is a very important factor in limiting body fat accumulation. Whether there is something special about fat that promotes obesity is controversial. What is clear is that fat has the most calories per gram of all foods. It adds more than twice the calories of the same amount of sugar. Added fats include foods such as oils, butter, margarine, salad dressing, mayonnaise, shortening, and oil for frying foods.

Weight Loss Principle Seven. Avoid Animal Products, Especially High Fat Animal Products.

Animal products, especially red meat, prepared meat and most poultry, are typically high in fat. This includes cheese and dairy, except for skim milk products. For details about animal products see Chapter 14 on protein.

Weight Loss Principle Eight. Exercise.

Exercise regularly. You should exercise for at least 30 minutes every other day, preferably 40 minutes every day. Exercise burns calories, increases insulin sensitivity, and increases metabolic rate. Resistance exercises, such as weight training, push-ups and sit-ups, preserve and build lean body mass, helping to naturally stimulate and maintain your metabolic rate.

CHAPTER 9

Burn Your Carbohydrate and Fat Away

Most of this book deals with calories coming into the body. This chapter deals with calories going out, or how to burn your carbohydrates and fats away.

When you burn calories, typically the first calories burned will be carbohydrate calories because they are the most readily available. However, in the long run, burning any calories will not only help you to burn off carbohydrates, it will also help tip the balance of calories in favor of weight loss and help you to reduce the amount of fat in your body.

There are three main things you can do to help accelerate the rate at which you burn carbohydrates and fat in your body. Couch potatoes can rejoice in knowing that not all of these ways involve heavy exercise. The first may surprise you, the second is obvious, and the third is not so obvious. Let's go through the three ways to burn carbohydrates and fat.

EAT CARBOHYDRATES TO BURN CARBOHYDRATES

The first way to increase the rate of carbohydrates being burned in your body may sound like a paradox, but eating carbohydrates actually helps you to burn carbohydrates. Studies have shown that eating carbohydrates increases your metabolic rate and helps you to use up calories. It has long been known that the act of eating anything causes the body to increase its rate of burning calories. After all, the act of eating and digestion takes energy. What researchers have found is that eating carbohydrates causes you to burn more calories than eating fat.

In 1982, an experiment done in Switzerland compared different diets with different ratios of fats to carbohydrates to compare the rate at which calories are burned in the body. Two experimental groups were used. Protein intake was kept the same in both groups in order to directly compare the effects of carbohydrates and fats in the diet. The first group of people was placed on a diet that was about 45 percent carbohydrate, 40 percent fat. The second group was placed on a diet that was approximately 75 percent carbohydrate, ten percent fat. After carefully measuring how many calories were burned after one day on the diet, researchers found that those who were on a high carbohydrate diet burned their calories at a significantly higher rate than those on the low carbohydrate, high fat diet. This effect of increased rate of burning calories continued through the night.

This study shows that eating carbohydrates can help you to burn carbohydrates, and calories in general. If you are on a high carbohydrate, low fat diet, it should be easier for you to lose weight than if you are on a high fat diet. Studies comparing body fat to what people eat over time confirm that those who eat more carbohydrates and less fat tend to weigh less. Just be sure that the carbohydrates that you use are good carbohydrates, because the negative effects of bad carbohydrates could override the increased metabolism you experience by eating carbohydrates in general. The Good Carbohydrate Plan shows you how to eat carbohydrates to burn carbohydrates away.

FAST BURN YOUR CARBOHYDRATES

A second obvious way to burn carbohydrates, fat, and calories is to exercise. Never underestimate the benefits of regular exercise for your overall health. Studies have shown that people who exercise regularly live longer, healthier, happier lives than those who do not. Exercise is the most important way to increase your metabolic rate. What may encourage those who haven't or aren't able to engage in vigorous exercise is recent research indicates that even light-to-moderate exercise improves health. In other words, any activity you do is better than none.

One of the many reasons that regular exercise improves your health is that it helps you to keep your blood sugar and insulin under control, in addition to helping you to burn off excess calories. The best kind of exercise for this purpose is called aerobic exercise. Aerobic means that it is exercise that makes you use oxygen. If you are healthy, this means to exercise enough to make you breathe harder, and increase your heart rate and break a sweat. (If you have health problems, or if you don't do much exercise to begin with, check with your doctor first to see how much exercise is right for you.) Exercising vigorously helps to start the process of burning the carbohydrates in your bloodstream and causes your body to start using up the carbohydrates that are stored away.

Directly burning calories isn't the most important benefit of aerobic exercise. In fact, the main effect of exercising takes place when we are not exercising at all! Here's how it works. If you exercise once a week, the effect of the exercise is gone within a day. You burn the calories you needed during the exercise and then continue to burn calories through a recovery period of several hours, but that's it. After the recovery period, the rate at which you burn calories drops down to where it was before you exercised.

By contrast, let's say that you exercise three to four times per week. This performs a bit of magic on your metabolic rate. It causes your metabolism to increase at all times. In other words, the rate at which you burn calories—even when you're not exercising—increases at all times, too. Regular exercise creates what I like to call the flywheel effect. A flywheel is a weighted wheel in a piston engine that keeps the engine running even while the piston isn't pushing the wheel. Regular exercise does the same for your body. It sustains momentum in your metabolism, causing it to burn calories at a faster rate even when you are not exercising.

Research performed at the University of Wisconsin showed that burning calories during exercise wasn't the only benefit of exercise. They measured the metabolic rates of people doing regular exercise on a regular basis at least every other day, and they found that in between exercise sessions—not just during exercise—calories were being burned at a faster rate than before thay started their regular exercise schedules. Additional calories were being burned even during sleep or sitting down and relaxing during the days between exercises. Other studies indicate that this is an effective way to help keep your metabolic rate high and your body fat low. What this means is that if you exercise regularly, your metabolic rate is reset at a higher level, so that you burn extra calories all the time, even when you are not exercising.

Aerobic Exercise Decreases Insulin Resistance

Aerobic exercise helps you to control your weight and control your blood sugar (in addition to directly burning calories) in another very important way, by decreasing insulin resistance. It helps your natural insulin work better so that your body doesn't need to use as much insulin to control your blood sugar. This is true whether you have diabetes or not. If you don't have diabetes, it means that your blood levels of insulin are as low as possible, which will help to prevent any of the problems that may be caused by high insulin levels. If you do have diabetes, it may mean that your blood sugar levels decrease so much that you might need to decrease the amount of medicine you need (with the help of your physician).

If you have Metabolic Syndrome, described in Chapter 13, decreasing insulin resistance may be the key to reversing a number of health problems related to high levels of insulin. This includes the reversal of high cholesterol and high blood pressure in addition to the improvement of blood sugar control.

SLOW BURN YOUR CARBOHYDRATES

A third way to burn carbohydrates and fats out of your body is not as obvious as simply using the calories through vigorous exercise. I call it the slow burning of carbohydrates, fats, and calories because it involves the slow and steady burning of calories by the cells in your body. This slow burning process is a result of the energy being burned by cells just to stay alive and perform the work they were intended to perform. This is sometimes called resting metabolic rate, or RMR. Here's the key: muscle tissue burns calories faster than fat tissue, so the more muscle you have, the more carbohydrate, fat and calories you are burning at all times.

Muscle cells burn more calories per minute than fat cells because muscle cells are much more active in their basic functions. Muscle cells constantly burn energy so the body can move, repair itself, grow in response to exercise, and replenish energy burned during activity. By sharp contrast, the only real function of fat cells is to store energy in the form of fat—this requires very little energy. Muscle cells, even if they are inactive, burn an average of 13 calories per kilogram per day, while fat cells burn an average of only 4.5 calories per kilogram per day. (When muscle cells become active they, of course, burn much more than they do at rest.) That is, muscle cells burn about three times as many calories as fat cells do when they are at rest and when you are asleep. Thus, the more muscle mass you have in your body and the less fat mass, the more calories you will burn at all times.

In order to preserve and build your muscle mass, it is important to do some resistance exercises such as weight lifting, push-ups, sit-ups and other similar muscle toning and muscle building exercises. These exercises will preserve and build up muscle tissue; increase the amount of muscle you have compared to body fat; and increase the rate of slow burning of carbohydrates, fat, and calories at all times.

HOW TO GET STARTED ON AN EXERCISE PROGRAM

Safety First

Here are some basics to get started on an exercise program to add to your Good Carbohydrate Plan. Before you begin any exercise program, you must consider your safety as your first priority. Consider your current health status and how much you can perform. If you have health problems or joint problems, this means talking with your physician to see how much exercise is right for you. In general, it is important to build up your exercise gradually. Don't be a fanatic and try to run a couple of miles on your first day of exercise if you haven't run even 100 yards in a while. Start with light exercise to see how much you can tolerate and set goals from there. It may be useful to talk to an exercise trainer if you have access to one.

Avoid Injury

For whatever exercise you do, take some steps to avoid injury. Have a good pair of exercise shoes that are comfortable and fit properly. This is especially important if you have diabetes and are therefore prone to foot infections that can be very serious even from minor injuries.

Stretching is important to help avoid muscle strains and tears. Always stretch the muscles you will be using before exerting them. Any sudden contraction of a muscle that is not stretched out before-hand may result in injury. This happens because the muscle simply is too tight and is not prepared for the strain that is placed on it when exercise begins.

Warming up is important because it allows your body to prepare itself for exercise. After stretching, jog in place a little or do any light activity in order to get your circulation going. Warming up prepares your body for exercise by increasing your heart rate a little, increasing circulation and getting all the blood chemistry, including blood sugar, ready for exercise. Sudden exertion without warming up could put undue strain on your heart, your muscle tissue, and your joints. It also generally stresses your body's metabolic systems unnecessarily.

Know your limits. After consulting with your doctor, pay attention to the limits that your doctor suggests to you. In addition, be aware of your own body and do not overexert yourself. If you become uncomfortable with your exercise, pay attention to your body and stop. Your increases in activity should be gradual. In doing these things, you help to ensure that your exercise is safe and most effective to help you accomplish your goals.

DO WHAT YOU ENJOY DOING

The best exercise in the world is not necessarily cross-country ski-ing, jogging, or swimming. The best exercise is one that you enjoy and will do on a regular basis. When I conduct my lectures, I always bring up the subject of exercise, and I can almost hear the groans from the audience. When, exactly, did exercise become a chore? Why is it that many of us see exercise as work to do? When we were kids, exercise was as natural as play. We used to chase each other around the schoolyard at recess time, play tag or have ballgames, and so on. If you visit an elementary school and watch the kids in the playground, you'll see how much energy they expend. And they're having fun. As we've grown up, however, many of us have lost the zest for physical activity.

So what is the best exercise in the world? It is the exercise that you enjoy, that you can do in a playful way. This means it is any exercise that feels like play rather than work. This kind of exercise is the best because you will do it regularly and keep doing it once you start. No exercise will help you if you will not engage in it consistently so that you reap the benefits.

If you can't think of anything right away, use the list below to give you some ideas. If you approach this with a playful attitude, exercise will become a time-out from the stresses of the day, a recess from responsibility and routine. You can easily get used to a play period during your day, simply because of the good feelings you get from doing it.

If you are interested in knowing how many calories are burned while doing various exercises, there are library sites on the Internet with this information. I found some by searching for "exercise and calories burned."

MAKE A REGULAR APPOINTMENT WITH YOURSELF

The most common excuse for not exercising is, "I don't have time." My patients tell me this and yet they have no trouble making appointments with other people who want their time. If you simply consider that you are as important as the people you make appointments with, you may realize that all you have to do is make an appointment with yourself for exercise and suddenly you will have time. If you will simply write in your calendar an appointment with yourself to do a little exercise daily or at least every other day, you have taken the first step towards regular exercise.

FEEL HOW GOOD IT FEELS

Once you have selected an activity that you feel you can do, and made an appointment with yourself to do it regularly, the next step is to just do it. Something wonderful happens when you start exercising. Your body's own chemistry makes it an enjoyable experience. Imagine yourself again as a child, running around with friends and doing a lot of physical activity during school recess or at a park during a picnic. Remember how exhilarated you felt? That feeling is more than simple childhood enthusiasm. Part of that feeling is your body secreting substances into your bloodstream, such as adrenaline and endorphins, that make you feel great. Even if it's a struggle at first to do exercise, once your body senses the energy you are using to do this exercise, it sets into motion a cascade of chemical reactions that can literally make you feel a natural high.

When your body feels some exertion, the hormone adrenaline kicks in. Adrenaline is usually associated with fight or flight body responses. It makes you feel wide awake and alert. Adrenaline causes your pupils to dilate and the blood vessels in your brain and muscles to open up to increase your blood flow to these vital organs and increase your sensory awareness. It also causes your heart to pump a little faster and your body to release stored carbohydrates into your bloodstream and replaces the blood sugar that you have been using during exercise. In these many ways this hormone gives you an initial burst of energy when you start your exercise.

After you have been exercising for a while, another set of natural substances is secreted in the brain, called endorphins. These substances act at the sites in your brain that turn off pain and give you a sense of euphoria. Morphine and other opiods act at these same sites, doing artificially what endorphins do naturally in your brain. Sustained exercise can help you feel great in a completely healthy way by causing the release of endorphins.

GET TO YOUR TRAINING HEART RATE

Once you have started exercising, try to keep the level of exercise high enough to give you the most benefit. You can use a simple formula that determines how vigorous your exercise should be to help weight loss. The idea is to get your heart pumping at your training heart rate; this ensures that your exercise is vigorous enough. *Again, if you have any health problems or haven't exercised in a while, see your doctor before undertaking any exercises in this book.* Your training heart rate is 60 to 85 percent of maximum heart rate. The more fit you are, the closer to 85 percent you should strive for; the less fit you are, the closer to 60 percent it should be. Following is a simple formula to find your training heart rate:

220 − age = maximum heart rate × 60 percent to 85 percent
= training heart rate

Example: For a person 35 years old, training heart rate would be 220 − 35 = 185 × .6 = 111,185 × 0.85 = 157

Thus, optimal exercise occurs when this 35-year-old's heart is beating between 111 beats/minute to 157 beats/minute, depending on fitness level. You can check your heart rate during exercise by counting your pulse against a watch or clock with a second hand. Then make sure that you exercise at least every other day for at least 30 to 40 minutes.

Remember that regular exercise helps you burn carbohydrates, fats and calories even when you are not exercising! You're finding your way back to the natural state of human beings, for we all require exercise in order to be healthy, happy, and FIT! So why not get started today?

CHAPTER 10

The Good Carbohydrate Plan

By now you can see that one of the most important ways you can improve your health, lose weight, and prevent disease is by eating a diet based on good carbohydrates. The principles of the Good Carbohydrate Plan are flexible; you can adapt them for your own personal needs. The most important point of the Good Carbohydrate Plan is to improve your carbohydrate sources—no matter what type of diet you are on.

The more closely you stick to the principles of the Good Carbohydrate Plan, the better results you will see. But it's not all or nothing. Every bad carbohydrate you replace with a good carbohydrate is an improvement in your diet. Every animal product, especially high fat animal product or fat/oil product you replace with a good carbohydrate is also an improvement in your diet. For a full explanation of why it is beneficial to replace animal protein and fat, see Chapters 14 and 15.

Adopt the Good Carbohydrate Plan in a way that best suits you. You can do it very simply and quickly or you can do it gourmet-style. You can shop in your local supermarket or you can shop in health food stores and specialty or ethnic food stores. The important thing is to tailor the plan to your tastes and your needs. Because the Good Carbohydrate Plan is flexible, it suits just about anyone's taste and can be done anywhere in the world.

BEFORE YOU BEGIN

As with any new eating plan, you should check with your doctor before starting if you have any health problems. This is especially true if you are on medication. Some individuals may need their medication adjusted while on this diet. Other individuals may also require monitoring of their symptoms, so a doctor's supervision is essential.

WHAT TO EXPECT ON THE GOOD CARBOHYDRATE PLAN

The first few days may be a period of adjustment for you. In my case, I changed my diet overnight from a high fast food/junk food diet to a diet rich in good carbohydrates. In making this transition, I experienced a number of changes that seem to be common among those who begin the Good Carbohydrate Plan.

For some, the transition is very easy, pleasant—even exhilarating. For others, the transition may be accompanied by an initial period of vague symptoms such as fatigue and headache, followed by a feeling of well-being and high energy. This usually occurs during the first three days as your body cleans itself out. It is for this reason I caution that if you have health problems, you must check with your physician before following the plan. I also recommend that you listen to your body, and if you become very uncomfortable during any part of the plan, as with any new eating plan, you should discontinue use and check with your doctor to make sure there aren't other causes for your discomfort.

Based on my personal experience as well as the experience of my patients, here are the most common effects of the Good Carbohydrate Plan.

Increased Energy

One of the most important benefits I noticed from following the Good Carbohydrate Plan was that feelings of fatigue began to disappear. Before following the plan, I usually became tired by early afternoon, and I would feel lethargic when I got home from work or school.

On the first day of following the Good Carbohydrate Plan, I didn't notice much other than a slight headache in the afternoon. On the second day, I felt a little fatigue in the morning, but I didn't experience my usual afternoon fatigue. By the fourth day, I woke up very early in the morning feeling so good that I had trouble getting back to sleep. This is when I really noticed a substantial change in my energy level.

Clear Thinking

On the Good Carbohydrate Plan, I also experienced a change in my thought processes. My thinking became very clear and my grades improved in graduate school. I began taking pre-med courses during the summers off from law school and the toughest science courses became interesting and easy to grasp. After I changed my diet, learning became exciting, fun, and easy. I was never much of a writer until after I changed my diet. While on the high carbohydrate diet that I adopted, I began to write well enough that a paper I wrote was published in the *Law Review,* and I have written eight books since that time.

Improved Digestion and Elimination

Because I was eating foods that were all plant-based, I learned to chew more than I used to. Remember that meat-eating animals don't chew their food. They simply tear flesh and swallow it because they don't really have the jaw structure or teeth for chewing. Humans have the teeth for chewing and grinding each mouthful of food and so this additional chewing brought me back to a more natural way of eating. This meant that I took a little longer to eat than usual. It turns out that this is good for the digestive system because it allows time for the digestive enzymes to work and slows the rate at which sugar is absorbed into the bloodstream.

My digestion also improved because of the fiber content. Having bowel movements once or even twice per day is not unusual with this diet. My patients who have constipation never fail to report that constipation disappears after they adopt the Good Carbohydrate Plan.

Less Sleep Required

For me, the most surprising result was that I didn't need as much sleep when I followed the Good Carbohydrate Plan. I was accustomed to sleeping nine hours per day. I would sleep from 11:00 P.M. to 7:00 A.M., a total of eight hours, and after a day of work or school, I would take a nap for about an hour. On the fourth day on this plan, a surprising thing happened to me—I woke up at 4:00 A.M. I was full of energy and I went through the whole day without needing a nap in the afternoon. This continued day after day to a point where I began going to sleep at 1:00 A.M. and waking at 6:00 or 7:00 A.M. I now need only about six hours of sleep.

Depression Disappeared

One of my patients taught me a lesson about the value of diet in dealing with emotions. He told me that, while on the standard American junk food diet, from time to time he felt a little depressed, almost for no reason. When he began to follow a diet based on good carbohydrates, he not only felt a boost in energy, but his bouts of depression disappeared. I believe this occurred because the Good Carbohydrate Plan improved the biochemistry of his brain (serotonin levels) and balanced his hormonal system (sex hormones, cortisol, and other hormones that can affect mood). The days of feeling depressed for no reason seem to have left him for good.

Tastes Changed

My tastes changed significantly after a few weeks on the diet. Sugary foods became too sweet, salty foods became too salty, and greasy foods became too greasy. Almost all the participants in our programs report the same change. "Candy is way too sweet for me now," is a typical comment from people who sample sweets after following the diet strictly. One participant told me that he couldn't stand the feeling of grease in and around his mouth when he ate a French fry.

Part of the reason for this is that taste buds become more sensitive when they are exposed to lower concentrations of substances such as salt and sugar. Conversely, this means that our sense of taste also becomes duller if we eat a lot of salt, fat, and sugar. Ironically, in America we are actually decreasing our ability to taste and enjoy food when we constantly eat very salty, very sweet, and very greasy foods.

Improvement in Overall Health

A number of people have reported improvement in health after following the program for three weeks. As we have described earlier, there are documented studies showing reduction in blood sugar, cholesterol, and blood pressure with this plan. Besides this, other health problems have been improved or reversed. Patients have reported a reduction in asthma, acne, arthritis, back pain, depression, headaches, fatigue, sexual dysfunction, menstrual cramps, as well as improvements in minor health conditions. Of course, the Good Carbohydrate Plan is not a substitute for medical care and you should see your doctor for any of these problems in addition to trying a good diet.

Adverse Effects

As with any new eating plan, individuals may respond differently when starting a new way of eating. Sometimes there are unknown food allergies, for example, that are uncovered with the introduction of new food. Your body has to adjust to the different source of calories and this transition may bring with it some symptoms. In any case, listen to your body. If you feel very uncomfortable with any symptom, discontinue the diet or engage in it more gradually. If any symptoms are severe, persistent or unusual, be sure to check with your doctor.

The most noticeable negative symptom that I experienced on this diet came on the first afternoon. I started getting a headache after eating lunch. I believe that this was a result of withdrawal from caffeine, since I used to drink coffee every day and I stopped when I began my diet. However, it may also have been a result of withdrawal from sugar. William Dufty, author of the book *Sugar Blues,* describes losing 50 pounds but having a migraine headache when starting a strict diet of whole grains and vegetables (good carbohydrates). He likened his experience to being a sugar addict and going through withdrawal when he eliminated all the added sugar from his diet.

Of course, if the symptoms are mild and if you are otherwise in good health, an over-the-counter headache remedy can be used. If symptoms are unusual or severe, check with your doctor. Be aware that for those on medication, a headache may be a sign that your medications are too strong and you must contact your doctor about any symptoms that you may experience.

In the first week or so, some individuals feel a little bloated. This is a result of the high fiber content of the diet, but this generally disappears by the second week. Some feel a little gassy, typically because their gut flora is not adjusted to the food. Try chewing your food more thoroughly as a remedy. If it is a result of the intake of legumes, make sure the legumes are adequately cooked, the soaking water poured off (this includes canned beans) and as a last resort, consider taking enzymes such as Beano® to aid in digestion.

After following this diet for three weeks or more, be careful if you decide to stray from it suddenly. You may undergo an adjustment period moving away from this eating plan. One of my participants reported that he ate a pork chop after following the diet strictly. He said he got a stomachache after eating the greasy fare and decided that his body was now beginning to reject what was unhealthy for it.

THE SEVEN STEPS OF THE GOOD CARBOHYDRATE PLAN

Step One. Learn the basics of the Good Carbohydrate Plan.

Learning the basics of the Good Carbohydrate Plan is important to keep you motivated. Read Chapter 3 to gain an understanding of the difference between good carbohydrates and bad carbohydrates and then look over the Twelve Principles for Finding Good Carbohydrates in Chapter 6. Understand the Good Carbohydrate Plan Pyramid in Chapter 7. Learn to use the lists of good carbohydrate foods in Chapter 7 or the Carbohydrate Quotient. Remember that in addition to diet, exercise and an overall healthy lifestyle are the key to good health and longevity.

Step Two. **Pick Your Plan.**

Once you understand the basics of the Good Carbohydrate Plan, you can pick your plan.

Plan A: The Easy Carbohydrate Repair

This is the easiest way to apply the Good Carbohydrate Plan. This approach is for those of you who want to use good carbohydrates but don't want to abandon all of your current eating habits. Every bad carbohydrate and bad fat that you replace with a good carbohydrate is an improvement. Just apply Step Three of the Good Carbohydrate Plan.

Plan B: The Three-Week Carbohydrate Cure

If you really want to see the value of eating good carbohydrates, I suggest that you follow this plan carefully and stick with it for at least three weeks. I call this the Three-Week Carbohydrate Cure because in 21 days, you learn how to cure yourself of bad carbohydrates with good carbohydrates.

If you are in a hurry, choose one of the Quick Start Plans described later in this chapter (see page 150). From there you can transition into a fuller version of the Good Carbohydrate Plan using a wide range of recipes from this book and adapting some of your own favorite recipes to fit the principles of the Good Carbohydrate Plan.

Plan C: The Good Carbohydrate Plan

If you decide to follow the Good Carbohydrate Plan completely, that's even better. Try the Three-Week Carbohydrate Cure and one of the menus in Chapter 11 of this book. You'll experience a full sampling of the different types of dishes you can enjoy while on the Good Carbohydrate Plan. Once you've learned the basics, go ahead and be creative. Season your food the way you like them. Adapt your favorite dishes or invent new ones, using the principles of the plan.

Step Three. **Replace Bad Carbohydrates with Good Carbohydrates.**

This is the biggest step you can take to make your diet a healthy one. Replacing the bad carbohydrates in your diet with good carbohydrates will be easy if you learn the simple recipes in this book. Whole grains, pilafs, pastas, whole grain breads, and potato dishes are some of the foods you can start with. You'll add to this a complement of delicious, nutrient-rich, high fiber foods that will fill you up and yet allow you to lose weight. Learn how to use the Five C's method of finding good carbohydrates. Then, learn how to prepare and use them in Chapter 11. Look at the list of foods to avoid below and replace these foods with good carbohydrates. This will help you to eliminate bad carbohydrates and bad fats from your diet. You'll also learn in Chapter 11 how to use some sweeteners in a way that will not adversely affect your blood sugar.

The Foods You Should Replace: White Flour and Refined Sugar

Minimize your use of products that contain white flour, especially white bread. If you must use white flour products, use pasta, pita bread, flatbread (chapati), or sourdough bread. When I talk about white flour I also mean white flour that is colored brown as in the typical commercial wheat bread. If it doesn't say whole wheat, you might be simply getting white flour that is colored brown to give you the appearance of whole wheat. Just look at the labels on these commercial soft brown breads and you will see what I mean. The first ingredient is probably enriched flour and there is some coloring agent to add the brown color to it. Physiologically, this is going to have the same effect on your blood sugar as white flour. Another type of food to be careful of is pastry. Pastries are really foods to help you put on weight. Not only do they have a high white flour content, they also contain sugar and fat.

Minimize your use of refined sugars. There is a difference between refined sugar and the sugar found in whole fruits and vegetables. Because the sugar in fruit is in a whole food, the effect of the sugar is blunted, making fruit a reasonably good source of carbohydrate. Limit the use of white sugar as much as possible. If you use any added sugar, consider using fructose instead of sucrose. It is better in terms of impact on blood sugar although it still can cause problems with bad cholesterol levels. Its main advantage is that it is sweeter than table sugar and you need less of it to have the same sweetness. Sweeteners such as barley malt, brown rice syrup, maple syrup, and blackstrap molasses are also better than refined white sugar because you will tend to get few calories from them because of the lower caloric density. If you want a sugar substitute, I recommend the herbal sweetener called stevia. It is a natural herb product that you can find at most health food stores where they sell herbs.

Be Careful of Packaged Foods

To help you make better food choices, take a close look through your kitchen cabinets and see how many items contain sugar. Be sure to read labels carefully. There is a lot of hidden sugar in prepared foods. Eliminate foods such as soft drinks, candies, cookies, white bread, pastries, white flour crackers, and sweet snack foods (including low fat specialty snacks). You may be surprised to find that most foods, which are packaged or canned in some way, have a fair amount of sugar in them. Packaged cereals are notorious for adding a great deal of sugar to their already high content of white flour. Whole grain cooked cereal is a much better choice.

If you are going to use packaged cereals, choose the type that has the least amount of added sugar, the most fiber, and/or the type that is fortified so that at least there is some redeeming value. Otherwise, you may be eating a product that is like candy disguised as a breakfast food. Learning the sugar content of the foods you are already eating gives you a head start in learning which foods you should replace. Oftentimes you can replace such foods with a fresh version, which doesn't have added sugar or chemical sweeteners.

If You're Going to Eat a Bad Carbohydrate ...

Remember, I'm not saying you should never eat any bad carbohydrates. Everyone at some time or another will consume bad carbohydrates. After all, the flavor of sweet is the flavor of carbohydrate and we should allow ourselves to enjoy this flavor from time to time. The problem is the massive quantities of bad carbohydrates the average person consumes today. Remember that in ancient times there was no refined sugar; the only way one could satisfy a craving for sweet was to eat whole fruit or on rare occasions to risk getting stung by a bee for some honey. So, realize that the flavor of sweet was never meant to be consumed all by itself. Other nutrients were meant to go along with it. With this in mind, be assured that just because a food is considered a bad carbohydrate, it doesn't mean you can't ever eat it. Below are eight ways to improve carbohydrate meals even if they contain some bad carbohydrates. These techniques will minimize the blood sugar and insulin effects of any meal.

1. If you are going to eat bad carbohydrates such as sugar or white bread, eat them in small amounts with large amounts of good carbohydrates. In other words, eat a substantial amount of good carbohydrates to blunt the effect of the bad ones.

2. Add high fiber foods or soluble fiber supplements to help slow the absorption of bad carbohydrates.

3. Pressure cooking grain helps to reduce its impact on blood sugar.

4. Keep your fat intake low to improve insulin sensitivity.

5. Add acidic foods such as lemon and vinegar to help slow the absorption of carbohydrate from other foods.

6. Exercise regularly to help control blood sugar and increase insulin sensitivity.

7. Eat smaller, more frequent meals. This helps to reduce the insulin response.

8. Eat more high Mass Index foods to automatically reduce the amount of calories and carbohydrates eaten, which in turn reduces the impact on blood sugar and insulin.

Step Four: Balance Your Diet.

Use the Good Carbohydrate Plan Pyramid and the lists of food in Chapter 7 for guidelines on how to include an adequate variety of food in your diet. Learn how to balance your diet with the different categories in the Good Carbohydrate Plan Pyramid. Load up your plate with vegetables (which are virtually all good carbohydrates and are low Carbohydrate Quotient foods) and some fruit. Fruits and vegetables represent the second tier of the Good Carbohydrate Plan Pyramid. The national Five-a-Day slogan is good advice for fruit and vegetable servings. Fruits and vegetables are important not only for their rich nutrient content but also for their bulk effect, coming from their rich fiber content. These foods help to slow down the rate of absorption of carbohydrates. They will also help to fill you up so that you automatically consume fewer calories.

Learn some of the vegetable recipes in Chapter 12. In your preparation, it's important that you choose whole, fresh vegetables when possible, although fresh frozen vegetables are a reasonable second choice. Try to add a serving or two at each meal when possible. These good carbohydrates will dilute any bad carbohydrate you may have and will add valuable nutrients and fiber to your whole diet.

Keep fresh, whole fruit on hand to fill out the food selections on the second tier of the Good Carbohydrate Plan Pyramid. Some examples include apples, oranges, grapefruits, peaches, apricots, and other fruit of this kind. Please refer to the Good Carbohydrate table in Chapter 7 or the Carbohydrate Quotient table in Appendix A for other fruit selections. Remember, turning fruit into juice increases its impact on blood sugar and insulin and makes it less desirable in the Good Carbohydrate Plan.

Add Non-Cholesterol Protein and Non-Dairy Calcium Foods

Complete your diet with foods from the third tier of the Good Carbohydrate Plan Pyramid, including the Non-Dairy Calcium group and the Non-Cholesterol Protein group. Make sure that you get a full range of nutrients by including some high protein good carbohydrates and high calcium good carbohydrates in your diet. Examples of high protein foods are lentils, beans, soy products, and nuts and seeds. Be careful about the use of nuts and seeds because of their high fat content. High calcium vegetables include kale, broccoli, watercress, collard greens, Chinese cabbage, mustard greens, and other dark leafy green vegetables. One of the easiest ways to obtain non-dairy calcium is to use dried seaweed, which is a surprisingly good source of calcium. If you can find dried wakame at your health food store or in the Oriental section of your grocery store, it is a simple way to obtain instant greens that you can add to any soup. Tofu is also a surprisingly good source of calcium and is also a good non-cholesterol protein food.

Limit Fat—Especially Animal Fat

Finally, it is important to limit your fat intake, especially animal fat. For weight control, limiting fat intake is even more important than limiting your intake of bad carbohydrates. Remember that there are two reasons for this. First, fats and oils must be limited for optimal effect because they may increase insulin resistance. Second, all fats, even added plant-based fats, will also add a lot of calories without adding much bulk, making it more difficult to control your weight. While sugar has a high concentration of calories at 4 calories per gram, fat is more than twice as concentrated at 9 calories per gram. As a rule of thumb, for weight control, I recommend a diet that is between 10 to 15 percent fat, which allows for 22 to 33 grams of fat on a 2,000-calorie diet.

If you must use oil, use oil high in monounsaturated fats such as extra virgin olive oil or macadamia nut oil because they are less likely to adversely affect your cholesterol levels. Replace as much of your animal protein intake as you can with foods from the third tier of the Good Carbohydrate Plan Pyramid, that is, beans, legumes, and soy products. This helps to reduce the amount of cholesterol and fat in your diet. You can use the recipes in this book to get started.

Step Five. Tailor Your Good Carbohydrate Plan to Your Needs.

If you are overweight, have heart disease, diabetes or other special conditions, you may need to make special adjustments to suit your needs. There are also different ways to follow the Good Carbohydrate Plan, depending on your use of the Optional Foods category of the apex of the Good Carbohydrate Plan Pyramid.

Read carefully Chapter 7 about the use of optional foods. You can follow the Good Carbohydrate Plan in a vegetarian or non-vegetarian way. You can simply add some good fats and some occasional sweets and still have an excellent vegan diet. You can have an occasional non-fat dairy and eggs and still have a vegetarian diet. You can add a small amount of seafood and have a healthy Asian-style diet. You can also add a little variation in animal products and have a healthy Mediterranean-style diet.

Step Six. Exercise.

Exercise is an important lifestyle step of the Good Carbohydrate Plan. Never underestimate the healthfulness of exercise. Exercise

helps to control blood sugar and insulin, and stimulates our metabolism, among other benefits. Check with your doctor to make sure
what level of exercise is okay for you. Follow the guidelines in
Chapter 9.

Exercise is a great healer. Exercise also helps to burn calories,
carbohydrates and fat, and sets in motion metabolic pathways for
your body to clean itself out. Those who score in the top 20 percent
of fitness have about one-eighth the chance of dying of heart disease compared to those who score in the bottom 20 percent.
Exercise also improves blood sugar control. If a person had difficulty with blood sugar, this may be improved to some extent simply
by engaging in regular exercise. Exercise helps blood sugar levels
by burning off some of the sugar in the blood. Exercise also helps to
improve insulin sensitivity (or decrease insulin resistance), that is, it
makes insulin more effective in controlling blood sugar. As a result,
your body requires less insulin to control blood sugar, so your
body's insulin level remains lower than it would without exercise.
This, in turn, helps to reduce the risk of coronary heart disease and
possibly obesity. These are some of the reasons that most effective
health and weight control programs, including programs for the
control of blood sugar and diabetes, include exercise.

Step Seven. Create a Healthy Lifestyle.

Health is not just diet and exercise. It includes taking supplements
when appropriate, seeing your physician if needed and taking medications as prescribed. Remember that creating a total healthy
lifestyle includes paying attention to your spiritual, mental, emo-
tional, and physical health.

Sleep

New research on the relationship between sleep and health suggests
that lack of sleep may make tolerance to carbohydrates worse. In
one study, individuals were allowed to sleep 12 hours per night in
the first trial, after which metabolic and blood tests were taken.
Then, they were allowed to sleep 4 hours per night and were tested
again. At the end of the study, the results were compared.
Researchers found that when the participants had inadequate sleep,

they had significantly worse glucose tolerance. Further testing showed that they had higher cortisol levels (which make blood sugar control more difficult) and a reduction in insulin sensitivity. Based on this study, adequate, regular sleep is likely to decrease your insulin resistance and improve your ability to handle carbohydrates. While this is just one study, and it's hard to draw too many conclusions from it, there is no harm in getting a good night's rest.

Supplements

For those who are not certain that they are getting enough nutrition through their diet, it may be prudent to add a reasonable supplement. If, despite your best efforts, you know that you are not obtaining the results you want, or getting the nutrients you need, consider herbs and supplements. For example, one of the most common deficiencies is calcium deficiency. While dairy is high in calcium, there are reasons to question whether it is the best way to obtain calcium. The Good Carbohydrate Plan recommends high calcium plant-based foods such as dark leafy greens and seaweed as the sources of choice. If you are not obtaining an optimal amount of these foods, I recommend calcium supplements as an alternative to dairy. For those who are not sure that they can obtain enough greens and who choose to avoid dairy in the Good Carbohydrate Plan, then a 500 mg supplement of calcium should be added.

However, I don't recommend mega doses of specific nutrients because of the uncertainty of what effect they may have on the body. If the amounts taken in are close to 100 percent of the RDA for a nutrient, that should be a safe level of nutrient to take. For those who have problems with blood sugar control, be sure to work with your doctor and consider supplements such as vanadium, magnesium, and chromium in case there are hidden deficiencies in this area. For those who decide to follow a strict Good Carbohydrate Plan with no animal products, a vitamin B12 supplement may also be wise, especially if one is following a strict vegan type of diet for a long period of time. Herbal supplements may also be helpful, but scientific documentation on the effectiveness of herbs is not always consistent. The use of supplements is described in Chapter 16 of this book.

Work with Your Physician

If you have trouble with blood sugar control or have any health problems, you must see your physician before you change your diet. Any change in diet may affect your need for medication and may require that your physician make adjustments in your overall diet and medication regimen. If you have diabetes, it is essential that you work with your doctor to decide the best overall plan of diet, exercise, and medication for your individual needs. While diet and exercise are the most important things you can do to combat the underlying disease, medications can help prevent harm from both short-term and long-term effects that may result from diabetes. It is possible to reduce or eliminate your need for some medications by following the Good Carbohydrate Plan, but this must be done gradually and in consultation with your doctor.

Stress Reduction/Positive Attitude/Spirituality

The Good Carbohydrate Plan is a whole person program. While the main point of this book is to help you make good food choices, it is important to remember that health is not just diet and exercise. It is the maintenance of harmony of body, mind, and spirit. The optimal Good Carbohydrate Plan includes all these elements.

Stress levels and mental attitude are very important to overall health. Just as carbohydrates can make you sick or make you well, mental attitude and stress can do the same. There is even evidence that stress can cause derangements in blood sugar control and may have an effect on lipid profiles, affecting your risk for coronary heart disease. In addition, there are a number of studies showing that people who have a good social support system and less stress tend to live longer and have fewer heart attacks.

Whatever you do to manage your own stress, I think everyone should consider the usefulness of meditation and the importance of prayer in their daily lives. Choose whatever means are helpful for you to manage your stress and keep a positive attitude. Don't forget the spiritual side of your life.

The last thing I want to do is to preach religion. Religion and spirituality are personal choices. However, I want you to know that they do have an impact on health if for no other reason than helping you to cope with stress. I also believe that spirituality in some form is important to everyone in more ways than just for their good health.

The optimal Good Carbohydrate Plan involves the whole person—body, mind and spirit—and includes having a good relationship with your doctor and with people who can support your healthy lifestyle. The Good Carbohydrate Plan is a flexible plan that you can use to suit your needs in different situations. Whether you have a weight problem, blood sugar problem, cholesterol problem or other health condition, the Good Carbohydrate Plan can help.

THREE QUICK-START PLANS

For those of you who are interested in a quick and easy trial of the Good Carbohydrate Plan, here are three different approaches.

Quick-Start Plan #1: Ten-Day Whole Carb Diet

THE WHOLE GRAIN TASTE TEST

To experience the flavor of whole grain, try chewing a mouthful of brown rice 50 to 100 times until it liquefies. You will notice that as you chew it, the flavor becomes slightly sweet and very pleasant. The longer you chew it, the more pleasant it becomes. By contrast, take a small bite of meat and chew it 50 to 100 times. You will notice that as you chew it, its taste becomes less pleasant and more like cardboard. The longer you chew, the less pleasant it becomes. In fact, the only reason the meat was tasty at all was the salt or other flavor that was added while cooking. Which do you think is the natural food choice for humans?

The Ten-Day Whole Carb Diet is probably the easiest way to start, although you have to learn how to use a few new foods. Bear in mind that this is very simple and not for everyone. If you want fancier fare, look to some of the other Good Carbohydrate meal plans in Chapter 11. This is similar to how I started on a good carbohydrate diet when I was a busy student with little time to cook. It borders on an Asian-style diet but has some obvious Middle American food choices in it.

Here's how I got started. The evening before the first day, I cooked a simple dinner, including a pot of brown rice for the next day's lunch and a vegetable stir-fry. I enhanced the taste with soy sauce when needed. The next morning I started with cooked oatmeal, which was very simple to prepare. I just boiled it in water and flavored it by sprinkling some raisins on it. A little cinnamon adds variety. Some mornings I also had a piece of fruit, such as a grapefruit or an apple. Brown rice (flavored with low sodium soy sauce) and some soup or leftover vegetables from the night before was another common breakfast. If you are adventurous, cooked buckwheat (kasha) also makes a tasty good carbohydrate breakfast.

For lunch, I brought to work some brown rice and vegetables from the previous night's dinner, and in the evening I cooked brown rice again for dinner, and also made enough for breakfast and lunch the next day. I had a simple stir-fry for dinner with some beans or lentils and some cooked greens. By keeping the number of dishes small I had a stir-fry almost every night for the first few days—I could cook it quickly and it became very convenient. Here is a sample of the beginning menu that I used for my first ten days.

Day 1

Breakfast:	Oatmeal with Raisins and Cinnamon, Fruit (While cooking breakfast, consider preparing grain and vegetable for lunch.)
Lunch:	Brown Rice, Steamed Vegetables with Dijon Sauce, Lentil Soup, Sweet Potato
Dinner:	Brown Rice, Broccoli Stir-Fry, Tofu, Fruit

Day 2

Breakfast:	Oatmeal or Kasha (Buckwheat), Fruit (Lentil Soup from lunch is optional.)
Lunch:	Brown Rice, Broccoli Stir-Fry (from last night), Fruit
Dinner:	Brown Rice Pilaf, Greens with 3221 Dijon Sauce, Miso Soup with Tofu and Seaweed

Day 3

> Breakfast: Brown Rice, Miso Soup with Tofu and Seaweed
> (from last night), Fruit
> Lunch: Brown Rice Pilaf, Salad, Fruit
> Dinner: Brown Rice with Wild Rice, Squash, Bean dish,
> Greens

Continue on this type of diet for ten days to see its full effect. Notice that there are no bad carbohydrates on this diet. In order to follow the Whole Carb Diet for the 21 days, I suggest after the first ten days you might start adding other foods to tailor the plan to your own personal desires.

Quick-Start Plan #2: The Mediterranean-Style Diet

The Mediterranean-style Diet is a little more lenient than the Whole Carb Diet. In this plan, you may not lose weight as quickly; however, it may be a little more familiar to most Americans. You still need to learn how to use cooked whole grains in your diet to replace some of the bad carbohydrates and fat calories that you want to avoid. However, you can also use pasta (preferably whole wheat) in some simple Mediterranean-style dishes. Stone ground whole wheat bread may also be included in this diet, although you must be sure not to use commercially-prepared whole wheat bread. Olive oil is also used in some of the dishes.

For a standard breakfast, start with cooked oatmeal and raisins. On occasion, you may use foods such as whole grain bread and no-sugar-added fruit preserves. You can add some whole fruit to your breakfast or eat it as a morning snack. For lunch, try a combination of salad with some soup. Use a dressing of extra virgin olive oil and vinegar as the basic ingredients. For dinner, try a vegetable stir-fry along with brown rice pilaf and some good carbohydrate beans and other vegetables such as squash, pumpkin and dark leafy greens. Here is a sample menu:

Day 1

> Breakfast: Oatmeal and Fruit
> Lunch: Lentil Soup, Salad, and Fruit
> Dinner: Pasta with Salad, Side Vegetable, and Hummus

Day 2

Breakfast: Sprouted Whole Wheat Toast with Fruit Preserves,
              Oatmeal
Lunch: Hummus Sandwich in Pita Bread, Barley Soup,
              Greens Steamed or in Salad, Fruit
Dinner: Brown Rice Pilaf, Squash, Bean Dish, Salad with
              Tomatoes, Fruit

Day 3

Breakfast: Oatmeal, Fruit
Lunch: Pasta with Vegetables, Salad, Fruit
Dinner: Savory Garbanzo Beans, Mixed Grains,
              Vegetables, Salad

Quick-Start Plan #3: Adding Optional Foods

Another way to start the Good Carbohydrate Plan is to add some of the optional foods. When eating optional foods, remember that the best are those that are still low in fat, sugar, and white flour. For example, you could start with a breakfast of Egg Beaters® or egg whites with vegetables mixed in for a vegetable omelet. You could have some brown rice on the side or you might have some new potatoes, sautéed with herbs and spices, without oil. You might add some good carbohydrate fruit to your breakfast. Morning snacks could include good carbohydrate fruits or vegetables.

For lunch, you might have some whole grain bread with soup or you might try a low fat, whole grain pasta accompanied by a salad (non-fat dressing). For dinner, you could enjoy a whole grain bean and rice dish such as Chickpeas à la King over a bed of brown rice. This could be accompanied by a plate of steamed vegetables or a salad of some kind. Here is a sample menu:

Day 1

Breakfast: Egg Beater® Omelet, Sprouted Wheat Bread, Fruit
              Preserves
Lunch: Soup, Salad, Fruit
Dinner: Pasta, Salad, Stone Ground Whole Wheat Bread

Day 2

Breakfast:	Oatmeal, Fruit
Lunch:	Sandwich, Soup
Dinner:	Rice Pilaf, Chicken Stir-Fry, Greens, Squash, Fruit

Day 3

Breakfast:	Stone Ground Whole Wheat Toast, Fruit Preserves, Fruit
Lunch:	Rice Pilaf, Soup, Salad
Dinner:	Broiled Fish, Brown Rice, Salad, Steamed Greens

COMPLETE YOUR 21-DAY PLAN

After trying the diet for ten days, you have the option of using the menus found in Chapter 11 for another 11 days, which will complete your 21-day trial period. Meanwhile, you should begin to learn a few new dishes each week to increase the variety in your new Good Carbohydrate Plan diet.

If you are committed from the beginning to learn the Good Carbohydrate Plan, simply start with one of the 11-day menus and add in selections from the Quick-Start menus to complete your 21-Day Plan. The beginning steps are similar in that you should learn how to prepare whole grains. Read the next chapter on setting up your kitchen and how to prepare yourself for a Good Carbohydrate Plan lifestyle.

The Quick-Start plans are generic and designed to be simple and easy. For the long term, you will want to learn a larger variety of dishes and to tailor the plan to your personal taste. Ideally, you should decide what your personal Good Carbohydrate Plan should look like. To a large extent it will be determined by how your body responds to food. Everyone has her or his own idiosyncrasies as to how they respond to certain foods and the flexibility of the Good Carbohydrate Plan allows you to accommodate your own body.

Now let's learn more about how to put the Good Carbohydrate Plan into action.

CHAPTER 11

How to Put the Good Carbohydrate Plan into Action

Planning, Menus, Shopping, and Preparing Good Carbohydrates

PLANNING YOUR GOOD CARBOHYDRATE MEALS

Planning your good carbohydrate meals ahead of time is important so you can get organized to know what you have on hand and what you need to buy. You can use the menus beginning on page 157 to get started or you can design your own.

For some of you there will be many new foods to experience on this plan. Use the Good Carbohydrate Plan Pyramid and food lists in Chapter 7 as your guide. It's best to use fresh food ingredients; next best is frozen, and then canned. These foods can be prepared in their raw form or baked, boiled, steamed, grilled, or stir-fried.

- It might be helpful to plan your menu at the same time every week, such as Sunday morning before going food shopping. Your meal planning doesn't need to take a lot of time or effort.

- Make sure to include a variety of ingredients, tastes, colors, and textures. Adding variety helps to curb cravings.

- Each meal should include grains and/or other staple foods. Eat eight to thirteen servings of these foods each day. Some grain choices for your menu could be wheat (including pasta and whole wheat bread), corn, oats, rice, and barley. Some less known grains you might include are amaranth, millet, buckwheat, and quinoa. Some staple vegetables you might choose are carrots, potato, sweet potato, taro, and yams. Convenience tip: When cooking grains or beans, it's good to make extra and use them in your menu throughout the week.

- Include a variety of fresh vegetables (at least three to five servings daily). You can eat as many vegetables as you want. They are the most neglected good carbohydrates. Vegetables fill up your stomach and provide the vitamins, minerals, micronutrients, and fiber your body needs. Some of the colorful and wonderful vegetable choices are asparagus, broccoli, cauliflower, cabbage, celery, cucumber, green beans, kale, onions, pumpkin, spinach, squash, summer squash, tomatoes, watercress, and zucchini.

- For your sweet cravings, plan to have whole fruit (two to four servings daily). If you want a sweet taste you can try some prepared desserts in this book. Fruits are high in vitamins, especially vitamin C, and fiber. Some fruit choices for your menu are apples, blueberries, cantaloupe, grapefruit, grapes, lemons, melons, nectarines, oranges, peaches, pears, plums, and strawberries.

- Be sure to use leafy green vegetables or non-dairy, high calcium vegetables in your menu daily (two to three servings per day). If possible, incorporate sea vegetables daily, such as dulse, hijiki, konbu, and wakame. Sea vegetables provide important minerals, including calcium. You can eat as many high calcium vegetables as you want. Some high calcium vegetable choices are broccoli, Brussels sprouts, cabbage, Chinese cabbage, endive, collard greens, green leaf lettuce, green onion, kale, mustard greens, spinach, Swiss chard, turnip greens, and watercress.

- Use beans or legumes as your main source of protein. Two to three servings a day of non-cholesterol protein foods, such as beans, can replace meat in your menu. You may eat as much as you want of the foods from the non-cholesterol, protein food group. Some choices for your menu are azuki beans, black beans, black-eyed peas, butter beans, chickpeas (garbanzo beans), great northern beans, green peas, kidney beans, lentils, lima beans, navy beans, pink beans, pinto beans, red beans, split peas, and white beans.

GOOD CARBOHYDRATE SAMPLE MENUS

There are three sets of sample menus I have prepared for you. Each set has a vegetarian and a non-vegetarian version. The recipes listed in these menus can be found in Chapter 12. The first menu set has more traditional foods—familiar foods we are comfortable with. The second set is more international and adventurous. The third set of menus is for those who follow the Mediterranean Diet Plan. The Mediterranean Diet Plan has more oil and bread. It is for the person who doesn't have a weight problem or a cholesterol problem. It can be used, minus the bread, for those who don't have a weight problem but have difficulty handling blood sugar after trying a lower fat Good Carbohydrate Plan.

GOOD CARBOHYDRATE PLAN
Traditional Vegetarian Sample Menu 1

Day	Breakfast	Lunch	Dinner
1	Oatmeal with Raisins and Cinnamon Soy or Skim Milk (optional) Fruit	Quick Chili Brown Rice or Baked Potato Vegetable Sticks Spinach and Tomato Salad Fruit	Pasta and Mushroom Marinara Sauce Steamed Greens Four-Bean Salad Whole Wheat Roll Fruit

Traditional Vegetarian Sample Menu 1 *(continued)*

Day	Breakfast	Lunch	Dinner
2	Whole Wheat Cereal Soy or Skim Milk (optional) Mixed Fruit	Vegetable Barley Soup Green Salad with Vinaigrette Dressing Whole Wheat Roll Fruit	Mushroom Vegetable Stew Brown Rice Spice Apple Crisp
3	Whole Wheat Bagel with Fruit-only Preserves Fruit	Whole Wheat Pita Bread with Vegetables and Simple Hummus Split Pea Soup Fruit	Chickpeas à la King Brown Rice Steamed Kale and Butternut Squash Green Beans Pumpkin Spice Cookies
4	Multigrain Cereal Soy or Skim Milk (optional) Fruit	Gardenburger Wrap with Fresh Vegetables using Whole Wheat Tortilla or Whole Wheat Chapati as wrap Brown Rice Fruit	Carol's Lasagna Green Salad with Non-fat Dressing (see recipes) Steamed Broccoli with 3221 Dijon Mustard Sauce Rainbow Gel Compote
5	Cream of Wheat Soy or Skim Milk (optional) Fruit	Stovetop Spanish Rice Vegetable Sticks and Tofu Dip Sauce Fruit	Barbecue Baked Beans Brown Rice and Barley Steamed Mixed Vegetables Cucumber and Tomato Slices Fruit

Traditional Vegetarian Sample Menu 1 *(continued)*

Day	Breakfast	Lunch	Dinner
6	Stone-ground Whole Wheat Toast with Fruit-only Preserves Fruit	Spicy Black Bean Soup Whole Wheat Roll Steamed Leafy Greens Garlic Baked Potato Fruit	Rice and Lentils Green Salad with Non-fat Dressing Steamed Carrots and Peas Rice and Sweet Potato Pudding
7	Kasha (Buckwheat) Soy or Skim Milk (optional) Fruit	Hurrito Burrito Green Salad with Non-fat Dressing (see recipes) Fruit	Pasta with Eggplant Sauce Whole Wheat Roll Steamed Swiss Chard Garden Green Salad with Non-fat Dressing (see recipes) Fruit
8	Multigrain Cereal Soy or Skim Milk (optional) Fruit	Ann's Corn Tomato Soup Americas Quinoa Salad on Leafy Greens Fruit	Black-Eyed Peas with Squash and Italian Mustard Greens Just Barley with Savory Gravy Green Salad and Non-fat Dressing (see recipes) Fruit

Traditional Vegetarian Sample Menu 1 *(continued)*

Day	Breakfast	Lunch	Dinner
9	Peachy Banana Muffins Mixed Fruit	Creamy Zucchini Soup Mixed Greens with Vinaigrette Dressing Whole Wheat Bread Fruit	Pasta with Roasted Vegetables Steamed Greens and Summer Squash Black Bean Salad "Pine" Apple Dessert
10	Oatmeal with Raisins and Cinnamon Soy or Skim Milk (optional) Fruit	Mixed Vegetable Curry Brown Rice Whole Wheat Bread or Tortilla Spinach Salad with Non-fat Dressing (see recipes) Pumpkin Spice Cookies	Tofu and Vegetable Stir Fry Basmati Brown Rice Oriental Ginger Gravy Creamy Mango or Peach Pudding or Fruit
11	Stone-ground Whole Wheat Toast with Fruit-only Preserves Fruit	Multigrain Fried Rice with Tofu Steamed Greens or Spinach Tomato Slices Fruit	Stuffed Peppers à la Español Rice and Lentils Steamed Kale Fruit

GOOD CARBOHYDRATE PLAN
Traditional Non-Vegetarian Sample Menu 1

Day	Breakfast	Lunch	Dinner
1	Oatmeal with Raisins and Cinnamon As is or with Soy or Skim Milk Fruit	Quick Chili Brown Rice or Baked Potato Vegetable Sticks Spinach and Tomato Salad Fruit	Herbed Mediterranean Chicken over Garlic Noodles Steamed Greens Four-Bean Salad Fruit
2	Egg Beaters® Omelette with Mushrooms and Vegetables Mixed Fruit	Vegetable Barley Soup Green Salad with Vinaigrette Dressing Whole Wheat Roll Fruit	Mushroom Vegetable Stew Brown Rice Steamed Leafy Greens Corn on the Cob Whole Wheat Roll Spice Apple Crisp
3	Whole Wheat Bagel with Fruit-only Preserves Fruit	Whole Wheat Pita Bread with Vegetables, Chicken Breast Chunks and Simple Hummus Split Pea Soup Fruit	Carol's Lasagna Green Salad with Non-fat Dressing (see recipes) Steamed Broccoli with 3221 Dijon Mustard Sauce Rainbow Gel Compote

Traditional Non-Vegetarian Sample Menu 1 *(continued)*

Day	Breakfast	Lunch	Dinner
4	All Bran Cereal Soy or Skim Milk Fruit	Black-eyed Peas with Squash and Mustard Greens Cooked Barley with Savo Gravy Green Salad with Non-fat Dressing (see recipes) Fruit	Shrimp Stir Fry Brown Rice Fruit
5	Cream of Wheat As is or with Soy or Skim Milk Fruit	Stovetop Spanish Rice Vegetable Sticks and Tofu Dip Sauce Fruit	Pasta with Eggplant Sauce Whole Wheat Roll Steamed Swiss Chard Green Salad with Non-fat Dressing (see recipes) Fruit
6	Whole Wheat Toast with Fruit- only Preserves Fruit	Spicy Black Bean Soup Whole Wheat Roll Steamed Leafy Greens Garlic Baked Potato Fruit	Rice and Lentils Green Salad with Non-fat Dressing Steamed Carrots and Peas Rice and Sweet Potato Pudding

Traditional Non-Vegetarian Sample Menu 1 *(continued)*

Day	Breakfast	Lunch	Dinner
7	Kasha (Buckwheat) As is or with Soy or Skim Milk Fruit	Hurrito Burrito Green Salad with Non-fat Dressing (see recipes) Fruit	Baked Fish Green Salad with Non-fat Dressing (see recipes) Steamed Broccoli with 3221 Dijon Mustard Sauce Rainbow Gel Compote
8	Multigrain Cereal Soy or Skim Milk Fruit	Ann's Corn Tomato Soup Americas Quinoa Salad on Leafy Green Lettuce Fruit	Barbecue Baked Beans Brown Rice and Barley Steamed Mixed Vegetables Cucumber and Tomato Slices Fruit
9	Peachy Banana Muffins Mixed Fruit	Creamy Zucchini Soup Mixed Greens with Vinaigrette Dressing Whole Wheat Bread Fruit	Pasta with Roasted Vegetables or Black Bean Salad Steamed Greens and Summer Squash "Pine" Apple Dessert

Traditional Non-Vegetarian Sample Menu 1 *(continued)*

Day	Breakfast	Lunch	Dinner
10	Oatmeal with Raisins and Cinnamon As is or with Soy or Skim Milk Fruit	Mixed Vegetable Curry Brown Rice Whole Wheat Tortilla Spinach Salad with Non-fat Dressing (see recipes) Pumpkin Spice Cookies	Garlic Chicken Stir Fry Basmati Brown Rice Green Salad with Non-fat Dressing (see recipes) Creamy Mango or Peach Pudding or Fruit
11	Stone-ground Whole Wheat Toast with Fruit-only Preserves Fruit	Multigrain Fried Rice with Tofu Steamed Greens or Spinach Tomato Slices Fruit	Stuffed Peppers à la Español Rice and Lentils Steamed Kale Fruit

GOOD CARBOHYDRATE PLAN
International Vegetarian Sample Menu 2

Day	Breakfast	Lunch	Dinner
1	Oatmeal with Raisins and Cinnamon Soy or Skim Milk (optional) Fruit	Quick Chili Brown Rice or Baked Potato Vegetable Sticks Spinach and Tomato Salad Fruit	Hearty Sweet Potato Stew Brown Rice Steamed Leafy Greens Black-eyed Peas Whole Wheat Roll Rainbow Gel Compote

GOOD CARBOHYDRATE PLAN

International Vegetarian Sample Menu 2 *(continued)*

Day	Breakfast	Lunch	Dinner
2	Kasha (Buckwheat) Soy or Skim Milk (optional) Mixed Fruit	Mediterranean Barley Salad Steamed Carrots and Green Beans Spice Apple Crisp	Cannellini Sauce over Pasta Whole Wheat Roll Steamed Greens and Summer Squash Green Salad and Non-fat Dressing (see recipes) Fruit
3	Whole Wheat Bagel with Fruit-only Preserves Fruit	Stuffed Tomatoes with Beans 'n' Rice Creamy Zucchini Soup Whole Wheat Bread Fruit	Chickpeas à la King Brown Rice Steamed Kale and Butternut Squash Pumpkin Spice Cookies
4	Hot Amaranth Cereal or Multigrain Cereal Soy or Skim Milk (optional) Fruit	Whole Wheat Pita Bread with Vegetables and Simple Hummus Split Pea Soup Fruit	Black-eyed Peas with Squash and Italian Mustard Greens Just Barley with Savory Gravy Green Salad with Non-fat Dressing (see recipes) Fruit

International Vegetarian Sample Menu 2 *(continued)*

Day	Breakfast	Lunch	Dinner
5	Cream of Wheat Soy or Skim Milk (optional) Fruit	Tabouleh Peasant Potato Salad Four-bean Salad Fruit	Carol's Lasagna Whole Wheat Roll Garden Green Salad with Non- fat Dressing (see recipes) Fruit
6	Whole Wheat Toast with Fruit- only Preserves Fruit	Spicy Black Bean Soup Whole Wheat Roll Steamed Leafy Greens Garlic Baked Potato Fruit	Rice and Lentils Green Salad with Non-fat Dressing Steamed Carrots and Peas Rice and Sweet Potato Pudding
7	Miso Soup Brown Rice Pickled Vegetables or Multigrain Cereal Soy or Skim Milk (optional) Fruit	Hurrito Burrito Green Salad with Non-fat Dressing (see recipes) Fruit	Barbecue Baked Beans Brown Rice and Barley Steamed Mixed Vegetables Raita (yogurt and cucumbers) Fruit

International Vegetarian Sample Menu 2 *(continued)*

Day	Breakfast	Lunch	Dinner
8	Quinoa Cereal Soy or Skim Milk (optional) Fruit	Ann's Corn Tomato Soup Americas Quinoa Salad on Leafy Greens Fruit	Colorful Millet-Stuffed Artichokes Baked Potato with Barbecue Baked Beans as topping Steamed Broccoli with 3221 Dijon Mustard Sauce Rainbow Gel Compote
9	Peachy Banana Muffins Mixed Fruit	Bean and Radicchio Salad with Raspberry Vinaigrette Whole Wheat Bread Fruit	Pasta with Roasted Vegetables Steamed Greens and Summer Squash Black Bean Salad "Pine" Apple Dessert
10	Oatmeal with Raisins and Cinnamon Soy or Skim Milk (optional) Fruit	Multigrain Fried Rice with Tofu Steamed Greens or Spinach Tomato Slices Fruit	Tofu and Vegetable Stir Fry Basmati Brown Rice Oriental Ginger Gravy Creamy Mango Pudding

International Vegetarian Sample Menu 2 *(continued)*

Day	Breakfast	Lunch	Dinner
11	Stone-ground Whole Wheat Toast with Fruit-only Preserves Fruit	Mixed Vegetable Curry Brown Rice Whole Wheat Bread Spinach Salad with Non-fat Dressing (see recipes) Pumpkin Spice Cookies	Stuffed Peppers à la Español Rice and Lentils Green Salad with Non-fat Dressing (see recipes) Fruit

GOOD CARBOHYDRATE PLAN
International Non-Vegetarian Sample Menu 2

Day	Breakfast	Lunch	Dinner
1	Oatmeal with Raisins and Cinnamon Soy or Skim Milk (optional) Fruit	Quick Chili Brown Rice or Baked Potato Vegetable Sticks Spinach and Tomato Salad Fruit	Hearty Sweet Potato Stew Steamed Leafy Greens Black-eyed Peas Whole Wheat Roll Rainbow Gel Compote
2	Egg Beaters® Omelette with Mushrooms and Vegetables Mixed Fruit	Mediterranean Barley Salad Steamed Carrots and Green Beans Spice Apple Crisp	Mango and Chicken Stir Fry Basmati Brown Rice Green Salad and Non-fat Dressing (see recipes) Fruit

International Non-Vegetarian Sample Menu 2 *(continued)*

Day	Breakfast	Lunch	Dinner
3	Whole Wheat Bagel with Fruit-only Preserves Fruit	Stuffed Tomatoes with Beans 'n' Rice Creamy Zucchini Soup Whole Wheat Bread Fruit	Rice and Lentils Italian Mustard Greens Steamed Carrots and Peas Rice and Sweet Potato Pudding
4	Hot Amaranth Cereal or Multigrain Cereal Soy or Skim Milk (optional) Fruit	Whole Wheat Pita Bread with Vegetables and Simple Hummus Split Pea Soup Fruit	Carol's Lasagna Whole Wheat Roll Garden Green Salad with Non-fat Dressing (see recipes) Ono Mango Crisp
5	Cream of Wheat Soy or Skim Milk (optional) Fruit	Hurrito Burrito Green Salad with Non-fat Dressing (see recipes) Fruit	Beans and Red Onion with Fish Brown Rice and Barley Oriental Ginger Gravy Steamed Mixed Vegetables Raita (yogurt and cucumbers) Fruit

International Non-Vegetarian Sample Menu 2 *(continued)*

Day	Breakfast	Lunch	Dinner
6	Stone-ground Whole Wheat Toast with Fruit-only Preserves Fruit	Spicy Black Bean Soup Whole Wheat Roll Steamed Leafy Greens Garlic Baked Potato Fruit	Pasta with Roasted Vegetables Green Salad with Non-fat Dressing (see recipes) Black Bean Salad "Pine" Apple Dessert
7	Miso Soup Brown Rice Pickled Vegetables Or Multigrain Cereal Soy or Skim Milk (optional) Fruit	Multigrain Fried Rice with Tofu Steamed Greens Tomato Slices Fruit	Garlic Chicken Stir Fry Basmati Brown Rice Steamed Kabocha Squash Fruit
8	Quinoa Cereal Soy or Skim Milk (optional) Fruit	Ann's Corn Tomato Soup Americas Quinoa Salad on Leafy Greens Fruit	Colorful Millet-Stuffed Artichokes Baked Potato with Barbecue Baked Beans as topping Steamed Broccoli with 3221 Dijon Mustard Sauce Rainbow Gel Compote

International Non-Vegetarian Sample Menu 2 *(continued)*

Day	Breakfast	Lunch	Dinner
9	Peachy Banana Muffins Mixed Fruit	Bean and Radicchio Salad with Raspberry Vinaigrette Whole Wheat Bread Fruit	Calico Wraps Brown Rice Steamed Kale Pumpkin Spice Cookies
10	Oatmeal with Raisins and Cinnamon Soy or Skim Milk (optional) Fruit	Tabouleh Peasant Potato Salad Four-Bean Salad Fruit	Herbed Mediterranean Chicken over Garlic Noodles Steamed Greens Black Bean Salad Fruit
11	Stone-ground Whole Wheat Toast with Fruit-only Preserves Fruit	Mixed Vegetable Curry Brown Rice Whole Wheat Bread Spinach Salad with Non-fat Dressing (see recipes) Pumpkin Spice Cookies	Barbecue Baked Beans Brown Rice and Barley Steamed Mixed Vegetables Raita (yogurt and cucumbers) Fruit

GOOD CARBOHYDRATE PLAN
Mediterranean Vegetarian Sample Menu 3

Day	Breakfast	Lunch	Dinner
1	Oatmeal with Raisins and Cinnamon Soy or Skim Milk (optional) Fruit	Minestrone Soup Stone Ground Whole Wheat Roll Fruit	Carol's Lasagna Whole Wheat Roll Garden Green Salad with Non-fat Dressing (see recipes) Fruit
2	All Bran Cereal Soy or Skim Milk (optional) Mixed Fruit	Mediterranean Barley Salad Steamed Carrots and Green Beans Spice Apple Crisp	Mushroom Vegetable Stew Brown Rice Steamed Leafy Greens Spice Apple Crisp
3	Ovo-vegetarians may try Egg Beaters® Omelette with Mushrooms and Vegetables Fruit	Stuffed Tomatoes with Beans 'n' Rice Green Salad and Non-fat Dressing (see recipes) Stone-ground Whole Wheat Bread Fruit	Pasta with Eggplant Sauce Whole Wheat Roll Steamed Greens and Summer Squash
4	Multigrain Cereal Soy or Skim Milk (optional) Fruit	Whole Wheat Pita Bread with Vegetables and Simple Hummus Onion Soup Fruit	Just Barley with Savory Gravy Steamed Greens Baked Butternut Squash Green Salad with Non-fat Dressing (see recipes) Fruit

Mediterranean Vegetarian Sample Menu 3 *(continued)*

Day	Breakfast	Lunch	Dinner
5	Cream of Wheat Soy or Skim Milk (optional) Fruit	Tabouleh Lentil Soup Stone Ground Whole Wheat Bread Fruit	Broiled Falafel Brown Rice Steamed Greens Fruit
6	Stone-ground Whole Wheat Toast with Fruit- only Preserves Fruit	Moroccan Salad Whole Wheat Roll Fruit	Rice and Lentils Italian Mustard Greens Steamed Carrots and Peas Baked Apples
7	Kasha (Buckwheat) Soy or Skim Milk (optional) Fruit	Vegetable Soup Steamed Leafy Greens Just Barley Tomato Slices Fruit	Herbed Italian Beans Steamed Mixed Vegetables Raita (yogurt and cucumbers) Tomato Slices Fruit
8	Multigrain Cereal Soy or Skim Milk (optional) Fruit	Stovetop Spanish Rice Green Salad garnished with Avocado, Olives, and Non-fat Dressing (see recipes) Fruit	Colorful Millet- Stuffed Artichokes Whole Wheat Roll Steamed Broccoli with 3221 Dijon Mustard Sauce Corn on the Cob Fruit

Mediterranean Vegetarian Sample Menu 3 *(continued)*

Day	Breakfast	Lunch	Dinner
9	Peachy Banana Muffins Mixed Fruit	Bean and Radicchio Salad with Raspberry Vinaigrette Stone Ground Whole Wheat Pita Bread Fruit	Pasta with Roasted Vegetables Steamed Greens and Summer Squash Black Bean Salad Fruit
10	Oatmeal with Raisins and Cinnamon Soy or Skim Milk (optional) Fruit	Greek Spinach Salad Tuscany Bean Soup Fruit	Pasta with Mushroom Marinara Sauce Green Salad with Non-fat Dressing (see recipes) Whole Wheat Roll Spice Apple Crisp
11	Stone-ground Whole Wheat Toast with Fruit-only Preserves Fruit	Gardenburger with Whole Wheat Pita Bread and Tomatoes, Lettuce, Olives, Sprouts, and Raita (yogurt and cucumbers) Fruit	Stuffed Peppers à la Español Rice and Lentils Green Salad with Non-fat Dressing (see recipes) Fruit

GOOD CARBOHYDRATE PLAN
Mediterranean Non-Vegetarian Sample Menu 3

Day	Breakfast	Lunch	Dinner
1	Oatmeal with Raisins and Cinnamon Soy or Skim Milk (optional) Fruit	Minestrone Soup Stone Ground Whole Wheat Roll Fruit	Herbed Mediterranean Chicken over Garlic Noodles Steamed Greens Four-Bean Salad Fruit
2	Whole Wheat Cereal Soy or Skim Milk (optional) Mixed Fruit	Mediterranean Barley Salad Steamed Carrots and Green Beans Spice Apple Crisp	Carol's Lasagna Whole Wheat Roll Garden Green Salad with Non-fat Dressing (see recipes) Fruit
3	Egg Beaters® Omelette with Mushrooms and Vegetables Fruit	Stuffed Tomatoes with Beans 'n' Rice Green Salad and Non-fat Dressing (see recipes) Whole Wheat Bread Fruit	Chickpea à la King Brown Rice Green Salad with Vinaigrette Dressing Fruit

Mediterranean Non-Vegetarian Sample Menu 3 *(continued)*

Day	Breakfast	Lunch	Dinner
4	Multigrain Cereal Soy or Skim Milk (optional) Fruit	Whole Wheat Pita Bread with Vegetables and Simple Hummus Onion Soup Fruit	Mediterranean Fish Just Barley with Savory Gravy Steamed Greens Baked Butternut Squash Green Salad with Non-fat Dressing (see recipes) Fruit
5	Cream of Wheat Soy or Skim Milk (optional) Fruit	Tabouleh Lentil Soup Stone Ground Whole Wheat Bread Fruit	Pasta with Eggplant Sauce Whole Wheat Roll Black Bean Salad Steamed Greens and Summer Squash Fruit
6	Whole Wheat Toast with Fruit-only Preserves Fruit	Moroccan Salad Whole Wheat Roll Fruit	Rice and Lentils Italian Mustard Greens Steamed Carrots and Peas Baked Apples

Mediterranean Non-Vegetarian Sample Menu 3 *(continued)*

Day	Breakfast	Lunch	Dinner
7	Kasha (Buckwheat) Soy or Skim Milk (optional) Fruit	Greek Spinach Salad Tuscany Bean Soup Fruit	Fish Kabobs with Mediterranean Salsa and Vegetable Kabobs and Marinades of Choice Brown Rice Green Salad with Non-fat Dressing (see recipes) Fruit
8	Multigrain Cereal Soy or Skim Milk (optional) Fruit	Stovetop Spanish Rice Green Salad garnished with Avocado, Olives, and Non-fat Dressing (see recipes) Fruit	Colorful Millet-Stuffed Artichokes Whole Wheat Roll Steamed Broccoli with 3221 Dijon Mustard Sauce Corn on the Cob Fruit
9	Peachy Banana Muffins Mixed Fruit	Mediterranean Chicken Salad Stone Ground Whole Wheat Bread or Whole Wheat Pita Bread Fruit	Pasta with Roasted Vegetables Steamed Greens and Summer Squash Black Bean Salad Fruit

Mediterranean Non-Vegetarian Sample Menu 3 *(continued)*

Day	Breakfast	Lunch	Dinner
10	Oatmeal with Raisins and Cinnamon Soy or Skim Milk (optional) Fruit	Vegetable Barley Soup Steamed Greens Tomato Slices Fruit	Spanish Chicken Casserole Whole Wheat Roll Garlic Baked Potato Steamed Greens and Summer Squash Spice Apple Crisp
11	Whole Wheat Toast with Fruit-only Preserves Fruit	Pasta and Mushroom Marinara Sauce Spinach Salad with Non-fat Dressing (see recipes) Fruit	Stuffed Peppers à la Español Rice and Lentils Green Salad with Non-fat Dressing (see recipes) Fruit

SNACKS

You can have snacks even though they aren't listed on the sample menus. Everyone gets hungry between meals at some time. Probably the best thing to do when you get hungry is to exercise first. When ancient humans had hunger pangs, it was a signal for them to go out and obtain food, which required exercise. This naturally suppressed hunger for a while. After effort was expended and the food was obtained, the hunger drive was so healthy that the simplest food tasted very good.

So that you don't find yourself choosing bad carbohydrates for snacking, it's useful to have some items handy that can be prepared quickly so that you can be ready when hunger strikes. Use the Carbohydrate Quotient table to find items that have a low Carbohydrate Quotient number and start with that. Have the fixings for some of the following items in your kitchen for snack emergencies. Some snack ideas are:

- Whole fruit: always keep some handy.

- Frozen seedless grapes: they taste like mini sherbet balls.

- Baked sweet potato: pre-cook some and keep handy in the refrigerator for a very filling sweet snack.

- Garbanzo beans from the can, rinsed: a great 15 percent fat substitute for 62 percent-fat boiled peanuts.

- Fresh cut vegetables with dip or non-fat dressing: make sure the dip is low fat such as a bean dip.

- Baked corn chips and bean dip or salsa.

- Baked pita chips with low fat hummus: cut a whole wheat pita into eighths and place in a toaster oven for chips. Use the low fat Simple Hummus in this book for the dip.

- Brown rice sprinkled with seaweed flakes: a traditional Asian favorite.

- Quick burritos: Use whole wheat tortilla, canned non-fat refried beans, fresh greens, and salsa.

- Instant or canned low fat soup: just add water or heat and serve. Add vegetables of your choice. Dried vegetables are also excellent additions, such as dried corn, peas, shiitake mushrooms, or seaweed.

APPLYING THE GOOD CARBOHYDRATE PLAN: GO SHOPPING!

Whether you choose a Quick-Start Diet Plan or the sample menus, the menus will help you to create a shopping list. You can find plenty of foods for the Good Carbohydrate Plan at a regular supermarket, although sometimes a wider variety is available at health food stores. Even some drug/variety stores are now featuring a health food section.

The Good Carbohydrate Plan Pyramid from Chapter 7 is another good tool to help you with your shopping. Start with the base of the Pyramid and work your way up. Go to your favorite food store and buy some whole grains as the main staple for your eating plan. I use brown rice because it is the most versatile. Whole grains such as oats, brown rice, bulgur wheat, buckwheat (kasha), and whole corn will be your staple foods. These foods will replace refined sugar and refined flour, which are eliminated on the Quick-Start Diet Plans found in Chapter 10.

Shopping Tips

- When preparing your shopping list, remember you want to stock your pantry with good carbohydrates such as grains (rice and oats, etc.), beans, pasta, and sea vegetables (dried or fresh). Grains, beans, and seasonings store easily in airtight containers.

- Condiments and bottled goods on your shopping list may be salad dressings (no oil), sauces (marinara sauce, pizza sauce, low-sodium soy sauce, hoi sin sauce, vegetarian stir fry sauce, A.1® Steak Sauce, barbecue sauce, Tabasco® Sauce, teriyaki sauce, and Dijon mustard), salsa, fruit preserves (no sugar added, no artificial sweetener), and no-oil marinated artichoke hearts.

- Include enough fresh vegetables, fruits, and other refrigerated foods for your first week of meals. Shop often for fresh ingredients.

- Stock up on quick foods. See the list of snack ideas (p. 179). Four instant foods for your shopping list are dried mushrooms, miso, and wakame (seaweed), vegetarian chicken-flavored broth powder.

- Stick to your list and avoid impulse buying. The store is where your diet begins and it can be also where it ends. Caution here.

- Don't shop when you're hungry.

- Try to shop at times when the store isn't busy.

- Shop at a familiar store. The better you know the store, the faster you can find what you need and check out.

- Get familiar with a good health food store that has whole foods (not just pills and powders). They tend to have a greater selection of whole grain and minimally-processed foods.

PREPARING YOUR GOOD CARBOHYDRATE MEALS

The Good Carbohydrate Plan requires no expensive kitchenware or appliances. You can start with what you have or you may like to add some appliances for additional convenience in preparing your good carbohydrates. How much time and money you spend setting up your kitchen is up to you.

Recommended Cookware and Appliances

Stainless steel cookware or enameled cookware is better than aluminum cookware because less of the metal from the pot is likely to get into the food. A wok, an electric wok or wok-like skillet is useful for stir-fry dishes. Two other appliances in particular are very helpful in preparing good carbohydrates: the automatic rice cooker and the pressure cooker.

The Electric Rice Cooker

An automatic rice cooker is the ultimate convenience appliance. (I think they should be called automatic grain and vegetable cookers because they are so versatile.) Simply place your rice and water in it, press the button and forget about it until it goes "bing," telling you your rice is done. No watching or burning rice ever again. The rice cooker knows how long to cook, and it always comes out perfect as long as you put in the right amount of water. It will do this with other grains and vegetables as well. Rice cookers come in small two-cup sizes all the way up to large family sizes.

The automatic rice cooker is probably the most underused appliance in America. The healthiest state in the U.S. is Hawaii, and just about every household in Hawaii has a rice cooker. The healthiest nation in the world is Japan, and just about every household in Japan has a rice cooker. Could it be that consuming rice, which typically has a lower Glycemic Index and Carbohydrate Quotient than bread, plays a part in keeping Hawaii and Japan's populations healthy?

The Pressure Cooker

If you want to speed up your cooking, a pressure cooker will help. A pressure cooker speeds up the cooking time for grains by about 10 minutes, takes less water, and locks in the natural flavor of the grain or other food. Pressure cooking apparently has an additional advantage beyond convenience and taste. Studies have shown that pressure cooked rice has a lower Glycemic Index and Carbohydrate Quotient than rice that is not pressure cooked. Thus, one of the ways to make carbohydrate meals better is to pressure cook your grains.

Don't be afraid of using a modern pressure cooker. The modern pressure cookers are designed to be very safe with pressure release valves and automatic locking devices that prevent you from opening the lid until the pressure is down. I prefer stainless steel pressure cookers over aluminum. To cook brown rice, take 2 cups of rice, add 3½ cups of water (instead of the normal 4 cups recommended in the grain chart), add a pinch of sea salt, and cover with the lid as directed by the manufacturer of the pressure cooker. Bring the pot to pressure (until it starts to make a "hissing" sound) on high heat, then lower to low heat and cook for 35 to 40 minutes. Remove from heat, let the pressure subside, then let stand for 5 to 10 minutes before opening. Stir and serve. To cook other grains, simply use the appropriate amount of water and cooking time as described in the grain-cooking chart below. To cook beans in a pressure cooker, follow the same procedure as pressure cooking grains. Use the water and cooking time described in the cooking chart for beans and legumes.

GRAINS

Whole Grains

The main sources of calories for the Good Carbohydrate Plan are whole grains. All whole grains are good carbohydrates and are high in fiber as well as rich in vitamins and minerals. Many civilizations have sustained themselves eating different grains. Try adding a variety of grains to your diet for a taste adventure. Here is a description of a number of different grains to give you an idea of the great variety that is available.

Amaranth

Rediscovered from South America, amaranth is a very small grain with a unique nutty flavor and higher protein content than almost all other grains. Amaranth is also very high in calcium, and contains three times more fiber and five times more iron than wheat. Just rinse it well under cold water before cooking. Do not soak. When cooking amaranth, it's best to cook it without salt for better water absorption. Amaranth can be used in the same way as any other grain, either by itself or combined with grains and vegetables to make stuffing, stews, soups, and casseroles. Amaranth can be ground up for breads or you can even toast the seeds in a dry skillet until they pop like popcorn. Popped amaranth can also be added to spice up stews and vegetables. Amaranth is very durable and will keep for several years in a dry, cool place in an airtight container. Amaranth, as with other grains, also stores well in the refrigerator.

Buckwheat (Kasha)

Technically, buckwheat is not a grain, but it is cooked like a grain and has been eaten as a staple food for centuries. Botanically, buckwheat is actually a seed that grows on short bushes and is related to rhubarb, not wheat, but it is quite similar in nutritional value to wheat. In America, buckwheat is most commonly found in the form of whole seeds called groats. These are cooked or roasted, to give them the deepest flavor. Buckwheat can also be cracked or coarsely ground into grits. It can be finely ground into flour and made into soba noodles, or used in pancakes, breads, and other baked goods. Buckwheat is prepared as cereal, a side dish, or used as stuffing. It can be added to salads, soups and casseroles, or it can be used as a substitute for potatoes or rice. Buckwheat combines very well with other grains, pastas, peas, and beans.

Barley

Barley has the lowest Carbohydrate Quotient and Gycemic Index numbers of all the grains. It is an ancient grain that was used as staple food by the Egyptians. Barley is similar in shape to rice but a little rounder. Hulled barley is the best kind to use because it is in the whole form. The pearled barley found in stores is polished, which means some of the fiber and bran have been removed. Barley has a good texture and a mild grain taste. It can be used in soups, stews, casseroles and salads, and it can be served alone or combined with other grains such as rice. Barley, like other whole grains, should be stored in an airtight container in a cool, dry place.

Brown Rice

Brown rice is the main food for more people in the world than any other grain and has been the staple food of Asia for millennia. In modern times, most people are accustomed to using white rice. Brown rice, however, is healthier because its bran, or outer layer, is still intact. Brown rice is a grain that everyone should learn how to use. Any form of brown rice is better than refined white rice, because it is the whole, unprocessed grain, which accounts for its rich, nutty color and chewy texture. That means none of the nutrition has been processed out and the grain contains its full complement of nutrients, such as vitamin B complex, vitamin E, and fiber.

Be aware that there is great variation in blood sugar effects of rice depending on the type you choose. If you must use white rice, use long grain rice, especially basmati rice, because it tends to be high in amylose, a starch that is slowly digested. Basmati rice, which means "lady of fragrance," has the added feature of having a very pleasant nutty fragrance when it is cooked. Of course, brown basmati rice is even better in terms of blood sugar effects than white basmati rice.

There are many varieties of brown rice including long, short, and medium grain. Some examples of other varieties include basmati rice (both brown and white), jasmine rice, Arborio, plain brown, Thai black, and wild rice. You can find most types of rice in health food stores or Asian groceries. You'll want to experiment with many simple rice dishes.

Brown rice takes longer to cook than the other grains. See cooking instructions for the rice cooker and pressure cooker given earlier in this chapter and the grain guide for cooking below. Simply plan ahead and cook enough brown rice to last for a day or two, store in an airtight container in your refrigerator, and you'll have it on hand to serve with many of your most wholesome and easy-to-make meals. (Cooked rice after first use should be kept in the refrigerator and not more than five days as it will spoil.) Rice is often eaten by itself or combines well with other grains and vegetables. Uncooked rice can be stored for many months in an airtight container or in the refrigerator or freezer.

Corn

Corn or maize was originally a Central and South American food, but is now found all over the world. Most of us have eaten corn in a variety of ways all of our lives. It's also one of the few grains that we are used to eating in its whole form, without being ground up into flour. Corn on the cob is quick, delicious, and easy to prepare. Just be sure to use seasonings such as lemon and soy sauce or A.1® Steak Sauce instead of butter or margarine. Corn grits, hominy (dried corn with the hull removed), cornmeal, popcorn, and corn kernels are other ways we eat the grain corn. Polenta, corn bread, and corn tortillas are foods made from cornmeal. In the South, grits are a common part of breakfast, as rice is in Hawaii. Storage depends on whether it's fresh whole corn (refrigerator), cornmeal (airtight container in cupboard or refrigerator), corn grits (airtight container in cupboard), corn tortillas (in refrigerator), frozen corn kernels (freezer), or canned corn kernels (pantry).

Millet

Although it is one of the oldest foods known to humans, millet is an uncommon food for Americans. Its main use here is as birdseed and cattle grain. Millet was used for centuries in ancient Egypt and other Middle Eastern and Eastern countries. It is currently the chief carbohydrate food of the Northern Chinese as well as many people in Africa and India. Millet is a small, round, light brown grain with the hull removed for human use. Millet is used as cereal or is ground up as flour for breads and other baked goods. Cooked or leftover millet may be used in casseroles, breads, stews, soufflés, or as a stuffing. Millet is very durable and can be kept for up to two years in an airtight container in a dry, cool place.

Oats

Oats are a quick, easy and familiar grain, especially for breakfast. Oats as we know them today were probably cultivated from wild oats by farmers in the Middle East and Europe around 4,500 years ago. Besides containing vitamins and minerals, oats are very high in fiber, both soluble and insoluble. We commonly eat oats in the form of oatmeal, from whole oats to rolled oats to instant oats. Whole oats, or steel cut oats, are the best for you, but they take a while to cook, just as it takes time to cook other whole grains, such as brown rice. Fortunately, rolled oats or old-fashioned oats (old-fashioned oatmeal) are quite good and can be prepared in as little as two to five minutes. I do not recommend instant oatmeal because it is a highly refined product similar to white flour or refined sugar. Oats (whole, steel-cut, or rolled) do best stored in the refrigerator. Oats mix well with other grains, fruits, and vegetables.

Quinoa

Quinoa, pronounced "keen-wah," is one of the world's most perfect foods. Grown and consumed for thousands of years on the high plains of the Andes Mountains in South America, this ancient grain is finding its way to North American tables, with delicious results. Quinoa is not a true cereal grain, but rather is the botanical fruit of an herb plant. It is, however, treated as a grain in cooking. It is best to buy quinoa that is refrigerated in the store for freshness. The grains are small, flattened spheres, approximately 1.5 to 2 mm in diameter, that range in color from yellow, dark brown, to near white. The larger, whiter varieties are most common and are considered superior. It's especially important to rinse this grain before cooking because there could be some bitter residue left from the hulling process. To bring out the best flavor, toast the quinoa in a hot, dry pan for about five minutes before cooking. Use the grain guide to complete the cooking process. Quinoa is tasty by itself or in combination with other grains, vegetables, and fruits. See the recipe chapter (Chapter 12, p. 208) for delicious combinations. Raw quinoa should be stored in the refrigerator or freezer so it doesn't become rancid.

Rye

Rye was first cultivated 2,000 to 3,000 years ago and is still extensively grown in northern Europe and Asia. Robust rye breads (dark rye and light rye) are found in all American supermarkets, but you may have to go to a health food store to get rye in its whole grain form as rye berries or rolled like oats as a cereal. Rye berries can be substituted in any dish that uses wheat berries. As with other grains, store in an airtight container in a cool, dry place.

Wheat

Wheat is another staple grain of very ancient origin. We use wheat as wheat berries or groats (whole form) as a breakfast cereal or combined with other grains in main dishes. Wheat berries have a delicious nutty flavor and pleasing chewy texture. Cracked wheat or bulgur wheat is the main grain used in Middle Eastern and Mediterranean dishes such as taboulleh salad rolled up as wheat balls. Whole wheat flour is used in crackers, flat and yeast breads, and pastas such as noodles and couscous. Kamut, spelt, and triticale are from other varieties of wheat, versus the hard red winter wheat that is typically sold in America.

Wheat berries generally aren't found in the supermarket. You may have to find them at a health food store, where they are sold both in bulk and packaged. You should be looking for a uniform deep russet color with no husks remaining. You can store wheat berries in a cool, dry, dark place or in the refrigerator if you live in a warm climate. Some recipes recommend soaking wheat berries, but it is not absolutely necessary. Soaking wheat berries makes them more digestible and allows them to cook more quickly.

Pasta

Pasta is another delicious staple food that is considered a reasonably good good carbohydrate. Even white flour pasta has a fairly good Carbohydrate Quotient number. Pasta raises insulin just slightly more than whole grains. Pasta is, of course, used in some of the most popular dishes in America. Because there is so much variety in how pasta is prepared, pasta dishes can range from very low to very high in fat. Pasta itself is made from flour, so I would recommend whole wheat, buckwheat (soba), or vegetable pastas. Unlike other foods that use flour, pasta has no added oil.

Italian Pasta

Regular Italian pasta, such as spaghetti, doesn't take long to cook and the cooking directions are on the package. Angel hair pasta cooks in seven minutes once the water is boiling. Cooking pasta requires a pot, water brought to boiling, and a pinch of sea salt to taste. Add pasta and push it down into the water while stirring, then cook for the required minutes stated on the package, being careful it doesn't boil over. Some people add the pasta to the boiling water, cover, and turn the heat to simmer or off and let the pasta cook slowly.

For a quick pasta dish, add a non-fat bottled sauce such as fat free spaghetti or marinara sauce with perhaps some fresh sliced mushrooms added to it. This will provide you with a low fat and tasty dish that is prepared from beginning to end in mere minutes.

If you want to add your own signature, start with a simple tomato-based sauce and add diced tomatoes (raw or cooked), peppers, thinly-diced onions, your favorite spices, and crushed and torn fresh basil or oregano to taste. You can add mushrooms, onions, garlic, vegetables, sun-dried tomatoes, or artichoke hearts (no-oil type). There are seemingly countless additions and side dishes for pastas. Use your creativity to select the ones that work best for you and your family. Don't forget that tomato-based sauces are only one way to eat pasta.

Moroccan Pasta

Couscous is a pasta from Morocco that is in the form of tiny grains about the size of millet. Couscous is used in Mediterranean and Middle Eastern dishes. It can be quickly prepared by bringing one-half cup of water to boil for every cup of couscous. When the water is boiling, add the couscous and boil for about a minute, stirring to keep it from sticking to the bottom and sides of the pot. Then let it stand briefly, fluff with a fork, and it's ready to serve. As with other pastas, I recommend you use whole-wheat couscous, which can be found in both health food stores and supermarkets. Couscous can be used in salads and in cooked dishes.

Asian Pasta

The three main types of Asian pasta dishes are fried pasta such as chow mein, soup noodles such as ramen, and cold noodles such as cold soba (buckwheat noodles) or somen. The fastest of these to prepare are the cold noodles and the cold noodle salad. The pasta used for these cold noodle dishes is soba noodles, made of whole grain buckwheat. You can find soba noodles in most supermarkets now, or in Asian markets and health food stores. Somen noodles, which are a very thin Japanese rice noodle, are made with white rice flour. Soba noodles take about six to eight minutes to cook after they are added to boiling water. For a quick dish, simply cook the noodles, cool quickly with cold water, and serve with a cold noodle sauce that can be found in a can or from scratch and with julienned (matchstick cut) vegetables, such as carrots.

You can easily make Asian pasta salads by adding fresh sliced vegetables and the low fat salad dressing (sauce) of your choice. Noodles can be flavored in a very simple way by adding pre-made soba sauce. For vegetarians, be aware that traditional soba sauce typically has some fish broth in it, as do other favorite Asian sauces that lend themselves well to noodle dishes. In many health food stores, you can now find vegetarian soba sauce. Or you can make your own Asian sauces in very little time. Simply dilute soy sauce and add rice vinegar and a natural sweetener such as honey, brown rice syrup, or other sweetener. If you only have soy sauce you can even just mix that with water and a little lemon juice for flavor. See the recipe chapter for more suggestions.

Basic Cooking Guide for Grains

This cooking guide should be helpful in cooking grains.

GRAINS COOKING GUIDE

1 Cup of Grain	Cooking on Stovetop or Rice Cooker		Cooking with Pressure Cooker		
	Cups Liquid	Simmering Time	Cups Liquid	Cooking Time	Yield (Cups)
Amaranth	2-3	20-25 min.	2	20 min.	3½-4
Barley (hulled) (soak)	3	1 hour	2¼	45 min.	4
Barley (pearled)	3	40 min.	2¼	30 min.	4

GRAINS COOKING GUIDE *(continued)*

| 1 Cup of Grain | Cooking on Stovetop or Rice Cooker | | Cooking with Pressure Cooker | | |
	Cups Liquid	Simmering Time	Cups Liquid	Cooking Time	Yield (Cups)
Brown Rice	2	45 min.	1½	40-45 min.	3
Buckwheat groats	2	20 min.	Do not pressure cook.		3
Bulgur (cooked)	2	15 min.	Do not pressure cook.		
Bulgur (boiling water)	2½	30 min. (sit)	Do not pressure cook.		3
Millet (pan toasted)	2½	25-30 min.	2	30 min.	3
Whole oats (groats)	4	2 hours	2½	50 min.	3½
Steel-cut oats	4	45 min.	3½-4	30 min.	3½
Rolled oats (oatmeal)	1½	10-15 min.	Do not pressure cook.		2½
Quinoa	2	15 min.	unavailable		3
Rye berries	3	45-60 min.	2½	40 min.	3
Wheat berries (soak overnight)	3	40-60 min. (uncovered)	2½	40 min.	3

1. Rinse the grain until the water runs clear (especially quinoa).
2. Put grain into a cooking pot and add the specified amount of water. Bring to a boil, cover, and add a pinch of sea salt for each

cup of grain; reduce heat and simmer. Remove from heat and let stand. Drain off excess water and serve.

3. When using a pressure cooker and the grain has been soaked, use approximately one quarter less listed in the Grains Cooking Guide (p.189–90) or follow the manufacturer's instructions.

4. When using a rice cooker follow the same table on cooking grains. The only difference is the rice cooker will automatically turn off when the rice or grain is done. Let stand with the cover on and then serve.

5. Follow the instructions for each recipe in combining grains with beans or other grains.

Grain Tips

Here are some grain tips I hope you will find useful:

- Try new grains every week. There are even more grains than listed above to be discovered in your health food store, supermarket, or on the Internet.

- You can buy many grains on the Internet and have them shipped to you for convenience or if your nearby stores do not carry the variety you might like.

- In the recipe chapter you will find gravies and sauces to accompany your grains for tasty variety.

- Quick and easy burritos or tacos can be made by adding grains and fresh vegetables to beans.

- Plain grains can be rolled into sushi rolls, or rice or grain balls.

- Simply by adding vegetables to grains you can make wonderful grain salads that are portable, ready-to-eat meals for travel or work.

- Make a cereal out of your grain by adding fruit and reheating with water, rice milk, or soy milk.

- Veggie burgers can be made out of grain and chopped vegetables like onions, carrots, celery, and a binder such as Egg Beaters® or vegetarian egg replacer (available in health food stores). Then bake or fry with cooking oil spray.

- You can "cream" a soup or stew by blending leftover grains or beans, such as lima beans.
- You can puree cooked grains with mushrooms, herbs, and seasonings to make gravy.

Vegetables

Vegetables which are on the second tier of the Good Carbohydrate Plan Pyramid, are the next largest category of good carbohydrates. Vegetables are important because they are a good source of vitamins and minerals and they help to slow down the absorption of carbohydrates from other sources—even bad carbohydrates. So make sure you have adequate amounts of vegetables in your daily fare.

Fresh vegetables are the best because most of their natural nutrition is retained if they are truly fresh and haven't been refrigerated too long. The next best choice is frozen vegetables and then canned vegetables. Vegetables are a perfect complement to grains. They can be eaten raw or baked, boiled, steamed, grilled, and fried. You can eat as many vegetables in a day as you want. You will find the Good Carbohydrate Plan more interesting if you try different ways of preparing your food throughout the week. In the recipe chapter you will find tasty sauces that don't add fat and make your vegetables even more delicious.

Vegetable Tips

Now that you want to do things differently, there are a few tips to observe in cooking your vegetables:

- Just a reminder, fresh vegetables have more of their original nutrition value than frozen or canned vegetables.
- For salads, the preferable dressings are those that are non-fat with vinegar or lemon juice in them. If there is any oil, the preferred oil is extra virgin olive oil.
- Just a reminder, buy fresh vegetables and cook them as soon as possible without letting them sit in the refrigerator too long.
- Try using different herbs and spices, fresh or dried, sprinkled

over your vegetables. For example, try the flavors of fresh ginger, garlic, and chili peppers with your vegetables.

- Use a variety of no fat or low fat dressings and sauces that will add zing and flavor. You no longer need to add butter or margarine to your vegetables. Lemon and soy sauce together is amazingly simple and tasty.

- Try using water or broth to sauté or stir-fry your vegetables instead of using oil. Vegetable broth is available in liquid and powdered form at health food stores and many supermarkets.

- All vegetables can be steamed with a little bit of water at the bottom of the pan or bowl (microwave) or by using a steamer tray or basket that keeps the vegetables above the water.

- When cooking a medley of vegetables, as in a stir-fry dish, add the heavier, denser vegetables first, such as carrots. Add each vegetable in the order of their required cooking time, such as celery and onions after carrots; then bok choy; and high calcium leafy greens, bean sprouts, or pea pods last.

- Don't overcook your vegetables. You retain more vitamin and mineral value if you cook vegetables lightly so they change color slightly but still retain their bright color and crispness, such as the green of green beans and broccoli.

- Root vegetables need to be cooked until a fork can pierce the skin easily.

- Low sodium soy sauce or tamari can substitute for salt.

- If you use a teaspoon of oil in the bottom of your skillet to sauté and the pan starts smoking, that means the oil is burned and you should rinse the pan and start over at a lower heat. Olive oil and sesame oil have the best heat tolerance.

- Cooked vegetables are good as leftovers or snack food. Cook extra and add a dressing and cooked grains for a quick, cold salad.

- Try cutting your vegetables up in attractive creative ways, such as on the diagonal or julienned (matchstick).

- Leftover vegetables can be put into a soup base to make a quick soup. Be creative: add some cooked grains, beans, other fresh vegetables, and garnish with fresh parsley, sliced green onion, sesame seeds, or nori (dried sea vegetable).

FRUIT

In Chapter 7 there is a list of some of the different varieties of fruit. However, this list isn't the only fruit you can eat. There are many other fruits available at the health food store or your supermarket that you are welcome to add to your menu.

Fruit Tips

Here are some fruit tips:

- Whole, fresh fruit is best. As we've learned in earlier chapters, the more refined a food is, the faster it enters our system and may raise blood sugar. For example, if you compare apples to applesauce to apple juice, it is recommended you eat the whole apple rather than drink apple juice.

- Whole fruit is typically low on the Carbohydrate Quotient scale and moderate to high on the Mass Index scale, which means it will help you to feel full without adding too many calories.

- When baking with fruit, it's better to use fructose rather than sugar. Juice is better to keep cakes moist, rather than butter or margarine.

- When making fruit pie, remember that most of the fat is in the crust. Consider using oatmeal flakes or grape nuts or other low fat foods in place of the crust.

- Fruit is delicious with your morning oatmeal, in salads with grains, and as a dessert (see Chapter 12 for recipes).

- Frozen fruit is an excellent substitute for sweet desserts. Frozen seedless grapes can be used as a snack. Frozen bananas can be processed through a juicer and turned into a dessert much like soft ice cream. Other frozen fruit can be blenderized into a sherbet-like dessert.

- Citrus fruit, because of its acidity, can help to reduce the blood sugar effect of other carbohydrates. For example, salad dressings that have lemon juice in them help slow the absorption of carbohydrates from the meal.

- Don't overdo fruit. Grains and other starchy staples should be your main source of calories because fruit sugar can directly raise LDL (bad cholesterol) and triglycerides even without raising insulin.

LEGUMES AND BEANS: THE NON-CHOLESTEROL PROTEIN FOODS

The non-cholesterol protein foods are excellent sources of protein, vitamins, minerals, and fiber. Nutritionists call beans a powerhouse food because they are unusually rich in nutrients and fiber but relatively low in calories. They are also inexpensive and versatile. Beans and legumes are a great substitute for flesh protein in your diet, and they have the advantage of having no cholesterol and very little fat.

Most people only know beans as canned goods. Fresh beans have a limited availability. If you want to prepare dried beans, rinse them well first in a colander or a pan. Pick out any discolored beans or little stones. From there put them in a pan and add water as guided in the cooking instructions, page 197. Beans can also be soaked before cooking. Here are some of the different ways you can cook beans:

1. Put the beans into a big bowl and add water to cover two inches. Cover and let stand for up to 24 hours. Beans should triple their size. If your kitchen is warm, refrigerate while soaking. Discard the soaking liquid and cook as directed below or follow your recipe directions.

2. For a quick soak (about an hour), put the beans into a big bowl, pour boiling water to cover two inches, and let sit until the beans swell up and have absorbed most of the water. Drain off the soaking liquid and discard, rinse beans again, then cook as directed below or follow your recipe directions.

3. Another quick-soak method is to place the beans in a saucepan, adding water to cover two inches. Heat the saucepan to boiling and then reduce the heat to simmer for two minutes. Let stand, covered, for one hour. Drain and discard the water. Rinse the beans again, and cook as directed below or follow your recipe directions. The risk in this method is the bean skins may break and the beans could break up.

4. A microwave soaking method is to put 4 cups of water and a pound of beans into a four-quart, covered casserole. Heat on high to boiling for 12 to 18 minutes. Turn to medium setting and cook for 2 more minutes. Stir and let stand, covered, for about an hour. Drain the liquid, discard, and rinse the beans again. Cook as directed below or according to your recipe directions for the final cooking.

5. Unlike dried beans, legumes such as dried whole green peas, split peas and lentils, require no soaking prior to cooking. They cook soft fairly quickly.

I have provided the cooking instructions for just some of the bean and legume possibilities. Other bean/legume choices are butter beans, cranberry beans, fava beans, great northern beans, green peas, lima beans, mung beans, pigeon peas, pink beans, and red beans. Check out your health food store, supermarket, or the Internet for even more bean varieties to try.

Basic Cooking Guide for Dried Beans

1. Rinse in a colander or pan under running water and pick out the discolored beans and little stones.

2. Soak beans using one of the methods above.

3. Drain water off, rinse again, and add the amount of water indicated above.

4. Bring to a boil and cover.

5. Add seasonings except anything acidic such as tomatoes.

6. Reduce heat and simmer.

7. When beans are almost tender, you can add the acidic ingredients such as tomatoes.

8. Keep the beans in their water until ready to serve. Drain off excess water and serve or add to another recipe.

DRIED BEAN GUIDE

(1 cup of dried beans generally yields 3 cups cooked beans)

1 cup of Dried Beans	Presoak	Stovetop Cooking		Pressure Cooking	
		Cups Liquid	Cooking Time	Cups Liquid	Cooking Time
Azuki Beans—small, rich, deep red, mild-tasting	Yes	3	45 min.	2½	30 min.
Black Turtle Beans—medium black-skinned ovals; earthy, sweet flavor with a hint of mushroom	Yes	3½	2-3 hrs.	2½-3	50 min.
Black-eyed Peas—medium-size, oval-shaped, creamy skin with black dot on one edge; distinct, savory flavor and light, smooth texture	Yes	3	2 hrs.	3	50 min.
Cannellini Bean—medium to large, oval-shaped white bean with a black dot; smooth and creamy; the white kidney bean	Yes	3	1½ hrs.-2 hrs.	3	50 min.
Chickpeas (garbanzo beans)—round, medium-size; beige color; nutlike flavor and firm texture	Yes	4	2-3 hrs.	3	1½ hrs.
Kidney Beans—kidney-shaped bean; deep or light reddish-brown; robust, full-bodied flavor with soft texture	Yes	3	1½ hrs-2 hrs.	3	50 min.
Lentils (green or brown)—small, flat, circular bean; earthy flavor and powdery texture	No	3	45 min.	3	30 min.

DRIED BEAN GUIDE (continued)

(1 cup of dried beans generally yields 3 cups cooked beans)

1 cup of Dried Beans	Presoak	Stovetop Cooking		Pressure Cooking	
		Cups Liquid	Cooking Time	Cups Liquid	Cooking Time
Lentils (red or yellow)—small, flat, circular bean; earthy flavor and powdery texture	No	3	45 min.	2½	30 min.
Lima Beans—flat-shaped, creamy white-colored beans; smooth, creamy, sweet flavor	Yes	3	1 hr.	3	30 min.
Navy Beans—small, white ovals; mild flavor with powdery texture	Yes	3	1 hr.	3	40 min.
Pinto Beans—medium ovals; mottled beige and brown color; earthy flavor and powdery texture	Yes	3	2 hrs.	3	50 min.
Soybeans—medium round bean; mild nutty flavor and green in color	Yes	4	3 hrs.	3	1 hr.
Split Peas—green or yellow peas; soft and creamy texture when cooked	No	3	45–50 min.	3	30 min.
White Beans—small oval-shaped bean; mild flavor and powdery texture	Yes	3	45 min.-1 hr.	3	40 min.

Pressure Cooking Beans

Beans cook much faster in a pressure cooker. Clean and soak your beans as described above. Put them into the pressure cooker with enough water to cover. Season as you like. Cook presoaked beans for one-fifth to one-quarter of the minimum cooking time listed in the cooking guide above. If not quite done for your tastes, you can simmer without pressure if needed.

Microwaving Beans

Soak the beans as recommended in the soaking instructions above. Place rinsed and drained beans (more than one cup) in a microwave-safe bowl with about three cups of water and any vegetables such as onions, carrots, or herbs and spices. To prevent boiling over, add two teaspoons of oil. Cover the bowl tightly with two layers of plastic wrap. Microwave the beans on high to boiling for 12 to 18 minutes, then on medium setting for 30 to 45 minutes, stirring two or three times. Check at 20 minutes, and throughout the cooking time.

Legume/Bean Tips

- If you've had trouble digesting beans in the past and they give you gas, try using a product such as Beano® to solve this problem and enjoy beans again. And be sure to soak your beans overnight.

- Beans are a nutritional bargain. A pound of beans can cost less than a dollar and when cooked yields up to six cups of beans or 12 half-cup servings.

- Cook large batches of beans. Use them during the week and freeze some in small packages so they are ready to be added to chili, dips, salads, pasta, soup, and casseroles. Cooked beans freeze well for up to six months.

- When time is tight, just open a can of beans and heat for a quick meal.

- Add a can of beans to any of your favorite vegetable and left-over meat creations.

- You can use canned beans or home cooked beans to add to your favorite chili or stew recipe.

- You can toss chickpeas (garbanzo beans), kidney beans, or any favorite beans with leftover cooked grains and vegetables, season with your favorite no fat or low fat dressing and herbs, and you have a main dish salad.

- You can combine one cup of baby lima beans, one cup of black beans, and a half cup of oil-cured sun dried tomatoes in a blender until smooth. Serve as a dip with whole wheat crackers, vegetables, or French bread.

- Ever thought of trying your baked beans on toast for breakfast?

- Black or pinto beans, seasoned with an eye-opening dash of salsa, can be wrapped in a warm tortilla for a Mexican-style breakfast.

- Try a new type of bean every week.

- According to the Adventist Health Study, eating beans may help protect against colon cancer and may be particularly effective in reducing the harmful effects of red meat on the colon.

Grow Your Own Bean Sprouts

You can sprout beans for your own bean sprouts. Typically the azuki, mung, and lentils are used for sprouting because they are smaller and sprout more quickly. You can make one-and-a-half cups of sprouts with about three tablespoons of beans.

1. Put your rinsed beans into a bowl and cover with two inches of warm, not boiling, water. Let stand for 24 hours and rinse and drain.

2. Place the beans in a sterile jar big enough to hold one-and-a-half cups of sprouts, cover with a double layer of cheesecloth, and secure the cheesecloth on the jar with a rubber band.

3. Twice a day rinse the beans by filling the jar with cool water and draining it off through the cheesecloth. Drain all the water out.

4. Shoots should appear in five days or so. On the last day give the jar some sun so the sprouts will green up.

5. Open the jar and throw away any beans that didn't sprout. Put sprouts into a plastic bag and store in the refrigerator until you need them.

SOY FOODS

Soy foods deserve special mention. Soybeans are a major source of protein in Japan, whose population enjoys the longest average life span in the world. The quality of the protein from soy foods is excellent. Recently there has been a great deal of interest in phytonutrients found in soy known as isoflavones. The well-known isoflavones include daidzien and genistein. These are beneficial as antioxidants and as estrogen analogues (analogue means they are similar to estrogen so they block the effects of having too much estrogen in the body). As antioxidants, isoflavones may contribute to the low rate of coronary heart disease in Japan. They may also contribute to lower risk of certain cancers, such as breast cancer. It is possible that the protection from breast cancer and coronary heart disease is a result of the mild estrogen-like effect of the isoflavones.

Tofu is one of the easiest soy foods to eat. Tofu is a soft, white soy product that you can now find in any supermarket. It is convenient because it can be eaten without cooking. Just add soy sauce and use it as a tasty side dish or a main protein source. It can be eaten hot or cold. Tofu is great in stir-fry dishes, casseroles, and vegetable dishes. It is one of the most versatile protein sources available.

OPTIONAL FOODS

The optional foods, which are not necessary for health, are low fat fish, poultry, or meat as protein/iron foods; non-fat dairy calcium foods; and fats, oils, and sweets. These foods are not part of the core of the Good Carbohydrate Plan but can be used to add variety to your diet. If you avoid the fish/poultry/meat group, you have a vegetarian diet. If you avoid that and the dairy group, you have a vegan diet.

Low Fat Fish/Poultry/Meat

Of these optional foods, the animal flesh foods are not considered carbohydrate foods because they have practically no carbohydrates in them. Before you choose to use these foods, see Chapter 14 on some of the perils of protein, especially animal protein, and how to minimize your risk.

DAIRY

Dairy is often used in preparing carbohydrates. For example, many people use milk on their oatmeal or cheese on their spaghetti. Dairy foods also contain lactose and, therefore, are a source of carbohydrate.

In general I discourage the use of dairy for a number of reasons, which I described earlier in Chapter 7. If you decide to use these foods on an occasional basis, the best would be those that are non-fat or made from skim milk. You can substitute dairy with rice milk or soy milk. In both cases, use a low fat or non-fat variety.

FATS/OILS/SUGARS

Fats/Oils

These foods are very low on the Mass Food Index, which means they can turn a weight loss food into a weight gain food if not used sparingly. All fats and oils pack nine calories per gram—twice as many calories as a gram of sugar. Some fats are better than others in terms of heart disease. For example, extra virgin olive oil, canola oil, and macadamia nut oil may be better than other oils in this regard. Remember that these oils still may contribute to obesity and insulin resistance because of their high calorie content. See Chapter 16 for a full discussion about this.

Sugars

Some foods in the sugar group are white sugar, brown sugar, honey, molasses, maple syrup, rice syrup, and candy. These foods are not recommended except in small amounts and on an occasional basis or with a large dose of good carbohydrates. For example, if there is a little sweetener in a salad dressing, and you eat a lot of greens as a result, the addition of the vegetables, which are invariably high in fiber, will blunt the effect of the sweetener in the dressing. For example, if you use a small amount of sugar in a stir-fry sauce for a dish that has a lot of vegetables, it may be a good way to enjoy some flavor and still have a minimal effect on your blood sugar.

If you have a choice, use the type of sweetener that is only partially refined. For example, the worst choices are granulated or powdered sugar. Honey, maple syrup, rice syrup, and barley malt are a little better simply because there are small amounts of other nutrients that come with these sweeteners and they are bulkier than pure sugar, so you are likely to consume fewer calories from these sources. Blackstrap molasses is a step above these other sweeteners because it has high concentrations of minerals such as calcium and iron.

There is also some benefit to using fructose in the place of table sugar. Because fructose is a natural sweetener, when you substitute it in recipes calling for sugar, there should be an improved effect on blood sugar levels. Fructose does not break down in cooking like some artificial sweeteners. The general rule of thumb is to use one-third less fructose than the amount of sugar called for. Fructose can be used in all diets, but diabetics should check with their doctors if there's any doubt about using it.

SUGAR TO FRUCTOSE EQUIVALENT

Sugar	Fructose
¼ cup	2½ tablespoons
⅓ cup	3½ tablespoons
½ cup	5 tablespoons
⅔ cup	7 tablespoons
¾ cup	½ cup
1 cup	⅔ cup

Consider Stevia as an Herbal Sugar Substitute

For those of you who want an artificial sweetener, consider the herb stevia. Stevia can only be purchased as an herb, not a food, at your local health food store. It is 200 to 300 times sweeter than sugar and has no calories. I discuss this further in Chapter 16.

EIGHT WAYS TO MAKE CARBOHYDRATE MEALS BETTER

Following the Good Carbohydrate Plan does not mean that you can never eat bad carbohydrates at all. There are a number of things you can do to include a wide variety of food on the Good Carbohydrate Plan, including a limited amount of bad carbohydrates, and still have a very healthy eating plan. Here are eight techniques you can use to make the blood sugar and insulin impact of your meals even better.

1. **Keep Your Fat Intake Low to Improve Insulin Sensitivity.**

    Insulin sensitivity is impaired on a high fat diet. If you can limit the total amount of fat in your diet to between 20 and 40 grams of fat per day, you are likely to get the most out of your insulin. This will help to reduce blood sugar and insulin levels in most people.

2. **Pressure Cook Grain to Help Reduce Its Impact on Blood Sugar.**

    Research comparing the difference between methods of cooking rice indicates that pressure cooking actually causes a decrease in the blood sugar response to rice. In this study, researchers used white rice. The Glycemic Index of traditionally cooked rice in this study was 43.7. The Glycemic Index of pressure-cooked rice turned out to be 36.9. These figures were compared against a white bread standard. Based on this study, pressure cooking grains helps to make its impact on blood sugar better. Of course, choosing whole grains such as brown rice would make the blood sugar response even lower.

3. **Good Carbohydrate Foods Will Blunt the Effect of Bad Carbohydrate Foods.**

    If you have some foods in your diet that are considered bad carbohydrates, that is, high Carbohydrate Quotient foods that are likely to raise your blood sugar, you can improve the overall meal by choosing good carbohydrate foods that are low on the

Carbohydrate Quotient scale. These foods help to neutralize the effect of bad carbohydrates by slowing their digestion and absorption to a more moderate rate. For example, if you are going to eat foods that contain sugar, eat them along with a meal that is high in vegetables, fruit, whole grain, or legumes. This will help to make the overall meal one that has a more moderate effect on your blood sugar and blood insulin.

4. **Add High Fiber Foods or Soluble Fiber Supplements to Help Slow the Absorption of Carbohydrates.**

The reason for this suggestion is similar to the reason for adding high Carbohydrate Quotient foods to your diet. I emphasize high fiber here because I want to give you a principle to follow if you didn't have a Carbohydrate Quotient or Glycemic Index table handy. Remember that fiber, especially soluble fiber, helps to slow the absorption rate of carbohydrates. This is why eating cooked whole oats (not instant oats) in the morning is a good idea. Adding oat bran or eating an all bran cereal is also useful. Eating legumes as a source of protein instead of meat is also a good idea because legumes are high in fiber. Legumes not only have a low Glycemic Index value but will help to slow the absorption of carbohydrates from other foods in a meal.

There is some evidence that fiber supplements can also help to slow the absorption of carbohydrates and help to improve a total meal. The best fiber supplements are soluble fibers such as psyllium, guar gum, and locust bean gum.

5. **Add Acidic Foods Such As Lemon and Vinegar to Help Slow the Absorption of Carbohydrate from Other Foods.**

As I discussed in one of the insights of the five principles (Five C's) of good carbohydrate choices, sour-flavored (acidic) foods improve the blood sugar effect of foods. This also holds true for a whole meal. Studies show that adding lemon or vinegar to a meal will help to reduce the glycemic response of the whole meal. In one study, four teaspoons of vinegar in a dressing reduced the blood sugar response of a meal by as much as 30 percent. The same seems to hold true for lemon juice. This may explain why some health enthusiasts suggest that cider vinegar helps to control blood sugar in some individuals. For people who are concerned about controlling blood sugar, it may be a good idea to eat their meal with a salad that has a vinegar-based dressing. Be careful, however, of dressings that have a lot of oil, such as oil and vinegar dressings. The oil may work against you in the long run by impairing your insulin sensitivity or contributing to excess weight.

6. **Exercise to Help Control Blood Sugar and Increase Insulin Sensitivity.**

   Don't underestimate the value of exercise in improving blood sugar control. Exercise not only burns calories, it also helps to make your insulin more effective. This has the added benefit of keeping your insulin levels low because you won't need as much to have the same effect on blood sugar. Exercise also helps to control your blood sugar by burning some of the calories from carbohydrate in your body. Regular exercise is an important part of your healthy lifestyle.

7. **Eat Smaller, More Frequent Meals or Snacks to Help Reduce the Insulin Levels Throughout the Day.**

   Eating smaller, but more frequent, meals is an additional strategy for managing your insulin levels. Very large numbers of calories eaten at one time can overwhelm your body's ability to handle the nutrients that you absorb. This may force your body into secreting more insulin than it needs. This can result in increased health risks and hypoglycemia, which may trigger an undesirable cycle of fatigue and hunger.

8. **Eat More High Mass Index Foods to Automatically Reduce the Amount of Calories and Carbohydrates Eaten to Reduce the Impact on Blood Sugar and Insulin.**

   Adding high Mass Index (or low calorie density) foods helps to fill up your stomach and make you feel satisfied so that you consume fewer calories. This will reduce your overall intake of carbohydrates and your Glycemic Load. In the long run, it will also help you to control your weight. Reducing your weight is another way to help improve your insulin sensitivity and will reduce your blood sugar and insulin levels. There is a fuller explanation on how this works in Chapter 8 on weight control.

LET'S GET STARTED

Once you have learned how to use the principles and tools of the Good Carbohydrate Plan, and learned how to prepare good carbohydrates, it's time to get started. Armed with the knowledge of how to find good carbohydrates, your choices are endless. Start with the recipes in this book and then, based on the five principles (Five C's) of the Good Carbohydrate Plan, you can find additional recipes to add to your Good Carbohydrate Plan. In the next chapter, you'll find recipes to get you started on your way.

CHAPTER 12

Good Carbohydrate Plan Recipes

BREAKFAST

HEARTY OATMEAL
(grains, fruit, legumes or nuts, vegetables)

4 cups water
¼ teaspoon salt
1 cup steel-cut oats
1 cup apple, chopped
⅓ cup raisins
½ teaspoon vanilla
⅛ teaspoon ground cinnamon
½ cup soy, rice, or almond milk
2 tablespoons pure maple syrup (optional)

In a medium saucepan bring water and salt to a boil. Stir in oats and stir frequently until the mixture thickens (about 3 minutes). Reduce heat and simmer, uncovered, for 20 minutes, stirring occasionally to prevent mixture from sticking to the bottom of the pan. Stir in apple, raisins, vanilla, and cinnamon. Continue to simmer for 10 minutes. Serve each serving with 2 tablespoons of soy, rice, or almond milk and ½ tablespoon of maple syrup, if desired. Makes 4 (1 cup) servings. *(1 serving = 243 calories, 3.4 grams fat, 6.5 grams dietary fiber: 12% protein, 75% carbohydrates, 12% fat.)*

HOT AMARANTH CEREAL
(grains, fruit)

1 cup amaranth
3 cups water
Pinch of sea salt
2 tablespoons raisins

Place amaranth, water, and sea salt in a nonstick saucepan and bring to a boil. Reduce heat to medium low, cover, and simmer for 25 minutes. Grains will absorb water and bind together. Makes 4 (½ cup) servings. *(1 serving = 182 calories, 3 grams fat, 0 grams dietary fiber: 15% protein, 69% carbohydrates, 15% fat.) (1 serving with raisins = 196 calories, 3 grams fat, 0 grams dietary fiber: 14% protein, 72% carbohydrates, 14% fat.)*

Note: For a sweeter flavor, add raisins or chopped dried fruit during cooking.

QUINOA CEREAL
(grains, fruit)

1 cup quinoa
2 cups water
¼ cup raisins
¼ teaspoon ground cinnamon
Pinch of sea salt

Toast quinoa in a dry skillet over medium-low heat. Rinse well and drain. Place quinoa, water, raisins, cinnamon, and sea salt in a saucepan and bring to a boil. Reduce heat to medium-low, cover, and simmer for 10 minutes. Remove from heat and let stand 5 minutes. Makes 4 (½ cup) servings. *(1 serving = 187 calories, 2.5 grams fat, 2.7 grams dietary fiber: 12% protein, 76% carbohydrates, 12% fat.)*

WHOLE OATMEAL WITH RAISINS
(grains, fruit, vegetables)

1½ cups whole rolled oats
2 cups water
Pinch sea salt
¼ cup raisins
1 tablespoon blackstrap molasses
3 teaspoons wheat germ

Measure the rolled oats into a skillet. Dry roast over medium heat for a few minutes, stirring constantly to prevent burning until the oats are fragrant. Add water and a pinch sea salt. Reduce heat and simmer for 10 to 15 minutes, until of desired consistency. Serve with molasses and wheat germ. Makes 3 (¾ cup) servings. *(1 serving = 236 calories, 3 grams fat: 13% protein, 77% carbohydrates, 10% fat.)*

KASHA (BUCKWHEAT)
(grains)

1 cup kasha (found in most health food stores)
2 cups water
Pinch sea salt

If you want to give the kasha extra flavor, dry roast lightly over medium heat in skillet until it smells toasty. Remove from heat. Bring the water to boil in a saucepan, add the kasha, reduce heat to medium low, and cook until soft (about 20 minutes). Makes 2 (1 cup) servings. *(1 serving = 75 calories, 0.5 grams fat: 14% protein, 81% carbohydrates, 6% fat.)*

WHOLE OAT GROATS
(grains)

1 cup whole oats
5 to 6 cups water
½ teaspoon sea salt

After washing the oats, dry roast them in a dry skillet until golden, stirring constantly to prevent burning. Pour water over the oats, add salt, and bring to a boil. Cover and let simmer over low heat for 2 hours.

For pressure cooking, roast the oats as above, add 2½ cups water and sea salt, and pressure cook for 1 to 1½ hours over low heat after the pressure comes up. If made the night before, the oats can be left in pressure cooker and reheated in the morning. Makes 4 to 5 (1 cup) servings. *(1 serving = 152 calories, 3 grams fat: 17% protein, 67% carbohydrates, 16% fat.)*

POTATO QUESADILLAS
(staple vegetable, vegetables, grains, dairy)

Here's one way to reduce the fat in a quesadilla—eliminate the cheese entirely. That's what the street vendors in Mexico City do when they serve potato quesadillas. Unfortunately, the vendors also fry the potatoes in a sea of oil or lard. To make a low fat version, simmer the spuds in vegetable stock instead.

1 medium onion, thinly sliced
1 cup vegetable broth
2 Yukon Gold potatoes or 1 large russet potato, thinly sliced
Salt and freshly ground black pepper to taste
8 8-inch whole wheat tortillas
1 medium ripe tomato, chopped
¼ cup diced green chilies
½ cup low fat sour cream (optional)

Preheat oven to 400°F. In a large nonstick skillet over medium heat, sauté onion in 3 tablespoons of the broth, stirring often, until golden brown (about 3 minutes). Stir in potatoes and cook for 1 minute. Add remaining broth, salt, and black pepper. Simmer, stirring frequently, until potatoes are tender and liquid has been absorbed (about 8 minutes).

Coat a large baking sheet with a nonstick spray. Arrange 4 tortillas on baking sheet. Spread potato mixture evenly on tortillas. Divide tomato and green chilies between tortillas. Top with remaining tortillas. Bake, turning once, until lightly browned and heated through (about 10 minutes). Cut each quesadilla into wedges. Serve with a dollop of sour cream, if desired. Makes 4 (1 quesadilla) servings. *(1 serving = 277 calories, 4.3 grams fat, 3.5 grams dietary fiber: 12% protein, 74% carbohydrates, 14% fat.)*

APPETIZERS OR SNACKS

HEALTHY RED PEPPER HUMMUS WITH WHOLE WHEAT PITA BREAD
(grains, legumes, vegetables)

½ cup fresh basil leaves, lightly packed
2 cloves garlic
2 15-ounce cans garbanzo beans, drained and rinsed
⅓ cup water
1 roasted red bell pepper, seeded and cubed
3 tablespoons fresh lemon juice
½ teaspoon salt

In a food processor chop basil and garlic. Add garbanzo beans, water, roasted bell pepper, lemon juice and salt. Process until smooth. Serve with assorted vegetables or whole wheat pita triangles. Makes 8 (½ cup) servings. *(1 serving = 102 calories, 1.8 grams fat, 5.1 grams dietary fiber: 18% protein, 67% carbohydrates, 15% fat.)*

Note: Roast whole bell pepper by spraying lightly with an oil spray. Preheat broiler. Place bell pepper on a sheet of foil about 3" to 4" from broiler unit. Broil until just charred (about 7 to 8 minutes). Turn once. Watch carefully.

VIETNAMESE SUMMER ROLLS WITH DIPPING SAUCE
(grains, vegetables, and seafood)

1½ ounces cellophane noodles (bean threads)
6 round rice paper wrappers
Water in atomizer bottle for spraying
6 leaves butter head or other tender lettuce, washed and dried
6 large shrimp, cooked, peeled, and split lengthwise in half
½ cup mung bean sprouts
½ cup cilantro leaves
½ cup fresh basil leaves
6 sprigs fresh mint
Summer Roll Dipping Sauce, Clear Dip, or Amber Dip

Put cellophane noodles into a large bowl and cover with hot water. Soak until pliable (about 3 minutes). Drain and cut with scissors into 2" lengths.

Moisten a clean kitchen towel and place a rice paper wrapper on it. Spray wrapper on both sides using an atomizer bottle of water. Repeat with remaining wrappers. Wrap in a clean kitchen towel, and place in a plastic bag for several minutes, just until they become flexible.

Put a lettuce leaf on each softened wrapper. Top with a shrimp half, equal servings of each of the remaining ingredients, and the other shrimp half. Fold the sides of the rice paper over the filling and roll up to form a snug roll about 1" in diameter. Serve with Summer Roll Dipping Sauce, Amber Dip, or Clear Dip. Makes 6 (1) roll servings. *(1 serving = 67 calories, 1.3 grams fat, 0.5 grams dietary fiber: 30% protein, 52% carbohydrates, 17% fat.)*

Note: Rice paper wrappers are made of white rice flour and water. They look like brittle plastic but when moistened they become translucent and pleasantly chewy. They are available, dried, in Asian markets.

SUMMER ROLL DIPPING SAUCE
(vegetables, fruit, seafood, sugar)

¼ cup nuoc nam fish sauce
2 cloves garlic, peeled and minced
2 tablespoons Sucanat or light brown sugar
¼ cup water
1 tablespoon daikon, red radish, or turnip, grated
2 tablespoons carrot, grated
Juice of 1 lime
Cayenne pepper, to taste

Whisk all ingredients together. Serve at room temperature. Makes about 1 cup or 16 (1 tablespoon) servings. *(1 serving = 34 calories, 0.2 grams fat, 0.2 grams dietary fiber: 29% protein, 70% carbohydrates, 0% fat.)*

AMBER DIP*
(legumes, vegetables, grains or sugar)

1 cup Chinese bean sauce
¼ cup barley malt, rice syrup, or sugar
2 cloves garlic, minced
½ cup water
Corn starch, as needed for texture

On medium heat, cook bean sauce, sugar, and garlic together for 3 to 4 minutes, stirring constantly. Add water and stir. Thicken with corn starch mixed with water, if necessary. Makes 20 (½ tablespoon) servings to be used with summer rolls. *(1 serving = 19.2 calories, 0.3 grams fat: 12% protein, 73% carbohydrates, 15% fat.)*

Note: Ground peanuts can also be added as a garnish. Just remember that using a lot of peanuts will increase the fat content of this dish.

*From *Dr. Shintani's Eat More, Weigh Less® Cookbook*, p. 281.

CLEAR DIP*
(vegetables, grains or sugar)

2 cloves garlic, crushed
6 tablespoons barley malt, rice syrup, or sugar
1 tablespoon lemon juice
1 tablespoon rice vinegar
4 tablespoons water
Fresh chili, to taste

Mix ingredients together and use as a dipping sauce for summer rolls. Makes 20 (½ tablespoon) servings. *(1 serving = 10.4 calories, 0.0 grams fat, 1% protein, 99% carbohydrates, 0% fat.)*

*From *Dr. Shintani's Eat More, Weigh Less® Cookbook*, p. 281.

HOMEMADE CHIPS
(grains)

1 dozen corn tortillas or 6 whole wheat pita breads
Cooking oil spray

Preheat oven at 450°F. Cut the stack of corn tortillas into four pieces like a pie or cut the 6 pita breads into fours and separate. Lay the chips on nonstick baking sheets or spray the baking sheets with cooking oil spray. Then lay the chips in single layers; avoid overlapping. Bake until lightly browned and sufficiently crisp (approximately 8 minutes). Cool and use with salsa and dip (see recipes below), and soups. Store in airtight bags and freeze for future use. Makes 12 (4 chip) servings. *(1 serving = 58 calories, 0.7 grams fat, 1.4 grams dietary fiber: 10% protein, 84% carbohydrates, 10% fat.)*

Note: As a variation, chips can be sprayed before baking with mild soy sauce and water, and lightly sprinkled with your favorite seasoning or furikake flakes.

BLACK BEAN DIP*
(legumes, vegetables)

2 onions, raw, chopped

3 cloves garlic, crushed

1 8-ounce can tomatoes

2 15-ounce cans black beans, drained

1 tablespoon chili powder

1 tablespoon chili con carne seasoning

2 teaspoons cumin

2 teaspoons coriander

¼ teaspoon cayenne

Sauté onions and garlic in nonstick pan with a touch of water, until soft. Add beans, heat through, move to blender, and blend to dip consistency. Add spices and tomatoes: continue to blend until thoroughly mixed.

Use with low fat crackers, chips, or spread onto a burrito or taco to make a bean base for your Mexican treats. You can be creative with this dip. Some people prefer to use fresh-cooked beans, others like the speed of using canned. You can add chopped tomato, pepper, more onion, or whatever suits your taste. Makes 6 (¼ cup) servings. *(1 serving = 225.7 calories, 1.4 grams fat: 24% protein, 71% carbohydrates, 5% fat.)*

*From *Dr. Shintani's Eat More, Weigh Less® Cookbook*, p. 326.

GOURMET SALSA
(vegetables, grain)

1 10-ounce can stewed tomatoes
1 4-ounce can olives, chopped
1 4-ounce can mushrooms, chopped
1 4-ounce can green chilies
1 teaspoon garlic salt
1 tablespoon extra virgin olive oil
3 tablespoons wine vinegar
8 green onions, chopped
Chili pepper flakes, to taste (optional)
¼ cup corn (optional)

Mix all ingredients together and refrigerate overnight. Serve as a dip or salsa. Makes 9 (½ cup) servings. *(1 serving = 47 calories, 2.9 grams fat, 0.8 grams dietary fiber: 7% protein, 43% carbohydrates, 49% fat.)*

SALADS

BEAN AND RADICCHIO SALAD WITH RASPBERRY VINAIGRETTE
(legumes, vegetables, oil)

2 red bell peppers
1 large red onion
1 15-ounce can black beans, rinsed and drained
1 15-ounce can small white beans, rinsed and drained
4 sun-dried tomatoes, chopped
2 tablespoons basil or parsley, finely chopped
Raspberry Vinaigrette
1 head romaine lettuce, thinly sliced

Preheat oven to 400°F. Cut ends off bell peppers, then cut in half lengthwise. Remove seeds and ribs. Peel onion and cut into eight wedges. Place bell peppers and onion on a baking pan lined with foil. Roast for 10 minutes. Cool slightly, then cut bell peppers into strips and onions into cubes. In a large bowl combine bell peppers, onion, beans, sun-dried tomatoes, basil, and Raspberry Vinaigrette; toss lightly to mix. Divide romaine lettuce between 6 salad plates and top with salad mixture. Makes 6 (2 cup) servings. *(1 serving = 229 calories, 1.8 grams fat, 7.8 grams dietary fiber: 23% protein, 71% carbohydrates, 7% fat.)*

RASPBERRY VINAIGRETTE

1 teaspoon extra virgin olive oil
2 cloves garlic, minced
1 shallot, minced
½ cup raspberry vinegar
¼ cup vegetable stock
½ teaspoon salt
¼ teaspoon black pepper, freshly ground
⅛ teaspoon red pepper, crushed

In a small skillet heat olive oil on medium. Sauté garlic and shallot for 2 minutes or until shallots are translucent. Add ¼ cup raspberry vinegar and boil until reduced by half. Add vegetable stock and boil for 2 minutes. Stir in remaining ¼ cup raspberry vinegar, salt, black pepper, and crushed red pepper. Remove from heat and set aside. Makes ½ cup or 4 (2 tablespoon) servings. *(1 serving = 19 calories, 1.1 grams fat, 0.0 grams dietary fiber: 5% protein, 59% carbohydrates, 36% fat.)*

MOROCCAN SALAD
(grains, legumes, vegetables, fruit, oil)

1 cup couscous
2 cups boiling water
2 tomatoes, peeled and chopped
1 15-ounce can red kidney or pinto beans, rinsed and drained
1 cup corn kernels, cooked
½ red bell pepper, chopped
3 green onions, thinly sliced
3 tablespoons fresh lemon juice
1½ teaspoons extra virgin olive oil
Salt and freshly ground black pepper to taste

Soak the couscous in boiling water, until all the water is absorbed. Set aside to cool. In a large mixing bowl combine couscous, tomatoes, kidney beans, corn, bell pepper and green onions; mix well. Stir in lemon juice and olive oil. Season to taste with salt and pepper. Refrigerate for at least 2 hours to let flavors blend. Makes 6 (1½ cup) servings. *(1 serving = 277 calories, 1.7 grams fat, 6.0 grams dietary fiber: 15% protein, 78% carbohydrates, 7% fat.)*

BLACK BEAN SALAD
(legumes, vegetables, fruit)

I 15-ounce can black beans, drained and rinsed
1 small avocado, peeled and coarsely chopped
Lemon juice for drizzling over cut avocado
½ cup sweet onion, chopped
1 large tomato, chopped
½ cup parsley, chopped
1 tablespoon jalapeño pepper, minced and seeded
12 whole lettuce leaves

Peel avocado and coarsely chop. Squeeze lemon juice over avocado
to prevent color change. In a large bowl combine all ingredients,
except lettuce leaves; chill. To serve, use lettuce leaves to wrap
black bean mixture. Makes 6 (⅓ cup bean mixture) servings. *(1 serving = 150 calories, 5.5 grams fat, 4.7 grams dietary fiber: 17% protein, 51% carbohydrates, 31% fat.)*

TABOULEH
(grains, legumes, vegetables, fruit, oil)

2 cups water
1 cup bulgur wheat
2 medium firm, ripe tomatoes, chopped
1 cup cucumber, chopped
1½ cups chickpeas (garbanzo beans), cooked or canned
¼ to ½ cup fresh parsley, chopped
1 bunch scallions, finely chopped
2 to 3 tablespoons fresh mint leaves, minced, or 2 teaspoons dried
   mint
¼ cup extra virgin olive oil
1 large lemon, juiced
1 clove garlic, minced
Salt and freshly ground pepper to taste

Boil 2 cups of water and pour over the bulgur. Cover and let stand
for about 30 minutes. The water should be absorbed and the bulgur

should have a chewy consistency. Allow the bulgur to cool some-what, then add the remaining ingredients. Mix thoroughly and chill for 1 to 2 hours before serving. Makes 6 (1½ cup) servings. *(1 serving = 325 calories, 13 grams fat, 9 grams dietary fiber: 12% protein, 52% carbohydrates, 36% fat.)*

CRISP CHAPATIS WITH MIXED SALAD
(grains, vegetables, legumes, fruit, honey)

6 whole wheat chapati
1½ cups chickpeas, cooked
    or 1 15.5-ounce can chickpeas, rinsed and drained
1 cup corn kernels, fresh, or frozen, thawed
1 cup peas, fresh, or frozen, thawed
2 green onions, thinly sliced
1 small carrot, shredded
2 stalks celery, thinly sliced
⅓ cup fresh cilantro, chopped
⅓ cup fresh lime juice
1 tablespoon brown rice syrup or honey
1 tablespoon tamari or low sodium soy sauce
2 cups romaine lettuce, shredded

Preheat oven to 375°F. Brush chapatis on both sides with about ½ cup warm water. Place 6 small ovenproof bowls upside down on baking sheet and drape each with a chapati. Place in oven and bake until chapatis are browned and resemble tostada shells, about 20 minutes. Remove from oven and let cool slightly before removing from bowls. In a medium bowl combine all remaining ingredients, except romaine lettuce. Place shredded lettuce in chapati shells and spoon in salad mixture. Makes 6 (1 cup) servings. *(1 serving = 221 calories, 3.0 grams fat, 6.2 grams dietary fiber: 14% protein, 74% carbohydrates, 12% fat.)*

GREEK SPINACH SALAD
(vegetables, legume or dairy, fruit, oil)

2 cups fresh spinach leaves, torn
2 medium tomatoes, cut into thin wedges
1 small Japanese cucumber, thinly sliced
1 yellow bell pepper, julienned
½ red onion, thinly sliced
2 tablespoons green onion, thinly sliced
1 ounce soy cheese or feta cheese, crumbled
4 Kalamata olives, thinly sliced
2 tablespoons fresh basil, chopped
3 tablespoons fresh lemon juice
1 teaspoon extra virgin olive oil
½ teaspoon Dijon mustard
1 clove garlic, minced
⅛ teaspoon sea salt, ground

In a large salad or mixing bowl combine spinach, tomatoes, cucumber, bell pepper, red onion, green onion, soy cheese, olives, and fresh basil; toss lightly to mix. In a small bowl, whisk together lemon juice, olive oil, mustard, garlic, and salt. Drizzle dressing over salad; toss lightly to coat. Makes 6 to 8 (1 cup) servings. *(1 serving = 48 calories, 2.4 grams fat, 1.6 grams dietary fiber: 15% protein, 45% carbohydrates, 40% fat.)*

AMERICAS QUINOA SALAD
(grains, vegetables, oil)

1 cup quinoa
2 cups water
⅓ cup red wine vinegar
2 teaspoons extra virgin olive oil
1 clove garlic, minced
¼ teaspoon black pepper, freshly ground
⅛ teaspoon salt
1 small green bell pepper, chopped
1 small red bell pepper, chopped
½ cup cucumber, chopped
¼ cup red onion, chopped
¼ cup parsley, minced
4 black olives, sliced

Rinse quinoa thoroughly. In a saucepan combine quinoa and water and bring to a boil. Reduce heat and simmer until water is absorbed (about 15 minutes). When cooked, the grains will be translucent and the outer germ ring will separate. Combine red wine vinegar, olive oil, garlic, pepper, and salt; blend well. In a large bowl combine quinoa and all the remaining ingredients. Pour dressing over the salad mixture and toss lightly to mix. Chill 2 to 3 hours before serving. Makes 4 (1 cup) servings. *(1 serving = 202 calories, 5.3 grams fat, 3.3 grams dietary fiber: 12% protein, 66% carbohydrates, 22% fat.)*

Note: Quinoa cooks up well in a rice cooker. See Chapter 11, pp. 189–190.

PEASANT POTATO SALAD
(staple vegetables, vegetables, fruit, tofu, oil)

2 all-purpose potatoes, such as Yukon Gold, peeled and cut into ⅛"
 slices
3 tablespoons fresh lemon juice
1 teaspoon extra virgin olive oil
½ teaspoon Dijon mustard
1 clove garlic, minced
⅛ teaspoon sea salt, ground
8 cups mixed lettuce, torn
1 tomato, diced
2 tablespoons tofu cheese, crumbled
Salt and freshly ground black pepper, to taste

In a medium saucepan boil potatoes in salted water for 6 to 8 minutes or until just tender; drain. Transfer to a large mixing bowl. In a
small bowl, whisk together lemon juice, olive oil, mustard, garlic,
and salt. Pour dressing over potatoes and toss lightly to coat. Add
lettuce, tomato, and tofu cheese; toss lightly to mix. Season to taste
with salt and pepper. Serve immediately. Makes 6 (2 cup) servings.
*(1 serving = 78 calories, 2.1 grams fat, 2.2 grams dietary fiber: 15%
protein, 63% carbohydrates, 2% fat.)*

RAITA (YOGURT WITH CUCUMBER)
(dairy, vegetables)

1½ cups non-fat yogurt
½ teaspoon cumin, ground
¼ teaspoon salt
½ cucumber, thinly sliced
1 green chili, seeded and chopped
2 tablespoons cilantro, chopped

In a small bowl whisk together yogurt, ground cumin, and salt. Stir
in the cucumber, green chili, and cilantro; mix well. Chill. Makes 4
(½ cup) servings. *(1 serving = 54 calories, 0.2 grams fat, 0.4 grams
dietary fiber: 38% protein, 58% carbohydrates, 4% fat.)*

TOFU VEGETABLES WITH GINGER DRESSING
(tofu, vegetables, grains or honey, oil)

2 tablespoons tamari
2 tablespoons fresh ginger, chopped
2 cloves garlic, minced
1 jalapeño pepper, seeded and chopped
2 tablespoons water
1 tablespoon rice vinegar
2 tablespoons cilantro, chopped
1 tablespoon tahini
½ teaspoon sesame oil
½ teaspoon brown rice syrup or honey
12 ounces firm tofu, drained
2 teaspoons oil
4 cups won bok, thinly sliced
2 cups watercress, rinsed and trimmed
½ cup alfalfa sprouts (optional)

In a food processor or blender combine tamari, ginger, garlic, and jalapeño pepper; finely chop. Remove 1 tablespoon of the mixture and set aside. Add water, rice vinegar, cilantro, tahini, sesame oil, and brown rice syrup to the food processor; blend until smooth. Cut tofu into four equal pieces and coat one side with reserved ginger mixture. Place tofu between two cutting boards and top with a weight. Press and let drain for 30 minutes. In a large nonstick skillet heat oil over medium heat and cook tofu until golden brown (about 3 to 4 minutes per side). Transfer to a plate and keep warm. Toss together won bok and watercress and divide between four plates. Top with tofu and drizzle with dressing. Garnish with sprouts, if desired. Serve immediately. Makes 4 (2 cup) servings. *(1 serving = 142 calories, 8.8 grams fat, 2.6 grams dietary fiber: 25% protein, 24% carbohydrates, 51% fat.)*

PEA SALAD
(legumes, vegetables, fruit)

10 ounces frozen baby peas or 2 cups of fresh young peas
1 7-ounce can water chestnuts
½ cup fresh snow peas, cut in thirds
2 stalks celery, chopped
½ cup carrots, grated
2 green onions, thinly sliced
1 cup bean sprouts
1 tomato, chopped (for garnish)
Parsley (for garnish)
4 lettuce leaves

Marinade:

2 tablespoons tomato juice
2 tablespoons red wine vinegar
1 tablespoon tamari
1 teaspoon Dijon mustard
1 clove garlic, minced
½ teaspoon paprika
1 teaspoon frozen unsweetened apple juice concentrate

Defrost frozen peas in a strainer under cold water or steam, and chill the fresh peas. Set aside. Drain and slice the water chestnuts. Combine the peas, snow peas, water chestnuts, celery, carrots, green onions, and bean sprouts.

Mix the marinade ingredients well and pour over the vegetables, stirring lightly. Cover and refrigerate for about an hour. Drain off the marinade before serving. Serve on a lettuce leaf and garnish with chopped tomatoes and a sprig of parsley. Makes 4 (1½ cup) servings. *(1 serving = 98 calories, 0.4 grams fat, 1.2 grams dietary fiber: 20% protein, 77% carbohydrates, 4% fat.)*

FOUR-BEAN SALAD
(legumes, vegetables, honey, oil)

1 15.4-ounce can red kidney beans
1 15.4-ounce can black beans
2 cups fresh green beans, lightly steamed, cut in bite-size pieces,
    or 1 15.4-ounce can garbanzo beans
½ cup carrots, cut into thin strips or shredded
½ large green pepper, diced
1 to 2 stalks celery, thinly sliced
½ medium onion, finely chopped
1 clove garlic, crushed
½ cup cider vinegar
2 tablespoons and 2 teaspoons honey
4 teaspoons extra virgin olive oil
Salt, to taste
Black pepper, finely ground

Drain canned or cooked beans in a colander. Mix the vegetables and beans together in a large bowl. Mix the onion, garlic, vinegar, honey, olive oil, salt, and pepper to taste. Pour dressing onto the beans and vegetables and mix thoroughly. Chill for 1 hour. Makes 12 (⅔ cup) servings. *(1 serving = 162 calories, 2.5 grams fat, 6 grams dietary fiber: 18% protein, 68% carbohydrates, 14% fat.)*

MEDITERRANEAN BARLEY SALAD
(grains, fruit, vegetables, nuts, oil)

½ cup onion, minced
3 cloves garlic, minced
¼ cup vegetable stock
2 cups barley, cooked and cooled
2 tablespoons mint, chopped
½ cup golden raisins
¼ cup sunflower seeds
Ground sea salt and black pepper to taste
4 cups romaine lettuce, shredded
3 medium tomatoes, diced
¼ red cup wine vinegar
1 teaspoon extra virgin olive oil

In a medium saucepan sauté onion and garlic in vegetable stock. Stir in barley, mint, raisins, and sunflower seeds. Season to taste with salt and pepper. Set aside. Arrange lettuce on four salad plates. Top with barley mixture. Combine wine vinegar and olive oil; blend well. Pour over salad. Garnish with diced tomatoes. Makes 4 (2 cup) servings. *(1 serving = 259 calories, 6.5 grams fat, 7.5 grams dietary fiber: 9% protein, 70% carbohydrates, 21% fat.)*

EGGPLANT SALAD WITH SESAME DRESSING
(vegetables, legumes, fruit)

1 red bell pepper, trimmed and seeded
1 green bell pepper, trimmed and seeded
1 small jicama, peeled
4 tablespoons rice wine vinegar
2 tablespoons tamari
1 teaspoon sesame oil
3 tablespoons fresh lemon juice
2 tablespoons sesame seeds, toasted
4 tablespoons green onions, sliced
4 tablespoons cilantro, chopped
4 cloves garlic, minced
2 long eggplants, quartered lengthwise and sliced

½ 15.4-ounce can garbanzo beans, drained
Ground salt and pepper to taste
Non-fat cooking spray

Diagonally slice red bell pepper, green bell pepper, and jicama into pieces approximately ¼" by 1 ½" wide and 2" long.

Combine and whisk together all the remaining ingredients into a dressing, except the garbanzo beans. Place quartered eggplant in another mixing bowl and sprinkle one-third of the whisked dressing; toss lightly. Preheat the broiler. Spray baking sheet with non-fat cooking spray. Place coated eggplant on sprayed pan and broil for 4 minutes on each side. In a large mixing bowl combine cooked eggplant, bell peppers, jicama, garbanzo beans, and two-thirds of the dressing. Toss lightly. Season with ground salt and pepper. Makes 6 (1 cup) servings *(1 serving = 99 calories, 3.1 grams fat, 2.7 grams dietary fiber: 15% protein, 60% carbohydrates, 26% fat.)*

WAKAME VINAIGRETTE SALAD*
(vegetables, high calcium sea vegetables)

1 ounce wakame
½ cup vegetables such as cucumbers, julienned carrots, sliced
    radish, or sliced daikon or any combination (optional)

Dressing:
½ cup sushi vinegar, to taste (available in Oriental food section)
    or use
¼ cup brown rice vinegar mixed with a sweetener such as ⅓ cup of
    barley malt
1 teaspoon sea salt, or to taste

Rinse and soak the wakame in water. Thinly slice or julienne the cucumbers, carrots, and any other vegetables. Mix with the sauce, let stand for 10 minutes so the flavor mixes with the vegetables. Serve as a cool, tangy salad or side vegetable. Makes 2½ (½ cup) servings. *(1 serving = 125 calories, 0.6 grams fat: 14% protein, 83% carbohydrates, 2% fat.)*

*From *Dr. Shintani's Eat More, Weigh Less® Cookbook*, p. 227.

PRAWN PAPAYA SALAD WITH THAI VEGETABLES
(seafood, vegetables, fruit, sugar, oil)

8 ounces mixed salad greens
12 ounces prawns or shrimp (16 to 20), peeled and deveined
Salt and white pepper to taste
2 teaspoons sesame oil
Thai Vinaigrette
1 firm, ripe papaya
½ large red bell pepper, julienned
Sprigs of cilantro for garnish

Rinse and dry mixed greens and refrigerate. Lightly season prawns with salt and white pepper. Heat a wok or skillet and sauté prawns in sesame oil, being careful not to overcook. Set aside to cool. Prepare vinaigrette. Peel papaya and cut into quarters. Remove seeds and cut each section into a fan or slices; chill. When ready to serve, place mixed greens on four plates. Artfully arrange chilled papaya slices and prawns on top of the greens. Drizzle with Thai Vinaigrette. Sprinkle with bell pepper and garnish with cilantro leaves. Accompany with remaining vinaigrette. Makes 4 (1 cup) servings. *(1 serving = 119 calories, 3.1 grams fat, 1.1 grams dietary fiber: 50% protein, 27% carbohydrates, 23% fat.)*

THAI VINAIGRETTE
(vegetables, fruit, seafood, sugar)

3 tablespoons fresh lime juice
2 tablespoons fish sauce
1 teaspoon sugar
¼ to ½ teaspoon chili paste, ground fresh
1 tablespoon cilantro, minced
1 tablespoon green onions, minced
½ tablespoon ginger, minced

Combine all ingredients in a jar and shake vigorously; set aside.

MEDITERRANEAN CHICKEN SALAD
(vegetables, poultry, oil, fruit)

3 cups water
1 medium onion, peeled and quartered
2 carrots, peeled and chopped
1 leek, white part only, or 3 scallions, white part only
1 teaspoon dried thyme
1 bay leaf
4 parsley sprigs or 1 tablespoon dried
8 black peppercorns
Salt
2 whole chicken breasts, about 2 pounds
¼ cup extra virgin olive oil
1 teaspoon dried oregano
Juice of 1 small lemon (use ⅓ lemon, taste, and use more if desired)
½ cup black olives
¾ cup celery, chopped
1 to 2 tablespoons capers, drained
8 cherry tomatoes, halved or 2 medium tomatoes in wedges
1 pound whole green beans, cooked
Salt and fresh pepper to taste

Measure 3 cups water in large kettle; add onion, carrots, leek or scallions, thyme, bay leaf, parsley, peppercorns, and salt to taste. Bring to boil and simmer uncovered 15 minutes. Add chicken, return to boil, reduce heat and simmer, partially covered, until chicken is done (about 20 minutes). Let chicken cool in broth. Remove chicken (save broth for soup). Discard skin and pull meat from bones. Tear meat into medium-to-large pieces and combine in a bowl with olive oil and oregano. Cover and let stand at room temperature for 1 hour.

Meanwhile, steam whole green beans until cooked to your liking (about 10 minutes).

Add remaining ingredients to the chicken, toss and season to taste with salt and pepper. Add green beans just before serving. Makes 8 (1 cup) servings. *(1 serving = 321 calories, 19 grams fat, 3 grams dietary fiber: 28% protein, 21% carbohydrates, 51% fat.)*

SALAD DRESSINGS

DIJON VINAIGRETTE*
(vegetables, grains)

½ cup balsamic vinegar
2 tablespoons Dijon mustard
2 tablespoons soy sauce
2 tablespoons maple syrup

Blend all ingredients on high in a blender until smooth, or place in a small bowl and whisk together. Let sit for at least 15 minutes to allow flavors to meld. Toss with your favorite green salad or pasta salad. Makes 7 (2 tablespoon) servings. *(1 serving = 39 calories, 0.3 grams fat: 6% protein, 88% carbohydrates, 7% fat.)*

*From *Dr. Shintani's Eat More, Weigh Less® Cookbook*, p. 197.

CALIFORNIA SUNSHINE DRESSING*
by Dick Allgire
(fruit, vegetables)

12 ounces fresh orange juice
2 cloves garlic
4 tablespoons soy sauce

Combine all ingredients in a blender and blend on high until smooth. Makes about 1 cup or 8 (2 tablespoon) servings. *(1 serving = 25 calories, 0.1 grams fat: 13% protein, 84% carbohydrates, 3% fat.)*

*From *Dr. Shintani's Eat More, Weigh Less® Cookbook*, p. 198.

THOUSAND ISLAND DRESSING*
(vegetables, tofu)

¼ cup water
⅛ teaspoon salt
⅛ teaspoon pepper

1 teaspoon seasoned salt
2 tablespoons tomato ketchup
1 cup soft tofu, crumbled
4 sprigs fresh parsley (optional)
1 tablespoon cucumber, chopped fine
1 tablespoon celery, chopped fine

Mix all ingredients except cucumber and celery in blender. Add cucumber and celery; blend until smooth. Chill and serve. Makes about 1½ cups or 12 (2 tablespoon) servings. *(1 serving = 14 calories, 0.6 grams fat: 28% protein, 35% carbohydrates, 37% fat.)*

*From *Dr. Shintani's Eat More, Weigh Less® Cookbook,* p. 194.

SOUPS

SPICY BLACK BEAN SOUP
(legumes, vegetables)

¼ cup vegetable stock
1 small onion, coarsely chopped
1 4-ounce can green chilies, diced
2 cloves garlic, minced
2 teaspoons chili powder
1 teaspoon ground cumin
1 15-ounce can black beans, undrained
1 14.5-ounce can tomatoes, undrained and diced
1 cup water
Cilantro for garnish, if desired

Heat a large stockpot on medium high. Sauté onion in vegetable stock until soft and lightly browned (about 2 to 3 minutes). Stir in green chilies, garlic, chili powder, and cumin. Add black beans, diced tomatoes, and water; stir well and simmer for 15 minutes. Sprinkle each serving with cilantro, if desired. Makes 4 (1½ cup) servings. *(1 serving = 188 calories, 1.1 grams fat, 6.2 grams dietary fiber: 22% protein, 73% carbohydrates, 5% fat.)*

YUKON GOLD POTATO SOUP
(staple vegetables, vegetables)

1 quart vegetable stock
1 pound Yukon Gold or other yellow potatoes, cut into ½" cubes
1 medium onion, finely chopped
1 cup leeks, sliced, white part only
½ teaspoon salt
¼ teaspoon ground white pepper
2 tablespoons parsley or chives, chopped

In a large saucepan combine stock, potatoes, onion and leeks. Bring
to a boil over high heat. Reduce heat, cover, and simmer for 10 to 12
minutes or until vegetables are tender. Cool slightly, then in a food
processor or blender, process until smooth. Season with salt and
pepper. Garnish each serving with chopped parsley. Serve warm.
Makes 4 (2 cup) servings. *(1 serving = 146 calories, 0.4 grams fat,
4.0 grams dietary fiber: 9% protein, 88% carbohydrates, 2% fat.)*

THAI PUMPKIN BISQUE
(vegetables, fruit, seafood, sugar)

1½ to 2 pounds pumpkin
2 cloves garlic, crushed
1 shallot, sliced
2 stalks lemon grass, peel off tough outer leaves and chop
2 cups vegetable stock
½ to 1 teaspoon roasted chili paste
1 cup coconut milk
1 tablespoon fish sauce
1 teaspoon sugar
White pepper to taste
2 small red chilies, seeded and thinly sliced (optional)
Sprigs of fresh cilantro for garnish
¾ cup shredded chicken breast (optional)
   or
¾ cup small shrimp (optional)

Peel pumpkin and cut into ½" cubes. In a food processor or mortar grind together garlic, shallot and lemon grass. In a wok or large saucepan bring stock to a boil. Stir in garlic mixture and chili paste. Add pumpkin and simmer for 15 minutes or until pumpkin is just tender. Stir in coconut milk and return to a simmer. Add fish sauce, sugar, and white pepper. Simmer for 5 minutes. Cool slightly and puree in a food processor or blender; strain. Serve warm or chilled. Garnish with red chilies and sprigs of cilantro. Optional: Shredded cooked chicken or small cooked shrimp could be sprinkled on the surface as a garnish. Makes 6 (1½ cup) servings. *(1 serving without chicken or shrimp = 134 calories, 9.7 grams fat, 2.3 grams dietary fiber: 7% protein, 34% carbohydrates, 59% fat.) (1 serving with 2 tablespoons chicken = 210 calories, 13 grams fat, 3 grams dietary fiber: 15% protein, 29% carbohydrates, 56% fat.) (1 serving with 2 tablespoons shrimp = 190 calories, 10 grams fat, 3 grams dietary fiber: 11% protein, 42% carbohydrates, 47% fat.)*

CREAMY ZUCCHINI SOUP*
(vegetables, legumes)

2 medium onions, sliced
2 zucchini, sliced (about 3 cups unpeeled)
6 cups vegetable stock or vegetarian chicken stock
2 crookneck squash
¼ cup green onion, chopped
2 cups lima beans (one 10-ounce package, frozen)
¼ cup corn, frozen
1 cup peas (½ of 10-ounce package, frozen)
1 tablespoon low sodium soy sauce, or to taste
Pepper, to taste

Place onions and zucchini in a 4-quart saucepan. Add the stock and bring to a boil. Add the other vegetables. Bring the mixture to a boil again, reduce heat and simmer for about ½ hour, or until the vegetables are soft. Add soy sauce and pepper. Puree mixture, reheat, and then serve. Makes 10 to 12 (2 cup) servings. *(1 serving = 91.1 calories, 0.5 grams fat: 25% protein, 70% carbohydrates, 5% fat.)*

*From *Dr. Shintani's Eat More, Weigh Less*® Cookbook, p. 174.

LENTIL SOUP*
(legumes, vegetables)

1 cup lentils
4 to 5 cups water
1 medium onion
1 stalk broccoli, chopped
1 stalk celery, sliced into ½" pieces
1 carrot, sliced into thin pieces
Sea salt or low sodium soy sauce
2 bay leaves
2 tablespoons parsley, chopped
Vegetables (burdock, potatoes, seaweed, daikon) (optional)
2 teaspoons cumin (optional)
Vegetable stock, miso stock, or powdered vegetarian chicken stock
    can be substituted for some of the salt or soy sauce

Wash lentils and place in saucepan with water. Bring to a boil and reduce heat to low. Simmer 20 to 30 minutes. Add diced onion, broccoli, celery, and other vegetables. Simmer until vegetables are soft, about another 15 to 20 minutes depending on the size of chopped vegetables. If cut in larger chunks, you will need to add them sooner so they cook longer. Add salt or soy sauce and other seasonings to taste. Makes 6 (1 cup) servings. *(1 serving = 135 calories, 3 grams fat: 30% protein, 67% carbohydrates, 3% fat.)*

*From *Dr. Shintani's Eat More, Weigh Less® Diet*, p. 247.

ANN'S CORN TOMATO SOUP
(grain, vegetables, oil)

1 medium onion, chopped
8 cloves garlic, minced
1 teaspoon extra virgin olive oil
9 medium tomatoes, coarsely chopped
6 large ears of corn, shucked, peeled and cut from cob
¼ teaspoon salt and cayenne pepper to taste
Fresh parsley or basil, minced, to taste

In a stockpot sauté onion and garlic in olive oil on medium heat. When onions are transparent, stir in tomatoes and corn. Add salt, cayenne pepper, and parsley to taste. Bring to a boil, stir well, then reduce heat and simmer for 30 minutes. For a creamier soup puree about half the soup in a blender, then return it to the stockpot. The soup will become bright orange. Please note not to let the soup boil too long; it will lose flavor. Makes 8 (2 cup) servings. *(1 serving = 105 calories, 1.8 grams fat, 4.1 grams dietary fiber: 11% protein, 75% carbohydrates, 13% fat.)*

SPLIT PEA SOUP*
(legumes, vegetables)

8 cups water
2 cups split peas
¼ cup barley
2 onions, chopped
2 bay leaves
2 stalks celery, diced
1 carrot, diced
1 teaspoon basil or ½ teaspoon marjoram
1 teaspoon thyme
¼ cup low sodium soy sauce or miso dissolved in hot water, to taste
Other vegetables (parsnips, burdock, or potato) (optional)

Wash split peas well and boil with barley, onions, and bay leaves (and parsnips, burdock, or potato, if any) in 4 cups of water for 30 minutes. Add other vegetables, herbs and spices, 4 cups of water, and simmer another 30 minutes. Add soy sauce or miso to taste before serving. Makes 6 (2 cup) servings. *(1 serving = 282 calories, 1 gram fat, 25% protein, 72% carbohydrates, 3% fat.)*

*From *Dr. Shintani's Eat More, Weigh Less® Diet,* p. 248.

VEGETABLE BARLEY SOUP*
(vegetables, grains)

3 cups vegetable broth
2 10-ounce cans tomato sauce
2 large carrots, sliced
1 medium onion, chopped
2 stalks celery
1 to 2 bay leaves
1 clove garlic, chopped
½ cup barley

Combine all ingredients in a large pot. Bring to a boil, cover, reduce heat, and simmer 1 hour. Remove bay leaves and serve. Makes 6 (1 cup) servings. *(1 serving = 118 calories, 0.7 grams fat: 18% protein, 77% carbohydrates, 5% fat.)*

*From *Dr. Shintani's Eat More, Weigh Less® Cookbook*, p. 181.

TUSCANY BEAN SOUP
(legumes, vegetables, oil)

½ tablespoon extra virgin olive oil
3 cloves garlic, minced
1 large red onion, chopped
5 cups vegetable or vegetarian chicken broth
2 stalks celery with leaves, finely chopped
3 fresh sage leaves, finely chopped, or 1 teaspoon dried sage
2 bay leaves
2 16-ounce cans cannellini beans (or red kidney beans and white
    navy beans)
½ cup canned crushed tomatoes with juice
½ teaspoon Chinese parsley, chopped
Salt and freshly ground pepper to taste

In a large saucepan, sauté olive oil, garlic, and onion until transparent. Add broth, celery, sage, bay leaves, beans, tomatoes, parsley, salt, and pepper. Cover and cook over medium-high heat for 1 minute. Reduce heat to medium low and cover. Simmer for 20 minutes, stirring occasionally. Makes 6 (2 cup) servings. *(1 serving = 208 calories, 2 grams fat, 5 grams dietary fiber: 20% protein, 70% carbohydrates, 10% fat.)*

MINESTRONE SOUP
(legumes, vegetables, grains, oil)

2 tablespoons extra virgin olive oil
1 medium onion, chopped
2 leeks, thinly sliced
3 to 5 garlic cloves, thinly sliced
1 15-ounce can Italian plum tomatoes, with liquid
1 15-ounce can cannellini or kidney beans
1 medium carrot, halved lengthwise and thinly sliced
2 teaspoons salt
½ teaspoon basil
1 teaspoon oregano
10 cups water
1 cup green beans, cut into 1" pieces
1 medium zucchini, halved lengthwise and thinly sliced
¾ cup elbow macaroni, uncooked

In a large saucepan, sauté the onion in olive oil. Add leeks and garlic and cook for 2 more minutes. Add tomatoes, beans, carrot, salt, basil, oregano, water and bring to boil. Reduce heat and simmer for 30 minutes. Add green beans, zucchini and macaroni, and simmer 15 minutes. Makes 8 (2 cup) servings. *(1 serving = 200 calories, 4 grams fat, 6 grams dietary fiber: 14% protein, 68% carbohydrates, 18% fat.)*

ONION SOUP*

2 medium onions, cut in thin crescents
½ teaspoon sesame oil
¼ teaspoon sea salt
2 cups vegetable broth
3 cups water
1 tablespoon soy sauce

Sauté the onions in sesame oil until they are transparent. Add the vegetable broth and the boiling water. Cover and simmer for 5 minutes. Add the salt, cover, and simmer for 30 minutes on a low heat *(still boiling)*. Add the soy sauce. Serve immediately. Makes 6 servings. *(1 serving = 37 calories, 0.5 grams fat: 21% protein, 67% carbohydrates, 13% fat.)*

*From *Dr. Shintani's Eat More, Weigh Less*® *Cookbook*, p. 165.

MISO SOUP WITH SPINACH
(tofu, vegetables, grains)

8 ounces firm tofu
4 cups water
6 to 8 dried shiitake mushrooms (about ½ ounce)
1½ tablespoons ginger, finely minced
¼ cup green onions, thinly sliced
⅓ cup miso
1 tablespoon mirin or dry sherry
2 cups packed fresh spinach, rinsed, stemmed and sliced
1 tablespoon low sodium soy sauce, if desired

Drain tofu and cut into ½" cubes; set aside. In a stockpot combine water, dried shiitake mushrooms, ginger, and 2 tablespoons of the green onions. Bring to a boil; reduce heat, cover, and simmer for 15 minutes. Remove mushrooms and set aside. Strain stock. When mushrooms are cool, remove stems and thinly slice. In a large saucepan heat broth and whisk in miso. Add tofu and mirin. Bring to a simmer and add mushrooms and spinach. Simmer for 2 to 3 minutes or until spinach is tender. Season with soy sauce, if desired. Garnish with remaining green onions. Serve immediately. Makes 8 (2 cup) servings. *(1 serving = 165 calories, 6.6 grams fat, 2.7 grams dietary fiber: 30% protein, 35% carbohydrates, 33% fat.)*

SAUCES AND GRAVIES

Dips and sauces

TOFU DIP SAUCE*
(tofu, vegetables, fruit, legumes)

16 ounces soft tofu
1 tablespoon onion, minced
½ cup vegetarian broth
2 tablespoons low sodium soy sauce, or to taste
1 teaspoon lemon juice
Fresh dill (optional)

Mash tofu and mix in other ingredients. Place in a blender and puree. Use this as a vegetable topping or a dip for steamed vegetables. Add fresh dill as a variation with the other ingredients. Makes 20 (2 tablespoon) servings. *(1 serving = 14 calories, 0.6 grams fat: 34% protein, 26% carbohydrates, 40% fat.)*

*From *Dr. Shintani's Eat More, Weigh Less® Cookbook*, p. 249.

TAHINI SAUCE*
(vegetables)

2 tablespoons tahini
2 tablespoons tamari
2 tablespoons water

Place all ingredients together in a pan and cook over low heat, stirring constantly until they have blended and have the consistency of cream. Drizzle over grains. Makes 6 (1 tablespoon) servings. *(1 serving = 33 calories, 2.7 grams fat: 17% protein, 16% carbohydrates, 68% fat.)*

*From *Dr. Shintani's Eat More, Weigh Less® Diet*, p. 240.

ORIENTAL GINGER SAUCE*
(vegetables, grains, legumes)

1 tablespoon arrowroot or corn starch
1 cup water
4 tablespoons low sodium soy sauce
1 tablespoon ginger, grated

Mix arrowroot or corn starch in ¼ cup of cool water. Add to a saucepan with the remaining water, soy sauce, and ginger. Heat at medium until thickened, and stir. Serve with steamed vegetables. Makes 10 (2 tablespoon) servings. *(1 serving = 6.9 calories, 0.0 grams fat: 21% protein, 78% carbohydrates, 1% fat.)*

*From *Dr. Shintani's Eat More, Weigh Less® Diet*, p. 240, and from *Dr. Shintani's Eat More, Weigh Less® Cookbook*, p. 244.

3221 DIJON MUSTARD SAUCE*
(vegetables, fruit, legumes)

3 tablespoons soy sauce
2 tablespoons Dijon mustard
2 tablespoons lemon juice
1 clove garlic, crushed

Mix all ingredients together. Blend well and serve as sauce for vegetables or dipping sauce. Makes 3 (2 tablespoon) servings. *(1 serving = 26 calories, 0.6 grams fat: 26% protein, 52% carbohydrates, 22% fat.)*

*From *Dr. Shintani's Eat More, Weigh Less® Cookbook*, p. 243.

MUSHROOM TERIYAKI SAUCE
(vegetable, grains, legumes, honey)

½ cup mushrooms
1 teaspoon arrowroot or corn starch
2 tablespoons water
2 tablespoons low sodium soy sauce or tamari

1 teaspoon molasses or honey
1 teaspoon ginger root, grated (optional)

Chop mushrooms into small pieces. Sauté mushrooms with soy sauce, honey, and ginger. Dissolve arrowroot in 2 tablespoons cool water and add to mushrooms. Add additional water for desired consistency and continue to sauté for a minute or so until the ingredients are blended. Use on vegetables in a sandwich, on beans, tofu, or mix with noodles. Makes 4 (3 tablespoon) servings. *(1 serving = 31 calories, 0.2 grams fat: 18% protein, 86% carbohydrates, 1% fat.)*

*From *Dr. Shintani's Eat More, Weigh Less® Cookbook*, p. 183.

BARBEQUE SAUCE*
(vegetables, honey, grains)

½ cup water
1 teaspoon soy sauce
1 large onion, minced
3 cloves garlic, minced
1 8-ounce can tomato sauce
1 cup tomato ketchup
1 cup water
1 tablespoon honey
1 teaspoon chili powder
2 tablespoons cider vinegar
1 teaspoon dry mustard
2 tablespoons tamari
½ tablespoon corn starch or whole wheat flour, dissolved in 2
    tablespoons water

In a large pan, heat water and soy sauce. Add minced onion and garlic. Cook over medium heat until the onion is soft. Add other ingredients and cook for 10 minutes. Stir often. Makes about 4 cups or 32 (2 tablespoon) servings. *(1 serving = 17 calories, 0.03 gram fat, 0.2 gram dietary fiber, 8 percent protein, 90% carbohydrates, 1% fat.)*

*From *Dr. Shintani's Eat More, Weigh Less® Cookbook*, p. 246.

SIMPLE CURRY SAUCE*
(vegetables, grains)

4 teaspoons whole wheat flour
2 teaspoons curry powder (choose milk, medium or hot, to taste)
1 cup vegetable broth
1 cup water
2 teaspoons ginger, finely chopped
1 medium onion, chopped
1 bay leaf
1 clove garlic, crushed

Blend all ingredients, then cook over medium heat until thickened. Simmer 10 minutes. Remove bay leaf. Makes 24 (2 tablespoon) servings. *(1 serving = 6 calories, 0.1 grams fat: 19% protein, 74% carbohydrates, 7% fat.)*

*From *Dr. Shintani's Eat More, Weigh Less® Cookbook*, p. 247.

MEDITERRANEAN HERB SAUCE*
(vegetables, honey)

1 clove garlic, minced
2 tablespoons Dijon mustard
½ cup red wine vinegar
1 teaspoon black pepper
½ cup basil leaves, chopped
½ teaspoon onion powder
1 tablespoon honey

Combine all ingredients and serve over steamed vegetables. Serve as a marinade, as sauce for vegetables, or over vegetable kebobs. Makes 7 (2 tablespoon) servings. *(1 serving = 17 calories, 0.3 grams fat: 8% protein, 80% carbohydrates, 12% fat.)*

*From *Dr. Shintani's Eat More, Weigh Less® Cookbook*, p. 250.

GARLIC SAUCE
(vegetables, legumes, grains)

3 tablespoons tamari
1 tablespoon rice vinegar
½ teaspoon sesame oil
2 cloves garlic, minced

Combine all ingredients; blend well. Makes ¼ cup or 2 (2 table-spoon) servings. *(1 serving = 31 calories, 1.2 grams fat, 0 grams dietary fiber: 35% protein, 35% carbohydrates, 31% fat.)*

MISO SAUCE
(vegetables, legumes, grains, fruit)

¾ cup water
¼ cup tamari
2 tablespoons tahini
1 tablespoon miso paste
1 teaspoon lemon peel, minced (optional)

In a small saucepan, combine water, tamari, tahini, and miso paste; simmer over low heat for 15 minutes, stirring occasionally. Stir in lemon peel. Makes 4 (4 to 5 tablespoon) servings. *(1 serving = 65 calories, 4 grams fat, 0.15 grams dietary fiber: 23% protein, 21% carbohydrates, 56% fat.)*

Gravies

SAVORY GRAVY*
(grains, vegetables)

2 cups vegetable broth
1 cup water
1 tablespoon Old Bay® seasoning (found in your health food store)
½ cup whole wheat flour, pan toasted
¼ teaspoon black pepper
¼ teaspoon garlic powder

Place flour in dry pan in oven at 300°F until it is lightly browned (about 10 to 15 minutes). Blend in all other ingredients, then cook in a saucepan, stirring until thickened. Cover and simmer (about 10 minutes). Makes 9 (5 tablespoon) servings. *(1 serving = 31 calories, 0.2 grams fat: 22% protein, 74% carbohydrates, 5% fat.)*

*From *Dr. Shintani's Eat More, Weigh Less® Cookbook,* p. 258.

SEASONED GRAVY*
(grains, vegetables)

2 cups water
1 teaspoon onion powder
¼ cup whole wheat or other whole grain flour, pan toasted
½ teaspoon salt, to taste
¼ teaspoon black lemon pepper
1 teaspoon corn starch or arrowroot dissolved in 2 tablespoons water

Lightly brown flour in a skillet over medium heat. Dissolve 1 teaspoon of corn starch or arrowroot in a little water. Blend all ingredients until thoroughly mixed and cook until mixture boils. Serve with baked potatoes, seitan dishes, or vegetables. This also makes a good base for stews and vegetable pot pies. Makes 6 (5 tablespoon) servings. *(1 serving = 18 calories, 0.1 grams fat: 15% protein, 81% carbohydrates, 5% fat.)*

*From *Dr. Shintani's Eat More, Weigh Less® Cookbook,* p. 259.

BROWN MUSHROOM GRAVY*
(grains, vegetables, legumes, nuts)

2½ to 3 cups water
1 cup mushrooms, chopped
½ onion, minced
3 tablespoons low sodium soy sauce or to taste
½ cup whole wheat pastry flour
1 tablespoon vegetarian chicken or beef stock powder
2 tablespoons corn starch or arrowroot
1 to 2 tablespoons peanut butter or other nut butter (optional)

Heat about ¼ cup of water in a pot and sauté onions and mushrooms with 1 tablespoon soy sauce until onions are translucent. Add in the flour and vegetarian powder and mix well while cooking for 3 to 4 minutes until slightly browned. Mix corn starch or arrowroot with 2 tablespoons cool water, add soy sauce, and add to the mixture.

Cook over medium heat and add the rest of the water while stirring to smooth texture. Add more water, if needed, to thin the gravy or more flour to thicken it, to taste.

As an option, add 1 to 2 tablespoons of peanut butter or other nut butter. Just be aware that nuts and nut butters are low in EMI and high in fat, so use with caution. Makes 12 (¼ cup) servings. *(1 serving = 56 calories, 0 gram fat, 0 gram dietary fiber: 7% protein, 91% carbohydrates, 2% fat.) (1 serving with 1 tablespoon peanut butter or nut butter = 69 calories, 1 gram fat, 5 grams dietary fiber: 12% protein, 75% carbohydrates, 13% fat.)*

*From *Dr. Shintani's Eat More, Weigh Less® Diet*, p. 238.

ORIENTAL GINGER GRAVY*
(vegetables, legumes)

¼ onion, minced, or ½ teaspoon onion powder
1 clove garlic or ¼ teaspoon garlic powder
2 cups water
2 tablespoons arrowroot
1 to 2 teaspoons low sodium soy sauce or tamari to taste
½ teaspoon ginger root, grated

Sauté the onions and garlic in ¼ cup of water in saucepan until onions are translucent. Dissolve arrowroot in ¼ cup of cool water. Mix all ingredients, and simmer, stirring over low heat until thickened. Serve over steamed vegetables, rice, meat substitutes, or even on toast or waffles. Makes 8 (¼ cup) servings. *(1 serving = 10 calories, 0.02 grams fat: 9% protein, 89% carbohydrates, 2% fat.)*

*From *Dr. Shintani's Eat More, Weigh Less® Diet,* p. 240.

JUST GRAINS

RICE-COOKER RICE*
(grains)

2¼ cups water
1 cup brown rice
Pinch sea salt or to taste

Rinse rice, add the water (adjust the water to your liking) and turn on the rice cooker (about 40 to 45 minutes). Let stand 10 minutes. Makes 2 (1 cup) servings. *(1 serving = 216 calories, 1.8 grams fat: 9% protein, 83% carbohydrates, 7% fat.)*

Steamed vegetables may be cooked in much the same way as rice.

*From *Dr. Shintani's Eat More, Weigh Less® Cookbook,* p. 62.

PRESSURE COOKER BROWN RICE*
(grains)

1⅓ to 1¾ cups water
1 cup brown rice
Pinch sea salt or to taste

Rinse rice and soak 2 to 6 hours, if you have time. Rice will take a little longer to cook if not presoaked.

Place rice and water into a pressure cooker (stainless steel if possible). Add salt and cover with lid as directed by manufacturer of pressure cooker.

Bring to pressure on high heat, then lower to low heat and cook for 30 to 40 minutes. Let pressure come down, then let stand for 5 to 10 minutes; stir and serve. Makes 2 (1 cup) servings. *(1 serving = 216 calories, 1.8 grams fat: 9% protein, 83% carbohydrates, 7% fat.)*

*From *Dr. Shintani's Eat More, Weigh Less® Cookbook*, p. 60.

STOVETOP BROWN RICE
(grains)

2¼ cups water
1 cup brown rice
Pinch sea salt or to taste

Rinse rice, put into a cooking pot, and add water. Bring to a boil, cover, add a pinch of sea salt for each cup of grain, reduce heat, and simmer (about 45 minutes). Remove from heat and let stand for 10 minutes, drain off excess water, and serve. Makes 2 (1 cup) servings. *(1 serving = 216 calories, 1.8 grams fat: 9% protein, 83% carbohydrates, 7% fat.)*

BROWN RICE AND WILD RICE, BARLEY, OR MILLET*
(grains)

4½ cups water
1½ cups brown rice
½ cup wild rice, barley, or millet

Wash and mix three parts brown rice with one part wild rice, barley, or millet. Use any of the rice cooking methods described above. Simmer for 45 to 50 minutes, and let sit for 10 minutes. Makes 6 (1 cup) servings. *(1 serving brown rice and wild rice = 216 calories, 1.8 grams fat: 9% protein, 83% carbohydrates, 7% fat.) (1 serving brown rice and barley = 226 calories, 1.6 grams fat: 10% protein, 84% carbohydrates, 6% fat.) (1 serving brown rice and millet = 235 calories, 2 grams fat: 9% protein, 83% carbohydrates, 8% fat.)*

*From *Dr. Shintani's Eat More, Weigh Less® Diet*, p. 162.

WHEAT BERRY RICE*
(grains)

4½ cups water (or 3⅓ if using pressure cooker)
2 cups long grain brown rice
2 pinches sea salt
¼ cup wheat berries (wild rice or quinoa)

Rinse rice in water and drain. Place in a pot. Add water, sea salt, and wheat berries. Bring to a boil on high heat and then simmer on low heat for 45 minutes (or 35 minutes in a pressure cooker). Makes 6 (1 cup) servings. *(1 serving = 226 calories, 1.8 grams fat: 10% protein, 83% carbohydrates, 7% fat.)*

*From *Dr. Shintani's Eat More, Weigh Less® Cookbook*, p. 64.

JUST BARLEY
(grains)

2½ to 3 cups water
1 cup barley (hulled)
Pinch sea salt

Rinse the barley until the water runs clear. Put the barley and water into a cooking pot. Bring to a boil and cover. Add a pinch of sea salt. Reduce heat and simmer (about 1½ hours). Remove from heat and let stand. Drain off excess water and serve.

When using a pressure cooker and the barley has been soaked, use half the water or follow the manufacturer's instructions.

If you use a rice cooker, put the barley, water and salt in and turn on. The rice cooker will automatically turn off when the barley is done. Let stand with the cover on for 10 minutes and then serve. Makes 3 to 4 (1 cup) servings. *(1 serving = 170 calories, 0.5 grams fat, 6 grams dietary fiber: 12% protein, 87% carbohydrates, 3% fat.)*

QUINOA*
(grains)

2 cups water or vegetable broth
1 cups quinoa, rinsed
¼ teaspoon salt, or to taste

Rinse quinoa thoroughly and drain. Boil broth in a 3- to 4-quart pan; add quinoa, salt to taste. Cover and simmer gently on low heat until liquid is absorbed and grain is tender. This dish can also be prepared in a rice cooker: add all ingredients, cover, and turn on the cooker; it will automatically turn off when the quinoa is cooked (see p. 190). Cool, then serve. Use as side dish, or as base for your own special pilafs. Makes 6 (⅔ cup) servings. *(1 serving = 117 calories, 1.7 grams fat: 17% protein, 71% carbohydrates, 13% fat.)*

*From *Dr. Shintani's Eat More, Weigh Less® Cookbook*, p. 75.

CORN ON THE COB*
(grains)

6 ears fresh corn, husked and cleaned
1 cup water

Place 1½ inches of water in a saucepan, add corn. Bring water to a boil, cover, reduce heat to low. Cook for 3 to 5 minutes, turning ears twice to ensure even cooking. Move corn to a platter and serve. Makes 6 (1 ear) servings. *(1 serving = 83 calories, 0.1 grams fat: 11% protein, 80% carbohydrates, 9% fat.)*

Note: You can eat the corn plain or sprinkle with salt, an herb condiment such as Spike®, Butter Buds®, or other favorite condiments. But stay away from margarine or butter, which are 99 percent fat.

*From *Dr. Shintani's Eat More, Weigh Less® Cookbook*, p. 50.

PASTA

GREAT SPAGHETTI SAUCE AND PASTA
(vegetables, grains, sugar, oil)

1 onion, chopped
4 cloves garlic, minced
1 teaspoon extra virgin olive oil
1 28-ounce can whole Italian peeled tomatoes
1 28-ounce can tomato sauce
1 teaspoon fresh or dried basil, chopped
1 teaspoon sugar
Sprinkle of chili pepper flakes
1½ cups water
Salt and pepper to taste
1 16-ounce package whole wheat, spinach, or vegetable pasta

Sauté onion and garlic in olive oil on medium heat (about 2 minutes). Add tomatoes, tomato sauce, basil, sugar, chili pepper flakes, and water. Simmer for 30 minutes. Season to taste with salt and pepper. Cook your favorite pasta according to package instructions. Spoon sauce over pasta and serve immediately. Makes 8 (1¾ cup) servings. *(1 serving = 373 calories, 2.9 grams fat, 5 grams dietary fiber: 15% protein, 78% carbohydrates, 7% fat.)*

PASTA WITH ROASTED VEGETABLES*
(grains, vegetables, fruit, oil)

1 pound asparagus, trimmed
1 zucchini, quartered
2 yellow crooked-neck squash, quartered
2 long eggplant or 1 round eggplant, peeled
12 plum tomatoes, quartered lengthwise
1 head broccoli, cut in bite-size pieces
1 basket mushrooms, cut in halves
1 small garlic head, minced
2 tablespoons extra virgin olive oil
1 tablespoon fresh basil
2 teaspoons fresh lemon juice
1 tablespoon fresh cilantro
Salt and pepper, to taste
1 pound pasta of choice

Place oven rack in lower third of oven. Preheat oven to 450°F. Cut asparagus, zucchini, yellow crooked-neck squash, and eggplant in 2" lengths. In large roasting pan, toss vegetables with basil, lemon juice, cilantro, olive oil, and garlic. Roast 20 minutes until vegetables are tender.

In large pot of boiling water, cook pasta until tender but firm, about 8 minutes. Drain and transfer to roasting pan. Toss gently to combine with vegetables. Serve immediately. Makes 8 to 10 (1½ to 2 cup) servings. *(1 serving = 234 calories, 2.1 grams fat: 18% protein, 74% carbohydrates, 8% fat.)*

*From *Dr. Shintani's Eat More, Weigh Less® Cookbook,* p. 126.

PASTA WITH EGGPLANT SAUCE*
(grains, vegetables, sugar, oil)

This is a great main dish for any gathering. Leftover sauce can be used over brown rice for lunch the next day.

½ teaspoon extra virgin olive oil
1½ pounds eggplant, unpeeled and in ½" chunks
1 large red onion, chopped
3 large garlic cloves, minced.
1 cup mushrooms, coarsely chopped
1 cup green peppers, coarsely chopped
2 to 3 16-ounce cans plum tomatoes
2 teaspoons dry basil
1 teaspoon dry oregano
1 teaspoon sugar
⅔ cup cilantro
Salt and pepper, to taste
1 pound pasta

Heat oil, add eggplant, onions, and sauté over medium heat until soft and lightly browned, stirring frequently. Add garlic, mushrooms, and green peppers, and continue to sauté. Add tomatoes, basil, oregano, and sugar. Cook covered for 10 minutes. Add cilantro. Season with salt and pepper. Cover and simmer 15 to 20 minutes.

Cook pasta. Pour hot pasta sauce over pasta and serve. Makes 6 to 8 (1½ to 2 cup) servings. *(1 serving = 266 calories, 2.0 grams fat: 19% protein, 75% carbohydrates, 7% fat.)*

*From *Dr. Shintani's Eat More, Weigh Less® Cookbook,* p. 125.

PASTA AND MUSHROOM MARINARA SAUCE
(vegetables, grains)

1 cup fresh mushrooms or canned mushrooms, or 2 ounces dried
   mushrooms (any type)
2 cloves garlic, peeled and pressed
1 large onion, thinly sliced
2 tablespoons fresh basil
1 tablespoon fresh rosemary
5 tablespoons fresh parsley
2 teaspoons fresh oregano
3 cups plum tomatoes, canned with juices
¼ cup red wine
Salt and black pepper, freshly ground, to taste
1 16-ounce package whole wheat or vegetable pasta*

Break the herbs apart. Twist the leaves or stems into ⅛" pieces or
slightly smaller. This is the best way to release the full flavor of
herbs. Put aside.

Slice or chop fresh mushrooms, as you prefer. If using canned,
sliced mushrooms, just drain. If using dried mushrooms, soak in 1
cup of hot water for 15 to 20 minutes. Drain, reserving soaking liquid. Strain the soaking liquid through and set aside. Rinse and chop
the mushrooms.

Heat a large nonstick skillet over medium heat. Water-sauté
fresh mushrooms, if needed. Set aside. Water-sauté garlic cloves and
onion; then quickly add basil, rosemary, parsley, and oregano.
When the herbs begin to wilt, add tomatoes with juice, wine, and
mushroom soaking water (if using dried mushrooms). Bring to a
boil, turn down heat, add salt and pepper to taste, and let simmer
(about 10 minutes).

Cook whole wheat or vegetable pasta according to package
directions. Drain and serve with sauce. Makes 6 (1¾ cup) servings.
*(1 serving = 483 calories, 3.5 grams fat, 13 grams dietary fiber: 15%
protein, 80% carbohydrates, 5% fat.)*

*If you use the 12-ounce package of pasta it makes 6 (1⅓ cup) servings. *(1 serving =
420 calories, 3 grams fat, 12 grams dietary fiber: 15% protein, 79% carbohydrates,
6% fat.)*

GARLIC NODDLES*
(grains, vegetables)

1 12-ounce package whole wheat noodles, such as fettuccine
3 cloves garlic, peeled and diced
¼ teaspoon salt (if needed)

Cook noodles according to package directions. If noodles do not have salt in their ingredients, add salt to the cooking water. While noodles cook, peel garlic and dice. When noodles are ready, strain and rinse with cool water, let drain. In a large skillet, sauté garlic in a small amount of sesame oil. Add cooked noodles and toss with garlic, heat through and serve. Makes 8 (1 cup) servings. *(1 serving = 150 calories, 0.6 grams fat: 16% protein, 81% carbohydrates, 3% fat.)*

*From *Dr. Shintani's Eat More, Weigh Less® Diet*, p. 190.

CANNELLINI BEAN SAUCE OVER PASTA
(legumes, vegetables, grains, oil)

2 teaspoons extra virgin olive
½ onion, chopped
2 cloves garlic, minced
1 red bell pepper, seeds removed and chopped
1 4-ounce can green chili peppers, chopped
1 15-ounce can cannellini beans (white kidney beans), rinsed and
   drained
8 ounces whole wheat pasta
Salt and freshly cracked black pepper to taste

Heat olive oil in a heavy skillet over medium heat. Add onion and garlic; sauté 2 minutes. Add bell pepper and green chili peppers; sauté 2 minutes more. Add cannellini beans and stir until heated through.
   Cook pasta until tender.
   Puree bean mixture in a food processor or blender until smooth. Season to taste with salt and black pepper. Serve over hot cooked pasta. Makes 4 (1 cup) servings. *(1 serving = 341 calories, 4.2 grams fat, 2.0 grams dietary fiber: 18% protein, 71% carbohydrates, 11% fat.)*

CAROL'S LASAGNA
(tofu, vegetables, grains)

2 10-ounce packages whole wheat lasagna
1 26-ounce jar low fat marinara sauce
4 cups fresh spinach or two packages frozen spinach
3 10.5-ounce packages firm tofu, drained
2 medium zucchini
1 teaspoon salt
¼ teaspoon fresh ground pepper
1 to 3 tablespoons balsamic vinegar
1 teaspoon onion powder
3 teaspoons marjoram
3 teaspoons basil
5 teaspoons garlic, minced

Wash, trim, and steam fresh spinach (about 2 minutes) or defrost frozen spinach. Drain well.

Place two boxes of tofu in a food processor and pulse until the mixture is lumpy. Break up the remaining tofu and add the salt, pepper, vinegar, and onion powder.

Cook the lasagna noodles following the package directions. Cook for about 6 minutes. Do not overcook. Drain and rinse under cold water. Cover with plastic wrap to prevent drying.

Wash, dry and slice zucchini into ¼" slices. Add minced garlic to the bottled sauce.

In a 13" × 10" baking pan, place a thin layer of sauce. Place three to four noodles over the sauce. Spoon on a thick layer of the tofu mixture. Lay the sliced zucchini and the spinach over the tofu mixture. Over this sprinkle marjoram and basil. Repeat this order, ending with a layer of three or four noodles and marinara sauce.

Cover with foil and bake for 45 minutes. Remove the foil and bake for 15 minutes. Cool for 15 minutes before serving. Makes 8 to 10 (1 cup) servings. *(1 serving = 383 calories, 10 grams fat, 12 grams dietary fiber: 26% protein, 51% carbohydrates, 23% fat.)*

SOBA NOODLES (BUCKWHEAT NOODLES) STIR-FRY WITH RED PEPPER SAUCE
(grains, vegetables, oil)

½ pound soba noodles
1 teaspoon vegetable oil
1 clove garlic, minced
1 cup zucchini, thinly sliced
1 cup yellow squash, thinly sliced
3 medium portobello mushrooms, stemmed and sliced
½ cup green onions, thinly sliced
1 small tomato, diced
12 cups loosely packed spinach, rinsed and stemmed
Red Pepper Sauce
Sprigs of fresh cilantro for garnish

Cook noodles according to package directions. Noodles should reach desired tenderness in about 4 to 5 minutes. Strain noodles and rinse well under running water. Heat oil in a large skillet or wok. Stir-fry garlic for 1 minute. Stir in zucchini, yellow squash, portobello mushrooms, green onions, and tomato; stir-fry for 1 minute more. Add spinach and stir-fry until spinach is wilted and vegetables are crisp-tender. Stir in noodles and Red Pepper Sauce. Cook, tossing constantly, until sauce is almost absorbed (about 3 minutes). Transfer to a serving platter and garnish with sprigs of cilantro.

RED PEPPER SAUCE
(vegetables)

2 tablespoons tamari
¼ cup tomato juice
½ teaspoon crushed red pepper flakes or to taste

Combine all ingredients and mix well; set aside.

Noodles and sauce make 4 (2 cup) servings. *(1 serving = 267 calories, 3 grams fat, 7 grams dietary fiber: 20% protein, 72% carbohydrates, 8% fat.)*

GRAINS, VEGETABLES, AND LEGUMES

OLD FASHIONED BARLEY CASSEROLE
(grains, vegetables, oil)

1 cup barley (hulled)
4 cups vegetarian chicken broth
1 carrot, sliced
1 small leek, sliced (white part only)
1 small onion, chopped
½ teaspoon thyme, crushed
½ teaspoon vegetable seasoning
Pinch crushed red pepper
Parsley, chopped (for garnish)
Nonstick oil cooking spray

Preheat oven to 350°F. Combine all ingredients and place in a non-stick 2-quart casserole dish (or a casserole dish prepared with non-stick cooking spray). Bake covered for about 2 hours, stirring from time to time while baking.

Remove lid and garnish with parsley and serve. Makes 4 (1½ cup) servings. *(1 serving = 205 calories, 1.7 grams fat, 7.8 grams dietary fiber: 12% protein, 81% carbohydrates, 7% fat.)*

RICE AND LENTILS*
(grains, legumes, vegetables)

1 cup brown rice, regular or long-grained
½ cup lentils
1 medium onion, minced
2 teaspoons ginger root, peeled and grated
1 clove garlic, crushed
1 tablespoon low sodium soy sauce
1 teaspoon turmeric
3 cups water, boiling
1 large onion, sliced

Wash the rice and lentils together in water. If you have time, leave them to soak for an hour.

Water-sauté onions, ginger, and garlic in a large skillet over medium heat, stirring occasionally until onions are translucent. Drain the rice and lentils thoroughly. Add them to the pan and sauté gently, stirring constantly for 2 minutes. Add soy sauce and turmeric, mix lightly and cook for 3 minutes.

Next, pour in enough boiling water to cover the rice and lentils by ¾". When water bubbles vigorously, cover pot, reduce heat to very low, and simmer for 35 to 40 minutes, or until the rice and lentils are cooked and all the water has been absorbed. Serve and garnish. Makes 4 (1 cup) servings. *(1 serving = 272 calories, 1.7 grams fat: 16% protein, 78% carbohydrates, 5% fat.)*

*From *Dr. Shintani's Eat More, Weigh Less® Diet*, p. 180.

THAI RICE*
(grains, vegetables, fruit)

2 cups brown basmati rice
¼ cup sweet yellow onion, chopped medium fine
2 tablespoons lime zest (finely grated lime peel)
2 tablespoons fresh lime juice
Several sprigs fresh mint
1 stalk lemon grass (optional, available at your Asian grocery or
   health food store)
Several sprigs fresh parsley
3 tablespoons brewed jasmine tea (prepared from teabag)
¼ cup golden raisins (optional)
Lime wedges, to garnish

Cook rice, steaming if possible, until fluffy and soft. (See recipes on
pp. 246–247.)

Chop onion into medium-fine pieces. Prepare lime zest, juice,
and lime quarters. Finely chop lemon grass, mint, and parsley.
Lightly sauté onions, lemon grass, and lime zest together over high
heat, in jasmine tea. This is the same process as sautéing in water.

Remember: To water sauté you simply place several tablespoons
of water in a heated skillet in place of oil, and watch a bit more
closely so the food doesn't stick.

Add precooked rice to skillet and mix well, just until heated
through and steaming. Be careful not to cook too long. Turn off
heat and quickly fold in chopped mint, parsley and golden raisins,
mixing well. Place in serving dish and garnish with lime wedges,
mint, and parsley sprigs. Serve hot. Makes 5 (1 cup) servings. *(1
serving = 307 calories, 2.6 grams fat: 8% protein, 85% carbohydrates, 7% fat.)*

*From *Dr. Shintani's Eat More, Weigh Less® Cookbook*, pp. 57-58.

STOVETOP SPANISH RICE
(grains, vegetables)

1 15-ounce can whole tomatoes, stewed
½ cup green pepper, diced
1 cup water
¾ cup vegetable broth
¾ cup brown rice, uncooked
½ teaspoon sea salt
2 teaspoons chili powder (or to taste)

Combine tomatoes, pepper, water, vegetable broth, salt, and chili powder in medium saucepan. Boil over medium heat. Add rice. Reduce heat to low, cover, and simmer until most of the liquid has been absorbed, about 45 minutes. Fluff rice, replace cover, and let stand 5 minutes before serving. Makes 4 (1 cup) servings. *(1 serving = 174.1 calories, 1.5 grams fat: 11% protein, 82% carbohydrates, 7% fat.)*

Note: You may also garnish this dish with finely diced uncooked tomatoes and green pepper, for extra texture and fresh taste. To be really creative, add a tiny bit of chopped fresh cilantro to the top of your served mounds of rice. *Olé!*

WILD RICE PILAF
(grains, vegetables, legumes)

3 cups vegetable or vegetarian chicken broth
1 medium mild yellow onion, diced (about ¼ to ⅓ cup)
3 cloves garlic, minced
1 stalk celery, diced (about ½ cup)
1½ cups fresh mushrooms, thinly sliced
1 cup wild rice
1½ teaspoon tamari
½ teaspoon sesame seeds, toasted
Pinch sea salt

Preheat oven to 350°F. In a nonstick skillet, sauté onions, garlic, celery, and mushrooms in a little broth over medium heat, stirring often, until onions are translucent. Add water only if this mixture begins to stick to pan. Add broth and tamari to the other ingredients, mix well, then place all in a casserole or baking dish. Cover and bake 1½ hours. Remove cover and bake another 15 to 20 minutes to remove any excess liquid. Sprinkle with sesame seeds and serve. Makes 3 (1 cup) servings. *(1 serving = 265 calories, 1.3 grams fat: 20% protein, 76% carbohydrates, 4% fat.)*

QUINOA PILAF*
(vegetables, grains)

½ cup mushrooms, sliced
½ cup onion, finely chopped
2 cups vegetable broth
1 cup quinoa, toasted (see below)
½ cup celery, chopped (about ½" segments)
½ cup carrot, shredded
⅓ cup green bell pepper, finely chopped
⅓ cup red bell pepper, finely chopped
⅓ cup yellow bell pepper, finely chopped
Dash sea salt, to taste

Toasted Quinoa: Rinse thoroughly under cool running water. Place in a 10" to 12" skillet over medium heat; cook, shaking pan occasionally, until quinoa dries and turns golden brown (about 15 minutes). Pour toasted quinoa from pan and let cool. Makes 1 cup.

Water-sauté onions and mushrooms in a large (10" to 12") skillet over medium heat, until onions are caramelized and mushrooms are golden brown. (To water sauté, simply put a few tablespoons of water into a skillet, let it heat, then add onions and mushrooms. Stir often. If it begins to stick, add a bit more water.) Add broth, quinoa, and all vegetables. Bring to a boil, lower heat, cover, then simmer until liquid is absorbed, stirring often (about 15 minutes). Makes 6 (1 cup) servings. *(1 serving = 134 calories, 1.8 grams fat: 17% protein, 72% carbohydrates, 12% fat.)*

*From *Dr. Shintani's Eat More, Weigh Less® Cookbook*, p. 69.

SOUTH OF THE BORDER PILAF WITH SALSA
(grains, legumes, vegetables, fruit)

2 cups water
1 cup bulgur, uncooked
1 16-ounce can black beans, kidney or pinto beans, rinsed and
   drained
1 cup Salsa or more to taste
¼ cup fresh cilantro, chopped
2 green onions, thinly sliced

In a large saucepan bring water to boil. Stir in bulgur and return to a
boil. Reduce heat to low, cover and simmer gently until water is
absorbed (about 15 minutes). Fluff bulgur with fork, and stir in
remaining ingredients. Increase heat to medium low and cook,
uncovered, stirring occasionally, just until heated through (about 5
minutes). Serve hot.

SALSA

¾ pound plum tomatoes
1 to 2 fresh serrano chilies, stemmed
½ cup onion, finely chopped
¼ cup cilantro, chopped
2 cloves garlic, minced
1 tablespoon fresh lime juice or to taste
2 teaspoons ground cumin
¼ teaspoon salt or to taste

Diced tomatoes and place in a mixing bowl. Cut chilies in half
lengthwise and scrape out seeds. Chop chilies and add them to the
tomatoes. Stir in onion, cilantro, and garlic. Season to taste with lime
juice, cumin and salt, then let stand for a little while to let flavors
blend. Makes 2 cups or 8 (¼ cup) servings.
   Pilaf and Salsa makes 6 (1 cup) servings. *(1 serving = 211 calories, 2.0 grams fat, 9.5 grams dietary fiber: 19% protein, 74% carbohydrates, 8% fat.)*

MULTIGRAIN FRIED RICE WITH TOFU
by Claudia Neeley
(grains, vegetables, tofu, legumes, oil)

1 cup brown rice
½ cup whole grain rye
½ cup spelt, kamut or other grains
3¾ cups water
Pinch sea salt
4 cardamom pods, crushed (optional)
2 ounces firm tofu
½ cup vegetable stock
2 teaspoons ginger root, grated
2 tablespoons low sodium soy sauce
½ medium onion, diced
2 medium carrots, julienned
1 teaspoon canola oil
½ cup peas, frozen

Prepare grains by gently rinsing them until water runs clear. Place in 2-quart stockpot. Add water, sea salt, and cardamom. Bring to a boil; reduce heat and simmer, uncovered, for 10 minutes. Cover pot and continue to cook on low for 40 minutes. Do not uncover grains while cooking. Remove from heat and let stand 10 minutes before using. Discard cardamom pods; they will be on the grain surface.

Drain tofu. Place a heavy plate on tofu to press out excess water while grains are cooking. Cut into ½" cubes. Combine vegetable stock, ginger, and soy sauce. Pour half of the mixture over tofu cubes.

In a large skillet, sauté onion and carrots in oil over medium heat. Add cooked grains and toss lightly. Add tofu, peas, and remaining stock mixture; mix gently. Makes 6 (1 cup) servings. *(1 serving = 171 calories, 2.5 grams fat, 4.2 grams dietary fiber: 16% protein, 72% carbohydrates, 12% fat.)*

COLORFUL MILLET-STUFFED ARTICHOKES
(grains, vegetables, fruit, oil)

½ cup millet, quinoa or couscous, cooked
¼ cup red bell pepper, chopped
2 tablespoons Chinese parsley, chopped
2 cloves garlic, minced
2 teaspoons vegetarian Worcestershire sauce
1 lemon, cut in half
1 large bowl ice water
4 medium artichokes
2 teaspoons extra virgin olive oil
½ cup water

Preheat oven to 350°F. In a small mixing bowl combine millet, red bell pepper, Chinese parsley, garlic, Worcestershire sauce, and 1 teaspoon fresh lemon juice; mix well and set aside. Squeeze remaining juice from lemon into a large bowl of ice water, and then add rinds; set aside.

Cut off the top part of each artichoke and discard. Trim off stem and break off tough outer leaves at the base. Using a spoon, scoop out fibrous choke and small purple-tipped leaves. Place whole artichokes in lemon water until ready to use (soaking only up to 2 hours). Drain artichokes. Gently pull leaves outward from center until leaves open slightly. Divide millet filling between the four artichokes.

Place artichokes in a baking dish. Drizzle tops with olive oil. Pour ½ cup water into baking dish and cover with foil. Bake until a wooden skewer pierces artichoke heart easily, adding more water if needed (about 45 to 55 minutes). Makes 4 (1 stuffed artichoke) servings. *(1 serving = 92 calories, 2.4 grams fat, 1.2 grams dietary fiber: 15% protein, 63% carbohydrates, 22% fat.)*

STUFFED PEPPERS À LA ESPAÑOL
(grains, vegetables, oil)

Vegetable cooking spray
2 cups fresh mushrooms, sliced
1 small onion, chopped
1 clove garlic, minced
1 14.5-ounce can tomatoes with jalapeño peppers, undrained and
   diced
¾ teaspoon paprika
¼ teaspoon cayenne pepper
1 cup cooked barley
1 cup corn kernels, fresh or thawed from frozen
4 bell peppers

Preheat oven to 375°F. Lightly mist a large skillet with vegetable
cooking spray and heat to moderate heat. Sauté mushrooms, onion,
and garlic for 1 to 2 minutes. Stir in tomatoes, paprika, and cayenne
pepper. Simmer for about 5 minutes or until mushrooms are tender.
Stir in the barley and corn. Remove from heat.

Cut around stem of bell peppers and remove center ribs and
seeds. Divide filling between peppers. Replace tops. Stand peppers
in a shallow baking dish and bake until peppers are tender, depending on the size of the peppers (about 30 to 40 minutes). Serve
immediately. Makes 4 (1 stuffed pepper) servings. *(1 serving = 135
calories, 0.6 grams fat, 5.4 grams dietary fiber: 12% protein, 84%
carbohydrates, 4% fat.)*

STUFFED TOMATOES WITH BEANS 'N' RICE
(legumes, high calcium vegetables, vegetables, grains)

6 medium ripe, firm tomatoes
6 ounces dry white beans (soak for at least 8 hours)
3 cups water
Vegetable oil cooking spray
1 tablespoon fresh ginger, peeled and chopped
2 cloves garlic, minced
1 small jalapeño pepper, seeded and chopped
½ pound fresh spinach, trimmed and washed
1 cup brown rice, cooked
1 teaspoon ground cumin
1 teaspoon curry powder
Pinch sea salt

Preheat oven to 375°F. Core tomatoes and cut off the smooth end of each tomato about one-fourth of the way down. Reserve the ends for lids. Scoop out tomatoes, leaving about ¼" around the edges; chop what you scooped out.

In a stockpot combine beans and water. Bring to a boil, reduce heat, and simmer until tender (approximately 1 to 1½ hours). Drain and place the beans in a large bowl.

Lightly spray a medium skillet with vegetable spray and heat on moderate heat. Add ginger, garlic, and jalapeño pepper; sauté for about 10 seconds. Then add the spinach and toss briefly. Cover the skillet and cook the mixture for 2 minutes, until the spinach is tender.

Combine the spinach mixture and chopped tomatoes with the beans and rice. Stir in ground cumin, curry powder, and sea salt. Stuff tomatoes and top each with the reserved lid. Place the tomatoes in a baking dish and bake for 30 to 40 minutes. Serve warm. Makes 6 (1 stuffed tomato) servings. *(1 serving = 151 calories, 1.0 grams fat, 2.6 grams dietary fiber: 21% protein, 73% carbohydrates, 6% fat.)*

TOFU AND VEGETABLE STIR-FRY
(tofu, vegetables, grains)

1 carrot
1 red bell pepper
1 teaspoon peanut or canola oil
8 ounces firm tofu, cut into ½" cubes
6 tablespoons vegetable stock
2 cloves garlic, minced
2 teaspoons ginger, minced
2 cups broccoli florets, blanched
2 tablespoons tamari
2 cups brown rice, hot cooked
1 teaspoon sesame seeds, toasted

Peel carrot and cut into julienne strips. Cut bell pepper lengthwise, remove seeds, and cut into julienne strips. In a large skillet or wok, heat oil on medium-high heat. Add tofu, stirring frequently for 3 minutes. Remove from skillet and set aside.

Reheat skillet and add 3 tablespoons of vegetable stock. Sauté carrot, garlic, and ginger for 2 minutes. Add broccoli florets and bell pepper; sauté for 2 minutes more or until vegetables are tender-crisp. Add remaining stock, tamari, and tofu; toss gently to coat. Stir gently for 1 minute. Serve over hot cooked brown rice. Sprinkle with toasted sesame seeds. Makes 4 (1 cup) servings. *(1 serving = 256 calories, 7.7 grams fat, 1.6 grams dietary fiber: 23% protein, 52% carbohydrates, 25% fat.)*

ASIAN GRILLED EGGPLANT WRAPS WITH GARLIC SAUCE
(grains, vegetables, legumes, oil)

8 whole wheat, low fat tortillas or chapatis
2 tablespoons tamari
1 tablespoon rice vinegar
¼ teaspoon sesame oil
2 cloves garlic, minced
4 Japanese eggplants (about 1 pound), cut into ½" thick slices
Vegetable oil spray
1 tablespoon sesame seeds, toasted

Preheat oven to 250°F. Wrap tortillas in foil and bake for 10 minutes or until heated through. In a small bowl, whisk together tamari, rice vinegar, sesame oil, and garlic. Preheat a large skillet to medium-high. Spray eggplant slices with vegetable spray in the skillet, turning several times until golden brown and tender (about 8 to 10 minutes). Remove from heat and pour in tamari mixture; toss lightly. To serve, place mixture in warm tortillas, sprinkle with toasted sesame seeds, and wrap tightly. Makes 8 (1 wrap) servings. *(1 serving = 123 calories, 2.9 grams fat, 1.1 grams dietary fiber: 12% protein, 68% carbohydrates, 21% fat.)*

PITA BREAD SANDWICH WITH VEGETABLES
AND SIMPLE HUMMUS
(vegetables, grains, legumes)

2 whole wheat pita bread pockets
1 medium tomato, sliced and cut into bite-size pieces
½ cup bean sprouts
¼ ripe avocado, sliced
2 leaves leafy green lettuce, torn to bite-size pieces
1 fresh portabella mushroom (or mushrooms of choice), sliced or
   diced
½ cucumber, thinly sliced
½ cup black beans, cooked and drained
½ cup Simple Hummus

Slice the pita bread in half to make four pockets. Stuff the pockets evenly with all the ingredients, topping each pita half with 2 tablespoons of Simple Hummus. Makes 2 (two half pita bread pocket) servings with avocado. *(1 serving = 402 calories, 11 grams fat, 4 grams dietary fiber: 15% protein, 61% carbohydrates, 24% fat.)*

One serving of two half pita bread pockets without avocado: *(1 serving = 363 calories, 7 grams fat, 3 grams dietary fiber: 16% protein, 67% carbohydrates, 17% fat.)*

One serving of one half pita bread pocket with avocado: *(1 serving = 200 calories, 5.5 grams fat, 2 grams dietary fiber: 15% protein, 61% carbohydrates, 24% fat.)*

One serving of one half pita bread pocket without avocado: *(1 serving = 181 calories, 4 grams fat, 2 grams dietary fiber: 16% protein, 67% carbohydrates, 17% fat.)*

SIMPLE HUMMUS*
(legumes, vegetables, fruit)

1 cup garbanzo beans (chickpeas), cooked
2 to 3 tablespoons lemon juice
1 tablespoon onion, minced
1 clove garlic, crushed
1 teaspoon cumin
Low-sodium soy sauce or salt, to taste
Pepper to taste
Water

Cook the dry garbanzo beans per package directions. (Also, see Dry Bean Guide in Chapter 11 on page 197.) You may use precooked canned beans instead, if you wish. Mash beans and mix ingredients together with enough water to keep a thick moist dip consistency. Makes 8 (2 tablespoon) servings. *(1 serving = 94 calories, 1.3 grams fat: 22% protein, 67% carbohydrates, 12% fat.)*

*From *Dr. Shintani's Eat More, Weigh Less® Cookbook*, p. 327.

BROILED FALAFEL IN PITA BREAD*
(legumes, grains, vegetables, poultry)

2 cups garbanzo beans, cooked (¾ cup dry)
½ cup parsley clusters
3 cloves garlic, pressed
2 tablespoons egg replacer
½ teaspoon dry mustard
1 teaspoon cumin
½ teaspoon chili powder
Celery salt, to taste
Salt and pepper, to taste
1 teaspoon Worcestershire sauce
2 to 3 pita pockets

Puree garbanzo beans and parsley in blender. Mix blended beans with all other ingredients. Place on a lightly oil-sprayed baking pan. Spread mixture on broiler pan, broil, and toss every 10 minutes. Fill ½ pita pocket with falafel, lettuce, tomato, onion, and salsa. Makes 4 to 6 (½ stuffed pita pocket) servings. *(1 serving = 206 calories, 2.7 grams fat: 19% protein, 69% carbohydrates, 11% fat.)*

*From *Dr. Shintani's Eat More, Weigh Less® Cookbook*, p. 324.

CALICO WRAPS
(legumes, vegetables, grains, oil)

Vegetable oil cooking spray
2 green bell peppers, cut into ½" cubes (about 2 cups)
3 cloves garlic, minced
2 teaspoons dried oregano
2 teaspoons ground cumin
2 14.5-ounce cans tomatoes with green chilies, undrained and diced
2 15-ounce cans black beans, drained and rinsed
3 tablespoons red wine vinegar
Salt and freshly ground black pepper to taste
8 8-inch chapatis or whole wheat, low fat tortillas

Preheat oven to 250°F. Spray a large skillet with vegetable spray and heat over medium heat. Add bell peppers, garlic, oregano and cumin. Sauté for 2 to 3 minutes, then add tomatoes, black beans, and vinegar. Cook, stirring occasionally, until thickened (about 15 minutes). Season with salt and pepper.

Heat chapatis or tortillas by wrapping in foil and baking for 10 minutes. To serve, spoon filling on chapatis or tortillas and wrap tightly. Makes 6 to 8 (1 wrap) servings. *(1 serving = 242 calories, 2.6 grams fat, 5.3 grams dietary fiber: 19% protein, 72% carbohydrates, 9% fat.)*

HURRITO BURRITOS
(grains, legumes, vegetables)

4 large whole wheat chapatis or tortillas
½ to ¾ cup basmati brown rice, steamed until tender and set aside
¾ to 1 cup non-fat refried beans
1 clove garlic, minced
3 tablespoons onion, chopped fine
½ teaspoon ground cumin, or to taste
½ tablespoon chili powder, or to taste
4 slices non-fat cheese (optional)
½ bell pepper, diced
1 tomato, chopped
¼ cup green onion, chopped
2 tablespoons prepared salsa
2 tablespoons cilantro, chopped

Lightly warm chapatis or tortillas in oven, watching carefully so they remain soft. Reheat rice. In the meantime, combine refried beans, garlic, onion, cumin, and chili powder in a saucepan. Simmer about 5 minutes, stirring frequently.

For each burrito, place about 2 tablespoons of rice and 3 tablespoons of the bean mixture in the warm chapatis or tortillas. As an option, add one slice of non-fat cheese to the warm ingredients. Add green pepper, tomato, green onion, salsa and cilantro and roll into a burrito. Makes 4 (1 burrito) servings. *(1 serving = 227 calories, 3.5 grams fat, 5 grams dietary fiber: 14% protein, 72% carbohydrates, 14% fat.)*

If you add the optional non-fat cheese *(1 serving = 268 calories, 3 grams fat, 5 grams dietary fiber: 26% protein, 63% carbohydrates, 12% fat.)*

QUICK CHILI
(legumes, vegetables)

½ cup onion, chopped
½ cup green pepper, diced
⅛ teaspoon garlic powder
¼ teaspoon cayenne powder
1 to 2 tablespoons chili powder
¼ teaspoon cumin
2 14-ounce cans kidney (or chili or pinto) beans, with liquid from 1
   can only, or sauce will be too thin)
1 8-ounce can tomato sauce

Sauté onions and green pepper in water in a heavy saucepan over medium heat. Add garlic powder, cayenne pepper, chili powder, and cumin. Add beans and tomato sauce. Simmer for 30 minutes. Makes 4 (¾ cup) servings. *(1 serving = 175 calories, 1 grams fat, 10 grams dietary fiber: 22% protein, 72% carbohydrates, 6% fat.)*

CHICKPEA À LA KING*
(legumes, vegetables, grains, nuts)

4 tablespoons water
1 medium onion, chopped
1 4-ounce can button mushrooms or 1 cup fresh mushrooms
3 cups water
¼ cup cashew pieces
4 tablespoons sesame seeds
3 tablespoons vegetarian chicken seasoning
½ cup whole wheat flour
1½ cups green peas (frozen)
2 ounces pimentos, chopped
1 15.4-ounce can chickpea (garbanzo) beans

Preheat oven to 350°F. Sauté onions and mushrooms in 4 tablespoons of water until translucent. Blend in the blender 3 cups of water, cashew pieces, sesame seeds, vegetarian chicken seasoning, and flour until smooth. Add blended ingredients to the onions and mushrooms. Add the peas, pimentos and garbanzo beans. Cook until thickened, stirring carefully to keep from scorching. Serve over brown rice, sprouted wheat toast, or whole wheat flat noodles. Or fold the cooked noodles into the sauce and bake about 20 minutes. Makes 4 (1½ cup) servings. *(1 serving = 336 calories, 11 grams fat: 18% protein, 54% carbohydrates, 27% fat.)*

*From *Dr. Shintani's Eat More, Weigh Less® Diet,* p. 208.

BARBECUE BAKED BEANS*
(legumes, vegetables, oil, fruit)

1 cup onion, diced
3 14-16-ounce cans beans (kidney, black, navy, pinto, great
    northern, lima)
2 tablespoons blackstrap molasses
2 tablespoons apple cider vinegar
1 tablespoon dry mustard
½ teaspoon garlic powder
½ cup tomato ketchup
Canola oil cooking spray

Preheat oven to 350°F. Sauté onion in an oil-sprayed nonstick pan over medium heat. Pour off half the liquid from each bean can. Mix beans and remaining ingredients in large bowl and add onion. Mix thoroughly. Put into a 2-quart casserole dish and bake, uncovered, for 1½ hours, stirring after 1 hour. Makes 6 (1 cup) servings. *(1 serving = 279 calories, 1.6 grams fat: 18% protein, 77% carbohydrates, 5% fat.)*

*From *Dr. Shintani's Eat More, Weigh Less® Cookbook,* p. 320.

HERBED ITALIAN BEANS*
(legumes, vegetables, oil)

½ cup extra virgin olive oil
6 cloves garlic, minced
9 fresh sage leaves
1 sprig fresh thyme
1 bay leaf
2 16-ounce cans cannellini beans
3 cups canned plum tomatoes, chopped, with juice
Salt and freshly ground pepper to taste

In a large saucepan, heat oil at medium-high heat. Add garlic, sage, and thyme; cook for 1 minute. Add bay leaf, beans, tomatoes, salt, and pepper. Stir well and reduce heat to medium low. Cover and simmer, stirring occasionally until the beans are heated through (approximately 10 minutes). Makes 6 (1 cup) servings. *(1 serving = 351 calories, 19 grams fat, 5 grams dietary fiber: 13% protein, 41% carbohydrates, 46% fat.)*

*This recipe is designed for the Mediterranean menu as is. If you reduce the oil to ¼ cup, then it would be suitable for the other menus. *(1 serving = 271 calories, 11.5 grams fat, 5 grams dietary fiber: 16% protein, 53% carbohydrates, 31% fat.)*

BLACK-EYED PEAS WITH
SQUASH AND ITALIAN MUSTARD GREENS
(legumes, vegetables, high calcium vegetables, oil, fruit)

3½ cups vegetable stock
2 medium leeks, rinsed, white and light green parts sliced
2 cloves garlic, minced
¼ teaspoon red pepper, crushed
1½ cups black-eyed peas, cooked
½ teaspoon salt
¼ teaspoon black pepper, freshly ground
1 medium butternut squash, peeled, seeded and cut into ½-inch
    cubes
Italian Mustard Greens (recipe follows)

In a stockpot, heat 3 tablespoons of the vegetable stock over medium-high heat. Add leeks, garlic and crushed red pepper and cook, stirring frequently, until leeks start to brown, about 4 to 5 minutes. Add black-eyed peas, the remaining vegetable stock, salt and black pepper. Simmer for 5 minutes. Add butternut squash and cook, stirring occasionally, until squash is tender and most of the liquid has been absorbed, about 10 to 15 minutes. Serve with Mustard Greens. Makes 6 (¾ cup) servings.

ITALIAN MUSTARD GREENS

½ tablespoon extra virgin olive oil
2 cloves garlic, minced
1 pound fresh mustard greens, coarsely chopped
½ cup water
Salt and freshly ground black pepper to taste
Lemon wedges (optional)

In a large skillet, heat oil over medium heat. Add garlic and cook, stirring until fragrant (about 30 seconds). Stir in mustard greens and water. Season with salt and pepper; bring to a simmer. Cover and cook, stirring occasionally, until greens are tender (5 to 8 minutes). Serve hot, with lemon wedges. Makes 6 (1¼ cup) servings. *(1 serving including Italian Mustard Greens = 654 calories, 2.9 grams fat, 27.4 grams dietary fiber: 8% protein, 88% carbohydrates, 3% fat.)*

GARLIC BAKED POTATOES*
(staple vegetables)

4 potatoes
4 cloves garlic, sliced

Make one or more slits in each potato. Add slices of garlic cloves, and bake as indicated below.

To Bake: Preheat oven to 375°F. Scrub potatoes and puncture with a fork several times. Then place on a baking sheet and bake for approximately one hour. They're done when a fork easily penetrates through to the center.

To Microwave: Follow the cooking instructions that came with your machine. Each microwave is different, and what yields a fluffy perfect potato in one may deliver a burnt chunk of starch in another.

Makes 4 servings. *(1 serving = 145 calories, 0.2 grams fat: 8% protein, 91% carbohydrates, 1% fat.)*

*From *Dr. Shintani's Eat More, Weigh Less® Cookbook,* p. 147.

WARM KALE AND POTATOES
(staple vegetables, high calcium vegetables, vegetables, oil)

¾ pound small new potatoes
1 cup onion, coarsely chopped
2 teaspoons extra virgin olive oil
2 cloves garlic, minced
1 small jalapeño pepper, seeded and finely chopped
½ pound kale, torn into small pieces
2 tablespoons balsamic vinegar
1 tablespoon fresh oregano, chopped or 1½ teaspoons dried
    oregano
Salt and freshly ground black pepper to taste

Preheat oven to 400°F. Cut potatoes into ½" cubes, leaving skin on. In a medium bowl combine potatoes, onion, and 1 teaspoon of the olive oil; toss lightly to coat. Spread mixture on a baking sheet and roast until potatoes are tender, stirring occasionally (about 20 minutes). In a large skillet heat remaining olive oil over medium heat. Stir in garlic and jalapeño pepper and sauté for 30 seconds. Stir in kale, potatoes, and onions. Add balsamic vinegar. Cover and cook until kale is wilted (about 3 to 4 minutes). Add oregano, salt, and pepper. Toss lightly to mix. Serve warm. Makes 4 (1 cup) servings. *(1 serving = 150 calories, 2.7 grams fat, 4.6 grams dietary fiber: 9% protein, 75% carbohydrates, 15% fat.)*

STEAMED SWISS CHARD AND POTATOES*
(staple vegetables, high calcium vegetables, vegetables)

2 cups water
1 bunch Swiss chard, cut into pieces
2 cloves garlic, crushed
2 white or red potatoes, cut into chunks
2 teaspoons low sodium soy sauce, to taste
1 to 2 cups pinto beans or black turtle beans (optional)

Place water, chard, and garlic into saucepan and bring to a boil. Turn down to simmer, cover, and cook for 10 minutes. Add potatoes, then stir and cover. Cook for 25 to 30 minutes. Add soy sauce to taste. For variation, add 1 to 2 cups cooked pinto beans or black turtle beans. Makes 5 (¾ cup) servings. *(1 serving without beans = 27 calories, .07 grams fat: 18% protein, 80% carbohydrates, 2% fat.)* *(1 serving with beans = 79 calories, 0 grams fat, 5 grams dietary fiber: 20% protein, 76% carbohydrates, 0% fat.)*

*From *Dr. Shintani's Eat More, Weigh Less®® Cookbook,* p. 227.

MUSHROOM VEGETABLE STEW*
(staple vegetables, vegetables, legumes, grains)

1 medium onion, chopped
½ cup water
2 tomatoes, chopped
1 clove garlic, minced
3 carrots, cut into ½" slices
½ pound fresh mushrooms, small
1 small bell pepper, seeded and diced
3 medium red potatoes, unpeeled, cut into ½" cubes
1 bay leaf
½ teaspoon basil, dried
½ teaspoon oregano, dried
½ teaspoon fine herbs, dried (mixed Italian herbs)
Salt to taste
½ to 1 cup green peas, fresh or frozen
1 tablespoon corn starch mixed in 2 tablespoons water

Sauté onions in water until soft. Add other ingredients except salt and peas. Cover and simmer for 30 minutes until vegetables are just tender. Season to taste. Add peas and heat through. Remove bay leaf and thicken with corn starch mixture. Makes 8 (1 cup) servings. *(1 serving = 103 calories, 0.5 grams fat: 13% protein, 84% carbohydrates, 4% fat.)*

*From *Dr. Shintani's Eat More, Weigh Less® Cookbook,* p. 236.

HEARTY SWEET POTATO STEW
(staple vegetables, grains, vegetables, fruit, oil)

1 teaspoon extra virgin olive oil
1 large onion, chopped
2 cloves garlic, minced
2 cups cabbage, chopped
2 pounds cooked sweet potatoes, cut into ½" cubes or 1 18-ounce
  can sweet potatoes, drained and chopped
1 4.5-ounce can tomatoes, undrained and diced

1 cup tomato juice
½ cup apple juice
2 teaspoons ginger root, minced
¼ teaspoon red pepper flakes
Cooked brown rice, if desired

In a large frying pan heat oil on medium heat and sauté onion and garlic until golden brown and translucent (about 4 to 5 minutes). Stir in cabbage and cook, stirring occasionally, until cabbage is tender and crisp (about 4 minutes). Stir in cooked sweet potatoes, tomatoes, tomato juice, apple juice, ginger, and red pepper flakes. Reduce heat, cover, and simmer for 8 to 10 minutes. Serve with brown rice, if desired. Makes 6 (1 cup) servings. *(1 serving = 126 calories, 1.2 grams fat, 4.0 grams dietary fiber: 9% protein, 83% carbohydrates, 8% fat.)*

STEAMED SWEET POTATOES OR YAMS WITH ORANGE-DATE GLAZE*
(staple vegetables, fruit, grains, vegetables)

6 medium sweet potatoes or yams
Water to cover 1 inch deep in pan

Place whole sweet potatoes in steamer with 1" of water and steam until fork tender (approximately 15 minutes). Slice and serve. Or create glazed sweet potatoes by covering with the following sauce and baking for 5 more minutes. Makes 6 servings. *(1 sweet potato serving = 117 calories, 0.1 gram fat, 7% protein, 93% carbohydrates, 1% fat.) (1 yam serving = 127.8 calories, 0.1 gram fat, 5% protein, 94% carbohydrates, 1% fat.) (1 sweet potato serving with 1 serving orange-date glaze = 256 calories, 0.5 grams fat: 5% protein, 93% carbohydrates, 2% fat.)*

ORANGE-DATE GLAZE*

3 cups unsweetened orange juice
1 cup dates, pitted and blended to a mush
¼ teaspoon vanilla
½ teaspoon salt
½ teaspoon corn starch
¼ teaspoon cloves (optional)

Cook over a low heat, adding ingredients in the above order. Add corn starch last, stirring constantly as it begins to thicken. You want it to be the consistency of a thick syrup. Remove from heat and spoon over steamed yams or sweet potatoes. You can either serve directly, or place in a very hot oven and bake the flavors together for 5 minutes. Makes 6 (½ cup) servings. *(1 serving = 139 calories, 0.4 grams fat: 4% protein, 94% carbohydrates, 2% fat.)*

*From *Dr. Shintani's Eat More, Weigh Less® Cookbook*, pp. 157-58.

STEAMED TARO*
(staple vegetable)

2 to 4 medium taro roots
Water

Place in steamer and steam for 2 to 3 hours (depending on the size of the taro) until fork tender. Then scrape the skin off, slice, and serve. Pressure cooking for 1½ to 2 hours is another way to prepare taro. Makes 4 to 8 (¾ cup) servings. *(1 serving = 142 calories, 0.1 grams fat: 1% protein, 98% carbohydrates, 1% fat.)*

Very Important: Taro must be cooked well or the oxalate crystals will make your mouth itch. It can be eaten alone or with stews. Taro is a root vegetable that was the primary staple of ancient Hawaii and most of the rest of Polynesia. It is found on all continents including Asia, Africa, and the Americas.

*From *Dr. Shintani's Eat More, Weigh Less® Cookbook*, p. 160.

JUST VEGETABLES

OKRA GUMBO
(vegetables, oil)

1 teaspoon extra virgin olive oil
4½ cups okra, sliced lengthwise
¾ teaspoon white pepper
½ teaspoon black pepper
Pinch red pepper
1 cup onions, finely chopped
5 cups vegetable stock
1 teaspoon Old Bay® seasoning
1 cup fresh tomatoes, chopped
1 teaspoon salt
3 teaspoons garlic, minced
3/8 teaspoon onion powder
¼ teaspoon thyme
14 ounces Lightlife Soy Sausage®
Pam® cooking spray
½ cup green onions, chopped
Cilantro or Chinese parsley to garnish

Cut sausage into 8 slices. Quarter these slices and roll into individual balls (1″ in diameter). Spray skillet with Pam® and fry sausage balls until golden brown.

In a large Dutch oven, heat the olive oil and add 2 cups of okra. Cook for 3 to 4 minutes adding white, red, and black peppers. Stir and cook continuously for 10 minutes until okra is slightly brown. Stir in onions and cook for 5 minutes. Add 1 cup of vegetable stock and Old Bay® seasoning and stir well. Stir in tomatoes and cook for 5 minutes. Add another cup of stock and cook for 5 more minutes. Sprinkle in salt, garlic, onion powder, and thyme. Add remaining stock and stir well. Bring to full boil. Add soy sausage and simmer for 1 hour. Add the remaining okra and simmer for 10 minutes. Serve over brown rice and garnish with green onions and cilantro. Makes 6 (2 cup) servings. *(1 serving = 165 calories, 1 grams fat, 3.5 grams dietary fiber: 32% protein, 63% carbohydrates, 5% fat.)*

COLORFUL RATATOUILLE
(vegetables)

3 Japanese eggplants (about 1 pound)
¼ cup vegetable stock
1 red onion, thinly sliced
2 large tomatoes, cubed
1 yellow bell pepper, seeded and ribs removed
½ pound mushrooms, thickly sliced
2 cloves garlic, minced
½ teaspoon dried oregano
½ teaspoon dried thyme
¼ teaspoon black pepper, freshly ground
2 tablespoons fresh basil or parsley, chopped

Preheat oven to 400°F. Trim ends off eggplants and cut in quarters lengthwise, then in half. Place eggplant on a sheet of aluminum foil in a baking pan and roast for 15 minutes or until tender.

Meanwhile, heat vegetable stock in a large saucepan or skillet and sauté onion until soft (about 5 minutes). Stir in tomatoes, bell pepper, mushrooms, garlic, oregano, thyme, and black pepper; mix well. Simmer, covered, until soft (about 30 minutes), stirring occasionally to prevent sticking. Add baked eggplant and transfer to a serving platter and sprinkle with chopped basil. Serve hot or warm. Makes 6 (1 cup) servings. *(1 serving = 57 calories, 0.6 grams fat, 2.2 grams dietary fiber: 14% protein, 77% carbohydrates, 8% fat.)*

MIXED VEGETABLE CURRY*
(vegetables, grains)

2 carrots
1 stalk celery
2 potatoes
1 cup broccoli
1 cup cauliflower
1 onion, chopped into small pieces
3 cloves garlic, crushed
1 teaspoon soy sauce
1 tablespoon curry powder
1 teaspoon turmeric
½ teaspoon coriander
1 teaspoon ground cumin
¼ teaspoon dry mustard
¼ teaspoon chili powder
1 to 2 tablespoons whole wheat flour
1 green pepper, chopped into small pieces
½ cup fresh mushrooms, sliced
Soy sauce or salt to taste

Slice carrots; cut celery, broccoli, and cauliflower into medium-size pieces, and cut potatoes into chunks.

Place onion with crushed garlic in a saucepan over medium heat and sauté with water and a little soy sauce until translucent. Add spices and flour. Sauté for a few minutes, adding more water and stirring to form a sauce. Add carrots, celery, and potatoes. Cover and cook for 25 minutes. Add green pepper, mushrooms, and rest of ingredients and cook another 15 minutes. Add soy sauce or salt to taste. Serve over brown rice or as a filling for baked potatoes, or with whole wheat chapati (Indian flat bread). Makes 8 (1 cup) servings. *(1 serving = 68 calories, 0.5 grams fat: 15% protein, 80% carbohydrates, 5% fat.)*

*From *Dr. Shintani's Eat More, Weigh Less® Diet,* p. 206.

SPICY EGGPLANT (BAIGAN BHARTA)
(vegetables)

1 pound eggplant
¼ cup vegetable stock
1 large onion, finely chopped
1 teaspoon ground coriander
½ teaspoon ground turmeric
½ teaspoon chili powder
1 14.5-ounce can tomatoes, peeled and undrained
1 tablespoon cilantro, chopped
1 to 2 green chilies, seeded and chopped
½ teaspoon salt

Preheat broiler. Place eggplant on a piece of aluminum foil about 3 inches from the heat and cook, turning frequently until skin turns black and the flesh is soft (about 15 minutes). Cool slightly, then peel off and discard the skin; mash the flesh.

Heat the vegetable stock in a large skillet over medium heat and sauté onion until soft (about 4 to 5 minutes). Stir in coriander, turmeric, and chili powder. Add tomatoes, cilantro, chilies, and salt. Cook for 2 to 3 minutes. Add mashed eggplant and cook for 10 to 12 minutes more. Serve with chapatis. Makes 6 (¾ cup) servings. *(1 serving = 42 calories, 0.4 grams fat, 1.0 grams dietary fiber: 13% protein, 81% carbohydrates, 7% fat.)*

VEGETABLE KABOBS WITH MARINADES
(vegetables)

15 skewers
1 broccoli head, broken into flowerettes
20 cherry tomatoes
20 mushrooms, small, whole
1 cauliflower, broken into florets
10 green beans, cut in 1½" lengths
1 red bell pepper, stem and seeds, cut into large pieces
1 yellow bell pepper, stem and seeds, cut into large pieces
1 green bell pepper, stem and seeds, cut into large pieces

2 zucchini, cut in ½"-thick slices
20 whole small boiling onions
3 carrots, blanched and cut into 1" pieces
10 small new red potatoes, blanched 10 minutes and cut in half
1 sweet potato, cut into ½"-thick slices
Vegetable oil cooking spray

Soak skewers in water for one hour. Prepare charcoal grill or gas grill for at least 10 to 15 minutes to burn off starter fluid. Use clean grill so vegetables don't absorb burnt odors.

Prepare vegetables as indicated above. Whisk the marinade(s) of choice ingredients in a large glass bowl. You can add vegetables, toss to coat, and let stand for 5 to 10 minutes or add sauce while kabobs are cooking. Thread vegetables on skewers. Spray kabobs lightly with vegetable oil cooking spray so they won't stick on the grill and grill until tender (3 to 5 minutes). Turn skewers often, brushing with marinade. Make separate skewers of carrot, sweet potato, and new potatoes and grill them for 10 to 12 minutes. Makes 5 (3 kabob) servings. *(1 serving = 260 calories, 3 grams fat, 12 grams dietary fiber: 19% protein, 71% carbohydrates, 10% fat.)*

DIJON MARINADE
(vegetables, fruit)

2 tablespoons Dijon mustard (for variation, use other mustards)
3 tablespoons low sodium soy sauce or tamari
3 tablespoons lemon juice
2 cloves garlic, crushed

Mix ingredients together and use as marinade. Makes 4 (¼ cup) servings. *(1 serving = 15 calories, 0.1 gram fat: 33% protein, 64% carbohydrates, 3% fat.)*

TERIYAKI MARINADE
(vegetables, fruit)

⅓ cup low sodium soy sauce or tamari
2 tablespoons blackstrap molasses or honey
1 tablespoon ginger root, grated
1 clove garlic, crushed
2 teaspoons arrowroot or corn starch, mixed in 2 teaspoons water
   to dissolve
1 tablespoon sake or white wine (optional)
1 tablespoon lemon juice (optional)
2 tablespoons water

Combine dissolved arrowroot or corn starch with other ingredients in a saucepan. Bring to a boil and let cool. Makes 4 (¼ cup) servings. *(1 serving = 47 calories, 0 gram fat: 20% protein, 80% carbohydrates, 0% fat.)*

KOREAN BARBECUE SAUCE
(vegetables, fruit, oil)

⅓ cup low sodium soy sauce or tamari
2 tablespoons blackstrap molasses or honey
3 cloves garlic, crushed
2 teaspoons arrowroot or corn starch, mixed in 2 teaspoons water
   to dissolve
½ teaspoon sesame oil
1 tablespoon sake or white wine (optional)
1 tablespoon lemon juice (optional)
2 tablespoons water

Combine dissolved arrowroot or corn starch with other ingredients in a saucepan. Bring to a boil and let cool. Makes 4 (¼ cup) servings. *(1 serving = 51 calories, 0.6 gram fat: 17% protein, 72% carbohydrates, 11% fat.)*

WHITE WINE MARINADE
(vegetables, fruit)

1 cup white wine
¼ cup lemon juice
4 bay leaves
1½ teaspoons thyme
Pepper, to taste

Mix ingredients together and it's ready. Makes 5 (¼ cup) servings. *(1 serving = 37 calories, 0 gram fat, 0 dietary fiber: 3% protein, 95% carbohydrates, 2% fat.)*

BARBECUE MARINADE
(vegetables, fruit)

¾ cup ketchup
¼ cup lemon juice
3 tablespoons molasses or honey
¼ cup steak sauce (such as A.1® Steak Sauce)
½ teaspoon sea salt
Pepper, to taste

Mix ingredients together in a saucepan. Boil, cover, and simmer for 4 to 5 minutes. Use as marinade. Makes 5 (¼ cup) servings. *(1 serving = 100 calories, 0 gram fat, 0 dietary fiber: 5% protein, 94% carbohydrates, 1% fat.)*

(The marinades are from *Dr. Shintani's Eat More, Weigh Less® Diet* book.)

WAKAME WITH CARROTS (OR OTHER VEGETABLES)*
(vegetables, sea vegetables)

1 ounce dried wakame
2 cups carrots, cut in large chunks (or other vegetables such as
    cauliflower, turnips, daikon, celery burdock, or lotus root)
Water to cover vegetables
3 teaspoons low sodium soy sauce
Cilantro, scallions, chives or parsley for garnish, optional

Rinse and soak wakame. Slice into large pieces. Put the carrots (or other vegetables) into a pot and add water to half cover the carrots. Bring to a boil, cover, and reduce the heat to low. Simmer until the carrots are nearly done (about 20 to 30 minutes). Adjust cooking time for other vegetables. Then add the wakame and low sodium soy sauce to taste and simmer until carrots are done. Garnish. Makes 4 (½ cup) servings. *(1 serving = 40.8 calories, 0.2 grams fat: 11% protein, 85% carbohydrates, 4% fat.)*

*From *Dr. Shintani's Eat More, Weigh Less® Cookbook,* p. 290.

STEAMED KABOCHA SQUASH*
(vegetables)

Water to cover 1½" bottom of pan
1 kabocha squash or acorn squash

Scrub squash clean, cut in half, remove the seeds, then slice into quarters. Place in pot (in a steamer basket, if desired) into which 1½" of water has been added. Cover and slowly cook until it tests tender with a toothpick (about 20 to 30 minutes). Remove to a serving dish. Makes 2 (¾ cup) servings of acorn squash or 4+ (½ cup) servings kabocha squash depending on size. *(1 serving = 86 calories, 0.2 grams fat: 7% protein, 91% carbohydrates, 2% fat.)*

*From *Dr. Shintani's Eat More, Weigh Less® Diet,* p. 147.

SUMMER SQUASH AND ONIONS*
(vegetables)

1 medium summer squash
1 medium onion, sliced into crescents
2 tablespoons water

Scrub squash and cut into ½" rounds. Sauté the onions in 2 table-spoons of water until translucent and add the squash. Stir occasion-ally. Cover and cook over low heat until tender. Makes 2 (½ cup) servings. *(1 serving = 34 calories, 0 grams fat: 15% protein, 85% carbohydrates, 0% fat.)*

*From *Dr. Shintani's Eat More, Weigh Less® Diet*, p. 215.

SQUASH DELUXE
(vegetables, grains)

1 average butternut, acorn, or kabocha squash
1 tablespoon miso (optional)
1 teaspoon maple syrup or other sweetener
¼ cup water

Scrub squash until clean and cut into quarters.

Pressure Cooker: Place in 1" of water and cook by bringing it to pressure at high heat; then cook at low heat (about 2 to 3 minutes). Uncover and test to see if squash is tender. Cook a little longer if it is not.

Stovetop Cooking: Boil or steam the squash in a covered pot with about 1½" of water. To steam, insert steamer basket into pot, add water and squash, and cook until tender (about 15 minutes).

After cooking, cut squash into 1" to 2" chunks. Mix in a separate bowl the miso and maple syrup in ¼ cup of water. Return cut-up squash to the pot and the miso, maple syrup, and water mixture. Bring to boil and simmer with pot uncovered for 5 to 10 minutes. Serve on a platter garnished with parsley sprigs. Makes 2 to 4+ (½ cup) servings depending on squash's size. *(1 serving = 72 calories, 21 grams fat: 8% protein, 89% carbohydrates, 3% fat.)*

STEAMED GREENS AND SUMMER SQUASH*
(high calcium vegetables, vegetables)

Water
Pinch sea salt
2 large bunches kale greens, washed and chopped
2 to 3 medium summer squash, sliced or quartered

Pour about 1½ inches of water into a pan. Add a pinch of sea salt, the greens, and then the squash. Cover the pan and bring to a boil. Reduce heat to medium and cook for 5 to 8 minutes or until greens are bright green and tender. Remove from pan and serve. Makes 8 (½ cup) servings. *(1 serving = 28 calories, 35 grams fat: 21% protein, 69% carbohydrates, 9% fat.)*

*From *Dr. Shintani's Eat More, Weigh Less® Diet,* p. 216.

STEAMED LEAFY GREENS*
(high calcium vegetables)

4 cups greens of your choice (collards, kale, or a combination of
   the two; mustard greens; turnip greens)
1½ cup water (approximately)

Wash the greens thoroughly, and chop into bite-size pieces. Pour the water into a pan, add the greens, cover, and bring to a boil. Reduce heat and cook over low heat until just tender but still bright green. Remove to serving dish right away to retain bright green color. Use a dressing or condiment of your choice to season such as lemon and soy sauce, Dijon mustard, tofu dressing, or sesame salt. Makes 4 (1 cup) servings. *(1 serving Kale and Collard Greens = 22 calories, 0.3 grams fat: 21% protein, 70% carbohydrates, 9% fat.) (1 serving Collard Greens = 11 calories, 0.1 grams fat: 17% protein, 77% carbohydrates, 5% fat.) (1 serving Kale = 34 calories, 0.5 grams fat: 22% protein, 67% carbohydrates, 11% fat.) (1 serving Turnip Greens = 15 calories, 0.2 grams fat: 29% protein, 72% carbohydrates, 9% fat.)*

*From *Dr. Shintani's Eat More, Weigh Less® Diet,* pp. 212, 1137.

SAUTEÉD WATERCRESS
(high calcium vegetables, vegetables, oil)

2 large cloves garlic, minced
½ tablespoon extra virgin olive oil
1 pound watercress, rinse and discard coarse stems
Salt and pepper to taste

In a large skillet sauté garlic in oil over medium-high heat for 30 seconds. Add watercress and stir fry mixture to coat. Sauté, covered, for 2 to 3 minutes or until just wilted. Season to taste with salt and pepper. Makes 3 to 4 (½ cup) servings. *(1 serving = 16 calories, 0.1 grams fat, 2.7 grams dietary fiber: 53% protein, 42% carbohydrates, 6% fat.)*

STEAMED COLLARD GREENS WITH CARROTS*
(high calcium vegetables, vegetables)

3 cups collard greens
1 large carrot, thinly sliced on the diagonal
½ to 1 cup water
Pinch sea salt

Wash the greens. Drain, stack leaves, and slice down the center lengthwise. Then stack halves on top of each other and cut on the diagonal into bite-size pieces. Pour water into a pan, add sea salt, add the greens, then the carrots on top of the greens, cover and bring to a boil. Reduce the heat and simmer just until tender and greens are bright green (approximately 5 minutes). Don't stir. Remove to a serving bowl. Makes 4 (1 cup) servings. *(1 serving = 16 calories, 0.1 grams fat: 13% protein, 82% carbohydrates, 5% fat.)*

*From *Dr. Shintani's Eat More, Weigh Less® Diet*, p. 144.

PARBOILED GREENS*
(high calcium vegetables)

1 large bunch kale
1 large bunch collard greens
1 large bunch turnip greens
2 cups water

Wash greens thoroughly and slice on the diagonal into bite-size pieces. In a saucepan, place in 2 cups water, add greens, and cover. Bring to a boil. Reduce heat and simmer for 10 to 15 minutes or until greens are just tender but still bright green. Drain and remove to a serving dish to retain bright green color. Makes 6 (1 cup) servings. *(1 serving = 20 calories, 0.2 grams fat: 20% protein, 70% carbohydrates, 9% fat.)*

*From *Dr. Shintani's Eat More, Weigh Less® Diet*, p. 213.

CHICKEN AND FISH

MANGO AND CHICKEN STIR-FRY
(vegetables, poultry, fruit, legumes, grains)

1 pound boneless, skinless chicken breasts
1 large ripe mango, peeled and seeded
¼ pound thin asparagus
2 tablespoons fresh orange juice
2 tablespoons soy sauce
1 teaspoon brown rice syrup or honey
½ teaspoon corn starch
Cooking oil spray
2 cloves garlic, minced
1 tablespoon fresh ginger, minced
2 green onions, thinly sliced
¼ cup fresh mint or cilantro leaves
Hot, cooked brown rice, if desired

Cut chicken into ¼" strips. Cut mango into ½" cubes. Cut asparagus on the diagonal into 1" pieces.

In a small bowl, combine orange juice, soy sauce, brown rice syrup, and corn starch.

Just before serving, heat a nonstick wok or skillet over medium-high heat and spray with oil. Add the garlic, ginger, and green onions and stir-fry until fragrant (about 15 seconds). Add chicken and asparagus and stir-fry for 2 minutes. Stir in sauce and continue stir-frying until the chicken is cooked and nicely coated with sauce (about 1 to 2 minutes). Stir in the mango and mint leaves and cook for 10 seconds. Serve immediately over hot, brown rice, if desired. Makes 4 (1 cup) servings. *(1 serving = 182 calories, 5.1 grams fat: 1.8 grams dietary fiber: 44% protein, 31% carbohydrates, 25% fat.)*

GARLIC CHICKEN STIR-FRY
(vegetables, grains, poultry, legumes, oil, honey)

¾ pound boneless, skinless, chicken breast
1 tablespoon peanut oil
6 cloves garlic, minced
1 tablespoon fresh ginger, minced
4 green onions, thinly sliced
½ Maui or other sweet onion, thinly sliced
2 cups cabbage, cubed
1 red bell pepper, seeded and sliced
1 cup Chinese peas
½ cup vegetable broth
1 tablespoon soy sauce
½ teaspoon brown rice syrup or honey
½ teaspoon corn starch
½ teaspoon salt
Hot, cooked brown rice, if desired

Cut chicken into strips ¼" wide. Heat a nonstick wok or skillet over medium-high heat and heat oil. Add half of the minced garlic and all of the ginger and green onions. Stir-fry until fragrant (about 15 seconds). Add sweet onion and stir-fry until translucent (about 1½ minutes). Add chicken and cook until opaque (about 2 minutes). Add remaining minced garlic and stir. Add cabbage, bell pepper, Chinese peas, and ¼ cup of the broth. Cover and cook for 1 minute.

In a small bowl, blend the remaining ¼ cup broth, soy sauce, brown rice syrup, corn starch, and salt. Add sauce mixture to wok or skillet and stir until chicken and vegetables are coated with the thickened sauce. Serve immediately over hot, brown rice, if desired. Makes 4 (1 cup) servings. *(1 serving = 173 calories, 7.2 grams fat: 2.4 grams dietary fiber: 37% protein, 26% carbohydrates, 37% fat.)*

CHICKEN GUMBO
(poultry, vegetables, oil)

2 pounds fryer chicken, cut up
1 teaspoon salt

1 teaspoon garlic powder
1 teaspoon cayenne pepper
Pam® cooking spray
8 ounces Lightlife Soy Sausage®
1 teaspoon extra virgin olive oil
1 cup onions, chopped
1 cup bell pepper, chopped
½ cup celery, sliced ¼" thick
6 to 7 cups vegetarian chicken stock
¾ teaspoon white pepper
½ teaspoon black pepper
1 cup fresh tomatoes, chopped
1 teaspoon salt
3 cloves garlic, minced
½ teaspoon onion powder
¼ teaspoon thyme
½ cup green onions, chopped
Cilantro or Chinese parsley

Wash and trim chicken for excess fat. Mix salt, garlic powder, and cayenne pepper together, and rub on chicken pieces or put all in large Ziploc® or paper bag, close, and shake until coated. Place in baking pan and spray with Pam®. Bake for 1 hour or until golden brown.

Cut sausage into 8 slices. Quarter these slices and roll into individual balls (1" in diameter). Spray skillet with Pam® and fry sausage balls till golden brown.

In a large Dutch oven, heat olive oil and add onions, bell pepper, and celery. Cook for 3 to 4 minutes adding white and black peppers. Add 1 cup stock and stir well. Stir in tomatoes and cook for 5 minutes. Add another cup of stock and cook for 5 more minutes. Sprinkle in salt, garlic, onion powder, and thyme. Add remaining stock and stir well. Bring to full boil. Add chicken and soy sausage and simmer for 1 hour. Serve over brown rice and garnish with green onions and cilantro. Makes 8 (1½ cup) servings. *(1 serving = 265 calories, 4 grams fat, 4 grams dietary fiber: 50% protein, 37% carbohydrates, 13% fat.)*

SPANISH CHICKEN CASSEROLE
(vegetables, poultry, dairy, oil)

1 medium onion, chopped
2 to 3 cloves garlic, minced
1 teaspoon olive oil
½ pound fresh mushrooms, sliced
1 medium bell pepper, chopped
1 8-ounce can tomato sauce
1 6-ounce can tomato paste
½ cup white wine
½ cup pitted black olives
1 6-ounce jar water-marinated artichoke hearts, drained
1 teaspoon dried basil
1 teaspoon dried oregano
1 teaspoon salt
1 teaspoon pepper
¼ cup Parmesan cheese, freshly grated
2 to 3 pounds skinless, boneless chicken breast

Preheat oven to 350°F. In medium saucepan, sauté onion and garlic in olive oil. Add mushrooms, bell pepper, tomato sauce, tomato paste, wine, olives, and spices. Place chicken breast on the bottom of a 2-quart casserole dish. Cover with sauce. Bake uncovered for 50 minutes. Place artichoke hearts and cheese evenly over casserole for last 10 minutes of cooking time. Makes 10 (⅔ cup) servings. *(1 serving = 317 calories, 9 grams fat, 2.5 grams dietary fiber: 59% protein, 15% carbohydrates, 26% fat.)*

HERBED MEDITERRANEAN CHICKEN
(poultry, vegetables, oil)

1½ tablespoons extra virgin olive oil
1½ pounds skinless chicken breasts, cut into chunks
1 medium onion, sliced
2 cloves garlic, crushed
1 cup mushrooms, sliced
1 16-ounce can tomatoes, diced, with liquid
1 teaspoon dried basil
1 teaspoon dried oregano
½ cup ripe olives, pitted and sliced
⅓ cup red wine
1 teaspoon salt
1 teaspoon pepper
1 16-ounce package whole wheat medium noodles, rainbow
   radiatore, or egg bows

In a large skillet, heat oil and brown chicken. Add onion, garlic, and mushrooms; cook until vegetables are tender. Add tomatoes and liquid, basil, oregano, olives, wine, salt, and pepper. Simmer, covered, until chicken is tender, about ½ hour. To serve, arrange chicken and sauce over cooked noodles. Makes 8 (1¾ cups) servings. *(1 serving = 398 calories, 8 grams fat, 5.5 grams dietary fiber: 34% protein, 48% carbohydrates, 18% fat.)*

SHRIMP STIR-FRY
(vegetables, seafood, legumes, honey, oil, grains)

1 pound shrimp, peeled and deveined
1 teaspoon peanut oil
6 cloves garlic, minced
1 tablespoon fresh ginger, minced
4 green onions, thinly sliced
½ Maui or other sweet onion, thinly sliced
2 cups cabbage, cubed
1 red bell pepper, seeded and sliced
1 cup Chinese peas
½ cup vegetable broth
1 tablespoon soy sauce or tamari
½ tablespoon brown rice syrup or honey
½ teaspoon corn starch or arrowroot
½ teaspoon salt

In a nonstick wok or skillet, heat peanut oil. On high heat, add half the minced garlic, ginger, and green onions. Stir-fry mixture for 15 seconds. Add onions and cook for 1½ minutes. Add shrimp and cook until opaque (2 minutes). Stir in remaining garlic, cabbage, bell pepper, and Chinese peas with ¼ cup of the vegetable broth. Cover and cook for 1 minute. Combine the remaining ¼ cup broth, soy sauce, brown rice syrup, and corn starch in a small bowl. Add this to the shrimp and vegetables. Stir-fry until the mixture is coated with sauce. Serve immediately. Makes 4 (1 cup) servings. *(1 serving = 164 calories, 1.5 grams fat, 3 grams dietary fiber: 59% protein, 33% carbohydrates, 8% fat.)*

BEANS AND RED ONIONS WITH FISH
(legumes, seafood, vegetables, fruit, oil)

1 cup dried small white beans or great northern (soak for at least 8
  hours)
6 cups cold water
2 cloves garlic, crushed
Strips of lemon zest
¾ pound ahi (tuna) or other firm, white fish
1 medium red onion, thinly sliced
¼ cup red wine vinegar
1 teaspoon brown rice syrup
Juice of 1 lemon
1 teaspoon extra virgin olive oil
1 teaspoon fresh thyme, chopped, or ¼ teaspoon dried thyme
¼ teaspoon dried rosemary
Freshly ground black pepper to taste
Pickled onions (optional)

Rinse beans well. In a heavy saucepan combine beans, water, garlic, and lemon zest. Bring to a boil over high heat. Reduce heat, partially cover, and simmer for about 45 to 55 minutes or until tender. Drain beans and transfer to a mixing bowl. Discard garlic and lemon zest.

In a heavy saucepan combine onions, wine vinegar, brown rice syrup and lemon juice. Cook over medium heat for 8 to 10 minutes, stirring often, until onions are tender. Transfer to a bowl to cool.

Preheat broiler. Cut fish into 1" cubes. Place fish in a baking dish and coat with olive oil, thyme, rosemary, and black pepper. Broil for 2 minutes. Turn fish and broil 1 to 2 minutes more, until opaque. Do not overcook. Transfer beans to a serving dish. Arrange fish and pickled onions on top. Serve warm or cold. Makes 4 (1 cup) servings. *(1 serving = 261 calories, 5.0 grams fat, 0.7 grams dietary fiber: 39% protein, 44% carbohydrates, 17% fat.)*

Fish is just an additional, nonintegral part of recipe.

MEDITERRANEAN FISH
(seafood, vegetables)

1 pound fish fillets, fresh or frozen
2 tablespoons lemon juice
1 tablespoon garlic, minced
½ lemon, sliced and slices cut in half
¼ cup chopped onion
1 green bell pepper, chopped
2 fresh tomatoes, chopped
Salt and pepper to taste

Put fish in round glass casserole. Sprinkle with lemon juice. Add garlic. Arrange lemon slices on the fish and add onion, green bell pepper, and tomatoes covering the fish. Cover with plastic wrap, but leave a vent opening. Microwave on high 5 to 7 minutes turning dish during cooking. Spoon sauce over fish and microwave on medium 4 minutes more. Let stand 2 minutes before serving. Makes 3 (¾ cup) servings. *(1 serving = 202 calories, 6 grams fat, 1.5 grams dietary fiber: 58% protein, 16% carbohydrates, 26% fat.)*

FISH KABOBS WITH MEDITERRANEAN SALSA
(seafood, vegetables, fruit, oil)

10 bamboo skewers
1½ pounds firm-fleshed fish, such as halibut, sea bass, or shark
1 tablespoon plus 2 teaspoons extra virgin olive oil
Juice of 1 lemon
2 tablespoons fresh parsley, washed, dried, minced
1 tablespoon fresh thyme, washed, patted
1 teaspoon salt
Ground black pepper, to taste
2 to 3 large garlic cloves, minced
1 green bell pepper, washed, cored, seeded and cut into 1½"
   squares
1 large white onion, peeled and cut into 1½" squares
16 cherry tomatoes
Olive oil spray

Soak skewers in water for 1 hour. Rinse the fish in water, pat dry, and cut into 1½" cubes. In a medium bowl, combine olive oil, lemon juice, parsley, thyme, garlic, salt, and black pepper. Toss fish in mixture; cover and marinate for 30 minutes in refrigerator.

   Preheat grill. Remove fish from marinade; reserve marinade. Thread fish onto skewers alternately with tomatoes, bell peppers, and onion. Spray barbecue grids with olive oil spray. Place skewers on rack and grill, turning frequently (about 8 to 11 minutes). Spread Mediterranean Salsa on serving platter. Arrange kabobs on top. Serve immediately. Makes 5 (2 kabob) servings. *(1 serving = 231 calories, 8 grams fat, 2 grams dietary fiber: 52% protein, 17% carbohydrates, 31% fat.)*

MEDITERRANEAN SALSA
(vegetables, oil)

1 large red bell pepper, roasted
12 large basil leaves
2 to 3 large garlic clove, minced
1 jalapeno chili or other hot chili, washed, veins and seeds
    removed, finely minced
4 sun dried tomatoes, chopped
½ small red onion, peeled, ends removed, chopped
1 tablespoon extra virgin olive oil
1 tablespoon balsamic vinegar
1 tablespoon red wine vinegar
Salt to taste
Fresh ground black pepper to taste
2 large tomatoes, washed, seeded, diced
3 large black olives, pitted, chopped
3 large green olives, pitted, chopped

To roast bell pepper: Place oven rack 5" to 6" from broiler element. Preheat broiler. Line broiler pan or baking sheet with foil. Place red pepper on top. Roast on all sides until entire pepper is charred (about 15 to 20 minutes). Remove from oven and wrap the charred pepper in the aluminum foil used to line pan. Allow to rest 5 minutes. Remove foil and remove core and seeds and dice.

Fit a food processor with metal blade and process basil and garlic until finely chopped. Add jalapeno or other chili, sun dried tomatoes, and red onion; process 10 seconds. Add olive oil, vinegars, salt, and pepper; process 5 seconds. Carefully remove blade and stir in bell pepper, tomatoes, and olives. Makes 2 cups or 8 (¼ cup) servings. *(1 serving = 26 calories, 5 grams fat, 1 grams dietary fiber: 14% protein, 68% carbohydrates, 18% fat.)*

DESSERTS

SPICE APPLE CRISP
(fruit, grains)

Filling:

3 tablespoons whole wheat flour
1 teaspoon apple pie spice
Dash salt
3 apples, skinned and thinly sliced
1 to 2 pinch stevia powder

Preheat oven 350°F. Mix flour, apple pie spice, and salt together. Pour this mixture over apples. Sprinkle stevia over apples and taste for sweetness. If not sweet enough, add another pinch of stevia. (Caution: A little goes a long way). Place in 8″ pie tin and add topping.

Topping:

2 cups rolled oats
1 cup whole wheat flour
1 teaspoon apple pie spice
¾ cup apple juice concentrate

Mix rolled oats, whole wheat flour, apple pie spice, and apple juice concentrate. Stir with a fork and sprinkle on the top of apple mixture. Bake for 60 minutes. Serve warm or cool. Makes 8 (¾ cup) servings. *(1 serving = 209 calories, 1.9 grams fat: 4.1 grams dietary fiber: 11% protein, 82% carbohydrates, 8% fat.)*

RICE AND SWEET POTATO PUDDING
(grains, staple vegetables, legumes, fruit)

1 cup cooked sweet potato
1⅔ cups low fat soy milk
½ teaspoon stevia powder
2 cups brown rice (cooked)
1 teaspoon vanilla extract
1 teaspoon cinnamon
½ teaspoon nutmeg
¼ teaspoon salt
Mint (garnish)
4 orange slices (garnish)

Wash and cut up sweet potato into large chunks and place in steamer for 30 to 40 minutes. Blend cooked sweet potato, low fat soy milk, and stevia in a blender or food processor. In a saucepan, combine cooked brown rice and blended sweet potato mixture. Cook over medium heat for 15 minutes. Stir in spices, salt, and vanilla and cook for 2 minutes longer. Serve warm. Garnish with orange slices and sprigs of mint. Makes 4 (1 cup) servings. *(1 serving = 243 calories, 2.2 grams fat: 7% protein, 84% carbohydrates, 8% fat.)*

"PINE" APPLE DESSERT
(fruit, grains)

Bottom Layer:
6 medium apples (peeled and sliced)
½ cup crushed pineapple
¼ cup applesauce
1 pinch stevia powder

Topping:
¾ cup crushed pineapple or pineapple tidbits
¼ cup applesauce
1 teaspoon apple pie spice

1 cup whole wheat flour
¾ cup rolled oats
1 cup low fat, non-dairy whipped topping (garnish, optional)

Preheat oven at 350°F. Mix apples, crushed pineapple, and apple-sauce. Sprinkle stevia over mixture and taste for sweetness. If mixture is not sweet enough, add another pinch. (Caution: A little goes a long way.)

Mix the crushed pineapple, applesauce, apple pie spice, whole wheat flour, and rolled oats. Spread over the top of apple mixture. Bake for 60 minutes. Serve warm with non-dairy whipped topping. Makes 8 (1 cup) servings. *(1 serving = 157 calories, 1.1 grams fat, 4.7 grams dietary fiber: 9% protein, 86% carbohydrates, 6% fat.)*

ONO MANGO CRISP
(fruit, grains, fructose, vegetables, oil)

2 large ripe mangoes, sliced into ¼" slices; or peaches
¼ cup apple juice
1 to 2 teaspoons apple pie spice
2½ tablespoons fructose
1 teaspoon vanilla
1 tablespoon arrowroot
⅓ cup whole wheat pastry flour
⅓ cups old-fashioned oats
Butter-flavored cooking spray

Preheat oven to 375°F. Place mangoes, apple juice, apple pie spice, fructose, vanilla, and arrowroot in a small saucepan. Cook for approximately 10 minutes or until mangoes are tender. Place mixture in 1-quart shallow baking dish.

Combine flour, oats, and apple pie spice. Sprinkle over cooked fruit. Spray with butter-flavored spray. Bake for 30 minutes or until golden brown. Serve as dessert or for breakfast. Makes 4 to 6 (1 cup) servings. *(1 serving = 139 calories, 0.8 grams fat, 3.0 grams dietary fiber: 6% protein, 88% carbohydrates, 5% fat.)*

RAINBOW GEL COMPOTE
(fruit, vegetables)

2 cups green grapes
1 stick agar agar (red)
2¾ cups apple juice, organic
1 stick vanilla bean
2 15-ounce cans light fruit cocktail, chilled
Fresh mint (garnish)

Wash and freeze green grapes in a Ziploc® bag. Soak agar agar in apple juice and vanilla bean for ½ hour, then boil until agar agar is fully dissolved. Cook for 10 to 15 minutes longer. Remove vanilla bean. Chill the liquid in square 9″ x 9″ pan in the refrigerator for 45 minutes to 1 hour. Cut into ½″ squares and stir in fruit cocktail with syrup and frozen green grapes. Serve in individual tall-stemmed glasses. Garnish with sprigs of fresh mint. Makes 6 (1 cup) servings. *(1 serving = 286 calories, 0.6 grams fat, 0.6 grams dietary fiber: 2% protein, 96% carbohydrates, 2% fat.)*

CREAMY MANGO PUDDING
(tofu, fruit, vegetables)

2 12.3-ounce packages firm silken tofu
3 cups fresh mangoes, chopped
1 tablespoon lemon/lime juice
Fresh mint (garnish)
8 (or 4 cut in half) maraschino cherries (garnish)

Blend or process the above in a blender or food processor. Refrigerate until firm (approximately 2 hours). Garnish with cherries and mint. Makes 8 (1 cup) servings. *(1 serving = 194 calories, 7.9 grams fat, 3.4 grams dietary fiber: 27% protein, 40% carbohydrates, 33% fat.)*

PEACHY BANANA MUFFINS
(fruit, grains, vegetables, oil)

2½ cups oat flour*
1 cup baker's bran or oat bran
2 teaspoons baking soda
1 teaspoon salt
1 teaspoon cinnamon
½ cup apple juice concentrate
½ cup peach puree
2 teaspoons vanilla
1 cup water
1 large banana, diced
1 peach, diced
Butter-flavored cooking spray

*To make oat flour, place rolled oats in a blender and blend until the oats become a fine flour.

Place muffin tins in the oven and heat oven to 350°F. Combine oat flour, baker's or oat bran, baking soda, salt, and cinnamon in a large mixing bowl. In another bowl, stir apple juice concentrate, peach puree, vanilla, and water. Stir this mixture into the dry ingredients. Add diced fruit and stir until moistened. Do not overmix. Remove heated muffin tins from the oven and spray with butter-flavored cooking spray. Spoon batter into muffin tins. Bake for approximately 30 to 40 minutes. Makes 18 (1 muffin) muffins. *(1 serving = 98 calories, 0.6 grams fat, 1.3 grams dietary fiber: 10% protein, 85% carbohydrates, 5% fat.)*

PUMPKIN SPICE COOKIES
(grains, vegetables, fruit, legumes, nuts, fructose, oil)

2½ cups whole wheat pastry flour
2 teaspoons baking powder
½ teaspoon baking soda
½ teaspoon salt
2 teaspoons apple pie spice
2½ tablespoons fructose
¼ cup applesauce
1 cup pumpkin
½ cup low fat rice or soy milk
¼ cup raisins (plumped)
2 teaspoons vanilla
¼ cup walnuts, chopped
Butter-flavored cooking spray

Preheat oven to 350°F. In a large mixing bowl, combine flour, baking powder, baking soda, salt, and apple pie spice. In another bowl, mix fructose, applesauce, pumpkin, rice or soy milk, raisins, vanilla, and nuts thoroughly. Place this mixture in the large mixing bowl and stir well. Spray baking sheet with butter-flavored cooking spray. Drop dough by tablespoons onto baking sheet. Bake for 15 minutes or until bottoms are lightly browned. Remove from baking sheet and cool on racks. Makes 2 dozen cookies or 12 (2 cookie) servings. *(1 serving = 124 calories, 1.8 grams fat, 1.4 grams dietary fiber: 9% protein, 77% carbohydrates, 13% fat.)*

APPLE PEACH FREEZE
(fruit, vegetables)

2 cups apple juice
2 cups fresh peaches
2 pinches stevia powder
4 (or 2 cut in half) maraschino cherries (garnish)
Fresh mint (garnish)

Blend apple juice, peaches, and stevia together in blender or food processor. Pour into shallow trays and freeze until semisolid (approximately 2 hours). Remove from trays and put through blender or food processor until frothy. Serve immediately. Garnish with cherries and mint. Makes 4 (1 cup) servings. *(1 serving = 93 calories, 0.2 grams fat, 1.6 grams dietary fiber: 3% protein, 95% carbohydrates, 2% fat.)*

CHAPTER 13

Tailoring the Good Carbohydrate Plan for You

The Good Carbohydrate Plan is not a "one diet fits all" diet. There are differences between individuals and how food affects them. The Good Carbohydrate Plan allows for this and is adaptable to individual needs. The Good Carbohydrate Plan's core foods, those that make up the first three layers of the Good Carbohydrate Plan Pyramid, are the foundation of just about all healthy diets. The optional apex part of the Good Carbohydrate Plan Pyramid provides options for you to modify the diet to suit your tastes and needs.

THE GOOD CARBOHYDRATE PLAN FOR VEGETARIANS OR WOULD-BE VEGETARIANS

Research shows that a diet made up entirely of Good Carbohydrates, that is, a whole foods, vegetarian-style Good Carbohydrate Plan is the ideal diet for good health for the majority of people. Studies on the Seventh Day Adventists, who are vegetarian, show that they live longer, have less obesity, less heart disease, less diabetes, and less cancer than those on a modern American, meat-inclusive diet.

The landmark China Diet Study, conducted by T. Colin Campbell of Cornell University, along with researchers from Beijing and Oxford University, found that the more a diet is based on plant foods, the less the risk of coronary disease. They found that there is actually no threshold to how much improvement can be obtained by reducing the amount of animal products in the diet. Vegetarian diets have also been shown to reduce the risk of coronary heart disease and diabetes.

While a strict, whole-food vegan (no animal/dairy/egg product) diet appears to have many health benefits, supplements of vitamin B12 may be required for those who are very strict. This is especially true for infants and small children, who need this vitamin for neurological development. This is easily obtained in infant formula and fortified cereals. Adults need a very small amount of B12 (2 mcg per day), and those on a strict vegan diet may need to take either an occasional B12 supplement or eat cereal fortified with B12 (more about this in the supplement chapter of this book). In all other instances, the purely Good Carbohydrate (vegetarian) diet is excellent for promoting good health and preventing disease.

THE GOOD CARBOHYDRATE PLAN FOR BLOOD SUGAR CONTROL

If your doctor has told you that you have borderline high blood sugar, it is very important that you work to manage your blood sugar before it gets out of control. Depending on the lab where you get your blood sugar analyzed, this means you have a fasting blood sugar that is over 110 to 120 mg/dl. It is highly likely that if you do nothing about your diet and lifestyle, your borderline blood sugar condition may progress to full-blown diabetes. Diabetes can be a devastating disease in the long run as it causes the blockage of small blood vessels (in addition to aggravating the blockage of large vessels caused by high levels of bad cholesterol) and is the leading cause of blindness, kidney failure, and foot amputations in this country. In addition, fully half of those with diabetes die of heart disease. Poor blood sugar control also suggests that you are exposed to high levels of insulin as your body attempts to handle the high blood sugar levels and increases the risk of coronary heart disease. Elevated insulin levels have been linked to hypertension, high cholesterol, high blood sugar, and obesity.

If you already have diabetes, I cannot emphasize enough the importance of working with your doctor in managing this disease. Make your dietary changes based on the Good Carbohydrate Plan in accord with your doctor's plan for medication and regular checkups to monitor your blood sugar and any early signs of potential problems that may be caused by diabetes.

If you are already on medication for diabetes, do not begin the Good Carbohydrate Plan without medical supervision. Some participants who have followed the plan have reduced their need for medications so quickly that their medications needed to be adjusted on the first day. For diabetics, it is also very important to avoid bad carbohydrates, eat high fiber foods, keep fat intake low in order to decrease insulin resistance, and perform regular exercise to improve insulin sensitivity.

Eight Steps to Controlling Blood Sugar with the Good Carbohydrate Plan

Here's a review of the steps that I recommend for anyone who wants to control their blood sugar with the Good Carbohydrate Plan.

Step 1. Choose Foods Based on the Five C's and Twelve Insights of the Good Carbohydrate Plan.

Use the Five C's and Twelve Insights of the Good Carbohydrate Plan for choosing carbohydrates. When in doubt, choose low Carbohydrate Quotient foods. If you are unable to find all the foods that you are looking for on the Carbohydrate Quotient Table, try to pick as many moderate-to-high Mass Index foods as you can from the Mass Index column.

Step 2. Make Sure That Your Diet Is Balanced.

The Good Carbohydrate Plan Pyramid is the one to follow in order to optimize your diet. Pay special attention to the additional categories of foods beyond the base category: Whole Grains and Staple Foods. In controlling blood sugar it is very important to have enough servings of vegetables and some fruit to ensure that you have an appropriate mix of other nutrients besides carbohydrates. These nutrients include vitamins, minerals, antioxidants, and other phytochemicals that can help you to avoid heart disease and even some cancers.

Step 3. Include Foods That Contain a Lot of Fiber.

In ancient times, humans ate as much as 50 to 100 grams of fiber per day. Consuming fiber helps to control the rate at which carbo-hydrates are absorbed and therefore, helps to moderate the blood sugar response. Use the Carbohydrate Quotient Table in the back of the book to help you find foods that are high in fiber. Remember that whole, plant-based foods have a lot of fiber, such as beans (legumes), whole grains, whole vegetables, and whole fruit.

Step 4. Keep the Fat Content in Your Diet Low.

Dietary fat is known to increase insulin resistance. Low fat diets that are high in good carbohydrates have been shown to help insulin work better to process the carbohydrates that are consumed. Start with a diet that is 10 to 15 percent fat, or 22 to 33 grams of fat per day (based on a 2,000-calorie diet).

Step 5. Exercise.

Exercise is one of the best ways to control blood sugar and to increase insulin sensitivity. It helps to make your requirement for insulin less and lowers your blood sugar levels because your body is burning off the glucose in your bloodstream. See Chapter 9 for suggestions on regular exercise.

Step 6. Work with Your Physician.

If you have diabetes, you should have a primary physician to moni-tor your blood sugar and your potential for complications of dia-betes. This includes regular eye exams, urine checks, blood sugar checks, blood pressure, cholesterol, other lipids (including HDL, LDL and triglycerides, hemoglobin A1C or glycosylated hemoglo-bin), and regular physical exams. In addition, consider working with your doctor to establish a program and a support system to set goals for continued management of your blood sugar and to evaluate the results of your efforts in controlling blood sugar.

> If you are on medication, you must check with your doctor before starting the diet. Have your doctor monitor you to determine whether you need to change or reduce your medications.

Step 7. Consider Supplements in Addition to Any Medication Prescribed by Your Doctor.

Make sure you work with your doctor in taking any supplements because of potential toxicity and interaction with medications. For example, some individuals respond very well to the mineral vanadium. However, there is some evidence of potential side effects from overconsumption of vanadium.

There is some evidence that people with diabetes do well with a very small dosage of chromium. In addition, dietary fiber supplements may help to control blood sugar, weight, and cholesterol levels. You can read more about supplements in detail, in Chapter 16.

Step 8. Individualize the Good Carbohydrate Plan for Blood Sugar Control.

Try the Good Carbohydrate Plan in its low fat form first. If you don't achieve the results you want, first examine your sources of carbohydrate. Make sure they are good carbohydrates. Some people are sensitive to refined carbohydrates, even if they are made from whole grains, so I suggest if you don't do well initially to try the Good Carbohydrate Plan with no added sugar and no flour products. Minimize baked goods such as bread. Second, make sure you are eating an adequate amount of vegetables and low Carbohydrate Quotient foods. It's easy to neglect the importance of balancing out your diet with a lot of foods that are higher in fiber and that may slow the absorption of the carbohydrates you eat. Third, make sure your fat content is low as described in Step 4.

For Difficult Blood Sugar Control: If your blood sugar is still difficult to control after implementing these suggestions, and you are working with your doctor on optimizing medical treatment, consider trying a Mediterranean-style diet of the Good Carbohydrate Plan. In order to follow this version of the Good Carbohydrate Plan, you must reduce your total carbohydrate intake and make sure that you minimize refined sugar and white bread. A moderate amount of pasta is allowed, preferably whole grain pasta. Replace some of your carbohydrates with whole, plant-based foods that have some low saturated fat oils in them, such as olives, tofu, nuts, and avocados; and add some extra virgin olive oil or other high monounsaturated oil to your cooking and dressings.

Adding more fat may make weight control more difficult, but may help to raise HDL (good cholesterol) levels while decreasing the amount of carbohydrates your body has to process. For those using animal products, it is very important to use very low fat animal products. For some individuals, reducing the total amount of carbohydrates may help with blood sugar control. However, decreasing carbohydrate intake with an increase in fat intake may require overall portion size and calorie limitations.

On this diet, you must be aware that because of the higher fat intake, calories are a concern. One thing you can do to counteract the higher fat intake is to add very high Mass Index foods, such as green vegetables, and high Mass Index fruit, such as grapefruit. Exercise is also important if you decide to add good fats because you need to counteract this increase in fat calories, which may contribute to obesity. Remember that with any diet that has a substantial amount of fat in it, you must watch your calorie intake because fats of all kinds make it easy to take in too many calories.

THE GOOD CARBOHYDRATE PLAN FOR LOWERING CHOLESTEROL AND RISK FOR CORONARY HEART DISEASE

Your cholesterol levels are the most important predictor of coronary heart disease. The higher your cholesterol level, the higher your risk of coronary heart disease. While the national guidelines say that cholesterol levels under 200 mg/dl are desirable, I believe that under 170 mg/dl is a better recommendation.

The good cholesterol (HDL) and bad cholesterol (LDL) levels are also very important. It is a good idea to keep total LDL cholesterol levels below 100 mg/dl. HDL levels should be kept relatively high in relation to the total cholesterol levels unless your total cholesterol is around 150 mg/dl or less, in which case your ratio becomes irrelevant. Ideally, you want your cholesterol:HDL ratio below three or at least below four. For example, if your total cholesterol is 200 mg/dl, you want your HDL to be between 50 to around 67 mg/dl. Dividing 200 by 67 would make your ratio 2.98. The national average is about 4.5. The higher your ratio, the higher your risk.

The best diet for high cholesterol is a very low fat, very low or no cholesterol diet that is high in good carbohydrates. This means a plant-foods diet based on the core Good Carbohydrate Plan. Limiting saturated fat intake is even more important than limiting cholesterol intake. Eliminating animal products is the best way to get rid of the saturated fat in your diet.

There is good evidence to support this conclusion. For example, beyond my own studies, two separate studies using similar diets have shown the ability to cause a similar substantial reduction in cholesterol and reversal of atherosclerosis. One study conducted in Germany utilizing a high carbohydrate, 20 percent fat diet and exercise showed a modest regression of atherosclerotic lesions in some patients. In another study, a high carbohydrate, very low fat (10 percent fat) diet, exercise and lifestyle modification was compared against a moderate 30 percent fat diet for its effects on heart disease. The study showed that the high carbohydrate vegetarian diet caused a reversal of the coronary artery lesions while the 30 percent fat, lower carbohydrate diet caused a progression of the disease. The regression in the 10 percent fat diet was greater than in the 20 percent fat diet, which suggests that total fat restriction is useful.

Overall, a very low fat diet will help to keep cholesterol as low as possible. It is also important to limit the intake of refined carbohydrates because they can cause an increase in cholesterol, or may at least contribute to a poor LDL:HDL cholesterol ratio by stimulating an excessive insulin response. Also remember that an excessive intake of fruit sugar can contribute to LDL, the bad cholesterol. If you have high triglycerides, focus on limiting not only fats and oil, but also refined carbohydrates such as sugar and white flour. For some people this means even avoiding whole wheat bread products because of their potential effect on insulin and triglycerides.

Ten Steps to Control Cholesterol

Step 1. Cut Down on Saturated Fats.

Saturated fats are the fats that are the most likely to raise your total cholesterol and your bad cholesterol, LDL. They are found in large quantities in animal products. The best way to avoid saturated fat is to avoid high fat foods, meats, poultry, and cheese. Other sources of saturated fats to avoid are tropical oils such as palm oil and coconut oil. I'm also placing trans fats in this category because they are artificially saturated or hydrogenated oils. These oils are the worst type of added fats and are found in a number of processed foods including margarine, candies, and other high fat food products.

Step 2. Give Up Added Fats.

Added fats such as oils, shortening, butter, margarine, and mayonnaise can increase cholesterol and contribute to the risk of obesity and other diseases. Dietary fats can contribute to insulin resistance, which forces your body to produce more insulin to control blood sugar. This can contribute to increased deposition of fat, which might be caused by the increased insulin levels. Of course, as mentioned above, the worst types of added fats are those containing trans fats. To avoid added fats, avoid fried foods, especially deep-fried foods, oil in salad dressings, butter, margarine, mayonnaise, and oils found in processed foods. Check the food label.

Although there is controversy about whether oils high in monounsaturated fats such as olive and canola oils are healthy or unhealthy in terms of cholesterol and heart disease, even the best oils are high in calories. All oils are nine calories per gram and all can promote obesity, which in turn increases risk of heart disease and diabetes.

Step 3. Reduce or Eliminate Your Intake of Cholesterol.

Cholesterol in your diet contributes to increased cholesterol levels in your blood (although it has less of an impact than saturated fat). Since cholesterol is found only in animal products, the ideal diet for reversing cholesterol-related diseases, such as heart disease, is one that is free of animal products, including dairy products. This has been demonstrated in long-term clinical trials.

Step 4. Eat More Good Carbohydrates.

A healthy amount of good carbohydrates should be the center of your diet. These include whole grains such as corn, oatmeal, brown rice, and whole wheat. See Chapters 6 and 7 for more about choosing good carbohydrates. Avoid bad carbohydrates and all foods that are high in white sugar and white flour. These are foods that will raise your insulin levels, allow you to consume too many calories, and increase your glucose load.

Step 5. Eat More Whole Foods.

Along with your good carbohydrate staples, consume generous helpings of whole vegetables and whole fruits. This includes vegetables of all kinds and fruits that have not been reduced to fruit juice. These foods add a large amount of the other good carbohydrate—dietary fiber—to your diet. Remember that dietary fiber acts as anti-calories, as well as an anti-blood sugar, because it not only helps to limit the amount of calories eaten, but also limits the impact of blood sugar by slowing down its absorption. Both of these factors will help reduce cholesterol levels and improve the profile of the good cholesterol, HDL, over the bad cholesterol, LDL.

Step 6. Maintain Ideal Body Weight.

Excess body weight is associated with higher cholesterol levels and higher risk of coronary heart disease. The Good Carbohydrate Plan is designed to help you achieve and maintain your ideal body weight. Remember that the Good Carbohydrate Plan includes diet and exercise, and is a whole-person program for total, lifelong health.

Step 7. Exercise Regularly.

Regular exercise, especially aerobic exercise, helps to keep your good cholesterol (HDL) level up. It also helps to keep your body weight down. Remember that exercise does not lower total cholesterol, so a good diet is essential for maximum protection from heart disease, as well.

Step 8. Stop Smoking.

Believe it or not, besides causing cancer and heart disease, smoking also causes a rise in cholesterol. If you want to control your cholesterol to the greatest extent possible, stop smoking.

Step 9. Consider Supplements to Help Control Cholesterol.

If you've tried diet and lifestyle changes and haven't achieved adequate success in controlling your cholesterol, consider taking some natural supplements. In Chapter 16, you'll find suggestions for supplements that help to control cholesterol and prevent heart disease, and fit in with the Good Carbohydrate Plan. Some of these supplements include fiber, niacin, herbal supplements such as garlic and gugulipid, and antioxidant supplements. In addition, the minerals vanadium and chromium may be helpful for some individuals who have trouble with blood sugar control. Control of blood sugar may help to control insulin levels and improve the cholesterol profile.

Step 10. Consider Cholesterol-Lowering Medication.

If you have tried a good diet and supplementation and still have a cholesterol profile that is unfavorable, you should see your physician. Many medications are currently available that control cholesterol and reduce risk of heart disease and stroke. While this is not ideal, some people have difficulty adopting and maintaining a healthy diet. When this is the case and the risk of coronary artery disease is high, see your physician and consider prescription medication under his or her guidance. This may be a prudent alternative.

THE GOOD CARBOHYDRATE PLAN FOR CONTROLLING SYNDROME X OR METABOLIC SYNDROME

If you have high blood sugar, hypertension, high cholesterol, low HDL, and high blood fat all at the same time, you may have what is known as Metabolic Syndrome. Obesity is another clue to Metabolic Syndrome, although it may not be present. The term Syndrome X was first coined by Dr. Gerald Reavan in 1988 when he used the term at the annual meeting of the American Diabetes Association. Syndrome X is also known as the Metabolic Syndrome or Syndrome of Insulin Resistance. Twenty-five to 30 percent of all people are susceptible to this variant of insulin resistance. Talk to your doctor if you have a combination of high blood sugar, abnormal cholesterol, and high blood pressure to see if you have Metabolic Syndrome.

The new NIH guidelines for the diagnosis of Metabolic Syndrome are that you must have any three of the following:

Risk Factor	Defining Levels
Abdominal Obesity	Men: waist size > 40 inches
	Women: waist size > 35 inches
Triglycerides	150 mg/dl or higher
HDL	Men: < 40 mg/dl
	Women: < 50 mg/dl
Blood Pressure	Systolic: 130 mm Hg or higher
	Diastolic: 85 mm Hg or higher
Fasting Glucose	110 mg/dl or higher

National Institutes of Health, NHLBI, ATP III Guidelines At-a-Glance Quick Desk Reference 2001.

If you do have Metabolic Syndrome, you should still try the low fat Good Carbohydrate Plan first. The recommendations for those with this syndrome against the use of carbohydrates are based on studies with bad carbohydrates. The good carbohydrates in the Good Carbohydrate Plan may be enough to induce excess weight loss and correct the abnormalities of Metabolic Syndrome. Exercise is especially important because it directly helps to reduce insulin resistance, which is the core problem in Metabolic Syndrome.

If you have tried the low fat Good Carbohydrate Plan, and you still have a hard time controlling your blood sugar and blood fat levels, try the Mediterranean version of the Good Carbohydrate Plan. This version is lower in total carbohydrates and helps to decrease the Glycemic Load. See Step 8 under Eight Steps to Controlling Blood Sugar with the Good Carbohydrate Plan on page 314.

THE GOOD CARBOHYDRATE PLAN FOR WEIGHT LOSS

If you have a weight problem, the best approach is to follow a very low fat version of the Good Carbohydrate Plan. Also, emphasize good carbohydrates in their most natural form—that is, the least refined, the better. Pay special attention to eliminating or minimizing low Mass Index foods such as fats, sugars, and baked white flour products. Because of the higher fat nature of the Mediterranean version of the plan, it can only be used with some calorie restrictions. For more detail, see Chapter 8, Losing Weight the Good Carbohydrate Way.

CHAPTER 14

What About Protein?

As we have seen, replacing bad carbohydrates with fat is not a good idea, due to the increased health risks seen with higher fat consumption, especially saturated animal fats. In this chapter, I will explain why it's also not a good idea to replace bad carbohydrates with large amounts of animal protein. While the best science indicates that the exclusively plant-based Good Carbohydrate Plan is ideal for most people, this doesn't mean that you have to be a vegetarian to benefit from the Good Carbohydrate Plan. For those individuals who are not ready to give up animal products, I want to provide you with a more complete picture of protein, its upside and its downside in this chapter. I also want to show you how to minimize the negative health effects of protein.

WHAT IS PROTEIN, ANYWAY?

Protein is one of the four ways you can get calories from your diet. The other sources are carbohydrate, fat, and alcohol. Protein is about four calories per gram; carbohydrate, in its pure form, is four calories per gram; fat is nine calories a gram; and alcohol is seven calories a gram. Carbohydrate, fat, and alcohol are similar to each other in that they burn cleanly. All that remains after the body uses these sources of energy is carbon dioxide and water, which is easy for the human body to dispose of.

Protein, unlike the other three forms of food energy, does not burn cleanly because it is a more complex molecule. Protein, rather than only providing energy for the body, also supplies the building blocks of the body's tissues, and the building blocks of the enzymes used in the myriad of chemical reactions that make up the human metabolism. Protein provides the basis of many of the complex tissues in the body, such as muscle tissue and organ tissue. Thus, it is very important that we obtain enough good quality protein for optimal health.

With respect to weight control, protein has another positive aspect. Studies suggest that unlike fat calories, which are associated with obesity, animal protein calories are neutral and plant proteins are correlated with leanness. However, the importance of protein and its association with leanness has caused some proponents to overemphasize the amount of protein we need. We actually don't need much protein and more is not necessarily better—as you will see in the explanation of the Thirteen Perils of Excess Animal Protein, below.

Proteins are made from long chains of amino acids. Amino acids contain carbon, hydrogen, and oxygen, as do the other three forms of energy, and unlike the other three forms of energy, amino acids all contain nitrogen. Some amino acids also contain sulfur, depending on the amino acid. Unlike fat and carbohydrate, there is no good way to store excess protein. Fats are easily stored as body fat. Carbohydrates can be stored, at least to some extent, as glycogen in the liver or muscle. Protein, however, must be used for producing or replacing some part of the body or some enzyme the body needs. Any excess protein is either converted to sugar and burned as energy, or converted into fat and its waste products eliminated through the kidneys.

PROTEIN PRODUCES TOXIC WASTE

When protein is metabolized, it cannot be burned cleanly into carbon dioxide and water as can carbohydrates and fat, because it contains nitrogen and sulfur. Some toxic substances, such as urea, are created during the breakdown process because of the nitrogen content. Sulfur, a by-product of the breakdown of amino acids, such as methionine and cysteine, also must be eliminated and is turned into sulfuric acid. These must be eliminated through the kidneys. Thus, one of the undesirable side effects of high intake of protein is that a tremendous load is put on the kidneys to eliminate the waste by-products.

PROTEIN RAISES INSULIN LEVELS

Your body requires insulin to process protein in much the same way as it requires insulin to process sugar. Protein is broken down into amino acids, its basic building blocks, by enzymes in the digestive tract. The amino acids are absorbed into the bloodstream. This rise in amino acids in the blood signals the pancreas to secrete insulin. The reason for this is that insulin is required to move amino acids into cells just as insulin is required to move blood sugar into cells. As I described earlier, insulin then stimulates the use of the amino acids to be used in the buildup of the body's tissues. Thus, while protein intake does not cause much of a rise in blood sugar, it does cause a rise in amino acids in the blood. This creates a demand for insulin in the body. In fact, protein stimulates the secretion of insulin as much as or more than some carbohydrates do. In Protein Peril #1, page 328, I describe this rise in insulin in a little more detail.

HOW MUCH PROTEIN DO WE NEED?

While many experts tout the value of protein, we must realize that the human body needs very little protein to thrive. The RDA for protein is about 50 grams for an average woman. Realize that the RDA provides a generous margin of safety, adding about 30 percent to the true minimum. Metabolic studies suggest that we need somewhere around 0.6 grams per kilogram of weight. In other words, for an average 175-pound person, the requirement is about 48 grams of protein. Other studies suggest that the minimum requirement for dietary protein to prevent loss of lean body mass is only about 35 grams of protein, which amounts to about 1¼ ounces of protein per day for an average person. (Exercise increases this requirement.)

This amount of protein is easily obtained from plant-based foods. When you look at the components of protein, the amino acids, you will find that eight of them are considered essential amino acids because the body cannot manufacture them. Despite what you may have heard in the past about animal protein being superior to plant protein, the truth is that plant proteins provide all eight essential amino acids and come with fewer hazards associated with them. Also, protein is found in all plants as well as in all animal products.

PROTEIN AND AMINO ACID TABLE

Essential Amino Acids (in Mg) Available in 2,200 Calories of Food (RDA for adult female)

Food	Protein	Trypto	Threo	Isoleu	Leucine	Lysine	Methio	Phenyl	Valine
RDA Female	50	250	450	650	950	800	425	475	650
Rice, Brown	51	714	2,130	2,465	4,815	2,222	1,308	3,009	3,414
Corn	73	542	3,072	3,072	8,312	3,283	1,596	3,584	4,427
Potato	46	776	1,810	2,047	2,995	3,017	776	2,279	2,801
Turnip	86	982	2,768	4,018	3,661	3,929	1,250	1,964	3,214
Kale	110	1,829	6,768	9,023	10,548	9,023	1,402	7,682	8,231
Broccoli	220	2,608	8,151	9,782	11,738	12,716	3,043	7,608	11,520
Beans, Kidney	129	1,467	6,846	8,976	13,583	11,736	1,576	8,726	9,584
Beef	132	1,994	7,798	8,016	14,098	14,838	4,568	6,965	8,673
Cheese, Cheddar	179	1,993	5,497	9,593	14,805	12,878	4,052	8,147	10,316
Rice, White	47	590	1,809	2,173	4,170	1,821	1,181	1,688	3,077

You can see from the table that it is virtually impossible to design a protein-deficient or amino-acid-deficient diet if whole grains and vegetables are utilized, and if adequate calories are provided. In this country there is virtually no protein deficiency. In fact, the problem that we have is that we consume far too much protein. Most Americans consume somewhere between 100 to 200 grams of protein per day. This is far, far in excess of what we really need on a daily basis, and can have negative effects in the body.

HIGH PROTEIN DIETS

Recent popular literature has generated a lot of interest in the idea that a high protein diet is ideal. The high protein proponents claim that since carbohydrate causes a rise in insulin and protein does not, we should increase our protein intake. Some of the diets are so drastic that they nearly eliminate carbohydrate intake and replace many calories with dietary fat, including saturated fat.

There are two main types of high protein diets. The first type is the ketogenic diet, which is an old diet that continues to recirculate. Examples of this type of diet are the Stillman Diet, the Scarsdale Diet, the Atkins Diet, and the Protein Power Diet, to name a few. The ketogenic diet advocates the consumption of a large amount of animal protein in the form of meats and cheeses; it allows the use of vegetables, and virtually eliminates the intake of carbohydrates. It is called ketogenic because it so severely restricts the intake of carbohydrates that the body switches to burning fat. The process of burning fat for energy produces ketone bodies in the bloodstream as a by-product. Ketone bodies usually appear in the bloodstream during starvation when the body is feeding off its own fat. They are responsible for some of the bad breath that people experience during fasting. Ketone bodies also tend to suppress hunger; this is one of the features touted by proponents of ketogenic diets.

Unfortunately, ketogenic diets also cause the body to break down its own protein. Because the brain is starving for carbohydrates, the body begins to digest its own muscle and protein to produce carbohydrates to feed the brain. Moreover, these diets are typically very high in fat and cholesterol. The high fat, cholesterol, and

protein content of these diets can cause a number of health problems, which we discuss later in this chapter. Thus, the ketogenic diet
may work for some people in the short run and may be useful on a
trial basis for individuals who are at high risk. However, it carries
with it a number of health risks, especially in the long run.

The second type of high protein diet is a little more moderate. It
increases protein intake but still has carbohydrates as its main
source of calories. It also advocates a moderate fat diet of about 30
percent. Examples of this diet are the Zone and the Sugar Buster's
diets. In the view of one of these diets, the optimal ratio of
macronutrient intake is 30 percent protein, 40 percent carbohydrate,
and 30 percent fat, with an emphasis on Omega 3 fatty acids.

However, if you follow the actual guidelines of this plan, all you
have is an unrealistic calorie-restricted diet. For example, if you take
the estimated protein requirement based on the guidelines of this
diet, an average 154-pound person would require about 59 grams of
protein. If you multiply by four to obtain protein calories, you have
236 calories from protein. If you now create a diet in which protein
is 30 percent of calories as they recommend, you will have a 787-
calorie diet, which is close to a starvation diet. Weight loss is
achieved simply by drastic calorie restriction, not by the elaborate
interaction between insulin and the body's metabolism that they
claim. The bottom line is that there is no magic in this high protein
regimen, and it is impossible to sustain such a calorie restriction in
the long run.

These high protein diets rely largely on recent studies indicating
that refined carbohydrates are associated with higher insulin levels,
as well as other studies indicating that high insulin levels are associated with increased risk of obesity, heart disease, and diabetes. The
proponents of these diets overextend the science behind these findings, generalizing the research on bad carbohydrates to all carbohydrates. Some of them also use the Glycemic Index mechanically
without regard to the proper context of the index. A number of the
Ten Carbohydrate Myths mentioned in Chapter 1 have come from
the high protein proponents' interpretation of these studies. I hope
to clear some of the misunderstandings about protein for you in this
chapter.

THIRTEEN PERILS OF EXCESS ANIMAL PROTEIN

An ancient Cherokee tale explains ". . . the need for medicine began because man profoundly offended the animals by killing them for food. . . ." It goes on to explain that the animals plotted their revenge and as punishment, they devised "a great variety of diseases that the animals would visit on their human enemy." (Maxwell)

Most of the perils of protein are primarily associated with animal protein, not vegetable protein. Animal protein typically comes along with a number of disease-causing substances. Also, as I illustrated in Chapter 2, it appears that humans are built to eat primarily, if not exclusively, plant-based foods. This may be why excessive animal protein intake is associated with negative health consequences. Judging by our anatomy and physiology, it seems that the human body is simply not equipped to handle large amounts of animal protein. The number of health problems associated with the intake of animal protein seems to be part of that revenge and a validation of the old Cherokee tale.

Protein Peril #1: Insulin

Since one of the health problems the Good Carbohydrate Plan helps to control is excessive insulin levels, let me describe to you the effect of protein intake on insulin first. Remember that high insulin levels can contribute to the risk of a number of health problems. Studies on insulin response to different foods found that beef intake raised insulin levels 27 percent higher than pasta. Remember that beef is high in fat and because fat slows down the absorption of sugar, it is also likely to reduce the insulin response. Fish, which has less fat, and more protein has a 47 percent higher insulin response than pasta.

When you consider that in the test amounts in this study comparing beef with pasta was 240 calories of each food, and that beef is typically more than half fat, you'll find that the amount of protein that stimulated this rise in insulin was just 17 grams of protein compared to 48 grams of carbohydrate from pasta. When you further consider the Mass Index of these foods, and that it takes less than twice as much beef to provide the same number of calories as pasta

INSULIN RESPONSE TO 240 CALORIES OF HIGH PROTEIN AND HIGH CARBOHYDRATE FOODS

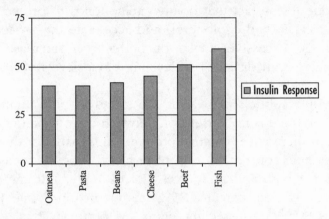

Adapted from: USDA Agricultural Handbook 456, *Am J Clin Nutr* (1997) 66: 1264-76, *Diabetes* (1997) 26:1179, and *Diabetes Nutr Metab* (2000) 13(1): 13-9.

or beans (the Mass Index of beef is 2.1 compared to 4.9 for pasta and 4.7 for beans), you'll realize that it is very easy to consume more calories from meat than from pasta or beans. Thus, the impact on insulin resulting from eating beef may well be even greater than it is from eating pasta or beans than the study indicates.

I want to keep in perspective the fact that not all carbohydrates enjoy this advantage over protein. A bad carbohydrate such as white bread would have an insulin response of 100 that is worse per 240 calories than the foods in the above graph. Also, there is not enough data on the insulin effects of protein to implicate protein as a cause of insulin resistance or diabetes. The main point is that protein is not a good substitute for good carbohydrates if the object is to keep insulin under control.

Protein Peril #2: Homocysteine

High intake of animal protein is associated with an increased risk of coronary heart disease. This may be due to an amino acid called homocysteine (pronounced homo-sis-téin). Homocysteine is formed from sulfur-containing amino acids, which are found in all protein.

Studies have shown that those with higher homocysteine levels in their blood have a higher rate of heart disease than those with low levels. The association of homocysteine with heart disease is probably due to the fact that homocysteine tends to promote the oxidation of LDL (bad cholesterol) and accelerate the process of atherosclerosis. Excessive intake of protein can increase the risk of coronary heart disease by elevating blood levels of the amino acid homocysteine.

While sulfur amino acids are found in both animal and plant protein, there is no correlation between plant protein and heart disease as there is with animal protein. One reason for this may be that the protein concentration in plant-based protein foods is much less than it is with animal sources. For example, 100 grams (about 3.5 ounces) of beef contains 25 grams of protein, while 100 grams of beans provides just eight grams of protein. Thus, plant protein sources are better from the perspective of homocysteine because they are less concentrated than animal protein sources and it is less likely that you will overconsume protein from these sources. Another reason plant protein is not associated with heart disease may be the content of folic acid and pyridoxine of plant-based foods. These vitamins can neutralize homocysteine by converting it to a safer form of amino acid.

Protein Peril #3: Calcium Loss from Protein

Increased risk of osteoporosis is another peril of protein. Studies show that people who consume large amounts of protein lose more calcium in their urine. The relationship between excessive protein and osteoporosis becomes even more alarming when you consider that the countries that consume the most animal protein have the most osteoporosis. For example, the Eskimo people eat a very high animal protein diet and they also have the highest rate of osteoporosis in the world.

Different studies have compared calcium balance on high and low protein diets. There is a consistent finding that people on high protein diets lose more calcium than they take in (negative calcium balance). This is true even if they have a high calcium intake. In contrast, there is a consistent finding that those on low protein diets actually gain calcium (positive calcium balance).

OSTEOPOROSIS VS. PROTEIN CONSUMPTION

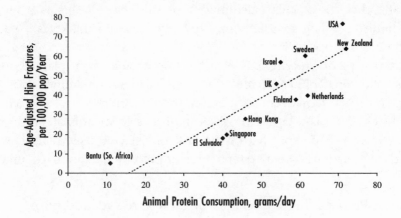

Adapted from: Cummings, Kelsey, Nevitt, and O'Dowd. *Epidemiologic Reviews* (1985) 7:178.

CALCIUM BALANCE ON LOW AND HIGH PROTEIN DIETS

Calcium Intake (milligrams)	Balance with Low Protein	Balance with High Protein
500	+31	-120
500	+24	-116
800	+12	-85
1,400	+10	-84
1,400	+20	-65

Adapted from McDougall, J., 1983

Why is protein intake associated with calcium loss? The answer may lie, again, in the sulfur-containing amino acids found in protein. When sulfur-containing amino acids are eaten in excess, they pass into the kidneys where they are broken down into sulfuric acid. Sulfuric acid is extremely acidic so the kidneys use calcium to neutralize it (in the same way we use TUMS®, i.e., to neutralize stomach acid). Thus, to compensate for a high protein diet, the body pulls calcium out of the bloodstream and releases it into the kidneys to neutralize the sulfuric acid. To replace the calcium in the blood-stream, the body pulls calcium out of the bones. This is a clear mechanism, which may explain why high protein intake is associ-ated with osteoporosis.

As for plant protein, it is possible that protein from plants could cause the same effect because there are also sulfur amino acids in plant proteins. However, once again, the concentration of protein is much less for plant-based proteins than it is from animal products. Thus, from the perspective of the risk of osteoporosis, plant-based good carbohydrates are a better source of protein than animal sources.

Protein Peril #4: Increased Risk of Cancer Associated with Excess Animal Protein

Excess animal protein is also associated with an increased risk for certain cancers. Population studies have shown that the countries where people consume the most animal protein also have the high-est rate of breast cancer, prostate cancer, and colon cancer. Studies are conflicting as to whether it is the protein that causes the cancer or something that is associated with a high animal protein lifestyle that increases the risk. However, recently, there has been interest in a substance that is similar to insulin called insulin-like-growth-factor I, or IGF-I, that is associated with an increased risk of certain can-cers. IGF-I, like insulin, stimulates cell growth and is suspected to be an important factor in the growth of tumors. IGF-I levels are higher in those who eat more animal protein than in those who eat less. In addition, laboratory studies conducted at Cambridge University showed that red meat, when exposed to colon bacteria, creates cancer-causing substances known as N-Nitroso compounds.

Dairy protein is also implicated in promoting certain cancers. Dr. T. Colin Campbell, Nutrition Biochemistry Professor of Cornell University and principal investigator of the landmark China Diet Study, has studied the relationship between over 200 biomarkers and cancer for decades. He indicates that dairy protein is associated with the development of a number of cancers such as prostate and breast cancer. He goes as far as saying that it may be time to evalu-ate dairy protein as a carcinogenic substance.

BREAST CANCER MORTALITY VS. PROTEIN CONSUMPTION

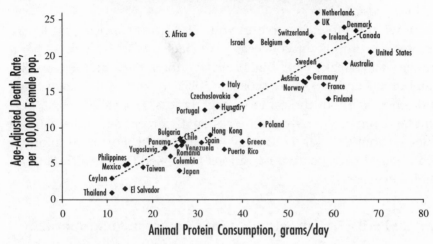

Adapted from: Carroll, et al. *Prog Biochem Pharmacol* (1975) 10:308.
Cited in Creasey, W.A. *Diet and Cancer*, 1985:52.

Protein Peril #5: Constipation

Protein from any source can be constipating if not accompanied by fiber. This is probably why carnivores such as lions, tigers, and dogs have short intestinal tracts. These carnivorous animals are built to handle their high animal protein diets, which tend to move very slowly through the intestines. A diet that is high in animal protein and devoid of a substantial amount of dietary fiber is inappropriate for the long digestive tract of humans and will result in constipation. Some of the health problems that are associated with this seemingly benign condition are diverticular disease, appendicitis, hemorrhoids, and colon cancer.

Protein Peril #6: High Total Fat Content in Animal Protein

Fat intake in America has been implicated as one of the causes of obesity and all the health risks that go along with obesity. High fat intake not only contributes to high cholesterol levels, it also thickens the blood, causing it to clot more easily. This increases the risk that a clot will form at the site of a cholesterol plaque and block the artery, causing a heart attack. In addition, high fat intake may be associated with insulin resistance, diabetes, and possibly, colon cancer and prostate cancer.

When the protein source in your diet is animal flesh, fat intake becomes an important concern. Most beef products, such as hamburgers and steaks, are higher in fat than they are in protein. Hamburgers and steaks are typically 55 to 70 percent fat. An average pork chop is about the same or slightly less. Hot dogs are 83 percent fat. Even chicken thighs are about 58 percent fat, and a chicken thigh without the skin is roughly 49 percent fat. For more information about the fat content of various foods see Chapter 15, Fat and Cholesterol Facts.

Protein Peril #7: High Saturated Fat Content in Animal Protein

One of the biggest problems with animal protein is that it is typically loaded with saturated fat, along with its high total fat content. Saturated fat raises cholesterol levels, especially LDL, the bad cholesterol, even more than cholesterol itself. This increases the risk of atherosclerosis and coronary heart disease. Lard (animal fat) is about 40 percent saturated fat. Chicken fat is 30 percent saturated fat. Compare this to olive oil, which is 13 percent saturated fat, and canola oil, which is 7 percent saturated fat. Of all the types of fat you can eat, the fats that come from animals promote coronary heart disease the most.

Protein Peril #8: High Cholesterol Content in Animal Protein

Animal protein also contains cholesterol. Did you know there is just as much cholesterol in lean meat as there is in fatty meat? Yes, there is just as much cholesterol in lean chicken, chicken without the skin and lean beef as there is in high fat beef. Although eating cholesterol doesn't raise blood cholesterol as much as saturated fat does, it is still a factor in increasing the risk of heart disease. Cholesterol is found in every cell in animals, in fat cells or muscle cells, in fatty tissue or lean tissue. Consuming animal flesh protein will always increase your cholesterol intake and consequently increase your risk for heart disease.

Protein Peril #9: Pollution in Animal Protein

While pollutants found in animal protein are present in relatively small amounts, some of them are potent carcinogens. The higher up you go in the food chain, the greater the concentration of pollutants. That's why vegetable foods have about one-tenth the amount of pesticides and other toxic chemicals as animal foods. Many of the pollutants will concentrate in the flesh of the animal, especially the fat. By eating the animal fat, you may get a concentration of pollutant that has accumulated over the life span of the animal.

In addition, some animals are treated with antibiotics and hormones in order to avoid illness, and to make the animals gain weight faster so they can be sold for a higher price for food. These antibiotics and hormones eventually end up in the flesh of the animal, where you eat them. One reviewer points out that, "The most contentious residues that occur in meat, milk, and eggs are antibacterial drugs, hormonal growth promoters and certain pesticides, heavy metals, and industrial chemicals." (McEwan)

Protein Peril #10: Parasites and Other Infectious Diseases in Animal Protein

As you have probably heard, a number of European meat products have been banned from the United States because there is concern that American beef may become contaminated with Mad Cow Disease. This disease is caused by cow cannibalism—the practice of feeding dead and diseased animal parts to other animals of the same species. Humans contract the disease by eating infected meat. Mad Cow Disease causes loss of memory, loss of bodily control, and death. While it appears that American beef is not contaminated, one way to be completely safe is to avoid meat.

Another group of diseases that can be contracted through eating infected meat are diseases caused by parasites. Trichinosis caused by the *Trichinella spiralis* worm is one such disease. Also, tapeworms and many other parasites can be contracted from eating contaminated meat.

Bacterial infection is another type of illness caused by eating contaminated meat. The best known examples are salmonella and

E-coli infections. Both can cause nausea, diarrhea, abdominal cramps, fever, vomiting, chills, and even death. The best way to minimize the risk from these diseases is to eat the pure plant-based version of the Good Carbohydrate Plan.

Protein Peril #11: Mystery Meat

When I was in college, we used to be served processed meats from time to time in the cafeteria, and the guys in my dorm would comment that they couldn't tell what type of meat it was. We jokingly called it mystery meat.

Because of the natural tendency of meat to putrefy, animal flesh turns a gray-green color soon after it is slaughtered. The meat processors prevent or hide this discoloration and keep the meat from further spoilage by adding food coloring, nitrates, sodium, and other preservatives. Some of the by-products of these preservatives, such as nitrosamines, have carcinogenic potential. The relationship between preserved meats and colon cancer was supported by scientific research reported in 2001 from the largest nutrition and health research project ever conducted, the European Prospective Investigation into Cancer and Nutrition (EPIC). This study, which included over 400,000 individuals in nine different countries in Europe, showed a significant relationship between processed meats and colon cancer. For all these reasons, the more mysterious the meat, the more caution I send to you against using it.

Protein Peril #12: Gout

One of my patients came to me with severe pain in his big toe. After a few minutes of talking with him, he told me he was on a high protein diet. I checked his uric acid levels and they were very high. He had gout, a painful disease caused by excessive amounts of uric acid crystallizing in the joints. While protein itself does not cause gout, a high intake of animal products puts you at risk because of the high content of a substance called purines. Purines come from the breakdown of nucleic acids from DNA and RNA in the nucleus of cells. Both plants and animals have purines; however, they tend to be much higher in animal products, especially organ meats and some seafood. Some of the foods that are very high in purines are sweetbreads (animal intestines), anchovies, sardines, liver, kidney, meat extracts, gravies, game meats, mackerel, and scallops. After using the principles of the Good Carbohydrate Plan, his uric acid returned to normal and the gout never bothered him again.

Protein Peril #13: Hormone-Related Disease

Animal products are also associated with hormone-related diseases. For men, this includes prostatic hypertrophy, and prostate cancer. For women, some examples are premenstrual syndrome, irregular menses, heavy menses, endometriosis, uterine fibroids, ovarian cysts, breast lumps, and breast cancer. The reason for this association is thought to be a result of chronically high male and female hormones in the blood. Animal products, especially animal fats, tend to cause the body to secrete more sex hormones. Obesity also plays a role in the conversion of estrogens to their active form. This can cause an overstimulation of the growth of certain organs and tissues and health problems may result. Vegetarians are known to have lower levels of these hormones and thus are at lower risk of these diseases. A higher intake of good carbohydrates reduces the body's sex hormone load and may provide some protection from these hormone-related diseases.

PLANT-BASED PROTEINS ARE ASSOCIATED WITH FEWER RISKS

The best source of protein is protein that comes from plant-based foods such as whole grains and beans (legumes). While protein from these sources are adequate in quantity and quality, they pose less of a risk of all thirteen perils that I describe. One of the main reasons for this is that the risks inherent to all protein are reduced because the concentration of protein from plant sources is less than the concentration from animal sources.

Here is a comparison of protein content of 100 grams (3.5 ounces) of different sources of protein. Note that even the relatively low content of protein in whole grain is adequate based on the RDA for calories and protein. Also the relatively high content of protein in the flesh foods are unnecessary for human needs and can result in a detrimental excess of protein.

Food	Calories	Protein	Fat	Fiber	Cholesterol
Beans	137	8.2 gm	0.5 gm	7.4 gm	0 mg
Tofu	75	8.1 gm	4.7 gm	1.2 gm	0 mg
Whole Grain	110	2.6 gm	0.9 gm	1.7 gm	0 mg
Beef	329	24.9 gm	26.9 gm	0 gm	92 mg
Chicken	234	26.9 gm	13.3 gm	0 gm	107 mg
Fish	140	26.7 gm	2.9 gm	0 gm	41 mg

Another positive aspect of plant proteins is the other food components that come with them. All plant-based proteins are accompanied by fiber. Of course, animal protein sources have no fiber. Plant-based proteins also tend to be low in fat and have no cholesterol. In addition, if you obtain protein from soy products, you may enjoy added health benefits from a substance called isoflavones. Mounting evidence suggests that these soy isoflavones are protective against coronary heart disease and certain cancers.

The Use of Animal Products

As you know, I don't recommend the use of animal products. However, the Good Carbohydrate Plan is flexible enough to include them. If you are going to use any animal products, here are some guidelines:

1. It should be the leanest cut possible.
2. Try to avoid processed meats because of their high content of fat, sodium, and preservatives.
3. The meat's fat profile should be similar to the fat profile of wild game, that is, with less than 20 percent of calories from fat and some Omega 3 fats.
4. Buying organically-fed animal products helps to minimize the amount of pollutants that may accumulate in the product.

Meats

In general, the guidelines above cut out just about all commercially produced beef or pork because both are actually produced in a way that encourages high fat content. An average cut of beef, for example, is somewhere between 60 to 70 percent of calories from fat. Don't be fooled when it says 9 or 10 percent on the label, because that typically means that it is 9 to 10 percent fat by weight.

Even when you trim excess fat from cuts of beef, the lean part of the beef is still roughly 50 percent fat, at minimum. The leanest hamburger is also still around 50 percent fat. Therefore it is very difficult to obtain beef that is reasonably healthy from the perspective of fat content. Probably the only red meats that could be acceptable would be wild game meats, such as venison, buffalo, and other such meats that are caught in the wild.

Typically, pork is as fatty as beef. However, it is possible to get some fairly lean cuts of pork. The lowest fat cuts of pork that I could find were the lean ham slices that some companies produce as low fat prepared meats. The caution here is that these are typically high in sodium and may contain preservatives that can be carcinogenic.

Poultry

Many health experts recommend poultry as a substitute for red meat because poultry tends to be lower in fat. However, do not be misled into thinking that poultry is generally low in fat. In fact, poultry, such as chicken, is typically high in fat compared to plant-based protein sources. It is promoted as healthy only in comparison to beef, which is very high in fat. For example, a typical cut of chicken is somewhere around 58 to 60 percent fat. Much of the fat is found in the skin of the chicken, thus, it is often recommended that the skin be removed. This helps, but still does not render the chicken very healthy because it is still around 48 percent fat.

The only cut of chicken that approaches being low in fat is skinless chicken breast, which is about 21 percent fat. However, remember that if the skin is removed after cooking, the fat melts into the meat and the meat still contains a fair amount of fat from the skin, in addition to the fat that is found in the lean part of the flesh of the chicken.

340 THE GOOD CARBOHYDRATE REVOLUTION

Turkey breast can actually be lower in fat than chicken breast if the skin is removed. A typical skinless turkey breast if it is skinned prior to cooking can be as low as five percent fat.

Dark meat from any poultry tends to be higher in fat than white meat. Thus, it is important to avoid dark meat from chicken, and other poultry as well.

Eggs

All the cholesterol and fat found in eggs are in the yolks. The egg white is essentially almost all egg albumin or a form of animal protein. Thus, the best way to use eggs is to use them without the yolk. Another way to use eggs is to use egg substitutes such as Egg Beaters®. Egg substitutes can be found in a carton in your local supermarket. They are made up of egg whites with beta carotene or some other food coloring to give them the appearance of regular eggs, and can be scrambled as you would prepare scrambled eggs. This type of food has 0 fat and 0 cholesterol. But remember not to overdo even egg whites, because many of the perils of protein still apply even though you remove the fat and cholesterol.

Recently there has been some debate about whether cholesterol from eggs actually causes a rise in cholesterol. This is because of some recent studies showing that adding eggs to a diet does not result in a substantial elevation of blood cholesterol levels. In my review of the literature, these studies were predominantly done with participants who start with very high cholesterol levels. When someone has a very high cholesterol level to begin with, adding eggs or other cholesterol foods may not raise cholesterol very much. There is good evidence that if people start at a low cholesterol level, eggs and other cholesterol and fat-containing foods will indeed cause a substantial rise in cholesterol levels and thus increase the risk of coronary heart disease.

Dairy

If you choose to use dairy foods, remember that most of the increase in coronary heart disease risk from dairy is caused by the high fat, high saturated fat, and high cholesterol content. If you use skim milk, all of that is removed. If you use two percent milk, you

still have 35 percent of calories coming from fat. If you use one percent milk, that still leaves about 25 percent of the calories coming
from fat. From the perspective of risk for coronary heart disease and
successful weight loss, the best milk to use is skim milk.

However, most people forget that milk's second main source of
calories is sugar, not protein. Milk is full of lactose, which is milk
sugar. Even when you are drinking skim milk, there is still a substantial amount of sugar present. For those who are lactose intolerant and for diabetics, this can pose a problem.

Lactose intolerance is one reason why some people prefer
yogurt and cheese as a source of their dairy. In both yogurt and
cheese, most of the lactose is consumed in the fermentation process.
When dairy is fermented to produce yogurt and cheese, the bacteria
cultured in the fermentation process uses up the lactose and produces the tangy flavor of yogurt and helps to congeal cheese into its
solid form. This leaves the lactose content of the remaining dairy
product at very low levels.

Before you run out and stock up on yogurt and cheese, remember that yogurt raises insulin more than most carbohydrates and
most cheeses are very high in fat. Cheddar cheese, for example, is
approximately 74 percent fat. It is also high in saturated fat and cholesterol. In fact, 2.5 ounces of cheese contains more cholesterol
(about 101 mg) than 3.5 ounces of beef (91 mg).

You can buy cheese made from skim milk that are very low in
fat. Check labels, and remember the way to evaluate the fat content
of anything: Calories from fat divided by total calories. Multiply that
number by 100 and you have the percentage of calories coming
from fat.

If you are allergic to dairy products, remember that dairy protein
is the allergen that causes a reaction. Thus, if you are allergic to
dairy, neither skimming the fat from the dairy product nor fermenting it will eliminate the problem. Dairy is one of the leading causes
of allergy in this country, and is associated with a number of health
problems such as postnasal drip, sinus congestion, asthma, rash,
and even aches and pains. Even autoimmune diseases such as Type
I diabetes may be linked to childhood dairy consumption. Because
of this link, it's plausible that dairy consumption could affect other
autoimmune diseases such as rheumatoid arthritis and lupus.

Remember that if you avoid dairy, which I do recommend, it is important to get your calcium from other sources, such as dark leafy greens, sea vegetables, tofu, and other high calcium foods. If you cannot get enough of these foods (which is very common), then I recommend obtaining calcium from supplements such as calcium citrate or calcium carbonate.

Seafood

If you are going to eat any flesh foods, seafood is probably the best to use because it is typically lower in fat. Studies done in Finland and the United States show that coronary heart disease rates are lower in those who eat more fish instead of meat, probably because fish and other seafood tend to be lower in fat content. Be aware that there are some wide differences in types of fish in terms of fat content. Darker meat fish tend to have higher fat content in the same way that darker meat poultry has a higher fat content than white meat poultry. Also, fish that come from cold water areas such as salmon and mackerel tend to have higher fat content. For example, salmon can have up to 50 percent of its calories from fat. However, one redeeming quality of the fat from fish that makes it better than red meat is its high proportion of Omega 3 fatty acids. Omega 3 fatty acids are known to help reduce the risk of coronary heart disease when they replace saturated fats. This is described in further detail in Chapter 15, Fats and Cholesterol Facts.

Although shellfish has a reputation of having high cholesterol levels, this comes from an error in measurement of cholesterol that occurred when the figures were first documented. Researchers mistakenly measured sterol as cholesterol in the shellfish and the original figures overstated the actual content of cholesterol. In reality, shellfish such as shrimp, lobster, and clams actually have only slightly more cholesterol than fish. In addition, they are typically as low in fat as the lowest fat types of fish. For example, shrimp has ten percent of its calories from fat.

Be very careful in how you prepare shellfish, however. Frying in oil can turn any low fat food into a very high fat food. Deep fried shrimp has up to 60 percent of calories coming from fat because of the oil that is added in the frying process. Thus, the best way to prepare any seafood, or any flesh food for that matter, is to avoid using any oil and to roast, broil, steam or bake the seafood or meat and use other sources of flavorings such as herbs, spices, and soy sauce.

Protein is a necessary part of the diet of humans. However, we don't really need much of it to be healthy and it is evident that too much of it can pose some significant health risks. The risks are magnified if the protein comes from high fat animal products. Whole, plant-based foods, in other words, Good Carbohydrate foods, are the best sources of protein. They are adequate in quantity and quality of protein and have components in them, such as dietary fiber and antioxidants, that may reduce the risks of a number of the health complications that may be caused by animal proteins.

CHAPTER 15

Fat and Cholesterol Facts

"What about fats and cholesterol?" my patients ask. We've heard so much information about fats in connection with dieting over the years that many of us are confused. I'm going to give you the straight facts on fat and cholesterol in this chapter.

FAT FACTS

Most of us are familiar with fats as that whitish greasy part of meats and poultry, or the oily liquid that is used for greasing pans and frying foods such as French fries. Fats and oils are terms that are used interchangeably. Technically, however, fats are solid at room temperature and oils are liquid at room temperature. What all fats and oils have in common is that they don't mix with water (that's why they have a greasy feel to them), and they are both loaded with calories.

Fats and oils are a part of our daily diet whether we like it or not. Not only is fat found in obvious food sources such as bacon grease and cooking oil, it is found in almost all foods. The most common sources of fat are foods such as meats, poultry, butter, margarine, cheese, nuts, salad dressings, and baked goods. Although it may be a small amount, there is fat in beans, fruits, vegetables, and grains, too. Here's a helpful, and perhaps eye opening, list of the fat content of some typical foods by percentage of calories:

Corn oil	100%
Olive oil	100%
Butter	99%
Margarine	99%
Mayonnaise	98%
French dressing	93%
Luncheon meat	83%
Hot dog	82%
Peanuts	80%
Cheddar cheese	74%
Hamburger meat	71%
Potato chips and corn chips	60%
Chicken thigh	59%
Whole milk	55%
French fries	49%
2% milk	35%
White bread	15%
Whole wheat bread	12%
Lettuce	10%
Broccoli	9%
Brown rice	7%
Apple	5%
Kidney beans	3%
White rice	2%
Potato	1%
Sugar	0%

There are five things I want you to notice about the fat content in these foods:

1. Almost all animal products are high in fat.

2. Almost all good carbohydrates are low in fat.

3. Some foods that you may think are low in fat aren't (2% milk is 35 percent fat).

4. Some foods that you may think have no fat do (white bread is 15 percent fat).

5. Just because something has no fat doesn't mean it's healthy (sugar has no fat).

Fats Make You Fat

The first thing you must know about fats is that they make you fat. While some experts debate whether there is anything special about fats that do this, they all agree that there are so many calories concentrated in all fats that it is easy to get too many calories by eating fat. Fats are the form of food in which plants and animals store calories for long-term needs. They contain the most calories for the least amount of weight of any food. For every gram of fat (a gram is the weight of a raisin) there are about nine calories of energy. This is true whether the fat is from animal or plant. Whether fat is saturated, monounsaturated, or polyunsaturated, they are all nine calories per gram and can contribute to obesity. By contrast, there are only about four calories per gram in pure carbohydrates and protein, and in good carbohydrates, there is about one calorie per gram or less.

Because fats are the most concentrated source of calories you can find, they are high in calorie density and they add to the calorie density of any food. In other words, they are low in Mass Index and adding fats to any food will lower its Mass Index value. The Carbohydrate Quotient, as you know, incorporates the Mass Index numbers of foods. This is why foods that are low on the Carbohydrate Quotient scale tend also to be low in fat.

Fats Affect Blood Sugar Control

The second thing I want you to remember about fats is that they have an impact on blood sugar control. In general, they can make your blood sugar control worse in most situations. The difficult thing to understand about fats is that by themselves, they don't raise blood sugar much and they don't raise insulin much. However, as I described in Chapter 3, fats tend to make insulin less effective and make it harder for your body to handle any carbohydrates you do eat.

Population studies also show that when people move from a low fat traditional diet to a higher fat modern diet, diabetes rates increase.

High Fat Diets Are Associated with Certain Cancers

Surveys comparing the cancer rates of various countries show an association between high fat diets and certain cancers. For example, the higher the intake of fat in a country, the higher that country's prostate cancer rate turns out to be. Colon cancer is also associated with high fat intake.

While this type of survey shows only that fat is *associated* with cancer and not necessarily that fat is the *cause* of cancer, other studies support the reasons for concern. For example, in clinical studies, high fat diets are associated with high levels of serum testosterone, which in turn is related to prostate cancer. Also, in animal studies, mice eating a diet high in fat have been shown to be more likely to develop breast tumors than those eating a diet lower in fat. In these studies, both saturated fat and polyunsaturated fat were associated with increased breast tumors, with polyunsaturated fats more closely correlated to these tumors.

Fats Affect Serum Cholesterol

Probably the most well-known effect of dietary fat is its effect on serum cholesterol. Most of the science about fats that we hear about is related to its impact on cholesterol levels and how they affect our risk of coronary heart disease. The countries that have the highest fat intakes tend to have the highest risk of coronary heart disease. In countries that have the lowest fat intakes, cholesterol levels and heart disease tend to be very low. There are a number of different types of fat. As I describe them below, I'll explain the potential effect of each type of fat on cholesterol levels.

But We All Need Essential Fats

We all need a small amount of dietary fat to survive, but not much! The fats absolutely necessary for life are called essential fats or essential fatty acids and are readily available in whole foods such as grains, vegetables, and legumes. These essential fats are known as linoleic acid and linolenic acid. Both are polyunsaturated fats, as described below. We require extremely small amounts of these fats, about two to five grams per day. Remember that a gram is about the weight of a raisin. These essential fats are available from whole foods without adding refined fats or oils such as vegetable oil, lard, margarine, or butter. The two to five grams per day of essential fats are easily obtained by eating whole, plant-based foods. There is a small amount of fat in vegetables, grains, legumes and fruit, but enough to supply our needs. For example, just two cups of cooked brown rice contains 1.1 grams of essential fats out of its 3.2 total grams of fat. There is a large amount in moderate-to-high-fat plant foods such as tofu, nuts, seeds, olives, and avocados. For example, one cup of tofu contains 5.9 grams of essential fats out of its 11.9 total grams of fat.

Fatty acid deficiency is virtually never seen in the general population because most of us have an ample supply of essential fats in our body fat. Just about the only time you will see fatty acid deficiency is in people who have malabsorption problems; in those who are on very unusual diets, such as alcoholics; or starvation situations, such as anorexia or end-stage disease.

FAT TERMINOLOGY

In order to better understand fats, let me describe some basic terms and define some words to help you to better understand how different fats affect you.

Fatty Acids

Fats are actually collections of different types of fatty acids, mostly in the form of triglycerides, which are groups of three fatty acids connected together. All natural fats are combinations of monounsaturated, polyunsaturated, and saturated fatty acids. Fatty acids are long chains of carbon atoms—some of them 16 to 18 carbons long. They are called fatty acids because chemically there is an acid component at one end of the molecule, but fats don't make things acidic because fats cannot be dissolved in water. The term fat is also loosely used to describe fatty acids when specific components of fats are described, such as monounsaturated fats and polyunsaturated fats.

FATTY ACID COMPOSITION OF VARIOUS OILS

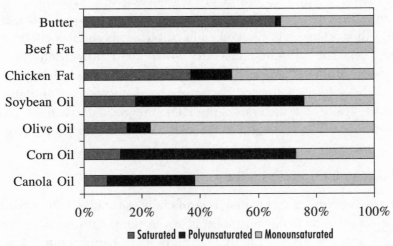

Data from: USDA Nutrient Database for Standard Reference, Release 12.

Saturation

Fats are classified based on the number of unsaturated bonds or double bonds they contain. There is at least one bond between each adjacent carbon atom. The term saturated comes from the fact that each carbon atom in the fat molecule has two extra binding sites in addition to the site that bonds it to the next carbon atom; these extra binding sites are saturated with hydrogen.

If a fat is saturated, it means there are no open binding sites for a double bond. If a fat is unsaturated, it means that some hydrogen atoms are missing and some binding sites are unoccupied and invariably creates a double bond between two carbon atoms. An unsaturated fat is one that has at least one double bond between two of the carbons in the chain. If there is one and only one double bond in the fat molecule, it is called a monounsaturated fat. If a fatty acid has two or more sites that have double bonds, it is called polyunsaturated fat.

THE BASIC TYPES OF DIETARY FAT

Saturated Fat

This is the natural fat found in fatty substances, which are solid at room temperature. Saturated fat is most often found in lard, butter and other animal fats, as well as in tropical oils such as coconut and palm oil. The saturated fats are worse than polyunsaturated and monounsaturated fats because they tend to raise cholesterol more than the others. Saturated fat raises total cholesterol and the bad LDL cholesterol. It also raises the HDL, the good cholesterol, but not enough to offset the significant rise it causes in bad cholesterol.

Hydrogenated, or Trans Fat

This is a term for a fat that is artificially saturated with hydrogen. They do this to make oils solid at room temperature. Basically, the manufacturers take a fat that is high in polyunsaturated fats and bubble hydrogen through it. The hydrogen saturates the fat and turns the double bonds into single bonds. As a result, you are left with a fat that is much like any saturated fat. Because of the artificial way the double bonds are formed, hydrogenated fats are often called trans fats.

Trans fats are associated with a higher risk of coronary heart disease than even saturated fat. Trans fats cause a decrease in HDL, or good cholesterol, as well as an increase in bad cholesterol. Studies have shown that heart disease rates are higher in people who consume more trans fatty acids.

Monounsaturated Fat

Fatty substances containing this type of fat tend to be liquid at room temperature. This is the type of fat that appears to be easiest on your heart and on your body in general, for that matter. You can find it in large amounts in olive oil, canola oil, and macadamia nut oil. Of all the various fats, monounsaturated fat tends to raise cholesterol the least. Be aware that it is possible that the low rates of heart disease associated with this oil may have been due in part to the antioxidants found in the extra virgin olive oil. Extra virgin olive oil is actually unfiltered olive juice, so much of the nutrients from the olive itself is mixed in with the oil.

Polyunsaturated Fats

Fatty substances containing this type of fat also tend to be liquid at room temperature. These are fats that have two or more double bonds in them. Foods that are high in this type of fat include vegetable oils such as corn oil, safflower oil, peanut oil, and other vegetable-based oils. As noted above, this is also the category of fat that includes the essential fatty acids, linoleic acid, and linolenic acid. Polyunsaturated fats are those that raise cholesterol very little and will cause a decrease in cholesterol if they are used in place of saturated fat.

Polyunsaturated fats are further categorized based on the location of the last double bond called the omega (the last letter in the Greek alphabet) double bond. A number is assigned to it depending on how far away it is from the tail end of the fatty acid. For example, an Omega 6 fatty acid has its last double bond six carbons away from the tail end of the fatty acid. Linoleic acid is an Omega 6 fatty acid and alpha linolenic acid is an Omega 3 fatty acid. When referring to linolenic acid, I am referring to alpha linolenic acid. This should not be confused with gamma linolenic acid, a similar but nonessential Omega 6 fatty acid.

The Omega 3 Fatty Acids—The Healthy Polyunsaturated Fat

Omega 3 fatty acids are polyunsaturated fatty acids found in large amounts in cold water fish, like salmon and mackerel. Its fatty acids have gotten a good reputation because of their association with low rates of heart disease, even among people who have a fairly high fat diet, such as the Eskimos of Greenland. The polyunsaturated oils that make up Omega 3 fat have the tongue-twisting names of docosahexaenoic acid (DHA) and eicosapentaenoic acid (EPA).

Probably the most important effect of Omega 3 fatty acids in the prevention of heart disease is that it limits the ability of platelets to form clots in the blood. In other words, like aspirin, it thins the blood. This helps to prevent heart attacks by preventing a clot from forming in an artery that is narrowed by cholesterol plaque, the final event that ultimately causes a heart attack. It also helps to reduce triglyceride levels. Omega 3 fatty acids can also help to reduce inflammation.

In general, I don't recommend taking fish oils because they add concentrated calories, there is a possible increase in the risk of a cerebral hemmorhage, and there are better ways to prevent heart disease, such as reducing your intake of saturated fat and increasing good carbohydrates. In addition, the cholesterol in fish can contribute to heart disease, although clearly, if you replace beef with fish you are better off. However, if you are at risk for heart disease and if you don't have a weight problem, then it is reasonable to eat a small amount of fish for Omega 3 fatty acids just as you might take aspirin. Make sure you consult your doctor so you don't thin your blood too much.

Alpha linolenic acid, an Omega 3 fatty acid from plants, is also considered by many to be a healthy fatty acid for a number of reasons. It has been shown to reduce LDL cholesterol slightly; however, it does not have the same triglyceride lowering or blood thinning effects of its fish-oil cousins. Any effect it may have is probably due to the fact that some of the linolenic acid is converted metabolically after it is ingested to EPA, the same fatty acid found in fish oil. There are claims that linolenic acid can help with a number of other health problems, such as inflammatory disease and blood sugar control, because of its effect on eicosanoids—a class of microhormones. There is also emerging evidence that linolenic acid may be useful in the prevention of headaches and even certain cancers.

Good sources of alpha linolenic acid are flaxseeds, soy beans, walnuts, and pumpkin seeds. They are also found in dark leafy greens. If you use flaxseed oil (linseed oil), keep in mind that it must be kept refrigerated, should never be heated, and should be used while fresh. Again, remember that these oils are still 9 calories per gram and can work against your efforts to lose weight.

THE CHOLESTEROL YOU EAT ALSO CONTRIBUTES TO YOUR CHOLESTEROL LEVEL

Cholesterol is found only in animal products. This is a very simple but not well-known fact. There is no plant with any appreciable cholesterol in it. (There are plant sterols that have cholesterol in their metabolic path, but the amount is insignificant.) Compared to saturated fat and trans fats, the cholesterol in your diet has less of an effect on cholesterol levels. Although the effect is actually less than saturated fats, make no mistake about it: Dietary cholesterol does indeed raise blood cholesterol levels, so it is a good idea to avoid animal products as much as possible.

What Is Cholesterol?

Cholesterol is a waxy substance that is not dissolvable in water. Biochemically, it is the nucleus of bile, steroid hormones, and vitamin D. It comes from the liver and is used in the digestive process to help in the digestion of fats. Cholesterol is important in providing the membrane fluidity of all human cells, and is an essential part of all animal cell membranes. Every animal, including humans, needs cholesterol to survive, but no animal needs to eat it to obtain it. Your body makes all the cholesterol it needs in your liver.

Good Cholesterol and Bad Cholesterol

Because cholesterol is not soluble in water it circulates in the bloodstream in little packets of substances that do mix with water called lipoproteins. There are different types of lipoproteins in the bloodstream that carry cholesterol and fats. Some of them are good because they carry cholesterol out of the plaques and make them smaller. Some of them are bad because they carry cholesterol into the plaques and make them worse. The good cholesterol is known as HDL, or high-density lipoprotein cholesterol. Because these particles carry cholesterol *away* from the plaque and the arteries, they are considered good cholesterol. A simple way to remember that HDL stands for good cholesterol is to think H for HEALTHY.

The bad cholesterol is known as LDL, or low-density lipoprotein cholesterol. LDL is larger than HDL because it is laden with cholesterol and fat to be deposited into the plaque in the arteries. The more LDL you have in your bloodstream, the more likely atherosclerosis will form in your arteries. This is why LDL cholesterol is considered bad cholesterol. A simple way to remember that LDL is the bad cholesterol is to remember the first "L" stands for LOUSY.

What Are Triglycerides?

A complete cholesterol checkup will include a measure of blood fats called triglycerides. They are so named because they are made up of three (tri) fatty acids attached to a glycerol (glyceride) backbone. Triglycerides are the forms in which most fats are stored and transported in the body. Generally, they are transported in lipoprotein particles in the same way as cholesterol. High levels of triglycerides in the blood are widely considered a risk factor for heart disease. In other words, while cholesterol, HDL, and LDL are the main players in predicting heart disease risk, high triglycerides also appear to be a factor.

As I described in Chapter 3, high blood insulin levels have been correlated with higher rates of coronary artery disease. High insulin levels also stimulate high blood triglyceride levels. It is not clear whether triglycerides are a direct risk factor for coronary disease or an indirect one—an innocent bystander alongside the real bad actors, such as high LDL levels, low HDL levels, or high insulin levels. In any case, it is better to have a normal triglyceride level than to have a high triglyceride level.

FATS AND THE GOOD CARBOHYDRATE PLAN

In general, the Good Carbohydrate Plan encourages a diet that is very low in fat and cholesterol. The reason for this is simple. Countries that have the lowest risk of the diseases that plague America are the countries that have diets that are lowest in fat and cholesterol. If you want to know more about the Good Carbohydrate Plan's recommendations for reducing your cholesterol and risk of heart disease, see Chapter 13. It's important to know that it is not just cholesterol or coronary heart disease that is of concern. The Good Carbohydrate Plan minimizes fat intake for most people to reduce the risk of other diseases as well. Good Carbohydrates are naturally low in fat and have no cholesterol. Low fat diets are associated with lower risk of certain cancers. In addition, low fat diets are also associated with lower rates of obesity and diabetes. Finally, it is important to remember that a low fat diet is likely to minimize insulin resistance so that you are better able to handle any carbohydrates that you may consume.

CHAPTER 16

Supplements for Health, Blood Sugar and Cholesterol Control

The best source of any nutrient, such as vitamins, minerals, and fiber, is whole food. As for weight control, blood sugar control, and cholesterol control, your diet is more important than any herb. But if you cannot maintain a good diet, are unsure if you are getting adequate amounts of essential nutrients, or if after your best efforts your weight, blood sugar and/or cholesterol is not under adequate control, supplements and herbs may be helpful.

The health benefits of many of the herbs and supplements are just beginning to emerge in the literature. Herbs and supplements are generally gentle and have minimal side effects when taken properly. Although they have marginally documented value, supplements are worth trying if you are having difficulty with blood sugar and/or cholesterol control. Please note: For safety, it is important to consult your physician before beginning any supplements.

FIBER SUPPLEMENTS

Dietary fiber is probably the supplement that is the best documented for control of insulin and blood sugar. (See Chapter 4 for a detailed discussion.) In general, dietary fiber supplements are useful in reducing blood sugar levels, as well as improving insulin sensitivity and controlling cholesterol. Whether dietary fiber as a supplement can induce weight loss is controversial.

Researchers at the Cleveland Clinic also found that fiber supplements can achieve a significant reduction in cholesterol and risk of coronary heart disease. In a double-blind study, a fiber supplement containing guar gum, locust bean gum, pectin, oat fiber, acacia fiber and barley fiber—in other words, a supplement high in soluble fiber—was tested against a placebo. The researchers found that after two months on a fiber supplement, participants' LDL cholesterol was nearly 10 percent lower than the LDL of those on a placebo.

Taking fiber supplements can be useful if you know you won't get adequate fiber from your diet. If you are considering taking fiber supplements, just be aware that the most commonly studied fiber supplements include oat bran fiber, psyllium fibers, and guar gum. Both oat bran fiber and guar gum were demonstrated to reduce insulin resistance and improve blood sugar control, while psyllium fiber supplementation produced mixed results. The dosages of guar gum used in the studies showing an improvement in insulin function ranged from 4 grams, twice a day to 10 grams, three times a day. Doses of guar gum higher than 10 grams per day should only be taken with physician supervision as there is a rare possibility of obstruction with very high doses of soluble fiber supplements.

VITAMINS

Biotin

Biotin, a member of the vitamin B family, has been shown to improve blood sugar levels and to decrease insulin resistance in experimental models of Type II diabetes. Although there aren't enough studies to be definitive about the use of Biotin in the treatment of diabetes, it is fairly gentle and is worth trying for specific cases on a trial basis. The dosages that are used in these studies ranged from 9 mg to 16 mg of Biotin per day. If you choose to try Biotin, I recommend that the source be one that includes other B vitamins, such as in a vitamin B complex.

Vitamin E

Vitamin E may be useful in increasing blood sugar control by improving the effectiveness of insulin. Clinical studies on the use of vitamin E to improve insulin sensitivity have shown conflicting results. Double blind studies showed that vitamin E supplementation is associated with improved glucose tolerance in people with Type II diabetes, but there have also been studies that show that vitamin E makes blood sugar control worse. Thus, vitamin E should be taken with caution, and with a view to individualizing its use. The dosage used in these studies was 600 mg per day. There are other potential benefits with vitamin E, such as the reduction in heart disease risk. The best source of vitamin E is whole grains.

Niacin

Large doses of niacin, or vitamin B3, should be avoided by anyone with glucose intolerance or diabetes. It has the potential to make blood sugar levels more difficult to control. Therapeutic amounts of niacin are sometimes recommended for cholesterol control. Good research has established that in some people, one to two grams of niacin per day will reduce cholesterol levels. However, niacin supplementation must be done under the supervision of a physician as it has a number of potential side effects. Flushing is the most common symptom, but this tends to lessen as time goes on. A more serious side effect is liver damage. Therapeutic amounts of niacin should be regarded as a medication that requires periodic blood testing for liver enzymes to monitor liver injury. Again, supplementation with niacin should only be done under the supervision of a physician.

Vitamin B12

Vitamin B12, or cyanocobalamin, is a vitamin that is required for the production of blood cells and for the development and maintenance of nerve tissue. This vitamin is produced by bacteria and animals accumulate it in their tissues from bacteria. Vegetables do not accumulate B12 and while there may be some B12 in fermented foods such as sauerkraut and miso (fermented soybeans), and sea vegetables, they are not reliable sources of B12.

Despite the requirement for B12, dietary deficiency of this vitamin is rare, even among vegetarians. Part of the reason for this is that the human body requires extremely small amounts of this vitamin. The RDA for B12 is 2 mcg (millionths of a gram) for adults. It is estimated that most people have a two to three years' supply of it in their bodies if they have not been strict vegetarians (vegan). For adults who are strictly vegan, if there are no symptoms such as fatigue or neurological problems or low blood count, an occasional B12 supplement may be prudent either in the form of a pill or fortified cereal. If there is any question, you can ask your physician for a B12 blood test to check the status of your B12 level.

Infants raised as vegans are at risk because they do not have any reserve B12 in their bodies and because B12 is crucial to neurological development at this stage. Thus, for infants, it is essential to check with a doctor to be sure that they are receiving adequate B12 through diet, infant formula, fortified cereal and/or supplements.

MINERALS

Calcium

I always encourage my clients to eat plenty of non-dairy high calcium foods such as greens and sea vegetables in order to obtain enough calcium. If this is not possible, then I recommend a calcium supplement. The most readily absorbed form of calcium is calcium citrate. Calcium carbonate is also fairly good. A supplement of 500 mg per day in order to cover shortfalls in calcium intake is reasonable.

Magnesium

Individuals with diabetes may have low magnesium levels, suggesting that magnesium is important in blood sugar control. However, magnesium supplementation produces mixed results in the control of Type II diabetes. There is evidence that magnesium supplementation helps to increase insulin production in some studies, but not in others. In short, while magnesium supplementation in people with diabetes may reverse the magnesium deficiency, the effect on blood sugar and insulin resistance is uncertain.

Chromium

Chromium is a mineral that is important in glucose metabolism. Some evidence indicates that chromium deficiency can contribute to insulin resistance and glucose intolerance. A well-known study examined the relationship between chromium picolinate and obesity. Two hundred micrograms of chromium picolinate was demonstrated to induce a small amount of weight loss in one study. Other studies have not shown similar results. In terms of blood sugar control, results are also conflicting. One placebo-controlled study involved 180 men and women who were randomly assigned to a placebo, 100 mcg of chromium, or 500 mcg of chromium twice daily. The results indicated that fasting glucose and insulin levels decreased significantly during the four months of the study in the group receiving the chromium. Other studies, however, showed no such improvement in a similar, double blind, placebo-controlled study. This is another supplement that might be very individual, and is probably best determined on a trial basis. The dosage used was about 200 mcg per day.

Vanadium

Vanadium is a trace mineral that is also used in blood sugar regulation. Some experts believe that poor blood sugar control is a result of vanadium deficiency. A number of studies suggest that for those with Type II diabetes, vanadium in the form of vanadyl sulfate helps to improve insulin sensitivity and blood sugar control. The amount used in these studies was 100 mg of vanadyl sulfate per day. There is some concern about the long-term safety of using vanadium. Vanadium is a pro-oxidant and can lead to irritation of mucosal lining such as in the eyes, nose, and throat. For this reason vanadium should be used with caution and under your doctor's guidance.

Alpha Lipoic Acid

Alpha lipoic acid is a powerful natural antioxidant that has improved insulin sensitivity in animal studies. Alpha lipoic acid has been shown to increase insulin sensitivity in some individuals with diabetes at doses of 600 mg per day.

HERBAL REMEDIES

Asian Ginseng

Asian Ginseng is an ancient, traditional, Chinese remedy for diabetes. It increases the release of insulin from the pancreas and possibly enhances insulin receptors. In a study published on diabetes care in 1995, a double blind study demonstrated that 200 mg of ginseng extract per day reduced blood sugar level significantly in patients with Type II diabetes.

Milk Thistle

Milk thistle, or *Silybum marianum,* has shown some value in specific situations for those with diabetes and alcoholic liver disease. In one study, 30 patients who were given 600 mg of *Silybum marianum* daily demonstrated a significant decrease in fasting blood sugar and fasting insulin levels after four months of therapy. The use of milk thistle on those without liver disease, but with diabetes, has not been studied.

HERBAL SUGAR SUBSTITUTE

Stevia

Stevia rebaudiana is one of the best-kept secrets of the herbal world. It is a Paraguayan herb that is also known as sweet leaf. It is an excellent substitute for sugar in sweetening beverages and food. Stevia has been used for centuries in Paraguay as a sweetener. In the United States it cannot be sold as a food product or a sugar substitute because it has not passed FDA regulations. It can, however, be sold as an herb because of FDA laws that allow for the sale of herbs that have traditionally been used in other countries, even though it has not gone through the rigorous FDA testing process.

Stevia can be found in the herbal section of health food stores, herb shops, and herb and vitamin shops. It is typically found in three forms: powdered, liquid drops, and tea. Be very careful when using this as a sugar substitute. It is 200 to 300 times sweeter than sugar! A minute amount is required for sweetening. Many natural health advocates prefer stevia to artificial sweeteners because it is not an artificially produced chemical, but rather a natural herb. While stevia is not known to improve insulin resistance or blood sugar control, it is very useful in reducing the need for using refined sugar of any kind.

KEEP SUPPLEMENTATION IN PERSPECTIVE

These are some of the supplements that are known to be useful in blood sugar and cholesterol control, and improving insulin resistance. Always remember that these supplements are just that, and they should be supplemental to a good diet and lifestyle. It is very important to first try a whole healthy lifestyle approach, which should include a good carbohydrate diet, exercise, a positive mental attitude, and a positive spiritual attitude. If you can adopt all of these lifestyle practices to optimize your health, supplements are ultimately not necessary. Always look at supplements as your second-line approach to improving your health, and put your best effort into improving your diet and lifestyle as your first-line approach to optimal health.

Epilogue

While this book is about one important aspect of health, I want to emphasize that total health is much more than just diet, exercise and supplements. Long ago, before I started medical school, I began studying ancient systems of health and healing. I learned the principles of various ancient cultural medical practices such as Oriental medicine. What I found was that these principles have withstood the test of time and are found in the traditional wisdom of ancient cultures around the world. I learned that everything is connected, and when we violate the laws of nature, it comes back to us. The Good Carbohydrate Plan is simply taking these lessons and applying them to modern science. Not only are these simple lessons worth learning but it is essential that we put them into practice if we are to truly do the best we can to optimize our health.

I wish you the best of health, and may God bless you and your family.

Me ke aloha pumehana (warmest aloha),

Terry Shintani, M.D., J.D., M.P.H.

APPENDIX A

The Carbohydrate Quotient

EXPLANATION OF THE CARBOHYDRATE QUOTIENT

The Carbohydrate Quotient is a table that helps to predict the impact of a food on blood sugar and insulin. It is based on two tables, the Glycemic Index, which measures the blood sugar impact and the calorie density of a food. Let me describe how I calculate the Carbohydrate Quotient. I've already described the basics of the Glycemic Index in Chapter 6, p. 77.

THE GLYCEMIC INDEX

To summarize, the Glycemic Index number is a number assigned to a food based on how high blood sugar levels rise as a result of the food compared to the blood sugar rise of white bread. Fifty grams of carbohydrate is used as the standard quantity tested. The blood sugar rise in response to white bread is used as a standard and is assigned the number 100. The blood sugar rise in response to 50 grams of carbohydrate from the test food is then measured and compared to that of white bread. A Glycemic Index number is assigned to that food based on the percent the blood sugar rises compared to the blood sugar rise induced by white bread. If the rise in blood sugar is 72 percent as high, the Glycemic Index number is 72. If it is 109 percent as high, the Glycemic Index number is 109. The Glycemic Index is useful in comparing apples with apples—or even comparing apples with oranges because they are similar types of foods.

DON'T USE THE GLYCEMIC INDEX MECHANICALLY

If you use the Glycemic Index to compare foods that are very different in type, you might mistakenly come to the conclusion that pumpkins are bad for you (with a Glycemic Index of 107). The reality is that this is one of the healthiest foods you can eat.

You might even conclude that a Snickers® candy bar, with a Glycemic Index of 59, is better for you than pumpkin, with a Glycemic Index of 107. The problem in using the Glycemic Index to evaluate these foods is that you are comparing foods that are very different in form. One is a highly refined, almost completely artificial food and the other, a whole natural food. If you were in an experimental situation, the Glycemic Index would give you an accurate measure of the comparative effect of 50 grams of carbohydrate from different sources.

On the other hand, this scenario is not very accurate in predicting the real life effect of foods because people eat very different amounts of carbohydrates, depending on the source. For instance, to get 50 grams of carbohydrates from pumpkin, you would have to eat 1.8 pounds of it. However, you'd only have to eat three ounces of a candy bar to obtain 50 grams of carbohydrate. In addition, the Glycemic Index fails to point out the fat content of the candy bar (43 percent of calories with 13 grams of fat per bar). It also fails to point out that the candy bar raises insulin 22 percent higher than white bread even though its blood sugar increase is 41 percent less.

THREE LIMITATIONS OF THE GLYCEMIC INDEX

How does the Glycemic Index make some foods that are good for you appear bad? There are three main limitations with the Glycemic Index in using it to make food choices. One of the limitations of the Glycemic Index is that it doesn't take into account the bulk effect of a food, or the calorie density. As a result, it may overestimate or underestimate how much a food will affect blood sugar in real life.

Remember that it is the Glycemic Load (Glycemic Index value times amount of food) that is more important than just the Glycemic Index of a food.

Glycemic Index Doesn't Measure Insulin

A second limitation of the Glycemic Index is that it doesn't measure how a food affects insulin. Remember that the Glycemic Index measures blood sugar and not insulin. When foods are measured for their effects on blood insulin, as described in the insulin response, you will see that whole foods such as brown rice and other whole grains raise insulin less than indicated by the Glycemic Index. Processed foods, such as candy, raise insulin much more than indicated by the Glycemic Index. In addition, protein raises insulin levels substantially, but does not raise blood sugar very much. As a result, from the perspective of the impact on insulin, the Glycemic Index misleadingly favors high protein foods, such as meat and yogurt, and misleadingly makes high carbohydrate whole foods, such as whole grains and pasta, look bad.

In the following graph comparing the insulin response and Glycemic Index of selected types of foods, you can see that the Glycemic Index doesn't always predict insulin response. Notice how it overestimates the insulin response of whole grains and underestimates its response for refined food such as candy.

GLYCEMIC INDEX VS. INSULIN RESPONSE

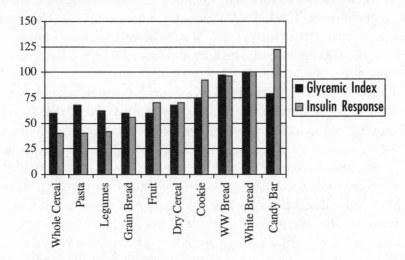

Data from: Noriega, E., *Diabetes Nutr Metab* (Feb 2000) 13(1):13-19; Holt, S.H.A., *Am J Clin Nutr* (1997) 66:1264-76; and Crapo, R.D., *Diabetes* (1977) 26:1179.

The Glycemic Index Only Compares Carbohydrates

A third limitation of the Glycemic Index is that it only tests carbohydrates. It is based on 50 grams of carbohydrate from whatever food source is being tested. There are other aspects of a food that are very important besides its effect on blood sugar. Probably the most important of these is fat. Fat actually slows the absorption of sugar. However, we know that eating too much fat is not good for us; it has a high number of calories and also decreases our sensitivity to insulin. Evaluating a fatty food's healthfulness using the Glycemic Index may be very misleading. For example, chocolate has a Glycemic Index of 70 while whole corn has a Glycemic Index of 79. This makes chocolate appear to be a healthier choice than corn, but we know there is more sugar and fat in chocolate and it has very little nutritionally redeeming value.

This is why the 5 C's are a better way to make your food choices. If you want to use a specific number for foods, then use the Carbohydrate Quotient, which, as I described, takes into account multiple aspects of food.

The Carbohydrate Quotient Is a Better Measure of Good Carbohydrates

If you want a specific number to find specific foods that are good carbohydrates, the Carbohydrate Quotient is a better measure than the Glycemic Index. The Carbohydrate Quotient describes the likely effect of how much a particular food will raise blood sugar over time. This is called the Glycemic Load. The Carbohydrate Quotient is based on three other tables, the insulin response, the Glycemic Index, and the Mass Index of food. The higher the Carbohydrate Quotient, the higher your blood sugar and insulin is likely to rise in response to that food. The Carbohydrate Quotient is essentially an adjusted Glycemic Index table that incorporates the benefit of the information from all three indexes.

Because the Carbohydrate Quotient factors in the caloric density, or bulkiness of foods, it is a better predictor of how much carbohydrate you will eat from a particular food. As I described before, you are much less likely to eat a whole bunch of carrots than you are to drink one and a third cans of soda, even though both of these provide 50 grams of carbohydrates. Since carrots are bulky and you tend to eat less of them, the actual effect of carrots on blood sugar is small.

As with the Glycemic Index, the Carbohydrate Quotient uses white bread as its standard, but it is adjusted downward if a food is very bulky compared to the number of calories in it. This bulk factor of a food is called the Mass Index. I created the Mass Index table because I believe that the concept of calorie density is very important but difficult to grasp because its units are calories per gram and most people aren't familiar with how much a gram actually is. So I converted this to pounds per daily calories and came up with the Mass Index of food. Thus, the Carbohydrate Quotient is a number that is based on the Glycemic Index but is adjusted by dividing the Glycemic Index by a factor determined by the Mass Index. This is why it is called a quotient.

By incorporating the Mass Index, the Carbohydrate Quotient provides a more accurate measure of how a food will affect your blood sugar in real life. When compared to insulin response studies, the Carbohydrate Quotient is a better predictor of insulin response than the Glycemic Index for most foods, and a better predictor of the overall healthfulness of foods in general. If you examine the table below, you will see that Carbohydrate Quotient numbers correlate more closely to insulin response than the Glycemic Index.

CARBOHYDRATE QUOTIENT VS. INSULIN RESPONSE

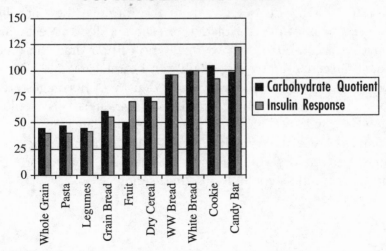

Data from: Noriega, E., *Diabetes Nutr Metab* (Feb 2000) 13(1):13-19; Holt, S.H.A., *Am J Clin Nutr* (1997) 66:1264-76; and Crapo, R.D., *Diabetes* (1977) 26:1179.

The Carbohydrate Quotient better represents the impact of a food because by factoring in the calorie density, it takes into consideration the three main weaknesses of the Glycemic Index. First, it adjusts for calorie density by giving foods that have a high calorie density an appropriately higher Carbohydrate Quotient number. Second, it accounts for other nutrients such as fat and protein by counting calories rather than just carbohydrates. Third, by factoring in the calorie density of a food, it winds up predicting its insulin response better.

You might ask, why don't we just use Insulin Index numbers. There are two reasons for this. First, there are still a very small number of foods on which insulin studies have been done so there isn't enough data to create a reliable, useful insulin index table. Second, because the insulin index is based on a set number of calories (240 calories per test food), it fails to account for calorie density.

How to Use the Carbohydrate Quotient Table

The Carbohydrate Quotient Table below are used to estimate the potential effect of a food on blood sugar and insulin. The higher the number, the greater the impact. Lower numbers are more desirable.

The table lists a limited number of foods because many foods have not been tested for Glycemic Index value. Because the Glycemic Index number is part of the formula, the Carbohydrate Quotient cannot be calculated on such a food. Meats are not included because they have virtually no carbohydrates in them and thus a Glycemic Index test would not be relevant. Also, beverages are not included because the calorie density of beverages are artificially low because of the great dilution by water. This would make the Carbohydrate Quotient numbers misleading. For dry cereal products, I use the straight Glycemic Index number because dry foods, such as dry cereals, have an artificially high calorie density and such numbers could also be misleading.

THE CARBOHYDRATE QUOTIENT TABLE

Food Item (White Bread = 100)	GI (bread)	Mass Index	CQ	Fiber (gm)/ 50 gm Carbs
All-Bran®, Kellogg's	60	1.4	62	22.5
Angel food cake	96	2.1	96	NA
Apple, dried	41	4.6	41	6
Apple, fresh	51	9.6	42	7
Apricot jam	79	2.0	96	NA
Apricots, canned, light syrup	91	8.7	77	3
Apricots, dried	44	4.6	44	6.5
Apricots, fresh	81	10.4	66	6
Bagel, white, frozen	103	2.0	105	1
Baked beans	69	5.1	44	10.5
Banana	76	6.0	70	3.5
Banana bread	67	1.7	75	NA
Barley, cracked	71	4.5	49	11.5
Barley, pearled	36	4.5	24	10
Beets	91	17.8	31	NA
Black beans	43	4.2	30	9
Black-eyed peas	60	5.1	39	21.5
Blueberry muffin	84	2.0	86	NA
Bran Buds®, Kellogg's	83	1.4	86	18
Bran Chex®, Nabisco	83	1.2	100	13.5
Bran Flakes®, Post	106	1.7	90	13
Bread stuffing	106	2.1	106	NA
Breadfruit	97	4.6	96	NA
Breads				
Bagel, white, frozen	103	2.0	105	1
Bread stuffing	106	2.1	106	NA
Bulgur (cracked wheat) bread	83	2.2	81	5.5
Corn tortilla	54	2.5	50	4
Croissant	96	1.4	117	NA
French baguette	136	2.0	139	2
Hamburger bun	87	1.9	92	2.5
Kaiser roll	104	1.9	110	3
Melba Toast, Old London®	100	1.4	122	5.5
Mixed grain bread	64	1.9	68	4

THE CARBOHYDRATE QUOTIENT TABLE *(continued)*

Food Item (White Bread = 100)	GI (bread)	Mass Index	CQ	Fiber (gm)/ 50 gm Carbs
Breads (continued)				
Oat bran bread	67	1.8	73	4
Pita bread, white	81	2.3	78	0.5
Pumpernickel bread, whole grain	73	2.2	71	7
Rye bread	93	2.4	87	6.5
Rye bread, American light	97	1.9	102	6.5
Rye bread, dark	109	2.2	106	4
Sourdough bread	74	2.1	74	2.5
Stone ground whole wheat bread	61	2.1	61	8
White bread	100	2.1	100	4
Whole wheat bread	99	2.2	96	7
Breakfast Cereals				
All-Bran®, Kellogg's	60	1.4	62	22.5
Bran Buds®, Kellogg's	83	1.4	86	18
Bran Chex®, Nabisco	83	1.2	100	13.5
Bran Flakes®, Post	106	1.7	90	13
Cheerios®, General Mills	106	1.3	118	5
Corn Bran®, Quaker	107	1.3	119	11.5
Corn Chex®, Nabisco	119	1.6	107	2
Corn Flakes®, Kellogg's	120	1.4	124	2
Cream of Wheat®, Instant, Nabisco	106	10.3	48	2
Cream of Wheat®, Nabisco	94	10.7	42	2
Golden Grahams®, General Mills	101	1.4	105	2
Grape-nuts®, Post	96	1.1	126	5.5
Grape-nuts Flakes®, Post	114	1.5	110	6
Life®, Quaker	94	1.4	98	6.5
Muesli, non-toasted	80	1.5	77	9.5
Muesli, toasted	61	1.5	59	9.5
Nutri-Grain®, Kellogg's	94	1.5	91	6
Oat Bran Cereal®, Quaker	71	1.5	69	9

THE CARBOHYDRATE QUOTIENT TABLE *(continued)*

Food Item (White Bread = 100)	GI (bread)	Mass Index	CQ	Fiber (gm)/ 50 gm Carbs
Breakfast Cereals (continued)				
Oat bran, raw	79	1.7	67	12
Oatmeal (porridge), old-fashioned	84	8.9	41	7.5
Oatmeal, one minute instant	94	8.9	46	7.5
Puffed Wheat®, Quaker	106	1.5	102	5
Rice Chex®, General Mills	127	1.8	102	1
Rice Krispies®, Kellogg's	117	1.4	121	0
Shredded Wheat®, Nabisco	99	1.5	95	6
Special K®, Kellogg's	77	1.4	80	0
Team Flakes®, Nabisco	117	1.4	121	0.5
Total®, General Mills	109	1.6	98	6.5
Wheat cereal	59	9.7	48	2
Wheat cereal, quick cooking	77	9.1	64	2
Broad beans	113	7.7	59	13
Buckwheat	77	6.0	46	5
Bulgur wheat	69	6.6	39	12.5
Bulgur (cracked wheat) bread	83	2.2	81	5.5
Butter beans	44	6.7	25	11.5
Cake				
Angel food cake	96	2.1	96	NA
Banana bread	67	1.7	75	NA
Pound cake	77	0.9	118	NA
Sponge cake	66	1.9	69	NA
Candy				
Chocolate candy	70	1.1	97	2.5
Jelly beans	114	2.3	109	0
Life Savers®	100	1.4	122	0
Mars Chocolate Almond Bar®, M&M Mars	97	1.2	129	1.5
M&M Chocolate Covered Peanuts®	47	1.1	65	3.5
Snickers®, M&M Mars	59	1.2	77	1.5
Twix®, Caramel, M&M Mars	63	1.1	87	2

THE CARBOHYDRATE QUOTIENT TABLE *(continued)*

Food Item (White Bread = 100)	GI (bread)	Mass Index	CQ	Fiber (gm)/ 50 gm Carbs
Cantaloupe	93	15.5	68	5
Carrots	101	12.7	41	16
Cheerios®, General Mills	106	1.3	118	5
Cherries	31	7.6	27	5
Chocolate candy	70	1.1	97	2.5
Cookies				
Oatmeal cookie	79	1.2	104	3
Shortbread cookie	91	1.1	126	0
Social Tea Biscuits®, Nabisco	79	1.4	96	NA
Vanilla wafers	110	1.2	146	0
Corn	79	5.5	49	7.5
Corn Bran®, Quaker	107	1.3	119	11.5
Corn Chex®, Nabisco	119	1.6	107	2
Corn chips	104	1.0	151	3.5
Corn Flakes®, Kellogg's	120	1.4	124	2
Corn tortilla	54	2.5	50	4
Cornmeal	97	1.5	115	2
Couscous	93	4.9	61	2
Crackers				
Graham crackers	106	1.4	129	2.5
Rice cakes	117	4.4	81	2
Rye crispbread, high fiber	93	1.4	114	13
Soda crackers	103	1.3	131	0
Stoned wheat thins	96	1.5	113	5
Wheat Crackers®, Breton	96	1.1	132	0
Cream of Wheat®, Instant, Nabisco	106	10.3	48	2
Cream of Wheat®, Nabisco	94	10.7	42	2
Croissant	96	1.4	117	NA
Dates	147	4.0	151	3.5
Doughnut, cake-type	109	1.3	138	1.5
Fava beans	113	6.9	62	NA
Fettucini, egg-enriched	46	3.9	34	2.5
Fish sticks	54	2.0	56	2.5

THE CARBOHYDRATE QUOTIENT TABLE (continued)

Food Item (White Bread = 100)	GI (bread)	Mass Index	CQ	Fiber (gm)/ 50 gm Carbs
French baguette	136	2.0	139	2
French fries	33	1.4	40	0
Fructose	33	1.4	41	0
Fruit and Fruit Products				
Apple				
Apple, dried	41	4.6	41	6
Apple, fresh	51	9.6	42	7
Apricots				
Apricot jam	79	2.0	96	NA
Apricots, canned, light syrup	91	8.7	77	3
Apricots, dried	44	4.6	44	6.5
Apricots, fresh	81	10.4	66	6
Banana	76	6.0	70	3.5
Breadfruit	97	4.6	96	NA
Cantaloupe	93	15.5	68	5
Cherries	31	7.6	27	5
Dates	147	4.0	151	3.5
Fruit cocktail, canned, light syrup	79	17.2	56	3.5
Grapefruit	36	18.3	25	3.5
Grapes	61	7.7	53	NA
Kiwi	74	9.1	62	11.5
Mango	79	8.3	67	3
Orange	61	11.6	48	10
Papaya	83	14.3	62	4.5
Peach				
Peach, fresh	40	12.8	31	7
Peaches, canned, heavy syrup	83	7.4	73	2
Peaches, canned, light syrup	74	10.2	60	3
Peaches, canned, natural juice	43	12.5	33	2
Pear				
Pear, fresh	51	9.3	43	8.5
Pears, canned in pear juice, Bartlett	63	11.1	50	3.5

THE CARBOHYDRATE QUOTIENT TABLE *(continued)*

Food Item (White Bread = 100)	GI (bread)	Mass Index	CQ	Fiber (gm)/ 50 gm Carbs
Fruit and Fruit Products (continued)				
Pineapple, fresh	94	11.1	75	5
Plum	34	10.1	28	NA
Raisins	91	3.6	96	3.5
Strawberry jam	73	2.0	89	NA
Watermelon	103	17.6	73	2.5
Fruit cocktail, canned, light syrup	79	17.2	56	3.5
Garbanzo beans, boiled (chickpeas)	47	5.2	30	6.5
Garbanzo beans, canned (chickpeas)	60	5.6	37	19.5
Glucose	139	1.4	171	0
Golden Grahams®, General Mills	101	1.4	105	2
Graham crackers	106	1.4	129	2.5
Grains				
Barley				
Barley, cracked	71	4.5	49	11.5
Barley, pearled	36	4.5	24	10
Buckwheat	77	6.0	46	5
Corn				
Corn	79	5.5	49	7.5
Corn chips	104	1.0	151	3.5
Corn tortilla	54	2.5	50	4
Cornmeal	97	1.5	115	2
Popcorn	79	1.3	100	12
Taco shells, corn	97	1.3	123	7
Millet	101	4.6	69	6.5
Oats				
Oat bran, raw	79	1.7	87	12
Oatmeal (porridge), old-fashioned	84	8.9	41	7.5
Oatmeal, one minute instant	94	8.9	46	7.5

THE CARBOHYDRATE QUOTIENT TABLE *(continued)*

Food Item (White Bread = 100)	GI (bread)	Mass Index	CQ	Fiber (gm)/ 50 gm Carbs
Rice				
Rice, brown	79	4.9	51	3.5
Rice, instant	130	5.6	80	1
Rice, specialty (mixed with wild)	79	5.4	49	1.5
Rice, white (high amylose)	80	5.0	52	1.5
Rice, white, Calrose (low amylose)	119	4.6	80	NA
Wheat				
Bulgur wheat	69	6.6	39	12.5
Wheat cereal	59	9.7	27	2
Wheat cereal, quick cooking	77	9.1	37	2
Grapefruit	36	18.3	25	3.5
Grape-nuts®, Post	96	1.1	126	5.5
Grape-nuts Flakes®, Post	114	1.5	110	6
Grapes	61	7.7	53	NA
Hamburger bun	87	1.9	92	2.5
Honey	104	1.8	113	0
Instant noodles, Mr. Noodle®	67	4.1	48	2.5
Jelly beans	114	2.3	109	0
Kaiser roll	104	1.9	110	3
Kidney beans, boiled	39	4.3	27	8
Kidney beans, canned	74	6.1	44	14.5
Kiwi	74	9.1	62	11.5
Lactose	66	1.4	81	0
Lentils, green and brown, boiled	41	4.7	28	10
Life Savers®	100	1.4	122	NA
Life®, Quaker	94	1.4	98	6.5
Legumes				
Baked beans	69	5.1	44	10.5
Black beans	43	4.2	30	9
Black-eyed peas	60	5.1	39	21.5

THE CARBOHYDRATE QUOTIENT TABLE *(continued)*

Food Item (White Bread = 100)	GI (bread)	Mass Index	CQ	Fiber (gm)/ 50 gm Carbs
Legumes (continued)				
Broad beans	113	7.7	59	13
Butter beans	44	6.7	25	11.5
Fava beans	113	6.9	62	NA
Garbanzo beans (chickpeas)				
Garbanzo beans, boiled (chickpeas)	47	5.2	30	6.5
Garbanzo beans, canned (chickpeas)	60	5.6	37	19.5
Kidney beans				
Kidney beans, boiled	39	4.3	27	8
Kidney beans, canned	74	6.1	44	14.5
Lentils, green and brown, boiled	41	4.7	28	10
Lima beans, baby, frozen	46	5.3	29	10
Navy (harcort) beans, boiled	54	3.9	40	7
Pinto beans				
Pinto beans, boiled	56	4.0	40	7.5
Pinto beans, canned	64	6.2	37	19.5
Soybeans	26	3.9	19	44.5
Split peas, yellow and green, boiled	46	4.7	31	20
Lima beans, baby, frozen	46	5.3	29	10
Linguini	70	3.9	51	2.5
M&M Chocolate Covered Peanuts®	47	1.1	65	3.5
Macaroni and cheese, boxed	91	3.6	70	1
Macaroni, boiled 5 minutes	64	3.9	47	3
Maltose	150	1.4	185	0
Mango	79	8.3	67	3
Mars Chocolate Almond Bar®, M&M Mars	97	1.2	129	1.5
Melba Toast, Old London®	100	1.4	122	5.5
Millet	101	4.6	69	6.5

THE CARBOHYDRATE QUOTIENT TABLE *(continued)*

Food Item (White Bread = 100)	GI (bread)	Mass Index	CQ	Fiber (gm)/ 50 gm Carbs
Mixed grain bread	64	1.9	68	4
Muesli, non-toasted	80	1.5	77	9.5
Muesli, toasted	61	1.5	59	9.5
Muffin, plain	89	1.8	96	NA
Muffins				
Blueberry muffin	84	2.0	86	NA
Muffin, plain	89	1.8	96	NA
Oat bran muffin	86	2.2	84	NA
Navy (harcort) beans, boiled	54	3.9	40	7
Nutri-Grain®, Kellogg's	94	1.5	91	6
Oat bran bread	67	1.8	73	4
Oat Bran Cereal®, Quaker	71	1.5	69	9
Oat bran muffin	86	2.2	84	NA
Oat bran, raw	79	1.7	67	12
Oatmeal cookie	79	1.2	104	3
Oatmeal (porridge), old-fashioned	84	8.9	41	7.5
Oatmeal, one minute instant	94	8.9	46	7.5
Orange	61	11.6	48	10
Papaya	83	14.3	62	4.5
Parsnips	139	6.8	77	7
Pasta				
Couscous	93	4.9	61	2
Fettucini, egg-enriched	46	3.9	34	2.5
Instant noodles, Mr. Noodle®	67	4.1	48	2.5
Linguini	70	3.9	51	2.5
Macaroni and cheese, boxed	91	3.6	70	1
Macaroni, boiled 5 minutes	64	3.9	47	3
Ravioli, Duram, meat-filled	56	4.4	38	2.5
Spaghetti				
Spaghetti, Duram	79	3.7	59	6.5
Spaghetti, white	59	3.7	44	2.5
Spaghetti, whole-wheat	53	4.4	37	5
Tortellini cheese pasta	71	3.3	57	3

THE CARBOHYDRATE QUOTIENT TABLE *(continued)*

Food Item (White Bread = 100)	GI (bread)	Mass Index	CQ	Fiber (gm)/ 50 gm Carbs
Pasta (continued)				
Vermicelli	50	3.0	42	2.5
Peach, fresh	40	12.8	31	7
Peaches, canned, heavy syrup	83	7.4	73	2
Peaches, canned, light syrup	74	10.2	60	3
Peaches, canned, natural juice	43	12.5	33	2
Peanuts	20	0.9	31	20
Pear, fresh	51	9.3	43	8.5
Pears, canned in pear juice, Bartlett	63	11.1	50	3.5
Peas	69	7.0	38	9
Pineapple, fresh	94	11.1	75	5
Pinto beans, boiled	56	4.0	40	7.5
Pinto beans, canned	64	6.2	37	19.5
Pita bread, white	81	2.3	78	0.5
Pizza, cheese	86	3.1	71	2.5
Plum	34	10.1	28	NA
Popcorn	79	1.3	100	12
Potato, baked	121	5.9	72	NA
Potato, boiled, mashed	104	6.2	61	3.5
Potato, canned	87	6.8	48	5
Potato chips	77	1.0	112	4.5
Potato, instant	119	7.0	65	3
Potato, new	89	6.8	49	NA
Potato, sweet	77	5.3	49	6
Potato, white, baked	86	5.9	51	NA
Potato, white, boiled	80	6.4	46	3.5
Potato, white, mashed	100	5.2	64	3.5
Potato, white, steamed	93	6.4	53	3.5
Pound cake	77	0.9	118	NA
Puffed Wheat®, Quaker	106	1.5	102	5
Pumpernickel bread, whole grain	73	2.2	71	7
Pumpkin	107	16.3	38	NA

THE CARBOHYDRATE QUOTIENT TABLE *(continued)*

Food Item (White Bread = 100)	GI (bread)	Mass Index	CQ	Fiber (gm)/ 50 gm Carbs
Raisins	91	3.6	96	3.5
Ravioli, Durum, meat-filled	56	4.4	38	2.5
Rice, brown	79	4.9	51	3.5
Rice cakes	117	4.4	81	2
Rice Chex®, General Mills	127	1.8	102	1
Rice, instant	130	5.6	80	1
Rice Krispies®, Kellogg's	117	1.4	121	0
Rice, specialty (mixed with wild)	79	5.4	49	1.5
Rice, white (high amylose)	80	5.0	52	1.5
Rice, white, Calrose (low amylose)	119	4.6	80	NA
Rutabaga	103	16.1	37	NA
Rye bread	93	2.4	87	6.5
Rye bread, American light	97	1.9	102	6.5
Rye bread, dark	109	2.2	106	4
Rye crispbread, high fiber	93	1.4	114	13
Sausages	40	1.7	44	NA
Shortbread cookie	91	1.1	126	0
Shredded Wheat®, Nabisco	99	1.5	95	6
Snack Foods				
Corn chips	104	1.0	151	3.5
Peanuts	20	0.9	31	20
Popcorn	79	1.3	100	12
Potato chips	77	1.0	112	4.5
Snickers®, M&M Mars	59	1.2	77	1.5
Social Tea Biscuits®, Nabisco	79	1.4	96	NA
Soda crackers	103	1.3	131	0
Sourdough bread	74	2.1	74	2.5
Soybeans	26	3.9	19	44.5
Spaghetti, Durum	79	3.7	59	6.5
Spaghetti, white	59	3.7	44	2.5
Spaghetti, whole-wheat	53	4.4	37	5
Special K®, Kellogg's	77	1.4	80	0

THE CARBOHYDRATE QUOTIENT TABLE *(continued)*

Food Item (White Bread = 100)	GI (bread)	Mass Index	CQ	Fiber (gm)/ 50 gm Carbs
Split peas, yellow and green, boiled	46	4.7	31	20
Sponge cake	66	1.9	69	NA
Stone ground whole wheat bread	61	2.1	61	8
Stoned wheat thins	96	1.5	113	5
Strawberry jam	73	2.0	89	NA
Sucrose (table sugar)	93	1.4	115	0
Sugars				
Fructose	33	1.4	41	0
Glucose	139	1.4	171	0
Honey	104	1.8	113	0
Lactose	66	1.4	81	0
Maltose	150	1.4	185	0
Sucrose (table sugar)	93	1.4	115	0
Taco shells, corn	97	1.3	123	7
Taro	77	5.1	50	NA
Team Flakes®, Nabisco	117	1.4	121	0.5
Tortellini cheese pasta	71	3.3	57	3
Tortilla, corn	84	3.0	71	4
Tortilla, flour	54	2.5	50	4
Total®, General Mills	109	1.6	98	6.5
Twix®, Caramel, M&M Mars	63	1.1	87	2
Vanilla wafers	110	1.2	146	0
Vegetables				
Corn	79	5.5	49	7.5
Peas	69	7.0	38	9
Pumpkin	107	16.3	38	NA
Vegetables, Root				
Beets	91	17.8	31	NA
Carrots	101	12.7	41	16
Parsnips	139	6.8	77	7

THE CARBOHYDRATE QUOTIENT TABLE *(continued)*

Food Item (White Bread = 100)	GI (bread)	Mass Index	CQ	Fiber (gm)/ 50 gm Carbs
Vegetables, Root (continued)				
Potato				
French fries	107	2.5	98	5
Potato, baked	121	5.9	72	NA
Potato, boiled, mashed	104	6.2	61	3.5
Potato, canned	87	9.2	42	5
Potato, instant	119	7.0	65	3
Potato, new	89	68	49	NA
Potato, sweet	77	5.3	49	6
Potato, white, baked	86	5.9	51	NA
Potato, white, boiled	80	6.4	46	3.5
Potato, white, mashed	100	5.2	64	3.5
Potato, white, steamed	93	6.4	53	3.5
Rutabaga	103	16.1	37	NA
Taro	77	5.1	50	NA
Yams	73	4.7	49	NA
Vermicelli	50	3.0	42	2.5
Waffles, Aunt Jemima®	109	2.8	94	2
Watermelon	103	17.6	73	2.5
Wheat cereal	59	9.7	27	2
Wheat cereal, quick cooking	77	9.1	37	2
Wheat chapati	39	3.2	31	7.5
Wheat Crackers®, Breton	96	1.1	132	0
White bread	100	2.1	100	4
Whole wheat bread	99	2.2	96	7
Yams	73	4.7	49	NA

Structure and Digestion of Carbohydrates

BASIC TYPES OF CARBOHYDRATES

Sugar molecules are the basic unit of all carbohydrates. In order for the body to use any carbohydrate, it must first be broken down into sugar. Carbohydrates are categorized into different types based on how many sugar molecules are in the carbohydrate and how the sugar molecules are linked together.

There are two main categories of carbohydrates. One category is *simple carbohydrates,* also known as "sugar." Sugars are typically one or two sugar molecules linked together. The other main category of carbohydrates is *complex carbohydrates,* which are long chains of sugar molecules linked together. Complex carbohydrates can be formed from dozens or hundreds of sugar molecules linked together in long, branching chains (see diagram). These long chains of complex carbohydrates are also commonly known as *starches.* Starches are found in large concentrations in grains, beans, and root vegetables such as potatoes, taro, and yams.

Most people are surprised to learn that fiber is another form of complex carbohydrate. Almost all fiber is made of nondigestible carbohydrates such as cellulose, pectin and gums. Fiber forms the structural part of plants and is an important substance that helps to control how fast sugar is absorbed. This is discussed in detail in Chapter 5, Fiber: The Other Good Carbohydrate.

CARBOHYDRATE FAMILY TREE

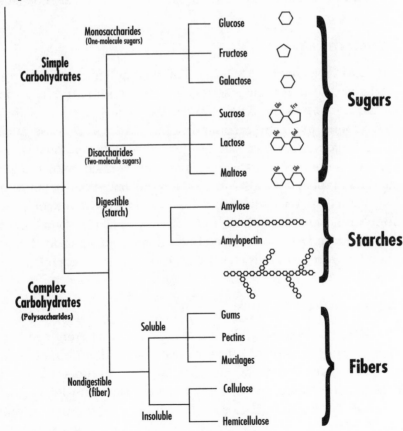

© Shintani 2000

Knowing the structure of carbohydrates helps you to understand why some sugars are absorbed so quickly and why it is important to know what type and form of carbohydrates you have in your diet.

Sugars

We think of sugar as the granulated white powder found in little packets on restaurant tables for spooning into coffee or in four-pound bags at grocery stores for cake baking and cookie making. But the type of sugar found in the supermarket is only one of several kinds of sugar. These sugars are divided into two main types. There are *monosaccharides,* those made up of a single-sugar molecule, and *disaccharides,* those made up of two-sugar molecules.

Monosaccarides

The monosaccharides that we eat include glucose, fructose, and galactose. Of these, glucose is the most common, both in food and in the body. It is the type of sugar that is at least one of the molecules found in all three common disaccharides. Glucose is also the basic building block of starches. Fructose, or fruit sugar, is another type of monosaccharide. Fruits typically contain both fructose and glucose. Fructose is also found in small amounts in some grains, such as corn. You won't find fructose in granulated or powdered form in most supermarkets, but you may find it in some health food stores. Galactose is an animal-based monosaccharide that is only found as part of the disaccharide lactose, or milk sugar.

Disaccharides

When two monosaccharides come together in different combinations, disaccharides are created. The most abundant disaccharide is sucrose, or table sugar. This is the kind that you find in the supermarket and that is used in most baking. It is a disaccharide that is a combination of glucose and fructose. Lactose is the kind of sugar found in milk. It is the only animal sugar and the only animal-based carbohydrate that we consume in any appreciable amount. It is formed by a combination of glucose and galactose. Malt sugar, or maltose, is formed by a combination of two glucose molecules. Maltose comes from grains and is found in sweeteners, such as barley malt.

Complex Carbohydrates

You'll often hear that it is good to eat your complex carbohydrates. Complex carbohydrates are called complex because they contain many sugar molecules—not just one or two. They are also called polysaccharides because they are large molecules made up of many (poly) sugar molecules (saccharides) linked together. They are linked together in long straight or branching chains in order to form a molecule of complex carbohydrate. There are two main types of complex carbohydrates—digestible and nondigestible.

Digestible Complex Carbohydrates

Digestible complex carbohydrates are also known as starches. They are found in plant-based foods, such as beans, grains, and root vegetables. Sometimes staple foods that are very high in complex carbohydrates are themselves called "starches," such as bread, rice, and potatoes. Refined complex carbohydrates can also be found in the supermarket, for example, as cornstarch. There are different types of digestible complex carbohydrates or starches, such as *amylose,* a straight-chained starch, and *amylopectin,* a branched-chain starch.

Nondigestible Complex Carbohydrates

There are also nondigestible carbohydrates, also known as dietary fiber. Dietary fiber makes up most of the nondigestible part of the plant. Dietary fiber is also called roughage, and is important in the normal functioning of the digestive tract. I discuss fiber in detail in Chapter 4.

Digestion and Absorption of Carbohydrates

The human body can only absorb carbohydrates one molecule at a time. Simple sugars are absorbed very quickly. Monosaccharides— single molecules of sugar—are absorbed directly through the walls of the digestive tract. No digestive enzymes are necessary for the body to absorb monosaccharides. Disaccharides—double molecules of sugar—must be divided into two single molecules of sugar before it can be absorbed. Because there is only one bond to break, disaccharides are almost immediately cut into two by digestive enzymes such as "amylase" (or "lactase," in the case of milk sugar), and absorbed as quickly as monosaccharides.

Complex carbohydrates are much larger than disaccharides, and as with disaccharides, they must be broken up and turned into sugar one molecule at a time before they can be absorbed. Thus, all digestible carbohydrates are absorbed as sugar whether they are simple sugars or complex carbohydrate starches. Once complex carbohydrates are broken down into sugars, they are absorbed as quickly as other sugars. Two types of enzymes work on these starches to break them down into sugar molecules. Salivary amylase, which is a digestive enzyme found in saliva, is one of them. It starts the process of digestion of carbohydrates in the mouth. Pancreatic amylase, produced by the pancreas and secreted into the intestines, is the other enzyme. This enzyme completes the digestion of carbohydrate in the small intestine.

These digestive enzymes cut off the sugar molecules one by one from the starch molecule. This enzyme works only at the ends of the starch molecule, and, therefore, takes a little more time to turn a complex carbohydrate into a digestible form. The fact that amylopectin has many branches, and therefore many "ends" where amylase can work, explains why it is absorbed more quickly than amylose, which is only a single straight chain and has only one "end."

Because complex carbohydrates cannot be absorbed until they are converted into sugar, some complex carbohydrates have the advantage of a slower absorption rate than some simple sugars. The sugar molecules that come from digested complex carbohydrates or starches, are available for absorption somewhat more slowly. For this reason, if the basic sugar molecules are the same in both, it is better to eat complex carbohydrates rather than simple carbohydrates.

Of course, it is not as simple as choosing complex carbohydrates over simple carbohydrates. The effect of carbohydrates on the human body is influenced by many factors. Sometimes, given the right conditions, complex carbohydrates have a blood sugar response curve that is actually steeper than that of simple carbohydrates. For example, sucrose, table sugar, causes slightly less of a rise in blood sugar than white bread, which is mostly highly refined complex carbohydrates. You can read more about how to find Good Carbohydrates in Chapter 6.

References

Chapter 1

Campbell, T. C. "The study on diet, nutrition and disease in the People's Republic of China." *Contemp Nutr* 14 (1989):6.

Chen, J., T. C. Campbell, J. Li, and R. Peto. *Diet, Life-Style, and Mortality In China: A Study of the Characteristics of 65 Chinese Counties.* Oxford, England: Oxford University Press, 1990.

Crews, D. E., and P. C. MacKeen. "Mortality related to cardiovascular disease and diabetes mellitus in a modernizing population." *Soc Sci Med* 16 (1982):175-81.

Garg, A., J. P. Bantle, R. R. Henry, et al. "Effects of varying carbohydrate content of diet in patients with non-insulin-dependent diabetes mellitus. *JAMA* 271(18) (1994):1421-8.

Gore, I., T. Nakashima, T. Imai, and P. D. White. "Coronary atherosclerosis and myocardial infarction in Kyushu, Japan, and Boston, Massachusetts." *Am J Cardiology* Sept (1962):400-6.

Hollenbeck, C. B., and A. M. Coulston. "Effects of dietary carbohydrate and fat intake on glucose and lipoprotein metabolism in individuals with diabetes mellitus." *Diabetes Care* 14(9) (1991):774-8.

Kagawa, Y. "Impact of westernization on the nutrition of Japanese: changes in physique, cancer, longevity and centenarians." *Preventive Medicine* 7 (1978):205-17.

Koike, G., O. Yokono, S. Iino, M. Adachi, et al. "Medical and nutritional surveys in the kingdom of Tonga; comparison of physiological and nutritional status of adult Tongans in urbanized and rural areas. *J Nutr Sci Vitaminol* 30 (1984):341-56.

Kumanyika, S. K. "Special issues regarding obesity in minority populations." *Ann Intern Med* 119(7 Pt 2) (1993):650-54.

Matsuoka, A., T. Yamaguchi, Y. Masuyama, et al. "Characteristics of dietary treatment of diabetes mellitus in Japan: comparison of dietary habits and diabetic pathology in Japanese and American diabetics." In S. Baba, Y. Goto, and I. Fukui, eds. *Diabetes Mellitus in Asia*. Amsterdam (*Excerpta Medica* (1976):265-69).

McGarvey, S. T. "Obesity in Samoans and a perspective on its etiology in Polynesians." *Am J Clin Nutr* 53 (1991):1586s-94s.

Nestle, M. "Animal v. plant foods in human diets and health: Is the historical record unequivocal?" *Proc Nutr Soc* 58(2) (1999):211-18.

Oiso, T. "Changing food patterns in Japan." *Nutrition in Health and Disease and International Development: Symposia From the XII International Congress of Nutrition*, Alan R Liss, Inc. (1981):527-38.

Prior, I., and A. M. Davidson. "The epidemiology of diabetes in Polynesians and Europeans in New Zealand and the Pacific." *New Zeal Med J* 65 (1966):375.

Shintani, T. T., S. Beckham, A. C. Brown, et al. "The Hawaii Diet: ad libitum high carbohydrate, low fat multi-cultural diet for the reduction of chronic disease risk factors: obesity, hypertension, hypercholesterolemia, and hyperglycemia." *Hawaii Med J* 60(3) (2001):69-73.

Shintani, T. T., S. K. Beckham, J. Tang, et al. "Waianae Diet Program: long-term follow-up." *Hawaii Medical J* 58 (1999):117-22.

Shintani, T. T., and C. K. Hughes. "Traditional diets of the Pacific and coronary heart disease." *Journal of Cardiovascular Risk* 1(1) (1994):16-20.

Shintani, T. T., C. K. Hughes, S. K. Beckham, and H. K. O'Connor. "Obesity and cardiovascular risk intervention through the *ad libitum* feeding of traditional Hawaiian diet." *Am J Clin Nutr* 53 (1991):1647S-51S.

Taylor, R. J., and P. Z. Zimmet. "Obesity and diabetes in Western Samoa." *Int J Obesity* 5 (1981):367-76.

Tsunehara, C. H., D. L. Loenetti, and W. Y. Fujimoto. "Diet of second-generation Japanese-American men with and without non-insulin-dependent diabetes." *Am J Clin Nutr* 52 (1990):731-38.

U. S. Department of Agriculture. *Agriculture Fact Book 2000*.

Whittemore, A. S., A. H. Wu-Williams, M. Lee, et al. "Diet, physical activity,

and colorectal cancer among Chinese in North America and China."
JNCI 82;11 (1990):915-26.

Wolever, T. M. S., et al. "Beneficial effects of low-glycemic index diet in
overweight NIDDM subjects." *Diabetes Care* 15 (1992):562-64.

Zimmet, P., M. Arblaster, and K. Thoma. "The effect of westernization on
native populations. Studies on a Micronesian community with a high
diabetes prevalence." *Aust NZ J Med* 8 (1978):141-46.

Chapter 2

Breazile, J. E., C. G. Beames, P. T. Cardielhac, et al. *Textbook of Veterinary
Physiology*. Philadelphia: Lea & Febiger, 1971.

Burkitt, D. P., and H. C. Trowell. *Refined Carbohydrate Foods and Disease:
Some Implications of Dietary Fiber*. London: Academic Press, 1975.

Campbell, T. C., B. Parpia, and J. Chen. "Diet, lifestyle, and the etiology of
coronary artery disease: the Cornell China study." *Am J Cardiol*
82(10B) (1999):18T-21T.

Cowan, C. W., and P. J. Watson. *The Origins of Agriculture*. Washington:
Smithsonian Institute Press, 1992.

Cunningham, J. G. *Textbook of Veterinary Physiology*, 2nd ed. Philadelphia:
W. B. Saunders Company, 1997.

Currie, W. B. *Structure and Function of Domestic Animals*. Boston:
Butterworths, 1988.

Deevy, E. S. "The human population." *Scientific American* 203 (1960):195-
204.

Dyce, K. M., W. O. Sack, and C. J. G. Wensing. *Textbook of Veterinary
Anatomy*. Philadelphia: W. B. Saunders Company, 1987.

Frandson, R. D. *Anatomy and Physiology of Farm Animals*. Philadelphia:
Lea & Febiger, 1981.

Frandson, R. D. *Anatomy and Physiology of Farm Animals,* 4th ed.
Philadelphia: Lea & Febiger, 1986.

Gribbin, J., and M. Gribbin. *Children of the Ice; Climate and Human
Origins*. Oxford: Basil Blackwell, Ltd, 1990.

Heiser, C. B. Jr. *Seed to Civilization*. San Francisco: W. H. Freeman and
Company, 1981.

Hildebrand, M. *Analysis of Vertebrate Structure,* 2nd ed. New York: John
Wiley & Sons, 1982.

Hodge, A. M., G. K. Dowse, P. Toelupe, et al. "The association of modernization with dyslipidaemia and changes in lipid levels in the Polynesian population of Western Samoa." *Int J Epidemiol* 26(2) (1997):297-306.

Huang, B., B. L. Rodriguez, C. M. Burchfiel, et al. "Acculturation and prevalence of diabetes among Japanese-American men in Hawaii." *Am J Epidemiol* 144(7) (1996):674-81.

Keith, A. *The Antiquity of Man,* Vol. I. London: Williams and Norgate, L.T.D., 1929.

Keith, A. *The Antiquity of Man,* Vol. II. London: Williams and Norgate, L.T.D., 1929.

Kent, G. C. *Comparative Anatomy of the Vertebrates.* St. Louis: Times Mirror/Mosby, 1987.

Keys, A. *Seven Countries. A Multivariate Analysis of Death and Coronary Heart Diseases.* Cambridge, Massachusetts: Harvard University Press, 1980.

MacNeish, R. *The Origins of Agriculture and Settled Life.* Norman: University of Oklahoma Press, 1992.

McMurry, M. P., M. T. Cerqueira, S. L. Connor, et al. "Changes in lipid and lipoprotein levels and body weight in Tarahumara Indians after consumption of an affluent diet." *N Engl J Med* 325(24) (1991):1704-8.

Mount, L. E. *The Climatic Physiology of the Pig.* London: Edward Arnold (Publishers), Ltd., 1968.

Passmore, R., and M. A. Eastwood. *Davidson and Passmore Human Nutrition and Dietetics,* 8th ed. London, England: Churchill Livingstone, 1986.

Polgar S., Ed. *Population, Ecology, and Social Evolution.* Paris: Mouton Publishers, 1975.

Prideaux, T. *Cro-Magnon Man.* New York: Time-Life Books, 1973.

Raskin, E. *World Food.* New York: McGraw-Hill Book Company, 1971.

Ravussin, E., M. E. Valencia, J. Esparza, et al. "Effects of a traditional lifestyle on obesity in Pima Indians." *Diabetes Care* 17(9) (1994):1067-74.

Reece, W. O. *Physiology of Domestic Animals.* Philadelphia: Lea & Febiger, 1991.

Richards, G. *Human Evolution.* London: Routledge and Kegan Paul, 1987.

Ronen A., Ed. *The Transition from Lower to Middle Paleolithic and the Origin of Modern Man.* Oxford: BAR-S151, 1982.

Ruckebusch, Y., L. P. Phaneuf, and R. Dunlop. *Physiology of Small and Large Animals*. Philadelphia: B. C. Decker, Inc., 1991.

Sack, W. O. *Essentials of Pig Anatomy*. Ithaca: Veterinary Textbooks, 1982.

Smith, E. G., K. A. Parsons, et al. *Early Man; His Origin, Development, and Culture*. Freeport: Books for Libraries Press, 1967.

Stedman, T. L. *Stedman's Medical Dictionary*, 25th ed. Baltimore: Williams and Wilkins, 1990.

Subcommittee on Swine Nutrition, Committee on Animal Nutrition, Board on Agriculture and National Research Council. *Nutrient Requirements of Swine*, 9th ed. Washington D.C.: National Academy Press, 1988.

Sunderman, F. W., and F. Boerner. *Normal Values in Clinical Medicine*. Philadelphia: W. B. Saunders Company, 1950.

Swenson M. J. *Dukes' Physiology of Domestic Animals*, 9th ed. Ithaca: Comstock Publishing Associates, a division of Cornell University Press, 1977.

Svendsen, P. *An Introduction to Animal Physiology*. Connecticut: The Avi Publishing Company, Inc., 1974.

Taylor R. J., and P. Z. Zimmet. "Obesity and diabetes in Western Samoa." *Int J Obesity* 5 (1981):367-76.

Tilton, R. C., A. Balows, D. C. Hohnadel, et al. *Clinical Laboratory Medicine*. St. Louis: Mosby Year Book, 1992.

Topping, D. L., J. M. Gooden, I. L. Brown, et. al. "A high amylose (amylo-maize) starch raises proximal large bowel starch and increases colon length in pigs." *Am Soc Nutr Sci* 127(4) (1997):615-22.

Tortora, G. J. *Principles of Anatomy and Physiology*, 9th ed. New York: John Wiley & Sons, Inc., 2000.

Towne, C. W., and E. N. Wentworth. *Pigs: From Cave to Corn Belt*. Oklahoma: University of Oklahoma Press, 1950.

Trewartha, G. T. A. *Geography of Population: World Patterns*. New York: John Wiley & Sons, Inc., 1969.

Trowell, H. D., and D. P. Burkitt. *Western Diseases: Their Emergence and Prevention*. Cambridge, Massachusetts: Harvard University Press, 1981.

Tsunehara, C. H., D. L. Leonetti, and W. Y. Fujimoto. "Diet of second-generation Japanese-American men with and without non-insulin-dependent diabetes." *Am J Clin Nutr* 52(4) (1990):731-38.

U.S. Department of Agriculture. *Agriculture Fact Book 2000*.

Chapter 3

Anderson, J. W. "High carbohydrate, high fiber diets for patients with diabetes." *Adv Exp Med Biol* 119 (1979):263-73.

Barnard, R. J., M. R. Massey, S. Cherny, et al. "Long-term use of a high-complex-carbohydrate, high-fiber, low-fat diet and exercise in the treatment of NIDDM patients." *Diabetes Care* 6(3) (1983):268-73.

Bassett, D. R., M. A. Abel, R. C. Moellering, et al. "Dietary intake, smoking history, energy balance, and 'stress' in relation to age, and to coronary heart disease risk in Hawaiian and Japanese men in Hawaii." *Am J Clin Nutr* 22(1969):1504-20.

Baxendale-Cox, L. M., and R. L. Duncan. "Insulin increases sodium (Na+) channel density in A6 epithelia: implications for expression of hypertension." *Biol Res Nurs* 1 (1999):20-9.

Burchfiel, C. M., R. D. Abbott, J. D. Curb, et al. "Association of insulin levels with lipids and lipoproteins in elderly Japanese-American men." *Ann Epidemiol* 8(2) (1998):92-98.

Castelli, W., M.D. "Framingham Heart Study." (May 1988).

Danao-Camara, T. C., and T. T. Shintani. "The Dietary Treatment of Inflammatory Arthritis: Case Reports and Review of the Literature." *Hawaii Med J* 58(5) (1999):126-31.

Dreon, D. M., B. Frey-Hewitt, N. Ellsworth, et al. "Dietary fat:carbohydrate ratio and obesity in middle-aged men." *Am J Clin Nutr* (United States) 47(6) (June 1988):995-1000.

Duncan, H., J. A. Bacon, and R. L. Weinsier. "The effects of high and low energy density diets on satiety, energy intake, and eating time of obese and nonobese subjects." *Am J Clin Nutr* 37(5) (1983):763-67.

He, J., M. J. Klag, B. Caballero, et al. "Plasma insulin levels and incidence of hypertension in African Americans and whites." *Arch Intern Med* 159(5) (1999):498-503.

Gibbons, G. F., K. A. Mitropoulos, and N. B. Myant. *Biochemistry of Cholesterol.* Amsterdam, New York, Oxford: Elsevier Biomedical Press, 1982.

Himsworth, H. P. "The dietetic factor determining the glucose tolerance and sensitivity to insulin of normal men." *Clin Sci* 2 (1935):68-94.

Hopkins, P. N., S. C. Hunt, and L. L. Wu. "Hypertension, dyslipidemia, and insulin resistance: links in a chain or spokes on a wheel?" *Curr Opin Lipidol* 7(4) (1996):241-53.

Kempner, K., B. C. Newborg, R. L. Peschel, et al. "Treatment of massive obesity with rice/reduction diet program." *Arch Intern Med* 235 (1975):1575-84.

Kempner, W., R. L. Peschel, and J. S. Scylar. "Effect of rice diet on diabetes mellitus associated with vascular disease." *Postgrad Med* 24 (1958):359-71.

Kushi, L. H., K. A. Meyer, and D. R. Jacobs. "Cereals, legumes, and chronic disease risk reductions: Evidence from epidemiologic studies." *Am J Clin Nutr* 70 (3 suppl) (1999):451S-458S.

Laakso, M. "Insulin resistance and coronary heart disease." *Curr Opin Lipidol* 7(4)(1996):217-26.

Lazarus R., D. Sparrow, and S. Weiss. "Temporal relations between obesity and insulin: longitudinal data from the Normative Aging Study." *Am J Epidemiol* 147(2) (1998):173-79.

Lempiainen, P., L. Mykkanen, K. Pyorala, et al. "Insulin resistance syndrome predicts coronary heart disease events in elderly nondiabetic men." *Circulation* 100(2) 1999:123-28.

Leonard R., ed. *Essential Medical Physiology.* Philadelphia: Lippincott-Raven, 1998.

Liese, A. D., F. J. Mayer-Davis, L. E. Chambless, et al. "Elevated fasting insulin predicts incident hypertension: the ARIC study. Atherosclerosis Risk in Communities Study Investigators." *J Hypertens* 17(8) (1999):1169-77.

Ludvik, B., J. J. Nolan, J. Baloga, D. Sacks, and J. Olefsky. "Effect of obesity on insulin resistance in normal subjects and patients with NIDDM." *Diabetes* 44(9) (1995):1121-25.

McDougall, J., K. Litzau, E. Haver, et al. "Rapid reduction of serum cholesterol and blood pressure by a twelve-day, very low fat, strictly vegetarian diet." *J Am Coll Nutr* 14(5) (1995 Oct):491-96.

Moellering, R. C., and D. R. Bassett. "Myocardial infarction in Hawaiian and Japanese males on Oahu—a review of 505 cases occurring between 1955 and 1964." *J Chron Dis* 20(1967):89-101.

Moller, L. F., and J. Jespersen. "Fasting serum insulin levels and coronary heart disease in a Danish cohort: 17-year follow-up." *J Cardiovasc Risk* 1995;2(3):235-40.

Ney, D., D. R. Hollingsworth, and L. Cousins. "Decreased insulin requirement and improved control of diabetes in pregnant women given a high-carbohydrate, high fiber, low fat diet." *Diabetes Care* 5(5) (1982):529-33.

Nicholson, A. S., M. Sklar, N. D. Barnard, et al. "Toward improved management of NIDDM: A randomized, controlled, pilot intervention using a lowfat, vegetarian diet." *Prev Med* 29(2) (1999 Aug):87-91.

Ornish, D., S. E. Brown, L. W. Scherwitz, et al. "Can lifestyle changes reverse coronary heart disease?" *Lancet* 336 (1990):129-33.

Ornish, D., L. W. Scherwitz, J. H. Billings, et al. "Intensive lifestyle changes for reversal of coronary heart disease." *JAMA* 280;23 (1998):2001-7.

Perry, I. J., S. G. Wannamethee, P. H. Whincup, et al. "Serum insulin and incident coronary heart disease in middle-aged British men." *Am J Epidemiol* (United States) 144(3) (Aug. 1, 1996):224-34.

Preiss, B. *Regulation of HMG CoA Reductase*. New York, London: Academic Press, Inc., 1985.

Reaven, G. M. "Role of insulin resistance in human disease (syndrome X): an expanded definition." *Annu Rev Med* 44 (1993):121-31.

Rolls, B. J., E. A. Bell, V. H. Castellanos, M. Chow, et al. "Energy density but not fat content of foods affected energy intake in lean and obese women." *Am J Clin Nutr* 69(5) (1999):863-71.

Sacks, F. M., W. P. Castelli, A. Donner, and E. H. Kass. "Plasma lipids and lipoproteins in vegetarians and controls." *N Engl J Med* 292(22) (May 29, 1975):1148-51.

Samsum, W. D. "The use of high carbohydrate diets in the treatment of diabetes mellitus." *JAMA* 86 (1926):178-81.

Scanlon, V. C. *Essentials of Anatomy and Physiology*. Philadelphia: F. A. Davis, 1999.

Shintani, T. *The HawaiiDiet*™. New York: Pocket Books, 1999.

Shintani, T. T., S. Beckham, A. C. Brown, and H. K. O'Connor. "The Hawaii Diet: *ad libitum* high carbohydrate, low fat multi-cultural diet for the reduction of chronic disease risk factors: obesity, hypertension, hypercholesterolemia, and hyperglycemia." *Haw Med J* 60(3) (2001):69-73.

Shintani, T. T., S. K. Beckham, J. Tang, et al. "Waianae Diet Program: long-term follow-up." *Hawaii Med J* 58(5) (1999):117-22.

Shintani, T. T., C. K. Hughes, S. K. Beckham, and H. K. O'Connor. "Obesity and cardiovascular risk intervention through the *ad libitum* feeding of traditional Hawaiian diet." *Am J Clin Nutr* 53 (1991):1647S-51S.

Sloan, N. R. "Ethnic distribution of diabetes mellitus in Hawaii." *J Am Med Assn* 183 (1963):419-24.

Trowell, H., and D. Burkitt, eds. *Western Diseases: Their Emergence and Prevention*. Cambridge MA: Harvard University Press, 1981.

U.S. Congress. "Current health status and population projections of Native Hawaiians living in Hawaii." *Office of Technology Assessment* April 1987.

Weinsier, R. L., M. H. Johnston, D. M. Doleys, and J. A. Bacon. "Dietary management of obesity: evaluation of the time-energy displacement diet in terms of its efficacy and nutritional adequacy for long-term weight control." *Br J Nutr* 47(3) (1982):367-79.

Zavaroni, I., L. Bonini, P. Gasparini, et al. "Hyperinsulinemia in a normal population as a predictor of non-insulin-dependent diabetes mellitus, hypertension, and coronary heart disease: the Barilla factory revisited." *Metabolism* 48(8) (1999):989-94.

Chapter 4

American Dietetic Association. "Position of the American Dietetic Association: health implications of dietary fiber." *J Am Diet Assoc* (United States) 97(10) (1997):1157-59.

Anderson, J. W. "High carbohydrate, high fiber diets for patients with diabetes." *Adv Exp Med Biol* 119 (1979):263-73.

Anderson, J. W. "High-fibre diets for diabetic and hypertriglyceridemic patients." *Can Med Assoc J* 123(10) (1980):975-79.

Anderson, J. W., N. J. Gustafson, C. A. Bryant, and J. Tietyen-Clark. "Dietary fiber and diabetes: a comprehensive review and practical application." *J Am Diet Assoc* 87(9) (1987):1189-97.

Anderson, J. W., and T. J. Hanna. "Impact of nondigestible carbohydrates on serum lipoproteins and risk for cardiovascular disease." *J Nutr* 129(7 Suppl) (1999):1457S-66S.

Anderson, J. W., B. M. Smith, and P. B. Geil. "High-fiber diet for diabetes. Safe and effective treatment." *Postgrad Med* 88(2) (1990):157-61, 164, 167-68.

Appleby, P. N., M. Thorogood, J. I. Mann, et al. "Low body mass index in non-meat eaters: the possible roles of animal fat, dietary fibre and alcohol." *Int J Obes Relat Metab Disord* (England) 22(5) (1988):454-60.

Bell, S., V. M. Goldman, B. R. Bistrian, A. H. Arnold, G. Ostroff, and R. A. Forse. "Effect of beta-glucan from oats and yeast on serum lipids." *Crit Rev Food Sci Nutr* 39(2) (1999):189-202.

Bennett, W. G., and J. J. Cerda. "Benefits of dietary fiber. Myth or medicine?" *Postgrad Med* (United States) 99(2) (1996):153-56, 166-68, 171-72 passim.

Burkitt, D. P., and H. C. Trowell. *Refined Carbohydrate Foods and Disease: Some Implications of Dietary Fiber.* London: Academic Press, 1975.

Gatti, E. "Clinical effects of a dietary fibre supplement. A review." *Eur J Clin Nutr* (England) 49(Suppl 3) (1995):S199-200.

Gibson, S. A. "Are high-fat, high-sugar foods and diets conducive to obesity?" *Int J Food Sci Nutr* (England) 47(5) (1996):405-15.

Heini, A. F., C. Lara-Castro, H. Schneider, K. A. Kirk, R. V. Considine, and R. L. Weinsier. "Effect of hydrolyzed guar fiber on fasting and postprandial satiety and satiety hormones: a double-blind, placebo-controlled trial during controlled weight loss." *Int J Obes Relat Metab Disord* 22(9) (1998):906-9.

Hylander, B., and S. Rossner. "Effects of dietary fiber intake before meals on weight loss and hunger in a weight-reducing club." *Acta Med Scand* 213(3) (1983):217-20.

Jacob, D. R., Jr., L. Marquart, J. Slavin, and L. II. Kushi. "Whole-grain intake and cancer: an expanded review and meta-analysis." *Nutr Cancer* 30(2) (1998):85-96.

Kaul, L., and J. Nidiry. "High-fiber diet in the treatment of obesity and hypercholesterolemia." *J Natl Med Assoc* 85(3) (1993):231-32.

Kushi, L. H., K. A. Meyer, and D. R. Jacobs. "Cereals, legumes, and chronic disease risk reductions: Evidence from epidemiologic studies." *Am J Clin Nutr* 70 (3 suppl) (1999):451S-458S.

McCrory, M. A., P. J. Fuss, N. P. Hays, et al. "Overeating in America: association between restaurant food consumption and body fatness in healthy adult men and women ages 19 to 80." *Obes Res* (United States) 7(6) (1999):564-71.

Morris, K. L., and M. B. Zemel. "Glycemic index, cardiovascular disease, and obesity." *Nutr Rev* (United States) 57(9 Pt 1) (1999):273-76.

Nuttall, F. Q. "Dietary fiber in the management of diabetes." *Diabetes* 42(4) (1993):503-8.

Pasman, W. J., W. H. Saris, M. A. Wauters, et al. "Effect of one week of fibre supplementation on hunger and satiety ratings and energy intake." *Appetite* (England) 29(1) (1997):77-87.

Pasman W. J., M. S. Westerterp-Plantenga, E. Muls, G. Vansant, J. van Ree, and W. H. Saris. "The effectiveness of long-term fibre supplementation on weight maintenance in weight-reduced women." *Int J Obes Relat Metab Disord* 21(7) (1997):548-55.

Purnell, J. Q., and J. D. Brunzell. "The central role of dietary fat, not carbohydrate, in the insulin resistance syndrome." *Curr Opin Lipidol* 8(1) (1997):17-22.

Ryttig, K. R., G. Tellnes, L. Haegh, E. Bøe, and H. Fagerthun. "A dietary fibre supplement and weight maintenance after weight reduction: a randomized, double-blind, placebo-controlled long-term trial." *Int J Obes* 13(2) (1989):165-71.

Salmeron, J., A. Ascherio, E. B. Rimm, G. A. Colditz, D. Spiegelman, D. J. Jenkins, M. J. Stampfer, A. L. Wing, and W. C. Willett. "Dietary fiber, glycemic load, and risk of NIDDM in men." *Diabetes Care* 20(4) (1997):545-50.

Salmeron, J., J. E. Manson, M. J. Stampfer, G. A. Colditz, A. L. Wing, and W. C. Willett. "Dietary fiber, glycemic load, and risk of non-insulin-dependent diabetes mellitus in women." *JAMA* 277(6) (1997):472-77.

Saltzman, E., and S. B. Roberts. "Soluble fiber and energy regulation. Current knowledge and future directions." *Adv Exp Med Biol* (United States) 427 (1997):89-97.

Sheu, W. H. "Coronary artery disease risk predicted by insulin resistance, plasma lipids, and hypertension in people without diabetes." *Am J Med Sci* 319(2) (2000):84-88.

Slavin, J. L., M. C. Martini, D. R. Jacobs, Jr., and L. Marquart. "Plausible mechanisms for the protectiveness of whole grains." *Am J Clin Nutr* 70(3 Suppl) (1999):459S-63S.

Stevens J. "Does dietary fiber affect food intake and body weight?" *J Am Diet Assoc* 88(8) (1988):939-42, 945.

Takahashi, M., S. Ikemoto, and O. Ezaki. "Effect of the fat/carbohydrate ratio in the diet on obesity and oral glucose tolerance in C57BL/6J mice." *J Nutr Sci Vitaminol* 45(5) (1999):583-93.

Ullrich, I. H., and M. J. Albrink. "The effect of dietary fiber and other factors on insulin response: role in obesity." *J Environ Pathol Toxicol Oncol* (United States) 5(6) (1985):137-55.

Vinik, A. I., and D. J. Jenkins. "Dietary fiber in management of diabetes." *Diabetes Care* 11(2) (1988):160-73.

Welsh, S., A. Shaw, and C. Davis. "Achieving dietary recommendations: whole-grain foods in the Food Guide Pyramid." *Crit Rev Food Sci Nutr* 34(5-6) (1994):441-51.

Willett, W. C. "Convergence of philosophy and science: the third international congress on vegetarian nutrition." *Am J Clin Nutr* 70(3 Suppl) (1999):434S-38S.

Wolever, C. M., S. Hamad, J. Gittelsohn, et al. "Low dietary fiber and high protein intake associated with newly diagnosed diabetes in a remote aboriginal community." *Am J Clin Nutr* 66 (6) (1997):1470-74.

Wursch, P., and F. X. Pi-Sunyer. "The role of viscous soluble fiber in the metabolic control of diabetes. A review with special emphasis on cereals rich in beta-glucan." *Diabetes Care* 20(11) (1997):1774-80.

Chapter 5

Bantle, J. P., S. K. Raatz, W. Thomas, et al. "Effects of dietary fructose on plasma lipids in healthy subjects." *Am J Clin Nutr* 72(5) (2000):1128-34.

Coulston, A. M., C. B. Hollenbeck, A. L. Swislocki, and G. M. Reaven. "Persistence of hypertriglyceridemic effect of low-fat high-carbohydrate diets in NIDDM patients." *Diabetes Care* 12(2) (1989):94-101.

Dufty, W. *Sugar Blues.* New York: Warner Books, Inc., 1976.

Food and Agriculture Organization of the United Nations and World Health Organization. *Carbohydrates in Human Nutrition Food and Nutrition, Paper 66.* Rome: Food and Agriculture Organization of the United Nations and World Health Organization, 1998.

Fryer, L., and D. Simmons. *Whole Foods for You.* New York, Mason & Lipscomb Publishers, 1974.

Institute of Food Technologists. "Sugars and Nutritive Sweeteners in Processed Foods." *Food Technology* (May 1979):1-5.

Levelle, G. A., and M. A. Uebersax, eds. "Fundamentals of food science for the dietitian: wheat products." *Dietetic Currents* 7(1) (1980):1-8. (Ross Laboratories, Columbus, OH.)

Passmore, R., and M. A. Eastwood. *Davidson and Passmore Human Nutrition and Dietetics*, 8th ed. London, England: Churchill Livingstone, 1986.

Pennington, J. A. T. *Bowes & Church's Food Values of Portions Commonly Used,* 16th ed. Philadelphia, PA: J. B. Lippincott Company, 1994.

Reiser, S. "Effect of dietary sugars on metabolic risk factors associated with heart disease." *Nutr Health* 3(4) (1985):203-16.

Shintani T. T., S. Beckham, A. C. Brown, et al. "The Hawaii Diet: *ad libitum* high carbohydrate, low fat multi-cultural diet for the reduction of chronic disease risk factors: obesity, hypertension, hypercholesterolemia, and hyperglycemia." *Hawaii Med J* 60(3) (2001):69-73.

Shintani, T. T., C. K. Hughes, S. K. Beckham, H. K. O'Connor. "Obesity and cardiovascular risk intervention through the *ad libitum* feeding of traditional hawaiian diet." *Am J Clin Nutr* 53 (1991):1647S-51S.

Steinbaugh, M. L., ed. "Fundamentals of food science for the dietitian: wheat products." *Dietetic Currents* 7(1) (1980). Ross Laboratories, Columbus, OH.

Swanson J. E., Laine D. C., Thomas W., et al. "Metabolic effects of dietary fructose in healthy subjects." *Am J Clin Nutr* 55(4) (1992):851-56.

Truswell A. S. "Food carbohydrates and plasma lipids—an update." *Am J Clin Nutr* 59(3 Suppl) (1994):710S-718S.

United States Department of Agriculture. USDA Nutrient Data Base for Standard Reference, Release 12, 1999.

Chapter 6

Blundell, J. E., V. J. Burley, J. R. Cotton, and C. L. Lawton. "Dietary fat and the control of energy intake: evaluating the effects of fat on meal size and postmeal satiety." *Am J Clin Nutr* 57(5 Suppl) (1993):772S-777S, discussion 777S-778S.

Blundell, J. E., S. Green, and V. Burley. "Carbohydrates and human appetite." *Am J Clin Nutr* 59(3 Suppl) (1994):728S-734S.

David, J. A., D. M. Jenkins, M. S. Thomas, et al. "Glycemic Index of Foods: A Physiological Basis for Carbohydrate Exchange." *Am J Clin Nutr* 34 (1981):362-66.

Edes, T. E., and J. H. Shah. "Glycemic index and insulin response to a liquid nutritional formula compared with a standard meal." *J Am Coll Nutr* 17(1) (1998 Feb):30-35.

Foster-Powell, K., and J. Brand Miller. "International Tables of Glycemic Index." *Am J Clin Nutr* 62 (1995):871S-93S.

Haber, G. B., K. W. Heaton, D. Murphy, et al. "Depletion and disruption of dietary fibre. Effects on satiety, plasma-glucose, and serum-insulin." *Lancet* 2(8040) (1977):679-82.

Holt, S. H., and J. C. Brand Miller. "Particle size, satiety and the glycaemic response." *Eur J Clin Nutr* 48 (1994):496-502.

Holt, S. H., J. C. Brand Miller, and P. Petocz. "An insulin index of foods: the insulin demand generated by 1000-kj portions of common foods." *Am J Clin Nutr* 66 (1997):1264-76.

Holt, S. H., J. C. Brand Miller, and P. Petocz. "Interrelationships among postprandial satiety, glucose and insulin responses and changes in subsequent food intake." *Eur J Clin Nutr* 50(12) (1996):788-97.

Indar-Brown, K., C. Norenberg, and Z. Madar. "Glycemic and insulinemic responses after ingestion of ethnic foods by NIDDM and healthy subjects." *Am J Clin Nutr* 55 (1992):89-95.

Jenkins, D. J., A. L. Jenkins, T. M. Wolever, et al. "Low glycemic index: lente carbohydrates and physiological effects of altered food frequency." *Am J Clin Nutr* (United States) 59(3 Suppl) (1994):706S-709S.

Jenkins, D. J., T. M. Wolever, J. Kalmusky, et al. "Low glycemic index carbohydrate foods in the management of hyperlipidemia." *Am J Clin Nutr* 45 (1985):604-17.

Lee, B. M., and T. M. Wolever. "Effect of glucose, sucrose and fructose on plasma glucose and insulin responses in normal humans: comparison with white bread." *Eur J Clin Nutr* 52(12) (1998):924-28.

Liu, S., W. C. Willet, M. J. Stompfer, et al. "A prospective study of dietary glycemic load, carbohydrate intake, and risk of coronary heart disease in US women." *AM J Clin Nutr* 71(6) (2000):1455-61.

Mayes, P. A. "Intermediary metabolism of fructose." *Am J Clin Nutr* 58(suppl) (1993):754S-65S.

O'Dea, K., P. J. Nestel, and L. Antonoff. "Physical factors influencing postprandial glucose and insulin responses to starch." *Am J Clin Nutr* 33 (1980):760-65.

Rasmussen, O., and S. Gregersen. "Influence of the amount of starch on the glycaemic index to rice in non-insulin dependent diabetic subjects of both sexes." *Am J Clin Nutr* 62 (1992):266-68.

Rolls, B. J. "Carbohydrates, fats and satiety." *Am J Clin Nutr* 61(suppl) (1995):960S-7S.

Rolls, B. J., and E. A. Bell. "Intake of fat and carbohydrate: role of energy density." *Eur J Clin Nutr* 53 Suppl 1 (1999):S166-73.

Shintani, T. T., *Dr. Shintani's Eat More, Weigh Less® Diet.* Halpax Publishing, 1993.

Shintani, T. *The HawaiiDiet* ™. New York: Pocket Books, 1999.

Shintani, T. T., S. Beckham, A. C. Brown, et al. "The Hawaii Diet: *ad libitum* high carbohydrate, low fat multi-cultural diet for the reduction of chronic disease risk factors: obesity, hypertension, hypercholesterolemia, and hyperglycemia." *Hawaii Med J* 60(3) (2001):69-73.

United States Department of Agriculture. USDA Nutrient Data Base for Standard Reference, Release 12. 1999.

Wolever, T. M. S., L. Kartzman Relle, A. L. Jenkins, et al. "Glycemic index of 102 complex carbohydrate foods in patients with diabetes." *Nutr Res* 14 (1994):651-69.

Wolever, T. M., and J. B. Miller. "Sugars and blood glucose control." *Am J Clin Nutr* 62(1 Suppl) (1995 Jul):212S-221S.

Chapter 7

American Dietetic Association. "Position of the American Dietetic Association: health implications of dietary fiber." *J Am Diet Assoc* 97(10) (1997):1157-9.

Eaton, S. B., and M. Konner. "Paleolithic Nutrition," *New Engl J Med* 312 (1985):283-289.

Elliott, R. B., D. P. Harris, J. P. Hill, et al. "Type I (insulin-dependent) diabetes mellitus and cow milk: casein variant consumption." *Diabetologia* 42(3) (March 1999):292-96.

Feskanich, D., W. C. Willett, M. J. Stampfer, and G. A. Colditz. "Protein consumption and bone fractures in women." *Am J Epidemiol* 143(5) (1996):472-9.

Kushi, L. H., E. B. Lenart, and W. C. Willett. "Health implications of Mediterranean diets in light of contemporary knowledge. 1. Plant foods and dairy products." *Am J Clin Nutr* 61(6 Suppl) (1995):1407S-1415S.

Lau, E. M., and J. Woo. "Nutrition and osteoporosis." *Curr Opin Rheumatol* 10(4) (1998):368-72.

Matlock, G. D. *Let's Live* (Dec 1966): cited in Kushi, M. *The Teachings of Michio Kushi*. Boston, MA.: The East West Foundation, 1972.

Messina, V. K., and K. I. Burke. "Position of the American Dietetic Association: vegetarian diets." *J Am Diet Assoc* 97(11) (1997 Nov):1317-21.

Muntoni, S., P. Cocco, G. Aru, et al. "Nutritional factors and worldwide incidence of childhood type 1 diabetes." *Am J Clin Nutr* 71(6) (2000):1525-29.

Pennington, J. A. T. *Bowes & Church's Food Values of Portions Commonly Used,* 16th ed. Philadelphia, P.A.: J. B. Lippincott Company, 1985.

Sahi, T. "Genetics and epidemiology of adult-type hypolactasia." *Scand J Gastroenterol* 29(Suppl 202) (1994):7-20.

Schrezenmeir, J., and A. Jagla. "Milk and diabetes." *J Am Coll Nutr* 19(2 Suppl) (2000):176S-190S.

Scrimshaw, N. S., and E. B. Murray. "The acceptability of milk and milk products in populations with a high prevalence of lactose intolerance." *Am J Clin Nutr* 48(4 Suppl) (1988):1079-159.

Turner, L. W., Q. Fu, J. E. Taylor, et al. "Osteoporotic fracture among older U.S. women: risk factors quantified." *J Aging Health* 10(3) (1998):372-91.

United States Department of Agriculture. USDA Nutrient Data Base for Standard Reference, Release 12. 1999.

Weaver, C. M., and K. L. Plawecki. "Dietary calcium: adequacy of a vegetarian diet." *Am J Clin Nutr* 59(5 Suppl) (1994):1238S-1241S.

Willett, W. C. "The dietary pyramid: does the foundation need repair?" *Am J Clin Nutr* 68(2) (1998):218-9.

Chapter 8

Astrup, A. "The American paradox: the role of energy-dense fat-reduced food in the increasing prevalence of obesity." *Curr Opin Clin Nutr Metab Care* 1(6) (1998):573-77.

Blundell, J. E., S. Green, and V. Burley. "Carbohydrates and human appetite." *Am J Clin Nutr* 59(3 Suppl) (1994):728S-734S.

Blundell, J. E., V. J. Burley, J. R. Cotton, C. L. Lawton. "Dietary fat and the control of energy intake: evaluating the effects of fat on meal size and postmeal satiety." *Am J Clin Nutr* 57(5 Suppl) (1993):772S-777S, discussion 777S-778S.

Blundell, J. E., C. L. Lawton, J. R. Cotton, et al. "Control of human appetite: implications for the intake of dietary fat." *Annu Rev Nutr* 16 (1996): 285-319.

Bolton-Smith, C. " Intake of sugars in relation to fatness and micronutrient adequacy." *Int J Obes Relat Metab Disord* 20 (Suppl 2) (1996):S31-3.

Burton-Freeman, B. "Dietary fiber and energy regulation." *J Nutr* 130(2S Suppl) (2000):272S-275S.

Dreon, D. M., B. Frey-Hewitt, N. Ellsworth, et al. "Dietary fat: carbohydrate ratio and obesity in middle-aged men." *Am J Clin Nutr* (United States) 47(6) (June 1988):995-1000.

Flatt, J. P. "Carbohydrate balance and body-weight regulation." *Proc Nutr Soc* 55(1B) (1996):449-65.

Green, S. M., and J. E. Blundell. "Effect of fat- and sucrose-containing foods on the size of eating episodes and energy intake in lean dietary restrained and unrestrained females: potential for causing overconsumption." *Eur J Clin Nutr* 50(9) (1996):625-35.

Hill, J. O., and A. M. Prentice. "Sugar and Body Weight Regulation." *Am J Clin Nutr* 62(1 Suppl) (1995 Jul):264S-273S.

Holt, S. H. A., J. C. Brand-Miller, P. Petocz, and E. Farmakalidis. "A satiety index of common foods." *Eur J Clin Nutr* 49 (1995):675-90.

Holt, S. H. A., J. C. Brand Miller, and P. Petocz. "An insulin index of foods: the insulin demand generated by 1000-kj portions of common foods." *Am J Clin Nutr* 66 (1997):1264-76.

Lachance, P A. "International perspective: basis, need, and application of recommended dietary allowances." *Nutr Rev* 56(4 Pt 2) (1998):S2-4.

Mokdad, A. H., M. K. Serdula, W. H. Dietz, et al. "The spread of the obesity epidemic in the United States, 1991-1998." *JAMA* 282(16)(1999):1519-22.

Mokdad, A. H., M. K. Serdula, W. H. Dietz, et al. "The continuing epidemic of obesity in the United States." *JAMA* 284(13) (2000):1650-51.

Morris, K. L., and M. B. Zemel. "Glycemic index, cardiovascular disease, and obesity." *Nutr Rev* 57(9 Pt 1) (1999):273-76.

Poppitt, S. D., and A. M. Prentice. "Energy density and its role in the control of food intake: evidence from metabolic and community studies." *Appetite* 26(2) (1996):153-74.

Rolls, B. J. "Carbohydrates, fats and satiety." *Am J Clin Nutr* 61(suppl) (1995):960S-7S.

Rolls, B. J., and E. A. Bell. "Intake of fat and carbohydrate: role of energy density." *Eur J Clin Nutr* 53 Suppl 1 (1999):S166-73.

Shintani, T. T., S. Beckham, A. C. Brown, et al. "The Hawaii Diet: *ad libitum* high carbohydrate, low fat multi-cultural diet for the reduction of chronic disease risk factors: obesity, hypertension, hypercholesterolemia, and hyperglycemia." *Hawaii Med J* 60(3) (2001):69-73.

Shintani, T. T., S. K. Beckham, J. Tang, et al. "Waianae Diet Program: long-term follow-up." *Hawaii Med J* 58(5) (1999):117-22.

Shintani, T. T., C. K. Hughes, S. K. Beckham, and H. K. O'Connor. "Obesity and Cardiovascular Risk Intervention through the *ad libitum* Feeding of Traditional Hawaiian Diet. *Am J Clin Nutr* 53 (1991):1647S-51S.

United States Department of Agriculture. *Agriculture Fact Book 2000.*

United States Department of Agriculture. USDA Nutrient Data Base for Standard Reference, Release 12. 1999.

Chapter 9

Bjorntorp, P. "Interrelation of physical activity and nutrition on obesity." In P. L. White and T. Mondeika, eds., *Diet and Exercise: Synergism in Health Maintenance.* Chicago, IL: American Medical Association, 1981:91-98.

Blair, S. N., H. W. Kohl III, R. S. Hafenbarger, et al. "Physical fitness and all cause mortality." *JAMA* (1989):262.

Bogardus, C., et al. "Familial Dependence of the Resting Metabolic Rate." *New Engl J Med* 315(2) (1986):96-100.

Borghouts L. B., and H. A. Keizer. "Exercise and insulin sensitivity: a review." *Int J Sports Med* (Germany) 21(1) (January 2000):1-12.

Elia, M. "Organ and Tissue Contribution to Metabolic Rate." In J. M. Kinney and H. N. Tucker, *Energy Metabolism* (New York: Raven Press, 1992), 61-79.

Fontaine, E., et al. "Resting Metabolic Rate in Monozygotic and Dizygotic Twins." *Acta Genet Med Gemellol* 43 (1985):41-47.

Garrow, J. S. "Exercise Diet and Thermogenesis." In M. Winick, ed., *Nutrition and Exercise.* (New York: John Wiley & Sons, 1986), 51-65.

Geliebter, A., M. M. Maher, L. Gerace, et al. "Effects of strength of aerobic training on body composition, resting metabolic rate, and peak oxygen consumption in obese dieting subjects." *Am J Clin Nutr* 66 (1997):557-63.

Goodyear, L. J., and B. B. Kahn. "Exercise, glucose transport, and insulin sensitivity." *Annu Rev Med* 49 (1998):235-61.

Gwinup, G. "Weight loss without dietary restriction: efficacy of different forms of aerobic exercise." *Am J Sports Med* 15:3 (1987):275-79.

Heini, A. F., and R. L. Weinsier. "Divergent trends in obesity and fat intake patterns: the American paradox." *Am J Med* 102(3) (1997):259-64.

Henson, L. C., et al. "Effects of exercise training on resting energy expenditure during caloric restriction." *Am J Clin Nutr* 46 (1987):893-99.

Hill, J. O., et al. "Effects of exercise and food restriction on body composition and metabolic rate in obese women." *Am J Clin Nutr* 46 (1987):622-30.

Hurni, M., B. Burnand, et al. "Metabolic effects of a mixed and a high-carbohydrate low-fat diet in man, measured over 24 hours in a respiration chamber." *Br J Nutr* 47 (1982):33-41.

Lennon, D., et al. "Diet and exercise training effects on Resting Metabolic Rate." *Int J Obes* (England) 9(1) (1985):39-47.

McArdle, W. D., F. I. Katch, and V. L. Katch. *Exercise Physiology*. Malvern, PA: Lea & Febiger, 1991.

McArdle, W. D., and M. Toner. "Application of exercise for weight control: the exercise prescription," In R. T. Frankle, and M. U. Yang, eds., *Obesity and Weight Control: The Health Professional's Guide to Understanding and Treatment* (Rockville, MD: Aspen Publishers, Inc., 1988), 254-74.

Nieman, D. C., J. L. Jaig, E. D. DeGuia, et al. "Reducing diet and exercise training effects on resting metabolic rates in mildly obese women." *J of Sports Med & Physical Fitness* 28 (1988):1:79-88.

Pi-Sunyer, F. X., and K. R. Segal. "Relationship of diet and exercise." In J. M. Kinney and H. N. Tucker, *Energy Metabolism* (New York: Raven Press, 1992), 187-210.

Pi-Sunyer, F. X. "Exercise in the treatment of obesity," In R. T. Frankle and M. U. Yang, eds., *Obesity and Weight Control: The Health Professional's Guide to Understanding and Treatment* (Rockville, MD: Aspen Publishers, Inc., 1988), 241-55.

Pollock, M. L., and J. H. Wilmore. *Exercise in Health and Disease*. Philadelphia: W. B. Saunders Company, 1990.

Rockhill, B., W. C. Willett, J. E. Manson, et al. "Physical activity and mortality: a prospective study among women." *Am J Public Health* (United States), 91(4) (Apr 2001):578-83.

Ryan, A. S., D. E. Hurlbut, M. E. Lott, et al. "Insulin action after resistive training in insulin resistant older men and women." *J Am Geriatr Soc* 49(3) (2001):247-53.

Saris, W. H. "Fit, fat and fat free: the metabolic aspects of weight control." *Int J Obes Relat Metab Disord* 22 Suppl 2 (1998):S15-21.

Schuler, G., and R. Hambrecht. "Regression and non-progression of coronary artery disease with exercise." *J Cardiovasc Risk* 3(2) (1996):176-82.

Simopoulos, A. P. "Diet, exercise, and calorie balance." *JAMA* 260(13) (1988):1953.

Sparti, A., J. P. DeLany, J. A. de la Bretonne, et al. "Relationship between resting metabolic rate and the composition of the fat-free mass." *Metabolism* 46:10 (1997):1225-30.

VanDale, D., P. F. M. Schoffelen, F. TenHoor, et al. "Effects of addition of exercise to energy restriction on 24-hour energy expenditure, sleeping metabolic rate and daily physical activity." *European J of Clin Nutr* 43 (1989):441-51.

Whatley, J. E., and E. T. Poehlman. "Obesity and exercise." In G. L. Blackburn and B. S. Kanders, eds., *Obesity Pathophysiology Psychology and Treatment* (New York: Chapman & Hall, 1994), 123-39.

Chapter 10

Arrighi, J. A., M. Burg, I. S. Cohen, et al. "Myocardial blood-flow response during mental stress in patients with coronary artery disease." *Lancet* 356(9226) (2000):310-11.

Blair, S. N., H. W. Kohl III, R. S. Hafenbarger, et al. "Physical fitness and all cause mortality." *JAMA* (1989):262.

Byrd, R. C. "Positive therapeutic effects of intercessory prayer in a coronary care unit population." *South Med J* (July 1988)1:826-29.

Calderon, R., R. H. Schneider, C. N. Alexander, et al. "Stress, stress reduction and hypercholesterolemia in African Americans: a review." *Ethn Dis* 9(3) (1999):451-62.

Dufty, W. *Sugar Blues.* New York: Warner Books, Inc., 1976.

Jiang W, M. Babyak, D. S. Krantz, et al. "Mental stress-induced myocardial ischemia and cardiac events." *JAMA* (United States) 275(21) (June 5, 1996):1651-56.

Labbate, L. A., M. Fava, M. Oleshansky, et al. "Physical fitness and perceived stress. Relationships with coronary artery disease risk factors." *Psychosomatics* 36(6) (1995):555-60.

Lerner, M. *Choices in Healing: Integrating the Best of Conventional and Complementary Approaches to Cancer.* Massachussetts: MIT Press, 1994.

Spiegel, K., R. Leproult, E. Van Cauter, et al. "Impact of sleep debt on metabolic and endocrine function." *Lancet* 354(9188) (1999 Oct 23):1435-9.

Zamarra, J. W., R. H. Schneider, I. Besseghini, et al. "Usefulness of the transcendental meditation program in the treatment of patients with coronary artery disease." *Am J Cardiol* 77(10) (1996):867-70.

Chapter 11

Himsworth, H. P. "The dietetic factor determining the glucose tolerance and sensitivity to insulin of normal men." *Clin Sci* 2 (1935):68-94.

Kent, N. L. *Technology of Cereals.* New York: Permagon Press, 1966.

Larsen, H. N., O. W. Rasmussen, P. H. Rasmussen, et al. "Glycaemic index of parboiled rice depends on the severity of processing: study in type 2 diabetic subjects." *Eur J Clin Nutr* 54 (2000):380-5.

Microsoft® Encarta® Online Encyclopedia 2000. "Oats."

Rombauer, I. S., M. Rombauer Baker, and E. Baker. *The All New All Purpose Joy of Cooking.* New York: Scribner, 1997.

Shintani, T. T. *Dr. Shintani's Eat More, Weigh Less® Cookbook.* Honolulu, HI: Halpax Publishing, 1995.

Chapter 12

Pennington, J. A. T. *Bowes & Church's Food Values of Portions Commonly Used,* 16th ed. Philadelphia, PA: J. B. Lippincott Company, 1994.

N-Squared Computing, *Nutritionist IV.* Salem OR, 1993.

Shintani, T. T. *Dr. Shintani's Eat More, Weigh Less® Cookbook.* Honolulu, HI: Halpax Publishing, 1995.

Shintani, T. T. *Dr. Shintani's Eat More, Weigh Less® Diet.* Honolulu, HI: Halpax Publishing, 1993.

Shintani, T. *The HawaiiDiet™.* New York: Pocket Books, 1999.

United States Department of Agriculture. USDA Nutrient Data Base for Standard Reference, Release 12. 1999.

Chapter 13

Fraser, G. E., and D. J. Shavlik. "Risk factors for all-cause and coronary heart disease mortality in the oldest-old. The Adventist Health Study." *Arch Intern Med* 157(19) (1997 Oct 27):2249-58.

Fraser, G. E., W. Dysinger, C. Best, and R. Chan. "Ischemic heart disease risk factors in middle-aged Seventh-day Adventist men and their neighbors." *Am J Epidemiol* 126(4) (1987 Oct):638-46.

Ornish, D., L. W. Scherwitz, J. H. Billings, et al. "Intensive lifestyle changes for reversal of coronary heart disease." *JAMA* (United States) 280(23) (Dec 16 1998):2001-7.

Schuler, G., R. Hambrecht, G. Schlierf, et al. "Myocardial perfusion and regression of coronary artery disease in patients on a regimen of intensive physical exercise and low fat diet." *J Am Coll Cardiol* (United States) 19(1) (1992 Jan):34-42.

Chapter 14

American Medical Association. Council on Foods and Nutrition. "A critique of low-carbohydrate ketogenic weight reduction regimens. A review of Dr. Atkins' diet revolution." *JAMA* (United States), June 4, 1973, 224(10)1415-19.

Arnesen, E., H. Refsum, K. H. Bonaa, et al. "Serum total homocysteine and coronary heart disease." *Int J Epidemiol* (England) 24(4) (Aug 1995):704-9.

Arpels, J. C. "The female brain hypoestrogenic continuum from the premenstrual syndrome to menopause. A hypothesis and review of supporting data." *J Reprod Med* 41(9) (1996):633-39.

Associated Press, "Red meat study offsets skepticism over fiber," in Honolulu Advertiser, June 24, 2001.

Barnard, N. D., A. Nicholson, and J. L. Howard. "The medical costs attributable to meat consumption." *Prev Med* 24(6) (1995):646-55.

Barnard, N. D., A. R. Scialli, D. Hurlock, et al. "Diet and sex-hormone binding globulin, dysmenorrhea, and premenstrual symptoms." *Obstet Gynecol* 95(2) (2000):245-50.

Campbell, T. C., B. Parpia, and J. Chen. "Diet, lifestyle, and the etiology of coronary artery disease: the Cornell China study." *Am J Cardiol* (United States) 82(10B) (Nov 26 1998):18T-21T.

Chai, A. U., and J. Abrams. "Homocysteine: a new cardiac risk factor?" *Clin Cardiol* (United States) 24(1) (Jan 2001):80-4.

Cheuvront, S. N. "The Zone Diet and athletic performance." *Sports Med* (New Zealand) 27(4) (April 1999):213-28.

Chhabra, S. K., V. L. Souliotis, S. A. Kyrtopoulos, et al. "Nitrosamines, alcohol, and gastrointestinal tract cancer: recent epidemiology and experimentation." *In Vivo* 10(3) (1996):265-84.

Coffey, D. S. "Similarities of prostate and breast cancer: Evolution, diet, and estrogens." *Urology* 57(4 Suppl 1) (2001):31-38.

Cummings, S. R., J. L. Kelsey, M. C. Nevitt, et al. "Epidemiology of osteoporosis and osteoporotic fractures." *Epidemiol Rev* 7(1985):178-208.

Deligdisch, L. "Hormonal pathology of the endometrium." *Mod Pathol* 13(3) (2000):285-94.

Delvenne, V., S. Goldman, F. Biver, et al. "Brain hypometabolism of glucose in low-weight depressed patients and in anorectic patients: a consequence of starvation?" *J Affect Disord* 44(1) (1997):69-77.

Elliot, B., H. P. Roeser, A. Warrell, et al. "Effect of a high energy, low carbohydrate diet on serum levels of lipids and lipoproteins." *Med J Aust* 1(5) (1981):237-40.

Galland, J. C. "Risks and prevention of contamination of beef carcasses during the slaughter process in the United States of America." *Rev Sci Tech* 16(2) (1997):395-404.

Goldin, B. R., H. Adlercreutz, S. L. Gorbach, et al. "Estrogen excretion patterns and plasma levels in vegetarian and omnivorous women." *N Engl J Med* 307(25) (1982):1542-47.

Grant, W. B. "Milk and other dietary influences on coronary heart disease." *Altern Med Rev* (United States) 3(4) (Aug 1998):281-94.

Hasselbalch, S. G., G. M. Knudsen, J. Jakobsen, et al. "Brain metabolism during short-term starvation in humans." *J Cereb Blood Flow Metab* 14(1) (1994):125-31.

Hirschel, B. "Dr. Atkins' Dietetic Revolution: a critique." *Schweiz Med Wochenschr* (Switzerland) 107(29) (July 23, 1977):1017-25.

Ingram, D. M., F. C. Bennett, D. Willcox, et al. "Effect of low-fat diet on female sex hormone levels." *J Natl Cancer Inst* (United States) 79(6) (December, 1987):1225-29.

Knekt, P., G. Alfthan, A. Aromaa, et al. "Homocysteine and major coronary events: a prospective population study amongst women." *J Intern Med* (England) 249(5) (May 2001):461-5.

Kushi, L. H., E. B. Lenart, and W. C. Willett. "Health implications of Mediterranean diets in light of contemporary knowledge. 1. Plant foods and dairy products." *Am J Clin Nutr* (United States) 61(6 Suppl) (June 1995):1407S-1415S.

Kushi, L. H., E. B. Lenart, and W. C. Willett. "Health implications of Mediterranean diets in light of contemporary knowledge. 2. Meat, wine, fats, and oils." *Am J Clin Nutr* (United States), 61(6 Suppl) (Jun 1995):1416S-1427S.

Lau, E. M., and J. Woo. "Nutrition and osteoporosis." *Curr Opin Rheumatol* (United States) 10(4) (July 1998):368-72.

Maxwell, J. A., ed. *America's Fascinating Indian Heritage.* Pleasantville, NY: Reader's Digest Assn., Inc., 1978.

McDougall, J. *McDougall's Medicine: A Challenging Second Opinion.* New Century Publishers, Inc. Piscataway, NJ, 1985.

McEwen, S. A., and W. B. McNab. "Contaminants of non-biological origin in foods from animals." *Rev Sci Tech* 16(2) (1997):684-93.

Nowak, R. A. "Fibroids: pathophysiology and current medical treatment." *Baillieres Best Pract Res Clin Obstet Gynaecol* 13(2) (1999):223-38.

Passmore, R., and M. A. Eastwood. *Davidson and Passmore Human Nutrition and Dietetics,* 8th ed. London, England: Churchill Livingstone, 1986.

Rein, M. S. "Advances in uterine leiomyoma research: the progesterone hypothesis." *Environ Health Perspect* 108(Suppl 5) (2000):791-93.

Schechter, D. "Estrogen, progesterone, and mood." *J Gend Specif Med* 2(1) (1999):29-36.

Sellmeyer, D. E., K. L. Stone, A. Sebastian, et al. "A high ratio of dietary animal to vegetable protein increases the rate of bone loss and the risk of fracture in postmenopausal women. Study of Osteoporotic Fractures Research Group." *Am J Clin Nutr* (United States) 73(1) (Jan 2001):118-22.

Snowdon, D. A., R. L. Phillips, and W. Choi. "Diet, obesity, and risk of fatal prostate cancer." *Am J Epidemiol* 120(2) (1984):244-50.

Stubbs, R. J., A. M. Prentice, and W. P. James. "Carbohydrates and energy balance." *Ann NY Acad Sci* 819 (1997):44-69.

United States Department of Agriculture. USDA Nutrient Data Base for Standard Reference, Release 12. 1999.

Whincup, P. H., H. Refsum, I. J. Perry, et al. "Serum total homocysteine and coronary heart disease: prospective study in middle aged men." *Heart* (England) 82(4) (Oct 1999):448-54.

Yu, H., and T. Rohan. "Role of the insulin-like growth factor family in cancer development and progression." *J Natl Cancer Inst* 20;92(18) (2000 Sep):1472-89.

Chapter 15

Alfieri, M., J. Pomerleau, and D. M. Grace. A comparison of fat intake of normal weight, moderately obese and severely obese subjects. *Obes Surg* 7(1) (1997):9-15.

Appleby, P. N., M. Thorogood, J. I. Mann, and T. J. Key. Low body mass index in non-meat eaters: the possible roles of animal fat, dietary fibre and alcohol. *Int J Obes Relat Metab Disord* 1998;22(5):454-60.

Ascherio A., and Willett W. C. "Health effects of trans fatty acids." *Am J Clin Nutr* (1997):66(4 Suppl) 1006S-1010S.

Bartsch, H., J. Nair, and R. W. Owen. "Dietary polyunsaturated fatty acids and cancers of the breast and colorectum: emerging evidence for their role as risk modifiers." *Carcinogenesis* (England) 20(12) (Dec 1999):2209-18.

Bittner V. "Correlates of high HDL cholesterol among women with coronary heart disease." *Am Heart J* 139 Pt 1(2)(2000):288-96.

Blundell, J. E., and J. I. MacDiarmid. "Fat as a risk factor for overconsumption: satiation, satiety, and patterns of eating." *J Am Diet Assoc* 97(7 Suppl) (1997):S63-69.

Bray, G. A., and B. M. Popkin. "Dietary fat intake does affect obesity!" *Am J Clin Nutr* 68(6) (1998):1157-73.

Caggiula, A. W., and V. A. Mustad. "Effects of dietary fat and fatty acids on coronary artery disease risk and total and lipoprotein cholesterol concentrations: epidemiologic studies." *Am J Clin Nutr* 65(5 Suppl) (1997):1597S-1610S.

Carmichael, H. E., B. A. Swinburn, and M. R. Wilson. "Lower fat intake as a predictor of initial and sustained weight loss in obese subjects consuming an otherwise *ad libitum* diet." *J Am Diet Assoc* 98(1) (1998):35-39.

"Carbohydrates in human nutrition." Report of a Joint FAO/WHO Expert Consultation. FAO *Food Nutr Pap* (Italy) 66 (1998):1-140.

Castelli, W. P. "Lipids, risk factors and ischaemic heart disease." *Atherosclerosis* 124 (Suppl) (1996):S1-9.

Castelli, W. P. "The triglyceride issue: a view from Framingham." *Am Heart J* 112(2) (1986):432-37.

Chan, J. K., B. E. McDonald, J. M. Gerrard, et al. "Effect of dietary alpha-linolenic acid and its ratio to linoleic acid on platelet and plasma fatty acids and thrombogenesis." *Lipids* 28(9) (1993 Sep):811-7.

Connor, W. E., C. A. De Francesco, and S. L. Connor. "N-3 fatty acids from fish oil. Effects on plasma lipoproteins and hypertriglyceridimic patients." *Ann NY Acad Sci* 683 (1993):16-34.

Duncan, K. H., J. A. Bacon, and R. L. Weinsier. "The effects of high and low energy density diets on satiety, energy intake, and eating time of obese and nonobese subjects." *Am J Clin Nutr* 37(5) (1983):763-67.

Dyerberg, J., and H. O. Bang. "Lipid metabolism, atherogenesis, and haemostasis in Eskimos: The role of the prostaglandin-3 family." *Haemostatsis* 8 (1979):227-233.

Fair, W. R., N. E. Fleshner, and W. Heston. "Cancer of the prostate: a nutritional disease?" *Urology* (United States 50(6) (Dec 1997):840-8.

Golay, A., and E. Bobbioni. "The role of dietary fat in obesity." *Int J Obes Relat Metab Disord* 21(Suppl 3) (1997):S2-11.

Grant, W. B. "Milk and other dietary influences on coronary heart disease." *Altern Med Rev* 3(4) (1998):281-94.

Grundy, S. M. "Management of high serum cholesterol and related disorders in patients at risk for coronary heart disease." *Am J Med* 102(2A) (1997):15-22.

Harris, W. S. "n-3 fatty acids and serum lipoproteins: human studies." *Am J Clin Nutr* 65(5 Suppl) (1997):1645S-1654S.

Jenkins, D. J., C. W. Kendall, E. Vidgen, et al. "Health aspects of partially defatted flaxseed, including effects on serum lipids, oxidative measures, and ex vivo androgen and progestin activity: a controlled crossover trial." *Am J Clin Nutr* 69(3) (1999 Mar):395-402.

Kannel, W. B., and P. W. Wilson. "Efficacy of lipid profiles in prediction of coronary disease." *Am Heart J* 124(3) (1992):768-74.

Katan, M. B. "Vegetarian diet: panacea for modern lifestyle diseases?" *Am J Clin Nutr* 66(4 Suppl) (1997):974S-979S.

Katsouyanni, K., Y. Skalkidis, E. Petridou, et al. "Diet and peripheral arterial occlusive disease: the role of poly-, mono-, and saturated fatty acids." *Am J Epidemiol* 133(1) (1991):24-31.

Kromhout, D., et al. "The inverse relationship between fish consumption and 20 year mortality from coronary heart disease." *NEJM* 312;9 (1985 May 9):1205-1209.

Leiter, L. A. "Low density lipoprotein cholesterol: Is lower better?" *Can J Cardiol* 16(Suppl A) (2000):20A-22A.

Lissner, L., B. L. Heitmann, and C. Bengtsson. "Low-fat diets may prevent weight gain in sedentary women: prospective observations from the population study of women in Gothenburg, Sweden." *Obes Res* 5(1) (1997):43-48.

Longcope, C., S. Gorbach, B. Goldin, et al. "The effect of a low fat diet on estrogen metabolism." *J Clin Endocrinol Metab* 64(6) (1987):1246-50.

Passmore, R., and M. A. Eastwood. *Davidson and Passmore Human Nutrition and Dietetics,* 8th ed. London, England: Churchill Livingstone, 1986.

Purnell, J. Q., and J. D. Brunzell. "The central role of dietary fat, not carbohydrate, in the insulin resistance syndrome." *Curr Opin Lipidol* 8(1) (1997):17-22.

Reddy, B. S. "Dietary fat and its relationship to large bowel cancer." *Cancer Res* (United States) 41(9 Pt 2) (Sep 1981):3700-5.

Reimer, L. "Role of dietary fat in obesity. Fat is fattening." *J Fla Med Assoc* 79(6) (1992):382-84.

Rutledge, J. C., D. A. Hyson, D. Garduno, et al. "Lifestyle modification program in management of patients with coronary artery disease: the clinical experience in a tertiary care hospital." *J Cardiopulm Rehabil* 19(4) (1999):226-34.

Schuler, G., and R. Hambrecht. "Regression and non-progression of coronary artery disease with exercise." *J Cardiovasc Risk* 3(2) (1996):176-82.

Schuler, G., R. Hambrecht, G. Schlierf, J. Niebauer, et al. "Regular physical exercise and low-fat diet. Effects on progression of coronary artery disease." *Circulation* 86(1) (1992):1-11.

Slattery, M. L. "Diet, lifestyle, and colon cancer." *Semin Gastrointest Dis* (United States) 11(3) (Jul 2000):142-6.

Thomas, J. A. "Diet, micronutrients, and the prostate gland." *Nutr Rev* (United States) 57(4) (Apr 1999):95-103.

Tzonou, A., A. Kalandidi, A. Trichopoulou, C. C. Hsieh, N. Toupadaki, W. Willett, and D. Trichopoulos. "Diet and coronary heart disease: a case-control study in Athens, Greece." *Epidemiology* (United States) 4(6) (Nov 1993):511-6.

Vartak, S., R. McCaw, C. S. Davis, et al. "Gamma-linolenic acid (GLA) is cytotoxic to 36B10 malignant rat astrocytoma cells but not to 'normal' rat astrocytes." *Br J Cancer* 77(10) (1998):1612-20.

Wagner, W., and U. Nootbaar-Wagner. "Prophylactic treatment of migraine with gamma-linolenic and alpha-linolenic acids." *Cephalalgia* (Norway) 17(2) (Apr 1997):127-30.

Wolk, A., R. Bergstrom, D. Hunter, et al. "A prospective study of association of monounsaturated fat and other types of fat with risk of breast cancer." *Arch Intern Med* 158(1) (1998):41-45.

Chapter 16

Anderson, R. A. "Chromium, glucose intolerance and diabetes." *J Am Coll Nutr* 17(6) (1998):548-55.

American Diabetes Association. "Magnesium supplementation in the treatment of diabetes. *Diabetes Care* 15(8) (1992):1065-67.

Badmaev, V., S. Prakash, and M. Majeed. "Vanadium: a review of its potential role in the fight against diabetes." *J Altern Complement Med* 5(3) (1999):273-91.

Balon, T. W., J. L. Gu, Y. Tokuyama, et al. "Magnesium supplementation reduces development of diabetes in a rat model of spontaneous NIDDM." *Am J Physiol* 269(4 Pt 1) (1995):E745-52.

Bierenbaum, M. L., F. J. Noonan, L. J. Machlin, et al. "The effect of supplemental vitamin E on serum parameters in diabetics, post coronary and normal subjects." *Nutr Rep Internat* 31 (1985):1171-80.

Brichard, S. M., and J. C. Henquin. "The role of vanadium in the management of diabetes." *Trends Pharmacol Sci* 16(8) (1995):265-70.

Coggeshall, J. C., J. P. Heggers, M. C. Robson, and H. Baker. "Biotin status and plasma glucose in diabetics." *Ann NY Acad Sci* 447 (1985):389-92.

Eriksson, J., and A. Kohvakka. "Magnesium and ascorbic acid supplementation in diabetes mellitus." *Ann Nutr Metab* 39(4) (1995):217-23.

Florholmen, J., R. Arvidsson-Lenner, R. Jorde, and P. G. Burhol. "The effect of Metamucil on postprandial blood glucose and plasma gastric inhibitory peptide in insulin-dependent diabetics." *Acta Med Scand* 212 (1982):237-39.

Gaut, Z. N., R. Pocelinko, H. M. Solomon, and G. B. Thomas. "Oral glucose tolerance, plasma insulin, and uric acid excretion in man during chronic administration in nicotinic acid." *Metabol* (1971):1031-35.

Grafton, G., and M. A. Baxter. "The role of magnesium in diabetes mellitus. A possible mechanism for the development of diabetic complications." *J Diabetes Complications* 6(2) (1992):143-49.

Hallfrisch, J., D. J. Scholfield, and K. M. Behall. "Diets containing soluble oat extracts improve glucose and insulin responses of moderately hypercholesterolemic men and women." *Am J Clin Nutr* 61 (1995):379-84.

Jacob, S., Ruus P., Hermann R., et al. "Oral administration of RAC-alpha-lipoic acid modulates insulin sensitivity in patients with type-2 diabetes mellitus: a placebo-controlled pilot trial." *Free Radic Biol Med* 27(3-4) (1999):309-14.

Kelly, G. S. "Insulin resistance: lifestyle and nutritional interventions." *Altern Med Rev* 5(2) (2000 Apr):109-32.

Landin, K., G. Holm, L. Tengborn, and U. Smith. "Guar gum improves insulin sensitivity, blood lipids, blood pressure, and fibrinolysis in healthy men." *Am J Clin Nutr* 56 (1992):1061-65.

Maebashi, M., Y. Makino, Y. Furukawa, et al. "Therapeutic evaluation of the effect of biotin on hyperglycemia in patients with non-insulin dependent diabetes mellitus." *J Clin Biochem Nutr* 14 (1993):211-18.

Molnar, G. D., K. G. Berge, J. W. Rosevear, et al. "The effect of nicotinic acid in diabetes mellitus." *Metabol* 13 (1964):181-89.

Paolisso, G., A. D'Amore, D. Giugliano, et al. "Pharmacologic doses of vitamin E improve insulin action in healthy subjects and non-insulin dependent diabetic patients." *Am J Clin Nutr* 57 (1993):650-56.

Paolisso, G., A. D'Amore, D. Galzerano, et al. "Daily vitamin E supplements improve metabolic control but not insulin secretion in elderly type II diabetic patients." *Diabetes Care* 16 (1993):1433-37.

Paolisso, G., and M. Barbagallo. "Hypertension, diabetes mellitus, and insulin resistance: the role of intracellular magnesium." *Am J Hypertens* 10(3) (1997):346-55.

Preuss, H. G., and R. A. Anderson. "Chromium update: examining recent literature 1997-1998." *Curr Opin Clin Nutr Metab Care* 1(6) (1998):509-12.

Rimm, E. B., M. J. Stampfer, A. Ascherio, et al. "Vitamin E consumption and the risk of coronary heart disease in men." *N Engl J Med* 328 (1993):1450-56.

Rodríguez-Morán, M., F. Guerrero-Romero, and G. Lazcano-Burciaga. "Lipid- and glucose-lowering efficacy of plantago psyllium in type II diabetes." *Diabetes Its Complications* 12 (1998):273-78.

Saris, N. L., E. Mervaala, H. Karppanen, J. A. Khawaja, and A. Lewenstam. "Magnesium. An update on physiological, clinical and analytical aspects." *Clin Chim Acta* 294(1-2) (2000):1-26.

Schwartz, S. E., R. A. Levine, R. S. Weinstock, et al. "Sustained pectin ingestion: effect on gastric emptying and glucose tolerance in non-insulin-dependent diabetic patients." *Am J Clin Nutr* 48 (1988):1413-17.

Skrha, J., G. Sindelka, J. Kvasnicka, and J. Hilgertova. "Insulin action and fibrinolysis influenced by vitamin E in obese type 2 diabetes mellitus." *Diabetes Res Clin Pract* 44 (1999):27-33.

Sotaniemi, E. A., E. Haapakoski, and A. Rautio. "Ginseng therapy in non-insulin dependent diabetic patients." *Diabetes Care* 18 (1995):1573-75.

Stampfer, M. J., C. H. Hennekens, J. E. Manson, et al. "Vitamin E consumption and the risk of coronary disease in women." *N Engl J Med* 328 (1993):1444-9.

Stephens, N. G., A. Parsons, P. M. Schofield, et al. "Randomized controlled trial of vitamin E in patients with coronary disease: Cambridge Heart Antioxidant Study (CHAOS)." *Lancet* 347 (1996):781-86.

Swain, R. "An update of vitamin B12 metabolism and deficiency states." *J Fam Pract* 41(6) (1995):595-600.

Verma, S., M. C. Cam, and J. H. McNeill. "Nutritional factors that can favorably influence the glucose/insulin system: vanadium." *J Am Coll Nutr* 17(1) (1998):11-18.

von Schenck, U., C. Bender-Gotze, and B. Koletzko. "Persistence of neurological damage induced by dietary vitamin B-12 deficiency in infancy." *Arch Dis Child* 77(2) (1997):137-39.

Vuksan, V., J. L. Sievenpiper, V. Y. Koo, et al. "American ginseng (Panax quinquefolius L) reduces postprandial glycemia in nondiabetic subjects and subjects with type 2 diabetes mellitus." *Arch Intern Med* 160(7) (2000):1009-13.

White, J. R., Jr., and R. K. Campbell. "Magnesium and diabetes: a review." *Ann Pharmacother* 27(6) (1993):775-80.

Yaworsky, K., R. Somwar, T. Ramlal, et al. "Engagement of the insulin-sensitive pathway in the stimulation of glucose transport by alpha-lipoic acid in 3T3-L1 adipocytes." *Diabetologia* 43(3) (2000):294-303.

Zhang, T., M. Hoshino, et al. "Ginseng root: Evidence for numerous regulatory peptides and insulinotropic activity." *Biomed Res* 11 (1990):49-54.

Index